1

Indeterminacy of Literary Meaning and Medieval Culture, 1100–1500

Critical Orientation: Medieval Studies and Literary Theory

A recent theorist of literature has written about the activity of literary interpretation as an adventure comparable to the quest of a romance-hero: "Art, like Romance, teaches us to interrupt. Only, like a hero in Romance, the interpreter must ask the right question. If he asks it wrongly, or at the wrong time, he wakes into emptiness."[1] This passage, from Geoffrey Hartman's book *The Fate of Reading*, probably refers to the *Conte del Graal* of Chrétien de Troyes: its hero, Perceval, indeed fails to ask the right questions at the right moment in the Grail-castle, which is empty when he tries to ask his questions the next morning.[2]

It may seem odd that Hartman, usually identified with the avant-garde of twentieth-century literary theory, should find his paradigmatic interpreter in a twelfth-century romance, but I propose to take his comparison seriously. Perceval, in this episode as elsewhere, must engage in the interpretation of his world just as a critic interprets the story of Perceval's adventures. An understanding of the mysteries of either the world of the romance or the romance text is not easily acquired; the truth is elusive, and Perceval's attempts to achieve it fail not only at the Grail-castle but consistently, as we shall see in chapter 2. At the same time, the interpreter of his adventures faces similar problems: definitive, authoritative meaning is constantly deferred in this romance, and though readers may believe they have found it, each such reading invariably comes into conflict with others equally plausible. Interpreting, then, for the critic as for the hero, never quite satisfies the desire to know the truth, and yet interpretation is all they have to guide their attempts at understanding.

The literary works I will be examining in this book reproduce for the reader this "sense of baffled involvement in a mystery" which, when experienced by its characters, has been called one of the defining characteristics of romance.[3] For the reader, however, this experience is not limited to romance: medieval literature of all genres after 1100 abounds in the semantic "gaps" or "blanks" found by certain literary theorists in works of other periods, gaps that require the reader's participation in supplying what is missing from the text. As Wolfgang Iser puts it: "The reader will only begin to search for (and so actualize) the meaning if he does not *know* it, and so it is the unknown factors in the text that set him off on his quest."[4] And these medieval works are not merely conceptually incomplete; they insist upon their own incompleteness, upon the gaps that make interpretation not only possible but necessary, and necessarily indeterminate.

The indeterminacy of meaning and the undecidability of interpretation are also, of course, the concern of many postmodern theorists of language and literature. A number of the most influential of these theorists have themselves been influenced by medieval literature, or at least began their careers as medievalists: Julia Kristeva, A. J. Greimas, Tzvetan Todorov, Umberto Eco, Hans Robert Jauss—these critics, identified in the minds of most academics primarily with various modes of poststructuralist discourse, have all at one time or another written with particular interest on medieval literature.[5]

In examining the ways medieval studies and recent literary theory are related, the work of Jacques Derrida, like that of Hartman and Iser, may prove helpful, especially the "messianic"[6] opening chapter of the *Grammatology*, in which Derrida announces the advent of writing as free play:

> There is not a single signified that escapes, even if recaptured, the play of signifying references that constitute language. The advent of writing is the advent of this play: today such a play is coming into its own, effacing the limit starting from which one had thought to regulate the circulation of signs, drawing along with it all the reassuring signifieds, reducing all the strongholds, all the out-of-bounds shelters that watched over the field of language.[7]

Readers of Derrida have seized on this notion of the free play of writing as an important Utopian element in Derrida's thought, one that emerges "anarchically" in later texts like *Glas*.[8] *Glas* itself closely resembles, in its typographical layout, medieval manuscripts in which the commentary interpenetrates with the text.[9]

I do not wish to claim that Derrida's project is a repetition of medieval modes of thought, and in fact shall be arguing against critics who do so. The postmodern rejection of the transcendental signified is not the same thing as the late medieval conception of a God who cannot be known by

MEDIEVAL INTERPRETATION

Models of Reading in Literary Narrative, 1100–1500

Robert S. Sturges

Southern Illinois University Press
Carbondale and Edwardsville

Library of Congress Cataloging-in-Publication Data

Sturges, Robert Stuart, 1953–
    Medieval interpretation: models of reading in literary narrative,
1100–1500 / Robert S. Sturges.
        p. cm.
    Includes bibliographical references.
    1. French literature—To 1500—History and criticism—Theory, etc.
2. English literature—Middle English, 1100–1500—History and
criticism—Theory, etc. 3. Literature, Medieval—History and
criticism—Theory, etc. 4. Arthurian romances—History and
criticism. 5. Grail—Legends—History and criticism. 6. Reader-
response criticism. 7. Narration (Rhetoric) I. Title.
PQ151.S78   1991
840.9′001—dc20   89-26357
ISBN 0-8093-1556-4   CIP

Dedicated to the memory of
Hilda Anderson Mackey
(1888–1981)
and
Clifford William Sturges
(1915–1969)

CONTENTS

ACKNOWLEDGMENTS

More intellectual debts are incurred during the years it takes to complete a project like this one than can possibly be acknowledged in the space traditionally allotted to words of thanks. Many people have read or listened to all or part of this book since I first began working on it. With my apologies to any who may have been omitted inadvertently, a partial list of those who offered advice or encouragement, or who simply asked the right question at the right time, would include the following.

Elizabeth Kirk, whose expertise has been of benefit to my thinking about these issues ever since I was a graduate student, must come first. Good advice, all of which I took, was also offered at an early stage in this project by the late Morton Bloomfield. More recently, Don Berke, E. Jane Burns, Jerry Burns, William Calin, Marjorie Curry, Carolyn Dinshaw, Peter Dunn, Judith Ferster, Anne Hunsaker Hawkins, Sherman Hawkins, Maureen Quilligan, Jeff Rider, Barbara Herrnstein Smith, Gayatri Spivak, Khachig Tölölyan, Siegfried Wenzel, Steven White, and an anonymous reader for Southern Illinois University Press have all made helpful suggestions, and students in my seminars on medieval literature and literary theory have forced me to sharpen and clarify my presentation of this material. I regret that my original inspiration in the study of medieval literature, Russell Griffin, did not live to see this project completed.

All of the institutions at which I have taught—M.I.T., Wesleyan, and the University of New Orleans—have been generous with the financial support and time off without which this book could not have been finished, and a Mellon Faculty Fellowship at the University of Pennsylvania allowed me to complete a first draft of it. I also wish to thank the library staffs of all of these institutions, as well as those of Harvard, Yale, Loyola, and Tulane, especially Bob Heriard of U.N.O. Portions of chapter three have previously appeared, in different form, as "Texts and Readers in Marie de France's *Lais*," *Romanic Review* 71 (1980), 244–64, and as "Speculation and Interpretation in Machaut's *Voir-Dit*," *Romance Quarterly* 33 (1986), 23–33, published by the University Press of Kentucky, and have been reprinted here with permission. My editors at Southern Illinois have been enthusiastic in their encouragement, and diplomatic in their criticism. My friend and colleague Susan Krantz generously helped read the proofs.

More personal thanks go to my mother, Barbara Sturges, and my sister, Linda Ard, for help of too many kinds to list. Thanks finally to my dear friends Marlena G. Corcoran and especially Barbara A. Johnson. Their intellectual companionship over the years has improved my manuscript in many concrete ways; and only they fully understand what it means for me to have written this book.

MEDIEVAL INTERPRETATION

Models of Reading in Literary Narrative, 1100–1500

humans, and the self-consciousness with which Derrida destabilizes texts is not the same thing as manuscript *mouvance*, though the terms in each of these comparisons do have obvious similarities. The Middle Ages had not experienced modern positivism and hence had no need to reject it, as postmodern thinkers have done.

Nevertheless, the deconstructive free play of writing may have something in common with, and something to tell us about, interpretation in the Middle Ages, which may have been governed less by any positivist notion of the author's intentions for the integrated text than by something more closely resembling this free play. For medieval as for postmodern writers, the author, text, and reader can easily seem less distinct from one another than we have been trained to conceive of them, and indeed they might be regarded less as separable entities than as three literary functions that continuously interact in various combinations.

Mouvance, the process by which texts in a manuscript culture inevitably change with each new manuscript produced, is not merely an effect of scribal error; it is a fact of medieval text production in more important ways as well.[10] Authors do not stake exclusive claims to their works in the Middle Ages; thus the prose *Lancelot* seems to have been conceived as a collaboration,[11] while Chaucer felt free to produce *Troilus and Criseyde* in part simply by translating whole sections of Boccaccio's *Filostrato*:[12] the literary community as a whole is responsible for such works. Texts themselves, then, are also necessarily less stable. Poems such as *Piers Plowman*, of course, exist in multiple versions apparently by the same author,[13] but even the most authoritative of texts, the Bible, was subject to violation as well. Like other written authorities, it was frequently preserved in the form of preaching handbooks, verses taken out of context and rearranged according to subject matter.[14] Mosaic-like works drawn from many sources were theorized as the genre of *compilatio*.[15]

Medieval readers could have a kind of power over the texts they read unknown to their modern counterparts. Scribes not only copied works but also read and edited them according to their own standards.[16] And in a culture in which print does not confer authority, any reader's marginal jottings, or extended commentary, at least have the potential to be incorporated into the text the next time it is copied. The distinction between reading and writing cannot have been as clear as it seems to us; any reader could become a writer simply by writing. Perhaps this potential is what stands behind the frequent rhetorical appeals to the reader found in high and late medieval narrative, as when Marie de France informs us that the readers can supply their own meaning for her text,[17] or when Chaucer asks that his works be corrected by his readers. These are conventional appeals, no doubt; but like most conventions, they are rooted in what was actually possible. Certainly medieval readers took Chaucer's appeals seriously and corrected *The Canterbury Tales* by continuing it with further tales or with commentary.[18] And, as we shall see, the reader's additions to the text can become a new text, to be interpreted and rewritten by new readers/writers.

Thus when Derrida produces a new work, *Glas*, in part by juxtaposing pre-existing texts in a new way, or when he quotes, bit by bit, the entire article by John R. Searle to which he is responding in "Limited, Inc a b c . . . ,"[19] he is performing operations in an ironic and self-conscious mode comparable to those medieval authors or compilers performed as a matter of course. When Stanley Fish writes, "Interpreters do not decode poems; they make them,"[20] he is participating in a merging of author and audience like that taken for granted by the medieval literary community. That these relations become self-conscious in the postmodern period does, of course, make a difference. The similarities are striking nonetheless: the free circulation of signifiers was not unknown in the Middle Ages. Medieval thinkers like St. Bonaventure asked, like Michel Foucault, "What is an author?" and, like Paul Ricoeur, "What is a text?"[21]

As Derrida suggests, the free circulation of language, independent of specific authors and texts, also implies a freedom of meaning from authorial intention and from the limits imposed by the coherent text. And turning to medieval literature, we find Robert Hanning's suggestion that the invasion of text by commentary inevitably implies a conflict or competition of coexisting meanings: "The idea that a gloss manipulates rather than explains its text may seem a peculiarly modern one, but medieval scholars and satirists were by no means unaware of the possibilities of such textual harassment."[22] The instability of texts is also the instability of meaning. Perhaps, then, our methods of interpreting these texts must be re-evaluated. Another recent literary theorist, Gerald Bruns, has suggested that indeterminate meanings must be one result of the existence of literary works in multiple manuscript versions rather than in an authoritative printed text. Bruns suggests, developing an argument first made by Eugène Vinaver,[23] that *all* writing in a manuscript culture, and specifically in the later Middle Ages, can be regarded as "textual intervention" or commentary; late medieval works are always written in the margins, as it were, of an earlier work or works. He goes on to suggest how this state of affairs affects interpretation:

> My argument would be that in a manuscript culture the text is not reducible to the letter; that is, a text always contains more than it says,

or more than what its letters contain, which is why we are privileged to read between the lines, and not to read between them only but to write between them as well, because the text is simply not complete—not fully what it could be, as in the case of the dark story that requires an illuminating retelling (that is, by one who understands). This is why it is important to remember that the grammarian's embellishment is an art of disclosure as well as an art of amplification. Or, rather, amplification is not merely supplementation but also interpretation: the act of adding to a text is also the act of eliciting from it that which remains unspoken.[24]

It is not only a question of finding what is hidden in a text but of adding to it that which is not yet there, just as medieval authors frequently ask us to do.

Similar comparisons between the medieval and the postmodern have been taken up recently in several important books on medieval literature.[25] These studies have been both valuable and, in two different ways, problematic. Certain critics, notably those like Gellrich and Bloch who take an anthropological approach, tend to present medieval culture as essentially unified and monolithic. Thus for Gellrich, only literature is able to escape the control of signification and the stabilization of hierarchical thought evident in every other aspect of medieval culture, whether language theory, theology, or even architecture or music. Bloch's more historically nuanced view suffers from a similarly essentialist reading of the culture as a whole; his book simply presents a change in medieval civilization from one essential structure (vertical and linear, concerned with origins as the determinants of meaning) to another (a circular one in which meaning is more diffuse), in a massive epistemic break. As we shall see, however, these modes of thought, which I will be calling determinate and indeterminate, actually compete with each other throughout the Middle Ages, in all areas of culture. Brian Stock has shown that oral and literate modes of thought compete with and influence each other in the eleventh and twelfth centuries; and his work also implies that determinate and indeterminate modes operate within the oral as well as the literate. Writing can act as a guarantee of factuality, in legal matters, for example ("Men began to think of facts not as recorded by texts but as embodied in texts"); but since writing can also be falsified, oral communication, with both parties undeniably present, can also act as a guarantee of truth, while writing lies.[26] The two modes coexist from the twelfth through the fifteenth centuries, though I will be contending that the indeterminate mode becomes stronger throughout the period.

The other fault with which recent critics might be charged is ahistoricism.

For critics such as Ferster (who in her introductory chapter to *Chaucer on Interpretation* spends more time discussing modern hermeneutic theory than medieval culture)[27] and Burns, the insights of poststructuralist theory have not been fully assimilated in historical terms.[28]

I hope to avoid both of these problems in the remainder of this chapter, which will examine long-term developments in a number of medieval disciplines. In all of them, the possibility of a mode of thought that does not seek to control signification and that renders all interpretation potentially indeterminate impinges on more determinate modes. Although the former becomes more and more powerful between the twelfth and fifteenth centuries, it never completely displaces the latter; despite important historical changes in all these aspects of medieval culture, the two modes of thought remain in competition throughout the period. I hope, then, to contribute to an awareness of the complexities, both synchronic and diachronic, of certain areas of medieval intellectual history. In doing so, I will emphasize problems of interpretation rather than analyzing structures of thought. My concern throughout this book is with the history of reading.

The Early Middle Ages: Neoplatonism and the Directed Vision in Literature

The neoplatonic Christian tradition passed on to the medieval period by thinkers like St. Augustine and pseudo-Dionysius the Areopagite held that true knowledge of God and of the created universe is accessible to human beings: the Incarnation of Christ had redeemed the human faculties, including speech, so that language, for the Christian believer, provides a true mirror of reality—at least in the traditional interpretation.[29] In this view, language is the means by which human beings can move beyond the limits of their understanding and toward the unmediated vision of God, as in the famous passage in Augustine's *Confessions* in which he and his mother attain a brief vision of divine reality: "And while we spoke of the eternal Wisdom, longing for it and straining for it with all the strength of our hearts, for one fleeting instant we reached out and touched it. Then with a sigh, leaving our spiritual harvest bound to it, we returned to the sound of our own speech."[30] The human speech of Augustine and Monica is fully adequate to its object, bringing them into the presence of that of which they speak, eternal Wisdom. God, in fact, guarantees the meaning of human language, regulating the circulation of signs and insuring their natural relationship with their objects. As R. Howard Bloch suggests, "it is as if language, for Augustine, were transparent because its eternally subsistent object always draws words to their natural mark. . . . they point inevitably to the same predetermined truth. Tongues may vary and the means of verbal expression may be hopelessly rooted in material reality, yet all language is about God and leads to God."[31]

In this reading of Augustine's theory of language, verbal signs, though limited, signify truly within their limits. Given God's participation in the world, interpretation, for the Christian believer, can hardly go wrong in the Augustinian system; thus, in another well-known passage from the *Confessions*, Augustine suggests that a multiplicity of interpretations for a Biblical passage does not mean that the passage's meaning is unclear or indeterminate. Instead, all possible meanings are to be held equally admissible, as long as they conform to Christian doctrine: even if they cannot have been intended by the passage's human author, its ultimate author, God, can inspire the interpreter as he inspired the human author.

> How can it harm me that it should be possible to interpret these words in several ways, all of which may yet be true? How can it harm me if I understand the writer's meaning in a different sense from that in which another understands it? All of us who read his words do our best to discover and understand what he had in mind, and since we believe that he wrote the truth, we are not so rash as to suppose that he wrote anything which we know or think to be false. Provided, therefore, that each of us tries as best he can to understand in the Holy Scriptures what the writer meant by them, what harm is there if a reader believes what you, the Light of all truthful minds, show him to be the true meaning? It may not even be the meaning which the writer had in mind, and yet he too saw in them a true meaning, different though it may have been from this.[32]

Another recent trend in interpreting Augustine's writings, not only the *Confessions* but *De doctrina Christiana* as well, suggests, however, that meaning in language is less fully controlled by its divine origins than may at first appear. For Peggy A. Knapp, for example, Augustine's concern with the difficulty of interpretation—with the need for the study of languages and history as guides to understanding the Bible, or with the possibility of errors in interpretation—"undercuts the absoluteness and stability of the received word, deferring to language study, judgment, likelihood, comparison, and human authority."[33] Taking our cue from these critics, we might ask of the passage just cited, What might happen if the multiplicity of interpretations there encouraged by Augustine were released from the conditions governing it? What if it were applied to secular literature rather than to Scripture, so that it could be released from the guidance of Christian doctrine? What if it were also released from an epistemology guaranteeing accurate, intuitive knowledge of the truth? The result might well be a literature that accepts, and even insists upon, its own indeterminacy. Such an observation, however, would be accurate only as long as the divine origin of language, and hence the divine guarantee of signification, were temporarily bracketed or left to one side. Purely human language, if it were separate from God, might well be subject to this indeterminacy, even for Augustine; but as we have seen, it is not separate from God, but is rather a way to him. Early medieval theorists of language are acutely aware of the dangerous possibility of indeterminacy in human language; the multiplication of instances of the "inexpressibility topos" noted by Curtius,[34] which claims that language is not adequate to its object, usually the praise of a ruler, may suggest that this awareness is present in literary works as well. But as Gellrich has pointed out, the response of early medieval grammarians to language's potential for indeterminacy is an attempt to guarantee signification as strictly as possible: "linguistic signification is, to a certain extent, an errant child who must be curtailed by the parental rod, or a sick body in need of grammar's medicine."[35] The parental rod is the appeal to divine origins that we have observed in Augustine's *Confessions;* it reflects what Gellrich calls the "inclination to protect signification from dissemination."[36] The possibility that language can be semantically indeterminate if cut off from divine control, then, is recognized in the early medieval period; but the postmodern critic's urge to perform this separation is resisted, for the time being. As we shall see, however, later medieval philosophers became more and more willing to bracket God's role in linguistic signification, to make good on the possibility recognized much earlier.

Before the twelfth century, however, the neoplatonic strain remains dominant in medieval thought; most important for our purposes is the theory of symbolism and interpretation proposed by John Scotus Eriugena in the ninth century. An especially significant text for Eriugena is St. Paul's declaration that "the invisible things of [God], from the creation of the world, are clearly seen, being understood by the things that are made" (Romans 1:20). The visible creation is a sign of God's *invisibilia*, of divine reality, which is thus accessible by means of the human senses and interpretive faculty. Eriugena, indeed, moves beyond Paul's generalization and proposes a more totalizing formula: "there is nothing among visible and corporeal things that does not signify something incorporeal and intelligible."[37] It is as if Augustine's insistence on the divine guarantee of linguistic signification had been expanded to include the meaning of the entire created universe as well as of language more narrowly defined; indeed, with Eriugena, the created universe becomes a language, a code that can be interpreted by Christians. The world is a book like the Bible, to be read with similar confidence by those who understand the code.

The influence of this mode of thought on the medieval view of the world is enormous; examples can be chosen almost at random, but perhaps most tellingly from among pre-twelfth-century historical writings, especially those concerned with unusual occurrences in the natural order. The eleventh-century *Historia Ecclesiastica* of Orderic Vitalis, for instance, theorizes the problem of interpreting the created universe:

> The human mind needs to be constantly occupied with useful learning if it is to keep its keenness; it needs too by reflecting on past and interpreting present events to equip itself with the qualities necessary to face the future. . . . Often events that seem incredible come to the ears of the ignorant; and strange things occur unexpectedly to the men of our time; shallow minds find them obscure and can only understand them by reflecting on past events.[38]

As Stock points out, the world is here treated as a text for interpretation,[39] but this interpretation is still predetermined by the *invisibilia* that are its object. What Stock says of Rodulf Glaber's *Historiae* is true of much historical writing from this period: "The natural, human, or supernatural agencies which periodically wrought destruction were all considered from an eschatological standpoint."[40]

For a more concrete example of how such interpretations operate, let us turn to a text dating from before Eriugena's theorization of the problem: the sixth-century *Historia Francorum* of Gregory of Tours. "In that year lightning was observed to flicker across the sky, just as we saw it before Lothar's death."[41] Such observations appear regularly throughout the *Historia*, interspersed with the political and military events being recounted, so that even the most common natural events can be quickly decoded as signifying the events in the human world which follow them; thus the lightning's portent, whose meaning is hinted at in the reference to Lothar's death, is soon explained further in the advice St. Germanus gives another king, Sigibert: "If you set out with the intention of sparing your brother's life, you will return alone and victorious. If you have any other plans in mind, you will die. This is what God announced through the mouth of Solomon: 'Whoso diggeth a pit (for his brother) shall fall therein.' "[42] This interpretation is finally confirmed by Sigibert's own death.

Interpretation here is clear and unequivocal, because the language of the book of nature, like the transparent verbal language imagined by Augustine, is controlled by a predetermined Christian meaning derived ultimately from God. Divine authority over signification is exercised vertically, as in Bloch's understanding of early medieval culture.[43] Both the natural sign (the lightning) and the linguistic sign (the quotation from Proverbs) can be correctly interpreted by the Christian reader (St. Germanus, or Gregory of Tours himself, or Gregory's readers), and can thus provide reliable information not only about the divine author of both books, but also about proper behavior, or the consequences of improper behavior, in the purely human political realm. The world speaks a language intelligible to those whose beliefs must inevitably bring them into contact with God, those correct interpreters mentioned by Orderic Vitalis. Curtius and Stock suggest that the world is conceived as an interpretable text in the high Middle Ages, but here we see a much earlier example, suggesting that it is Gellrich who is correct to see "the idea of the Book" as a transhistorical medieval phenomenon.[44]

It is not only the Book as a metaphor that is important here, however; the literal book written by Gregory also participates in this transparency. Writing is here seen as a guarantee of reliability; it preserves an account of the divine Book that can be confidently interpreted by his own readers. Once again, Stock has shown how this issue is theorized by Orderic Vitalis some centuries later: it is the preservative function of writing that is emphasized here, the view that texts allow the continued presence over time of that which would otherwise be lost. Writing in this sense does not destabilize signification, as it does for Derrida; just the opposite is true, in fact: writing is seen as the only source of stability in the flux of human life. "With the loss of books the deeds of old men pass into oblivion, and can in no wise be recovered by those of our generation, for the admonitions of the ancients pass away from the memory of modern men with the changing world."[45] This type of stabilized interpretation may be seen as one example of a widespread phenomenon described by Stock, the growth of "textual communities," in which interpretation is controlled from above, in a hierarchical fashion. Stock uses the example of heretical and reformist movements, in which the possibility of individual interpretation is strictly controlled by the movement's leaders,[46] but from another point of view the entire body of Christian readers might be seen as such a textual community, united in its directed interpretations of historical and literary, as well as religious, texts. Such communities find recent counterparts in the interpretive communities theorized by Hans Robert Jauss and by Stanley Fish.[47]

Gregory's book, of course, is an example of *"historia,"*[48] the genre that finds Christian significance in the course of human history, and it is also this genre that in turn provides, as Stephen Nichols has pointed out, a model for other kinds of literary narrative in the earlier Middle Ages. Nichols observes the operation of Eriugena's doctrine of *theosis*, "the manifestation of God in humans,"[49] in this genre, which he sees, with Rodulf Glaber, as a concept of narrative based on "a metonymic mechanism capable of equating the changing face of actuality—'the diversity and multiplicity of things,' as he puts it—into the unchanging, eternal order, a mechanism capable of embracing both history and Scripture and of showing how they must necessarily signify one another."[50] The resulting historical work will thus incorporate the directions for its own proper interpretation by the audience, which, like the members of Stock's textual communities, must find in it the same meanings its author found in the book of the world. Nichols goes on to trace the workings of this process in other literary forms, especially the *chanson de geste*, demonstrating that a poem like the *Chanson de Roland* also operates on the principle of directed vision: "The interest of this work, its freshness, lies in its refusal to reveal its ultimate purpose immediately. It accepts the risks of misreading . . . in favor of a gradual revelation of purpose, one that comes primarily through the intuitional progress of Roland."[51] Though interpretations other than the one that demonstrates Roland's *theosis* may be possible, they would be misreadings, results of a failure to attend to the poem's "directed vision."

I would suggest, with Bloch, that this state of affairs begins to change in the twelfth century, that it has changed drastically by the fourteenth and fifteenth centuries, and that these changes are reflected in the differences among early, high, and late medieval literature. Unlike Bloch, however, I would suggest that it is less a question of a massive epistemic break than of a continued competition among determinate and indeterminate modes of thought, though the indeterminate modes certainly gain ground in this period. Even in the early Middle Ages, we shall see evidence of a greater indeterminacy of meaning than may at first appear, or at least of its possibility: though Ganelon's false semiology is a perversion, it is nonetheless conceivable; and although there is a correct interpretation of the *Chanson de Roland*, others are, of course, possible, as is suggested by its "refusal to reveal its ultimate purpose immediately." It should also be pointed out that even Gregory of Tours does not himself draw any one-to-one relationships between the heavenly portents he describes and subsequent historical events, but simply juxtaposes them and allows the audience to draw whatever implications of a relationship there may be.

Such reticence on the part of both Gregory and the *Roland* suggests the possibility that, in literary texts as in language theory, a competition between indeterminate and determinate modes, between an "undirected" and a "directed vision," is conceivable even before the twelfth century. The competition is nowhere emphasized; it remains only an intriguing possibility. The reader's freedom is still severely limited. After the twelfth century, however, the "undirected vision" becomes more and more widespread, until it becomes the dominant (though never the exclusive) mode by the fourteenth and fifteenth centuries. I now turn to its appearance in several different areas of medieval thought.

Literal Meaning and the Rise of Indeterminacy: Exegesis, Rhetoric, Ethics

One innovation in twelfth-century thought was a new emphasis on literal reality: the historical rather than the allegorical level of Scripture, the verbal surface of literature rather than its potential for moralization, the natural world in itself rather than its potential symbolic meaning. The literal facts were still investigated for signs of divine immanence and will, but thinkers were also beginning to ask what they meant in themselves. The decisive impetus for this modification of attitudes toward the created universe (including human creations) was the introduction of Aristotle to Western thinkers, through the twelfth-century Latin translations of his works and those of his Arabic followers, particularly Averroës. For the first time, a coherent system of thought other than neoplatonic idealism became available to the West, allowing this world to become a more legitimate object of study in its own right, not only in its symbolic relation to divine reality.

Like the created universe, verbal texts also began to be read in this new way, whether the object of study was the Bible or the classical secular *auctores*, or even contemporary poetry: the rhetoricians began to suggest that new literary works could legitimately be created with an emphasis on their own surface beauty and the aesthetic pleasure they could give, rather than on any spiritual truths to be discovered through symbolic deep reading. This is also the period in which, as Minnis has shown, the Bible began to be read for the contributions of its human as well as its divine authors, thus linking it, too, to the interpretation of human creations. The novelty of these approaches can best be understood through a comparison of earlier and later trends in each of these disciplines.

Traditionally, Scriptural exegetes had read the Bible as Eriugena had read

God's other book, the created universe: as an allegory, whose literal or historical level served most importantly to orient the interpreter toward the more profound spiritual truths that were concealed in it and symbolically revealed by it. Exegetes after St. Augustine neglected his advice to study languages, natural history, etc., in order to understand the literal level, and their response to the doctrine that language can lead the Christian to God was to interpret even the most unlikely texts in such a way as to make this connection as directly as possible.[52]

Exposition was thus divided into the literal and the more important spiritual levels; and the spiritual could be further subdivided into various kinds of symbolic meaning. The best-known system is the ancient fourfold one derived from St. John Cassian, consisting of the literal (or historical) and three spiritual levels:

> Jerusalem, according to history, is a city of the Jews; according to allegory [referring to the life of Christ or the Church] it is the Church of Christ; according to anagoge [referring to Last Things and the after-life] it is that heavenly city of God *which is the mother of us all* (Gal. iv.26); according to tropology [referring to morality] it is the soul of man.[53]

Minnis has suggested that even in the twelfth century, there was little change in this state of affairs:

> It would seem, then, that twelfth-century exegetes were interested in the *auctor* mainly as a source of *auctoritas:* the human writer of Scripture was important in proportion to the extent to which he had provided (perhaps unwittingly) part of the vast pattern of meaning supposed to lie behind the literal sense of Scripture. It was this pattern which the exegetes strove to describe, not the individual contribution of any human *auctor*.[54]

To some extent this is true; nevertheless, the twelfth century also saw the beginnings of interest in the literal level itself. Beryl Smalley finds the origins of this movement in the Victorine interpreters of the twelfth and early thirteenth centuries.[55]

The implications of this shift in emphasis are suggested by Hugh of St. Victor. Although Hugh continually refers to the historical sense as merely a small part of exegesis, he also sees it as necessary: "Nor do I think that you will be able to become perfectly sensitive to allegory unless you have first been grounded in history. Do not look down upon these least things. The man who looks down on such smallest things slips little by little."[56] But

Hugh can also give us a sense of why the literal level was scorned, why even he and his fellow Victorines felt it to be such a small thing compared to allegory; and the reason for this discomfort with the literal level will in turn suggest an important parallel with the growth of semantic ambiguity in secular literature.

The spiritual level—what Hugh calls "the divine deeper meaning"—is so valuable because it is unitary; this is the level of singular, authoritative truth: "The deeper meaning admits no contradiction, is always harmonious, always true."[57] As in the literary genres that Nichols examines, the reader who perceives the spiritual level is directed to unified, divine truth. Even when a passage has more than a single "deeper meaning," they cannot contradict one another, because Scripture on this level reveals only meanings that are "consonant with sound faith."[58] Again, allegory insures the Augustinian doctrine that many interpretations are admissible, but only as long as they are consonant with Christian belief; it provides a persuasive example of the impulse to totalization that Gellrich finds throughout medieval culture. Eco poses the problem in slightly different terms; for him, the medieval view of the Bible is a "beautiful example of unlimited semiosis":

> Thus, both Testaments spoke at the same time of their sender, their content, and their referent, and their meaning was a nebula of all possible archetypes. The scriptures were in the position of saying everything. Everything, though, was rather too much for interpreters interested in truth.
>
> The symbolical nature of sacred scripture had therefore to be tamed. Potentially, the scriptures had every possible meaning; so the reading of them had to be governed by a code.[59]

The literal sense, then, is not so clear-cut as the spiritual senses; for Hugh of St. Victor, it contains "everything the sacred writer meant to say," which, as Eco points out, might include entirely too much. If the "deeper meaning" is necessarily univocal, the literal sense may be open to the confusing possibility of contradictory interpretations: "In the [literal] sense, as has been said, many things are found to disagree."[60] In Hugh's example of the different levels of meaning to be found in one Scriptural passage (Isaiah 4:1), he admits that the literal sense may allow two opposed interpretations: "You do not know what the Prophet wanted to say, whether he promised good or threatened evil."[61] Allegorical reading must necessarily produce a single, clearly directed vision of divine truth, but the literal sense can direct the reader in two opposite directions at once, producing a confusing ambiguity. Meaning is indeterminate on the literal level, and its indeterminacy can be resolved only by recourse to allegory.

Thirteenth-century exegetes approached this problem from the perspective of what was intended by the human authors of Scripture. Whereas Hugh of St. Victor, despite the Victorine critique of allegorical readings that neglect the literal level, both acknowledged the undecidability of meaning existing in the purely literal level, and seemed relieved to pass from that level to the clarity and harmony of allegory, St. Albert the Great completed the shift of emphasis that the Victorines had begun, concentrating on the literal level and even dismissing some conventional spiritual interpretations as absurd or irrelevant.[62]

Given Hugh of St. Victor's view that the literal level is the level of disharmony and ambiguity, it is not surprising that the movement toward the literal reading of Scripture should also imply a movement away from the traditional emphasis on unity. Minnis suggests that, rather than insisting on the totalizing harmony of the Bible, thirteenth-century exegetes drew new distinctions among its various authors: "It would seem that a writer's diverse talents are presupposed and exploited by God. As a result, the differences between the personalities and the various *modi agendi* of the human *auctores* of Scripture can be fully recognized."[63] This revised view of how Scripture was created also involves a new way of thinking about how it is to be interpreted; rather than being shunned, multiple literal meanings are now welcomed. Aquinas refers to the passage from Augustine cited above: "Now because the literal sense is that which the author intends, and the author of holy Scripture is God who comprehends everything all at once in his understanding, it comes not amiss, as St. Augustine observes, if many meanings are present even in the literal sense of one passage of Scripture."[64] No single human explanation is adequate to divine truth. St. Thomas's formulation of the question can be seen as an invitation to multiple and continual acts of interpretation.

At the same time, it should be noted that the difference between the divine and the human authors' intentions does not imply any disharmony between them. A possible indeterminacy of meaning is still kept in check by Christian doctrine. As Minnis points out, following Nicholas of Lyre, "the mind of God and the mind of man concur."[65] But Minnis suggests as well that this new way of conceiving of Biblical authorship also influenced the reading of secular, pagan authors, and that in their case, while some thinkers found that the ancients could be of use to the Christian faith, others strongly objected to the possibility that secular literature could be read like the Bible. Vincent of Beauvais exemplifies both trends: in his *Speculum historiale,* he situates the opinions of pagan authors side by side with those from Scripture, without trying to make them agree, but nevertheless asserting that the Christian ones have greater authority.[66] On the one hand, a multiplicity of contradictory interpretations suggests an indeterminacy of meaning; on the other, an assertion of the greater authority of revealed truth suggests a predetermined, directed reading. Once again, a method that determines meaning ahead of time conflicts with one that seems to remove knowledge from the exclusive control of Christian doctrine.

Only the Bible, according to Aquinas, could be read on a spiritual as well as the literal level; neither the book of nature nor the books of secular authors were to be interpreted on any level but the literal.[67] The emphasis on the literal level of interpretation, then, leads us to the notion of a secular literature existing only on that level, free of the *theosis* that directs the reading of the *chanson de geste* toward spiritual reality. Hugh of St. Victor's characterization of the literal level as undecidable suggests that such a literature would not resolve its surface meanings in a higher truth; and indeed, just such a literature was theorized by the rhetoricians of the twelfth and thirteenth centuries.

We have seen, with Nichols, that earlier genres (*historia, chanson de geste,* saint's life) orient their audience toward an awareness of divine immanence, as allegorical interpretation of the Bible reveals singular, divine truths beneath the ambiguous literal surface. This spiritual orientation is consistent with the Church's suspicion of purely secular literature. Indeed, from the earliest times, Christian writers typically condemned an interest in secular literature as a dangerous distraction from the Word of God. James J. Murphy characterizes this controversy as a "contrast between *Verbum* (Word of God) and *verbum* (word of man)" and cites various early Christian reactions against secular literature.[68] This distrust of literature that had no spiritual function may be related to the more general distrust of literacy documented by Stock and by M. T. Clanchy; both forms of suspicion on the part of traditional thinkers emphasize the potential for falsification implicit in texts generally, and specifically in poetic texts.

Clanchy suggests the possibility that the forgery of such legal documents as charters may have been the rule rather than the exception in the twelfth century, and thus that written documents (as opposed to oral custom) may have tended to falsify the past more than to preserve it: "A good oral tradition or an authentic charter might be rejected by a court of law because it seemed strange, whereas a forged charter would be acceptable because it suited contemporary notions of what an ancient charter should be like.

. . . Forgers recreated the past in an acceptable literate form."[69] Writing itself, then, necessarily widens the gap between language and reality.[70]

This tendency of language, especially written language, to falsify reality, was seen as particularly dangerous when the truth being falsified was religious truth. Late in the twelfth century, the influential Alain de Lille expressed the problem thus: "Can it be that thou dost not know how poets expose naked falsehood to their hearers with no protecting cloak, that they may intoxicate their ears, and, so to speak, bewitch them with a melody of honeyed delight; or how they cloak that same falsehood with a pretense of credibility?"[71] Whether Alain de Lille's own honeyed language can be taken at face value or not, he repeats here a position familiar to medieval readers: unless a literary work could be allegorized in order to yield up a singular Christian truth (and the efforts of, for example, the "classicizing friars" of the fourteenth century suggest that this continued to be possible even after Aquinas's insistence that only the Bible has a spiritual level of meaning),[72] it was a seductive trap. As in the Bible, then, the literal level of secular works—the only level many readers thought such works had—lacks the singular and harmonious truth of God's (allegorical) Word. Although a literary work might touch on a philosophical truth, the beauty and eloquence of its style was more likely to result in confusion:

> Of this sort are all the songs of the poets—tragedies, comedies, satires, heroic verse and lyric, iambics, certain didactic poems, fables, and histories, and also the writings of those fellows whom today we commonly call "philosophers" and who are always taking some small matter and dragging it out through long verbal detours, obscuring a simple meaning in confused discourses—who, lumping even dissimilar things together, make, as it were, a single "picture" from a multitude of "colors" and forms.[73]

Rhetoricians like Matthew of Vendôme and Geoffrey of Vinsauf in their works opposed, at least tacitly, this view of literature, and recommended precisely the tropes, the "colors of rhetoric," the verbal detours of *amplificatio*, which Hugh condemns. There is no mention of truth, divine or otherwise, in the *artes poeticae* of the twelfth and thirteenth centuries; language is here used for the sake of the aesthetic pleasure it can give the audience: "When meaning comes clad in such apparel, the sound of words is pleasant to the happy ear, and delight in what is unusual stimulates the mind."[74] In the repetition and amplification advocated by the rhetoricians, the multiplicity of words, rather than the singular Word of God, is emphasized, as is the literal surface of that purely human creation, the verbal text, rather than the spiritual significance of God's two books, the Bible and the Book of Nature. A human activity with its many meanings is perceived as a valid object of interest, whereas before it had been seen only as a distraction from the authoritative Truth. Alexandre Leupin sees Geoffrey of Vinsauf's *Poetria nova* in these terms: "While magically transforming black into white, negative into positive, and tarnish into luster, Geoffroi de Vinsauf turns theology's malediction into the metaphorical and improper fount of his new poetics."[75] As we shall see in chapter 2, Aquinas was far from alone in denying that any literary creation not directly inspired by God could have an allegorical, spiritual meaning. Human works could be read on the literal level alone, where conflicting, contradictory meanings abound.

This valorization of the literal surface with its multiplicity of words thus seems, almost inevitably, also to lead to an interest in the possibility of multiple meanings to be found in a literary work, in semantic indeterminacy or undecidability. At least one literary scholar in this period seems to have distinguished poetry, or poetic narrative, from history and philosophy, precisely by the multiple interpretive possibilities that poetry allows. Arnulf of Orléans, in his commentary on Lucan's *Pharsalia*, takes up this subject in passing, suggesting that whereas philosophers and historians, in their search for the authoritative truth, state their own views, a poet makes no attempt to solve the problem of differing interpretations, but rather suggests possibilities without affirming any of them.[76]

Arnulf practices what he preaches: he frequently provides a series of possible interpretations for a given passage in Lucan, drawing upon various sources, and usually refrains from choosing among them, as his editor, Berthe M. Marti, notes.[77] The effect of his method is to imply that one interpretation of a poet's work is as good as another, and furthermore that this multiplicity of possible interpretations is precisely the aspect of literature that makes it literary.

It is but a short step from the multiplicity of possible meanings in human language to the possibility that the interpreter of language—the hearer, receiver, or reader—contributes to its meaning; and, before the fourteenth century, that step is taken most decisively by Peter Abelard, under the influence of Aristotle. R. Howard Bloch has discussed Abelard's departure from theological tradition most suggestively:

> In [*De Unitate et Trinitate divina*] Abelard's appeal to reason—"human understanding"—poses the possibility of interpretation independent

not only of the exegetical past, but of doctrine itself. The book on the Trinity, based upon explanation rather than tradition, constitutes a heresy of reading; and when, in the trial which follows its publication, Abelard offers "to explain," his accuser, Albert of Rheims, pretends to "care nothing for human explanation or reasoning in such matters, but only for the words of authority." The essence of Abelard's heresy is, then, the substitution of the "logic of words" for authority.[78]

This is the logical step that earlier theologians refuse to take: the bracketing of spiritual authority in favor of an examination of the purely human faculties' interpretive abilities. Reason is, for the duration of this examination, detached from the control of doctrine, or divine guarantees. Logic, in fact, is for Abelard concerned primarily with language, and a clear distinction is drawn between the right use of language and any essential truth: logic is "the *altercatio* of some people who seek after the probability (or provability) of certain propositions, not after some real truth."[79] Language, in fact, no longer refers to things, but to the intellections or mental images of things: "According to Abelard, language and the ontological categories of the real are no longer coterminous principles, and the etymological effort to arrive at the nature even of physical reality is severely compromised."[80] Meaning, then, is not inherent in language or even in the intentions of the speaker. Stock points out some of the implications of this position: "Signification arises only when the sense intended by the speaker and heard by the listener are agreed to be the same. As this cannot be determined from the speaker alone, he prefers, with Aristotle, to refer significance ultimately to the hearer's understanding (*ad intellectum audientis*)."[81]

The intellectual conditions of the high Middle Ages would now seem to be prepared for a literature of indeterminate meanings: Abelard's bracketing of the traditional divine guarantees of signification releases language from the authority of the signified and opens it to the hearer's interpretation, while rhetoricians, classical scholars, and theologians recognize a secular literature existing on the purely literal level, the level characterized by ambiguity and undecidability. While more determinate modes of thought continue to exert their influence—in the impulse to bring language under the control of the divine guarantees through allegory and *theosis*, in the distrust of textuality and of poetic language, in the accusations of heresy brought against Abelard—the stage has also been set for the emergence of indeterminate forms. However, before turning to a comparison of the *chanson de geste* with romance, the new genre embodying these possibilities, one further contribution of Abelard's should be considered.

The implications not only of his thoughts on the interpretation of language but of those on the interpretation of human behavior as well, seem to be worked out in twelfth- and thirteenth-century romance. His influential "ethic of intentions" is conveniently summed up by Gilson: "For good as for evil, the morality of the act is identical with the morality of the intention."[82] Although Abelard concerned himself primarily with the theological implications of this theory, the emphasis on intentions, like the emphasis on literal reality, almost inevitably produces a corollary emphasis on indeterminate interpretation. Unlike actions, the intentions that alone provide their true meaning cannot be known with certainty by any observer except God. Human interpreters must deduce intentions from external signs, from the actions which in themselves may be good or bad, regardless of the morality of the intentions that produced them. For literary artists after Abelard, the world of human behavior represented in their works would come to seem confusing, even incomprehensible, in just this way: how could actions in that world be correctly interpreted without insight into the intentions that produced them? And how could such insight be achieved? If readers of such works confront in them multiple, conflicting possible meanings, the readers' confusion, and their need to interpret without any divine "directed vision" to guarantee accurate knowledge, are reflections of the similar need (and frustration) experienced by those works' characters as they confront their own social worlds. Like linguistic signs in Abelard's system, the meaning of human behavior in romance must be supplied by the observer, and there are no guarantees that such interpretations will be correct.

Indeterminacy and Interpretation: The Semiology of Epic and Romance

Turning at last to literary narrative itself, the major development of the twelfth century is what Eugène Vinaver has called "the rise of romance": "A series of French verse romances produced at that time established a new literary genre which, together with the influence of early Provençal poetry, 'determined,' as [W. P. Ker] puts it, 'the forms of modern literature long after the close of the Middle Ages.' "[83] Vinaver, like Ker before him,[84] and like most literary historians, sees the development of this new genre partly in terms of the decline of the previously dominant French form, the *chanson de geste* described in neoplatonic terms by Nichols. The distinction between these two genres seems to be a sound one, and they may be seen as yet another example, now in a poetic rather than a philosophical or exegetical context, of the competition between determinate and indeterminate modes of thought in this period. If, as Nichols so convincingly argues, the proper interpretation of the *chanson de geste* should take its clue from the neoplatonic "directed vision" theorized by Eriugena, then one of the distinguishing characteristics of romance is the very different kind of interpretation it seems to require. It might be described as a much less directed, or even as an "undirected" vision, having more in common with the trends just discussed than with the neoplatonic thought of Augustine and Eriugena. It should be useful at this point to compare the kind of interpretation demanded by these two genres.

In a passage from the *Chanson de Roland* that Nichols does not discuss, the Christian and pagan standard-bearers do battle (according to some editors).[85] This battle of signifiers has unambiguous results; the pagan leader sees his banner brought down in defeat and knows immediately how this sign is to be read: "il ad tort e Carlemagnes dreit."[86] Not only Charlemagne's signs, but his entire semiology as well, is superior, as the poem demonstrates over and over again: the battle itself is a transparent sign of that superiority. Signs by their very nature signify truly, and signifiers have an inherent, necessary relationship to what they signify in the world of the *chanson de geste*. This point is clarified even further in the scene of Ganelon's trial by battle. Although his prosecution is "difficult" for reasons of feudal law,[87] God's direct intervention in it establishes a singular, authoritative truth,[88] and, to use Abelard's terminology, makes Ganelon's intentions public.

Obviously, signs can be falsified in the *Chanson de Roland*, most notably by Ganelon himself. But the moral judgment attached to such falsification is revealing: it is invariably perceived as an abuse of signification, not as an inherent component of it. Wicked characters like Ganelon can pervert signification, but the true and normal nature of signs is to be transparently interpretable. Virtuous characters communicate immediately by the use of such signs, as when Charlemagne instinctively understands the true meaning of the sound of Roland's olifant. The audience, too, shares in this immediate knowledge of the truth: we are not fooled by Ganelon, because we have witnessed his negotiations with the heathens, and we know that Charlemagne's reading of the horn is correct, because we have witnessed the circumstances in which Roland sounded it. In the poem as in the standard-bearers' battle, Charlemagne's semiology, its signs fully adequate to their objects, triumphs over Ganelon's and the heathens' more indeterminate one.

This kind of semiology, in which transparent signs allow unmediated knowledge of the truth, is, as Nichols suggests, consistent with an Augustinian epistemology that claims that Christian charity allows human beings to attain knowledge:

> Just as God brings to the act of hearing the discourse the grace which may, if bestowed on the speaker, produce theosis, so man-the-audience must bring to the act of listening the human equivalent of grace, that is charity. If the discourse is authentic, that is, "true," then there will be the same coincidence between the intention of human minds, the speaker's and the listener's, as between human and divine intention.[89]

Just as the "spiritual" meanings of Scripture, dictated by God and discovered by interpreters versed in the doctrines of the Church, all unite in a singular, divine Truth, so perfect communication is possible among human beings linked by charity. As Augustine says in the *Confessions*, "But charity believes all things—all things, that is, which are spoken by those who are joined as one in charity—and for this reason I, too, O Lord, make my confession aloud in the hearing of men. For although I cannot prove to them that my confessions are true, at least I shall be believed by those whose ears are opened to me by charity."[90]

In romance, we find a very different set of values, requiring a new kind of interpretation. It should not be surprising to find multiplicity and indeterminacy of meaning playing a major role in these narratives. Whether seen in relation to the Victorines' method of reading Scripture, the principles of the rhetoricians, Arnulf's multiple interpretations of Lucan, or Abelard's ethic of intentions, the romances of the high Middle Ages, originating in the twelfth century along with these developments in other fields, should reveal a semiology contrasting with that of the confidently neoplatonic *chanson de geste* and should encourage a very different kind of reading. Recent theories about the genre as a whole, regardless of historical period, make similar points. Patricia A. Parker, for example, in a study of romance after the Middle Ages, characterizes the genre "primarily as a form which simultaneously quests for and postpones a particular end, objective, or object."[91] It is the genre, then, in which achievement of the goal is always deferred for the characters, and therefore in which authoritative meaning, like Derrida's transcendental signified, is always deferred for the reader. Departing from Northrop Frye's definition of romance as "a sequential and processional form,"[92] Parker goes on to suggest: "One of the implications of the sequential, however, is that it remains, like time itself, within a frame in which presence, or fulfillment, is always in some sense placed at a distance."[93] Indeterminacy of signification and a multiplicity of possible interpretations are, then, the norm in romance, often preventing the solution of the mystery and keeping the text's semantic gaps from being filled in. Interpretation in such texts is necessary, for the reader as for the characters, but since signification has been released from divine control it is also necessarily uncertain or undecidable. It is, in fact, this absence of divine control that defines romance.[94] Romances often thematize their own mysterious indeterminacy—their similarity to the Victorines' literal level of Scripture, on which there are simply too many possible meanings—by presenting characters involved in interpretive activities not so very different from those demanded of the reader by the text's semantic gaps.

Certain scenes in an early romance, the *Chevalier de la charrette* of Chrétien de Troyes, are comparable to those in the *Chanson de Roland* just mentioned. *Roland* was probably composed, in the form preserved in the Oxford manuscript, at the tail-end of the eleventh century, and the *Charrette* most likely around the year 1180.[95] Much less than a century separates them, but in terms of signification and interpretation, both represented within the poems themselves and as experienced by the audience, they are worlds apart.

Turning to Chrétien's poem, we find the romance-hero himself engaged in manipulations very similar to Ganelon's. Far from understanding the truth about Lancelot from the beginning, as we do with Ganelon, the reader is kept entirely in the dark about him, even as to his name, until about halfway through the romance (the original title referring not to his name but to the cart that carries him). The cart, indeed, can be taken as a concrete example of romance semiology, comparable in that way to the banners of the *Chanson de Roland*. As in that poem, two competing semiologies, one determinate and one indeterminate, govern the potential interpretation of all signs. If the view of Arthurian society as depicted in the *Charrette*, rather than Lancelot's own view, is taken as normative, the cart ought to serve the same identifying and judgmental functions as the banners and the trial by battle in *Roland*: as a sign, it is routinely associated with a single correct, socially conventional and agreed-upon meaning:

> qui a forfet estoit repris
> s'estoit sor la charrete mis
> et menez par totes les rues;
> s'avoit totes enors perdues,
> ne puis n'estoit a cort oïz,
> ne enorez ne conjoïz.[96]

The cart serves, in this society's conventional semiotic system, to identify and to judge its rider (he must be a criminal), just as the ensigns' battle in the *Chanson de Roland* identified and judged the political and moral stances of the two armies. But whereas the violator of conventional semiology in the *Roland* is a villain, in the *Charrette* it is Lancelot himself who, along with Guinevere, violates the system and reinterprets its signs in a manner precisely opposed to their conventional interpretation:

> Et la reïne li reconte:
> "Comant? Don n'eüstes vos honte
> de la charrete, et si dotastes?
> Molt a grant enviz i montastes
> quant vos demorastes deus pas.
> Por ce, voir, ne vos vos je pas
> ne aresnier ne esgarder."
> "Autre foiz me doint Dex garder,"
> fet Lanceloz, "de tel mesfet,
> et ja Dex de moi merci n'et
> se vos n'eüstes molt grant droit. . . ."[97]

In the lovers' interpretation it is the hesitation to ride in the cart, rather than the ride itself, that is a sign of criminality: they set up their own antisocial semiology based on a violation of social norms. Here as throughout this romance, such problems of interpretation can be associated with Abelard's ethic of intentions: although Lancelot's and Guinevere's actions are clear, the concealment of their motives invariably causes those actions to be misinterpreted. Knowledge of their intentions would force the other characters to revise their judgment of the couple; but since such knowledge would reveal their adultery, Lancelot and Guinevere resolutely prevent it. Hanning, in working out the problem of individuality in twelfth-century romance, has suggested that the protagonist must to some extent come into conflict with society and has also drawn suggestive connections with Abelard;[98] it is the effect of this new view of the self on interpretation that must now be explored.

This is the reason that Lancelot is such a mysterious figure in his romance. The social norm allows an immediate identification of individuals through references to their personal signs:

> Antr'ax diënt: "Veez vos or
> celui a cele bande d'or
> par mi cel escu de bernic?

C'est Governauz de Roberdic.
Et veez vos celui aprés,
qui an son escu pres a pres
a mise une aigle et un dragon?
C'est li filz le roi d'Arragon
qui venuz est an ceste terre
por pris et por enor conquerre."[99]

Lancelot, however, constantly appears in disguise, and is thus identifiable only to his partner in the transgression of sign-systems, Guinevere. In fact, in the tournament that concludes Chrétien's own contribution to the romance, which was completed by Godefroi de Leigni, she can identify him only by his willingness to violate the conventional code, and hence to do his worst, rather than his chivalric best, at her command. Such behavior, of course, renders him unidentifiable to the rest of his society. Unlike Baligant in the *Chanson de Roland*, the spectators can only misinterpret this battle, and their misinterpretation is not rectified when Guinevere changes her mind and orders Lancelot to do his best: he escapes, still unrecognized, at the end of the tournament. The court continues to respond inappropriately to Lancelot throughout the romance, even when he defeats Meleagant in Guinevere's trial by battle. A comparison of this final conflict with Ganelon's similar trial by battle in the *Chanson de Roland* reveals the growth of literary indeterminacy as regards God's will as well as such purely human concerns as identity.

Whereas the meaning of the trial by battle in the *Roland* is clearly determined by God and serves as a reliable decoding device for all who observe it, quickly unmasking Ganelon's false significations and itself serving as the true signifier of a transcendental signified, the trial by battle in the *Charrette* provides no such resolution of the romance's many deceptions, either for the observers within the poem or for the poem's audience. It is true that the accusation against which Lancelot defends the queen is technically inaccurate, and that therefore Lancelot deserves to win: Meleagant, misinterpreting the evidence of the queen's bloody sheets, has accused her of sleeping with the wounded Sir Kay, when in fact she has slept with Lancelot himself, after he was injured breaking in through her barred window. Thus Lancelot's final victory does reveal the truth about Meleagant's claims; but it also serves an even more important second purpose, that of concealing the queen's and Lancelot's own real guilt. As in the *Chanson de Roland*, the courtly spectators proclaim the victor:

> Li rois et tuit cil qui i sont
> grant joie an demainnent et font.
> Lancelot desarment adonques
> cil qui plus lié an furent onques,
> si l'en ont mené a grant joie.[100]

But in this case the jubilation is heavily ironic: Lancelot has betrayed the king who here leads the acclaim; he really is, from society's point of view, a criminal, as so many have perceived him after the episode of the cart, though not in the way they believe.

In the world of the romance, God's hand can no longer be forced by human legal institutions; the trial is no longer a *deus ex machina* as it was in the *Chanson de Roland*. Here we find a poetic parallel, once again, to the Victorine reading of the Bible's literal level. The spiritual interpretation could resolve such ambiguities; but if divine immanence is withdrawn from the world, or only from the literary work, authoritative truth and certain knowledge must also withdraw from the realm of human action, to be replaced by multiple human interpretations of the ambiguities that result.

God was the guide in the *Chanson de Roland*: he intervened directly in human history by means of the trial by battle or even, as in the concluding *laisse*, by means of a heavenly messenger, forcing Charlemagne into battle once again, much against his will.[101] The emperor may not like what he hears, but Gabriel's language has transparent and authoritative meaning, which cannot be either mistaken or ignored. High medieval rhetoric, however, posited works of literature existing purely in the realm of human words, without reference to the singular Word of God. Uncontrolled by divine immanence, such works cannot be read with any certainty of finding the truth. Interpretation under these conditions cannot be undertaken as confidently as in the neoplatonic tradition, in which the truth can be known.

At the level of interpretation also, the reader is faced with undecidable choices: how are we to regard Lancelot, for example? Is he a great and admirable hero? A traitorous criminal? A ridiculous butt of Chrétien's satire, with his absurd submission to Guinevere's whims? We know how various other characters regard him (Guinevere, Meleagant, Arthur), but which, if any of them, is right? We might even agree that Lancelot is all these things, but what are we to make of a hero who is also a criminal, or of a butt of satire who is also heroic? The truth about Lancelot is as multiple and indeterminate as the truth about Ganelon or Roland is singular and authoritative: "A chacun son Lancelot."[102] Our vision of him is directed in so many different ways that the truth cannot be decided.

Indeterminacy in Late Medieval Science and Philosophy

Whereas the high medieval cultural developments most relevant to our purposes here focused, for the most part, on texts of various kinds, the fourteenth and fifteenth centuries saw an expansion of interest in indeterminate modes of thought to disciplines less directly concerned with language and writing. In late medieval science, or natural philosophy, for example, the attempt to know this world in itself, produced by the introduction of Aristotle to the West, led eventually to the same multiplicity of interpretations in reading the Book of Nature that we have traced in attitudes toward verbal texts. Edward Grant discusses a convenient example of this trend in an article on two fourteenth-century philosophers at the University of Paris, Jean Buridan and Nicole Oresme. These two scientific investigators provide a useful contrast of two possible philosophical positions with regard to the created universe observed in its own right and not as a divine symbol: whereas Buridan produced confident interpretations of natural phenomena in order to arrive at a formulation of the laws of nature, Oresme made a point, according to Grant, of arriving at different, but equally logical, interpretations of the same phenomena, precisely in order to demonstrate the lack of absolute validity inherent in all scientific knowledge.[103] The determinate mode of thought represented by Buridan thus faced competition from one in which the human mind seemed less and less able to arrive at certainty or even at valid knowledge, and more and more subject to what it could not know.

This lack of confidence in human knowledge is related to a larger philosophical tendency, affecting investigations in more areas than the physical sciences alone, especially in the work of the fourteenth century's most influential philosopher, William of Ockham. It influences his ontology, for one example: "every positive thing existing outside of the soul is by that very fact singular."[104] Ockham's philosophical world is inhabited by radically individual beings separate from all others. Since God is separate from humanity, human knowledge of God is severly limited in Ockham's scheme.[105] A related problem is Ockham's understanding of divine power. Ordinarily, God operates in the created universe by means of secondary causes, that is, through natural law, rather than by constant direct intervention; this is action through "ordained power," *potentia ordinata*, and because the laws of nature through which it operates are orderly, their principles can be discovered and predicted. However, God also has the "absolute power" (*potentia absoluta*) to intervene directly in the created universe.[106] He can, for example, transcend natural law and cause a perception of something that does not exist; Ockham writes that there can be an intuitive cognition of a nonexistent being.[107] Knowledge can thus be called into question in a universe in which God can intervene directly and miraculously, without the knowledge of human beings. For any scientific or philosophical conclusion about the created universe to be valid, then, it must be assumed in any given instance that God is working only through his ordained, rather than his absolute, power; and there is no way of knowing whether or not this is actually the case. Marilyn McCord Adams has pointed out that Ockham does not pursue the implications of this view and therefore cannot be accused, as some have thought, of skepticism;[108] indeed, Ockham insists that the truths of faith are certain, though they are not knowledge.

Philosophy, that is, knowledge that is adequate to the created universe purely in itself, must thus be separated from theology, which renders such knowledge inadequate. Although created reality may be comprehensible in its own terms, the potential for divine intervention occurring without human awareness of it makes such comprehension radically contingent and uncertain. Knowledge as knowledge must therefore remain separate from religious belief.

Nevertheless, Ockham is determined "to guarantee natural knowledge while accommodating the truths of faith,"[109] and therefore holds that natural knowledge is indeed possible, though we cannot know in any given instance whether a cognition is actually the result of natural knowledge or of divine intervention. T. K. Scott puts the problem this way: "In brief, it seems to be suggested by his discussions that if all knowledge (in the strict sense) must be based on intuitive cognition, then even if we do sometimes know, we can never know that we know."[110] Ockham thus raises the possibility of skepticism without pursuing it; his followers, however, pursued it to far more radical conclusions than Ockham's own.

But before turning to those successors, Ockham's own contributions to two other fields, exegesis and language theory, should be stressed. The separation of human and divine, and the resulting unknowability of God, are related to Ockham's interest in the human authors of Scripture; it is *their* intentions that are expressed on the literal level, and their language thus deserves study in its own right. As Minnis suggests, Ockham followed other thirteenth- and fourteenth-century exegetes in finding the human authors' intentions a difficult problem of interpretation. Even deciding whether they express themselves figuratively or "properly," that is, straightforwardly, is difficult, yet doing so is necessary because the decision affects interpretation: "Unfortunately, many errors originate among the simple-minded who wish to accept all the statements of the *auctores* 'according to the property of speech' when they ought to be understood 'in accordance with authorial intention.' "[111]

Verbal signification, in fact, is a central problem in Ockham's thought. Universals, or general ideas, are natural signs abstracted from individual beings, but have no existence of their own outside the mind or as essences of the beings to which they refer. Words, in turn, have no natural relation to their referents at all, but are entirely artificial and conventional:

> The concept or impression of the soul signifies naturally; whereas the spoken or written term signifies only conventionally. This difference gives rise to another difference. We can decide to alter the signification of a spoken or written term, but no decision or agreement on the part of anyone can have the effect of altering the signification of a conceptual term.[112]

Words and things are thus separated from each other; we have come a long way from the transparent signification and confident interpretation of Augustine and Eriugena.[113]

William of Ockham's followers, very late in the period, provide the most striking examples of the indeterminate mode. Whereas Ockham emphasizes the possibility of natural knowledge, Nicholas of Autrecourt, for example, emphasizes the conclusion that we can never know that we know, or in other words, that knowledge is never certain (except for the principle of non-contradiction): "The thirteenth conclusion is that only opinion, not certainty, is had concerning things known by experience."[114] Thus, "if we admit that God can cause any appearance, we must either deny that judging evidently is knowing (and so abandon knowledge) or hold that one may know and yet be deceived, which is contradictory."[115] Ernest A. Moody sums up the conflict: Nicholas argues "that *if* we admit that an effect (be it intuitive cognition or any other natural occurrence) can be supernaturally produced without its natural cause, then we have no right to posit natural causes for any effects whatever," whereas Ockham "denies this consequence, and admits an order of natural evidence and necessity."[116]

The implications for interpretation of this denial of knowledge was far-reaching in the late Middle Ages. "God himself could deceive or mislead a man, making him believe what was not true and rewarding him for his belief. He would then be rewarded for his faith, which is independent of truth or falsity. . . . Revelation could therefore be falsified."[117] These "Ockhamists" of the later fourteenth century thus reinforced the separation of knowledge from belief, and found further limitations on knowledge.

Where Ockham accepted the necessity of causality at least as a proposition, though admitting also that God could suspend causes without suspending their effects, Nicholas argued that such a line of reasoning must prevent any certainty about natural causality, reducing it to mere probability.[118] Thus, whereas the *Chanson de Roland* showed divine intervention in the world to be the ultimate source of true and certain human knowledge, the "Ockhamist" emphasis on God's absolute power had just the opposite effect: divine intervention for many fourteenth- and fifteenth-century thinkers precisely precluded any possibility of certainty. For Nicholas, in fact, there could be no certain knowledge of the existence of substances themselves. This refusal of certainty about substance and causality implies a refusal of all natural knowledge except that which can be reduced to the principle of non-contradiction, a step never taken by Ockham himself.[119]

With the disagreement between William of Ockham and Nicholas of Autrecourt, we arrive at what is perhaps the closest parallel between medieval and postmodern theories of interpretation. The conflict between a thinker who believes that knowledge requires certainty, and therefore finds that knowledge is impossible, and one who is willing to accept uncertain knowledge as valid, has recently been revived in the pages of *The New York Review of Books*, the occasion being John R. Searle's review of Jonathan Culler's book *On Deconstruction*, in which Jacques Derrida's thought naturally plays a large part. To quote Searle: "There aren't in the way classical metaphysicians supposed any foundations for ethics or knowledge. . . . Derrida sees that the Husserlian project of a transcendental grounding for science, language, and common sense is a failure. But what he fails to see is that this doesn't threaten science, language, or common sense in the least."[120] Discussing Derrida's influence on literary theorists, scholars, and critics, Searle describes their "insistence that concepts that apply to language and literature, if they are to be truly valid, must admit of some mechanical procedure of verification. . . . the crude positivism of these assumptions I am criticizing is of a piece with Derrida's assumption that without foundations we are left with nothing but the free play of signifiers."[121] Searle here restates the current controversy over deconstruction in terms reminiscent of the fourteenth-century disagreement: he places Derrida in Nicholas of Autrecourt's position of denying the foundations of knowledge, and hence knowledge itself, while he himself takes Ockham's role, accepting the absence of such foundations while still claiming that knowledge can be valid even in their absence, that is, even without certainty. The competition between determinate and indeterminate modes of thought continues.

The following chapters examine the changing forms this competition takes in literary works from the twelfth to the fifteenth centuries; however, their order is logical rather than strictly chronological. My method is to examine what I term the "models of reading" proposed in a variety of major works, models for interpretation which the reader is invited to consider, accept, reject, or modify. The "gaps" in these narratives encourage the reader's participation in the creation of meaning for indeterminate or undecidable texts. However, the extent of this undecidability varies considerably with cultural changes, as does the extent to which it appears to be a desirable characteristic.

In chapter 2, the difference between allegory and romance helps us situate this conflict's literary aspects more clearly, while chapter 3, comparing a twelfth- and a fourteenth-century work, allows us to see how it develops between the high and the late Middle Ages. Chapter 4 explores a variety of solutions to problems raised by this competition in Chaucer's works, and chapter 5 investigates the issue of historical understanding and the growing radicalness with which knowledge was being questioned at the end of the Middle Ages.

2

Modes of Signification in Two Grail Romances

Some recent theorists of literature have suggested that allegory is, by its very nature, a mode of writing that destabilizes the meaning of language, drawing attention to the inadequacy of words to point toward a singular truth. Paul de Man asks,

> Why is it that the furthest reaching truths about ourselves and the world have to be stated in such a lopsided, referentially indirect mode? Or, to be more specific, why is it that texts that attempt the articulation of epistemology with persuasion turn out to be inconclusive about their own intelligibility in the same manner and for the same reasons that produce allegory?[1]

In the same article, he concludes that the nature of allegory is like the nature of language itself: "The notion of language as sign is dependent on, and derived from, a different notion in which language functions as rudderless signification and transforms what it denominates into the linguistic equivalence of the arithmetical zero."[2]

It is not my intention either to produce or to criticize a universal theory of allegory; for my purpose how allegory functions is less important than how medieval people perceived it. More helpful in this regard than either de Man or Miller is the work of Maureen Quilligan, who has demonstrated over and over again that a powerful tradition of thinking about allegory existed in the Middle Ages and the Renaissance, expressed in allegorical works themselves, and that this tradition was critical of language that does not point to a single transcendent truth: "Language for [Alain de Lille and Jean de Meun] is a force that must move society toward the Word at the center of the universe. Alain and Jean must be said to read that word: Chaucer must be said to hear it in the voices of creation. . . . for all three of these medieval writers it was critically possible and morally vital to perceive that Word in the world."[3] Allegory, then, was perceived by at least some medieval writers as a way of moving toward divine truth; far from being "a lopsided, referentially indirect mode," allegory was in this tradition a guarantee of language's adequacy to express the essential.

The danger of this view for modern readers lies in the suggestion, made frequently in the generation of scholars preceding that of de Man and Quilligan, that all medieval literature must be read as religious allegory. In this chapter I steer a path between the view that all medieval literature is geared toward such a transcendent reality and the view that no literary work, even an allegory, can be so directed. As I suggested in chapter 1, we shall find both views at work in twelfth- and thirteenth-century literature; the determinate mode of thought represented by medieval allegory competes with a more indeterminate mode represented by romance.

Because works like Chrétien's romances are to be read on the literal level alone, without reference to allegorical meanings, and because the literal level, as we have seen, lacks the divinely authoritative unity and harmony found by exegetes on the spiritual level(s), such works may seem mysterious or contradictory and thus require the reader's active participation in solving their mysteries, answering their unanswered questions, or filling in their "blanks" or "gaps." However, without the guidance that allegorical works find in church doctrine (and which even non-religious allegories provide, since their symbolic meanings determine their literal actions), the reader of such works can never be certain that any one interpretation is true or correct; these works remain to some extent ambiguous, their meaning indeterminate. Whereas allegories are didactic, imposing their interpretations as doctrinal truths about a higher level of reality, these other works are heuristic, inviting the reader's own interpretation as a way of exploring the mysteries of this world, this reality—and as a way of reflecting on that process. The interpretation of such works must be metonymic rather than metaphorical: rather than substituting one register (spiritual or abstract) for another (physical or concrete) in order to find a symbolic meaning harmonious with the literal, the reader must situate various pieces of information in their proper contexts on the same, literal level, in order to understand the various possible meanings. The reader's own uncertain speculations are reflected in those of the narratives' characters: their puzzling adventures become an event in, and an epitome of, our own mysterious world.

Even those works from this period that do recognize the instability of signification must still be seen in a more determinate context: the works of Chrétien de Troyes, like those of Marie de France (discussed in chapter 3), demonstrate not only an indeterminate mode of signification but the competition between that mode and the more determinate one prevailing in the earlier Middle Ages as well. Both of these writers are interested in semantic destabilization and in the audience's contribution to their works' meanings, but that this indeterminate view is still competing with a more determinate one in the twelfth century is suggested by the fact that they thematize indeterminacy, that is, they make it one of their own (determinate) meanings to be communicated to the audience. Not until the works of Machaut, in the fourteenth century (also discussed in chapter 3), does literature demonstrate a more thorough-going indeterminacy, one that playfully includes the reader but without imposing indeterminacy on the reader as a theme.

I address the problem of allegory by comparing two French romances on the Grail theme, giving this chapter a double purpose. First, it demonstrates that certain twelfth- and thirteenth-century romance writers were aware of the new ways of thinking about signification and interpretation—the interest in the physical or historical level of meaning theorized by the exegetes discussed in chapter 1, and recently examined by Minnis, for example[4]—and to some extent made them the theme of their works. Second, this chapter suggests that, whereas the *Queste del saint Graal* thematizes signification in order to encourage allegorical reading, Chrétien does so in his *Conte del Graal* in order to reject certain abuses of interpretation, one of which can be identified with allegory.

Modern critics are largely in agreement about one of these works, but not the other. The *Queste del saint Graal* is clearly allegorical and is almost universally accepted as such because it provides its own exegetical commentary on the romance fiction. The *Conte del Graal* of Chrétien de Troyes has provoked many allegorical readings but has just as often been read as a straight romance, without any allegorical superstructure. Scholars who read it (correctly, in my opinion) in this non-allegorical fashion emphasize its mysteriousness rather than insisting on a single specific meaning, as the allegorizers do; among these scholars is Jean Frappier, whose work on the *Conte* proclaims him the most sensible of Grail-scholars:

> Au vrai, Chrétien de Troyes n'a pas voulu donner au *Conte du Graal* une portée plus ou moins ésotérique ni le clarifier à l'extrême; à la lisière du mythe et de la vraisemblance, il a plutôt cherché à trouver un point d'équilibre entre la fantaisie et la raison. Le sens initial et profond du thème ne l'a pas tourmenté; mais son sujet lui permettait à merveille d'intriguer et de tenir ses lecteurs en haleine; il lui proposait des jeux d'ombre et de lumière.[5]

This position on Arthurian romance as a whole has been stated most fully by Robert Guiette in a somewhat impressionistic, but influential, article, and has been taken up by a number of more recent critics.[6] Few, however, have inquired just how this atmosphere of mystery is created, or how it affects the reader's response to the romance, or whether there is anything in the *Conte* that invites its readers to refuse allegory and to accept its mystery simply as mystery, or to provide their own solutions.

These are the questions I explore in this chapter by comparing the ways in which signification itself is thematized in these two romances. Both the *Queste* and the *Conte* are, to some extent, about the different ways in which it is possible to interpret the world and, by extension, the literary work that imitates it, but they use very different semiotic systems to call our attention to these issues. The *Queste*'s characters experience their world on various symbolic levels, as might be expected, each according to his or her own spiritual state, and the reader is encouraged to interpret the romance in a similarly allegorical manner. Its meaning is doctrinal and authoritative; its semiology is related to Cistercian allegoresis and perhaps to the moralizing of the classics in twelfth-century schools.[7] The *Conte*, it seems to me, places its emphasis very differently: its heroes must constantly adjust their perceptions of the world according to the circumstances in which they find themselves, but all the codes they learn or fail to learn coexist on the same, literal level of meaning. Indeed, attempts to read the world allegorically—interpretations like those the *Queste* provides for its own romance adventures—are shown in the *Conte* to be one of two hermeneutic procedures that cause failures of understanding. The reader is thus discouraged from allegoresis and instead is invited to experience the shifting perspectives on the world required of the two heroes. Interpretation here is related to such twelfth-century trends as the rhetorical tradition, the literal exegesis of Scripture, Arnulf's reading of Lucan, and the ethic of intentions. Allegory is thus not the only kind of interpretation thematized in the *Conte*; rather, Chrétien is concerned with a wide variety of responses to signification, of which allegory is only one.

Since the major emphasis of this chapter is on such a problematic work, the *Queste* is all the more useful as a standard of allegory against which the *Conte* can be measured, precisely because, in its self-interpretation, it is so clearly allegorical. But before dealing with the two romances themselves it should be useful to situate each of them in the medieval and modern debates about the existence of allegory outside of Scripture.

Medieval Literature: The Possibility of Allegory

The difference between a sensitivity to the presence of allegory and the unwarranted imposition of allegoresis is a persistent problem for interpreters of medieval literature. Many medieval works are clearly allegorical: the

Roman de la Rose and to some extent *Piers Plowman* (a more complex case, as it mixes its modes of signification) name their "characters" after the abstract qualities they represent, directly giving the reader a key to their interpretation; thus a figure named *Danger* is to be read not as a representation of a human personality but as one abstract characteristic of it. Dante provides a similar key in the *Divine Comedy*, not in its characters' names but in details of the landscape they inhabit, which represents certain of their qualities. Figures such as those in the *Rose* exhibit the "obsessive" or "compulsive" characteristics described by Angus Fletcher,[8] devoting their existence to the illustration of a single abstraction (though usually also providing enough mimetic complexity to keep the fiction interesting as fiction). Thus physical, sensory experience corresponds to the psychological or spiritual realities it reifies. Much medieval interpretation is also clearly allegorical: Scripture and the classics were consistently interpreted according to moral and doctrinal standards. St. Bernard's *Sermons* on the Song of Songs and the *Ovide moralisé* are two well-known examples.

In addition, some scholars (fewer today than twenty years ago, it seems, but more today than fifty years ago) believe in the existence of what might be called *concealed* allegory in medieval literature. Those who think that "medieval Christian poetry . . . is always allegorical"[9] necessarily find allegory where it does not obviously exist, that is, in works whose characters and iconographic details do not clearly represent abstractions. D. W. Robertson, Jr., though the best-known practitioner and promoter of the exegetical method by which all medieval works are interpreted as doctrinal allegory, is not alone: since before the publication of *A Preface to Chaucer*,[10] Urban T. Holmes and Sr. M. Amelia Klenke have tirelessly propounded their reading of one of the romances to be considered in this chapter, the *Conte del Graal* of Chrétien de Troyes, which they consider to be an allegory of the conversion of the Jews.[11] Despite the widespread influence of this method, it has always had its opponents as well, whose position has been summarized in part by Morton Bloomfield's response to the Holmes-Klenke thesis: "To suppose that medieval man would presume to put himself on the level of God in the writing of literature of whatever sort is surely most astounding."[12]

Bloomfield's opposition to the exegetical method in this statement is based on the fact that medieval readers themselves seem to have reserved such interpretations for Scripture (and to a lesser extent for classical literature)[13]; for a human poet to create such an allegory would therefore be presumptuous in its imitation of the divine creation of God's Word, and would put a mere human work on the same level as the Holy Bible. There is little evidence either that most medieval poets intended to do so, or that any medieval reader interpreted his or her contemporaries as the modern exegetes do. The great exception to both of these generalizations (the *Queste* is another, as we shall see) is, of course, Dante, whose well-known "Letter to Can Grande" (which may not be Dante's own work) introduces the reader to the fourfold exegesis of his *Commedia*, which was also widely interpreted as an allegory in the fourteenth and fifteenth centuries.[14] Dante, however, is a very unusual case: he appears to have conceived of the function of poetry in a new way (hence his designation of himself as *poeta*, the first time a vernacular poet used this term of himself).[15] Erich Auerbach, among others, has pointed out that Dante placed himself in a tradition not solely poetic but prophetic as well, and that "the *Commedia* is a special development of the tradition of the Gospels."[16] Eco has also suggested that for Dante, "poets continue the work of the scriptures, and his own poem is a new instance of prophetical writing; it is endowed with spiritual senses just as the scriptures are. The poet, moreover, is divinely inspired. He writes what love inspires him to, and his work can sustain the same kind of allegorical reading as the scriptures."[17] More recently, Minnis has lent his support to this position, showing that other medieval readers regarded Dante in a similar way.[18]

Dante's exceptional conception of his poetic function may, then, serve to confirm the generalization that there is little evidence of "concealed" religious allegory having been produced in medieval secular literature, or of medieval allegorical interpretation (or allegoresis) outside the classics and especially the Bible. Authoritative texts such as the *Glossa ordinaria*, indeed, deny that any merely human work could validly be subjected to allegorical exegesis:

> . . . this book [the Bible] is unique, because one literal passage contains many senses. The reason is that God Himself is the principal author of this book. He has the power not only to use words to signify something (since human beings, too, can and do do this), but He also uses the things signified by the words to signify other things. Therefore it is common to all books to signify something with words, but this book is unique in that the things signified by the words signify something else.[19]

St. Thomas Aquinas also states that no human work, but only Scripture, has any sense beyond the literal.[20] It is passages like these that Bloomfield had in mind when writing of the presumption necessarily involved in the creation of concealed allegory by medieval writers.

On the other hand, it would be rash to deny that any such allegories may have been written. The Robertsonians claim an even more formidable authority than Aquinas, finding in St. Augustine's *De doctrina Christiana* justification for the exegetical interpretation of all medieval literature.[21] It has often been pointed out that Augustine's attitudes toward secular literature and its allegorical interpretation range from the condemnatory (especially in *The City of God*) to the lukewarm (in the *Confessions*).[22] If his views can be summarized at all, it might be safest to say that he regards secular literature as distinctly dangerous but does grudgingly admit that it is less offensive if some concealed truth can be found in it: "For surely the fables of the poets and the penmen are better than the traps which [the Manichees] set! There is certainly more to be gained from verses and poems and tales like the flight of Medea than from their stories of the five elements disguised in various ways because of the five dens of darkness. These things simply do not exist and they are death to those who believe in them. Verses and poems can provide real food for thought."[23] Similar attitudes can be found in such thinkers as Isidore of Seville, John Scotus Eriugena, and Hugh of St. Victor,[24] and an important support for the allegorical view is to be found in St. Eucher of Lyons, apparently the one Church Father who explicitly allows the exegetical interpretation of secular works.[25] Indeed, St. Thomas himself, faced with the fact that secular authors do indisputably use figurative language, admitted that although such works could be interpreted only literally, the literal level itself could in those cases be polysemous.[26]

Nevertheless, it seems equally rash to insist that *all* secular medieval literature is necessarily concealed doctrinal allegory that would have been recognized as such by medieval readers, especially in the periods that concern us (the twelfth century and after), when so many denials of that possibility were being written. Allegory need not be doctrinal, as is demonstrated by Dante's interpretations of his own lyrics in the *Convivio*;[27] it has been pointed out that many medieval readers and scribes fail to recognize any allegorical intentions in such genres as the romance;[28] and Glending Olson has uncovered a venerable medieval critical tradition present even in some of the authorities cited by the exegetical school (Isidore of Seville, for example) that sees literature as primarily entertaining and therapeutic,[29] while Judson B. Allen found a similar tradition that places it in the category of ethics, reading it literally for examples of proper or improper human behavior.[30] In any case, only classical works, to return to the original point, seem to be under discussion when any of the authorities cited above mention allegorical readings of human creations.

The existence of allegory in any given literary work in the Middle Ages in which it is not obvious can, then, be neither automatically assumed nor automatically denied. Rosemond Tuve has distinguished between medieval allegory and modern allegorical interpretations: "We find the tight relations and complex networks of equivalents to be characteristics of modern interpretation but *not* of mediaeval presentation. . . . what we observe in the text itself is not a re-telling through a code of equivalents but instead, a loose juxtaposition that makes us connect the story we read with significance more universal because we see that it shadows a greater story in general drift of meaning." (She has just mentioned Chrétien's *Conte del Graal* as a romance which has been allegorized without "warrant from the author.")[31] One might justifiably ask how a reader can know when such a "loose juxtaposition" might be present, lacking a strict system of equivalents.

The Conte *and the* Queste *in the Debate on Allegory*

Following Tuve, we may continue to focus specifically on the *Conte del Graal* in trying to answer this question, for Holmes and Klenke are not alone in finding hidden symbolic meanings where none are signalled on the text's surface. And although Holmes and Klenke attracted some scholars (notably Mario Roques)[32] to various parts of their argument, many other allegorical interpretations of this romance, having nothing to do with the Ecclesia/Synagoga confrontation on which their reading is based, have also been proposed, ranging from allegories of orthodoxy and heresy to allegories of the Crusades and of current events in the Orient.[33] This is an old, in fact outmoded, debate, to be sure; but the allegorical readings have proven surprisingly tenacious, and in view of that fact, as well as my own assertion that the *Conte del Graal* is not only non-, but anti-allegorical, it is worthwhile to linger over the debate a bit longer.[34]

One might ask why this romance more than most others has attracted so much allegoresis in the absence of such interpretations within the text itself. There seem to be two related answers to this question, one more indirect than the other. The indirect answer approaches Chrétien's romance through some of its successors: the *Conte del Graal* inspired many subsequent Grail romances, either continuations of Chrétien's unfinished work, like Wolfram von Eschenbach's *Parzival*, or adaptations of its basic plot-line, including some that allegorize that plot, as both *Perlesvaus* and the *Queste del saint Graal* do. Allegoresis is thus one genuinely medieval response to the text, the one that sets a precedent for modern scholarly allegorizers (though the many non-allegorical versions suggest that this is not the only medieval response that could set a precedent).[35]

Perlesvaus and the *Queste*, as I have suggested, are self-interpreting romances; in them, and most consistently in the *Queste*, secular romance experience, indeed a plot derived ultimately from Chrétien, is given the kind of neoplatonic symbolic value that, as we have seen in chapter 1, was given to all earthly experience by theologians like Eriugena and historians like Gregory of Tours in earlier periods.[36] The existence of such self-interpreting romances (which is examined more closely later in this chapter) is a clear indication of how powerful the neoplatonic view of the created universe remained after 1100. But as we have also seen, it was not the only *Weltanschauung* available to writers of the twelfth and later centuries; even if Scriptural interpretation is taken as a model for literary creation (a risky proposition in itself after Hugh of St. Victor and the other twelfth-century thinkers we have examined), it must be recalled that this is the period in which the literal rather than the allegorical interpretation of the Bible is beginning to be recognized as valuable in itself.[37]

In any case, the *Queste*'s self-allegorization is spelled out for the reader; its secular, romance action is periodically interrupted while a holy man or woman explains its precise symbolic significance. Such explanations as appear in the *Conte del Graal*, on the other hand, are always literal, referring exclusively to the plot-line, elucidating it with new information, to be sure, but never reading it as a series of symbols or types. Its explanations are always on the same interpretive level as its actions, namely, the literal one. Even Scriptural interpretation can separate literal from allegorical, as exegetes were beginning to suggest at the same time that Chrétien was composing his romance.[38]

The second response to the question of why the *Conte del Graal* has attracted so much modern allegoresis has to do with the poem itself. It is an undeniably mysterious work, partly because it is unfinished,[39] and partly because it places so much emphasis on unexplained visions and unanswered (or even unasked) questions, especially in the central episode of Perceval's visit to the Grail-castle. One modern impulse—perhaps a natural human impulse—when faced with unexplained mysteries is to explain them away; if one can treat a mystery as a symbol *of* something, and so provide an authoritative decoding of it, one's desire for clarity and lucidity will be satisfied. This impulse may well have been as real for late medieval people as it is for us, judging from the medieval allegorizations of the *Conte del Graal*; but again, the opposite impulse, to allow as many possible explanations of a mystery and hence to let it remain mysterious, was also strong in the twelfth century, especially in literary studies, as is suggested by Arnulf of Orléans and his multiple interpretations of Lucan.[40]

All defenders of allegory (as distinct from critics who read non-allegorical works as if they were allegories) admit that allegory limits the reader's freedom to some extent. One of the more recent statements of this view is also the most nuanced: "The reader's involvement in allegory is perhaps more arduous than in any other genre, and if this intensity is lack of freedom, then it has its compensations; while the allegorist may limit the reader's freedom by showing him how his commentary ought to proceed, yet at the same time, that commentary becomes part of the fiction, and what the reader loses in freedom, he makes up in significance."[41] The wide range of allegorical responses to the *Conte del Graal* suggests that if it is an allegory it has failed in its allegorical purpose of teaching these readers how it is to be read properly; few scholars would agree on what its true concealed meaning might be. As I have suggested, these critics respond to the work's emphasis on the mysterious and the unexplained, assuming that all mysteries require a definitive solution rather than the interpreter's engagement with the multiple possibilities they imply.

One way in which this romance's mysteries are created is through the constant depiction of its characters reading, and frequently misreading or refusing to read, various kinds of signs. I would like to concentrate, not on finding one proper way of decoding these signs but on the act of sign-reading as Chrétien portrays it; it may be possible to locate the *Conte del Graal*'s thematic concerns not so much in what the Grail or the lance signify as in the very process of signification, of *how* they signify. I would propose, with Frappier and Guiette, that this romance invites the reader's participation in this process without orienting him or her toward any particular interpretive goal.

Signification as Theme in the Conte del Graal: *Perceval*

Chrétien involves us in acts of interpretation by showing his characters involved in similar acts. If Perceval wonders what the bleeding lance means without ever finding out, inevitably the reader wonders too, and with as little hope of satisfaction. In chapter 1 I showed how Lancelot disrupts his society's conventional semiotic systems in Chrétien's *Chevalier de la charrette*; the *Conte del Graal* has two heroes who do the same, though without intending to do so as Lancelot and the queen do, and in different ways (different not only from Lancelot but from each other as well). Perceval and

Gawain are complementary semiotic figures. Gawain tends to be flexible in his reading of signs, recognizing that unfamiliar circumstances have their own unfamiliar semiologies that the interpreter must be willing to learn in order to succeed in understanding. Those he encounters, however, are rarely as successful in reading Gawain himself because of their own interpretive rigidity: they try to read him according to their own semiotic conventions rather than learning his, and he therefore repeatedly becomes an enigmatic sign to his would-be interpreters.

Perceval, on the other hand, completely lacks Gawain's decoding powers and adaptability throughout most of his portions of the poem. Like Gawain, Perceval frequently finds himself in unfamiliar situations, but unlike that more sophisticated knight, he rarely adapts. Early in his adventures, Perceval consistently fails to recognize new contexts when he is involved in them, and naively applies inappropriate rules and conventions to them; he does not learn new social codes or sign-systems when necessary, and that single fact about him is the source of the rich comedy of those early adventures.

It is in these early scenes that the use of allegory in interpreting the world is confronted and rejected: several attempts to translate literal experience into the spiritual register are absurd failures and are recognized as such, at least by the reader. Other elements of the romance, including both chivalric action and the Grail itself, confirm this rejection of allegory in the way Chrétien reveals their meaning, or lack of it. Allegoresis over-interprets the world; but equally unsatisfactory is under-interpretation, the fascination with surface sensory impressions alone or with physical action pursued for its own sake, without any attention to the literal contexts that give them meaning. It is tempting to associate this second kind of faulty hermeneutic response with the rhetoricians' emphasis on literal surfaces; however, such a contrast of allegory and rhetoric as equally undesirable is too neat, for the rhetoricians never seek to abandon meaning altogether, as Perceval unwittingly does in his pursuit of adventures. Leupin has admirably demonstrated the relations between the rhetoricians and the Grail-romances;[42] nevertheless, proper interpretation in the *Conte del Graal* is closer to the Victorines' literal reading of Scripture or Arnulf's reading of the classics than to the rhetoricians' recommendations: it is shown that the world's phenomena can be understood in a variety of ways, according to the various contexts in which different individuals can situate them. We will examine these early scenes in greater detail below.

Later, when he has gained a certain sophistication, Perceval is at least able to recognize new circumstances when he sees them, and even the need for new rules of interpretation, as in the episode of the Grail-castle, but unlike Gawain, he never quite learns just what the new system might be nor how it is to be applied; hence his failure at the Grail-castle. He is still in the process of learning when he appears for the last time, in the episode of the hermit. In his own way, then, Perceval is as much a disrupter of conventional sign-systems as Gawain, and accordingly some characters misread him;[43] but for many of the important figures in his adventures, Perceval is a much more transparent sign than Gawain ever is: those who know the semiotic system that he fails to recognize or to learn usually see his inability for what it is and either educate or scold him for it.

The two heroes' roles as I have outlined them here are, of course, only tendencies; there are occasions on which Gawain is deceived (though even these occasions tend to become triumphs for him eventually), and occasions when Perceval is misinterpreted (although this usually occurs precisely because he does not know the conventions). But these are tendencies that are worked out consistently enough to form a genuine pattern of reflection on the reading and misreading of signs, and on the process of signification.[44] It is this process that interests me here. The *Conte del Graal* exposes it as arbitrary, but necessary. The world of society (and perhaps the natural world as well) is mysterious because its meanings change according to an individual's circumstances and surroundings; but it is nevertheless necessary to be alert to such changes, to be a responsive reader. The punishment for ignorance of the world's potential meanings, or for the refusal to respond to them, is failure and humiliation.

The young man whose name we later find to be "Perceval" seems at the beginning of the narrative itself to be a natural man, a prelapsarian Adam enjoying the Edenic life on his mother's estate in the "gaste forest" (line 75). This impression is almost immediately corrected by his encounter with a band of Arthur's knights:

> Li vallés oit et ne voit pas
> Ciax qui vers lui vienent le pas;
> Molt se merveille et dist: "Par m'ame,
> Voir se dist ma mere, ma dame,
> Qui me dist que deable sont
> Les plus laides choses del mont;
> Et si dist por moi enseingnier
> Que por aus se doit on seingnier,
> Mais cest ensaing desdaignerai,
> Que ja voir ne m'en seignerai,

> Ains ferrai si tot le plus fort
> D'un des gavelos que je port,
> Que ja n'aprochera vers moi
> Nus des autres, si com je croi." (lines 111–24)[45]

Perceval has already learned, we note, a fairly complex, though misleading, semiotic system: he has learned from his mother to interpret sensory experiences in moral and religious terms, and this method of interpretation, which he will continue to apply at certain points in his early adventures, causes his first (but far from his last) misreading of what his senses show him. The reader already knows that the noise is caused by "cinc chevaliers armez" (line 101), by knights and not by devils; the narrator's omniscience here guides us to an ironic reading of Perceval's interpretation of the auditory sign (that omniscient knowledge will be withdrawn from us at later, crucial moments).[46] His misreading is caused by the naive view that devils are ugly to the ear as well as to the eye, that angels are beautiful, and that physical or sensory appearances are an accurate clue to spiritual realities. This view could be called allegorical, as we shall see; in fact, though not all medieval writers would agree with de Man and Miller that allegory does not point toward a singular truth, Chrétien might: Perceval's allegorical readings of his world are very commonly misled by the multiplicity of possible readings for any given sign. The same interpretive method thus causes Perceval to reverse his original reading when the knights come into view:

> "Ha! sire Diex, merchi!
> Ce sont angle que je voi chi.
> Et voir or ai je molt pechié,
> Ore ai je molt mal esploitié,
> Qui dis que c'estoient deable.
> Ne me dist pas ma mere fable,
> Qui me dist que li angle estoient
> Les plus beles choses qui soient,
> Fors Diex qui est plus biax que tuit.
> Chi voi je Damedieu, ce quit,
> Car un si bel en i esgart
> Que li autre, se Diex me gart,
> N'ont mie de biauté la disme." (lines 137–49)[47]

The conflict of these aural and visual signs does not suggest that they must cancel each other out, from Perceval's perspective, nor does it cause him,

at first, to question his mother's advice or the sign-system of sensory/
spiritual equivalences he has learned from her.

Once he understands that the knights are not angels nor their leader
God, Perceval briefly demonstrates a second and potentially more fruitful
kind of interpretive response to what he does not understand: he now asks
for specific information about the visible signs of knighthood and tries to
understand what the knights tell him by fitting it into the literal context of
his own experience. As Bloch properly suggests, the text is "concerned
with—even defined by—the hero's attempt to read the signs of knightly
culture."[48]

> A sa lance sa main li tent,
> Sel prent et dist: "Biax sire chiers,
> Vos qui avez non chevaliers,
> Que est or che que vos tenez?"
> ". . . Sel te dirai, ce est ma lance."
> "Dites vos," fait il, "c'on la lance
> Si com je faz mes gavelos?"
> "Naie, vallet, tu iez toz sos!
> Ains en fiert on tot demanois."
> "Dont valt miex li uns de ces trois
> Gavelos que vos veez chi;
> Que quanques je weil en ochi,
> Oisiax et bestes au besoig,
> Et si les ochi de si loing
> Come on porroit d'un bojon traire." (lines 188–91; 197–207)

The leader of the knights understands his difficulty:

> "Il ne set pas totes les lois,"
> Fait li sire, "se Diex m'amant,
> C'a rien nule que li demant
> Ne me respont il ainc a droit,
> Ains demande de quanqu'il voit
> Coment a non et c'on en fait." (lines 236–41)[49]

Perceval doesn't know the laws, that is, the social codes by which the
knights live, and this clash of sign-systems and of the contexts which
produce them prevents communication. Perceval's ignorance of the chivalric context thus prevents proper understanding, but his attempt to find
literal meaning in these mysterious phenomena, rather than to translate
them into inappropriate spiritual terms, clearly brings him closer to a genu-

ine comprehension and suggests that a willingness to learn new contexts and their semiologies is necessary for successful interpretation.

Perceval's mother also tries to explain chivalry to him, in her long speech from lines 407 to 488, by situating it in a different context. Whereas the knights placed it in a practical, functional context relevant to their experience, producing a generally positive interpretation, Perceval's mother takes a very negative view of chivalry because of her own sad experience of it. These conflicting perspectives, each a valid reading in its own right, seem to be wasted on Perceval: later episodes detailing his ignorance of the proper use of armor (e.g., his attempt to remove the Vermilion Knight's, line 1120 ff.) suggest that he has ignored the practical context that the knights tried to provide; and that he is equally uninterested in the information recounted by his mother is demonstrated in his response to it:

> Li vallés entent molt petit
> A che que sa mere li dist.
> "A mengier," fait il, "me donez;
> Ne sai de coi m'araisonnez.
> Molt m'en iroie volentiers
> Au roi qui fait les chevaliers,
> Et je irai, cui qu'il em poist." (lines 489–95)[50]

Chivalry now has exactly the same meaning for him as it had before her recitation of the family's history of impoverishment, outrage, and death because of it. The context has no effect on Perceval.

Instead of adopting this contextualizing method of interpretation, then, Perceval demonstrates in his next adventures both a return to his earlier confusion of the literal and spiritual registers (a return prompted by the renewal of his mother's advice), and a third kind of response to new experiences: rejecting both of the two contradictory attempts to teach him chivalry's meaning by situating it in a context, he focuses instead on the pure sensory impressions it makes. As his response to his mother's speech suggests, he now simply wants to imitate the knights, to be like the beautiful objects he has encountered. His later admiration of, and desire for, the Vermilion Knight's armor suggests the same (e.g., lines 873–78, 994–97, etc.).

In these early scenes, Chrétien thus presents and evaluates at least three different ways of responding to the world's mysterious signs, only one of which allows genuine understanding. One can under-interpret them, valuing the sensory impressions they make purely for their own sake. This response is clearly inadequate, as is demonstrated by Perceval's comic inability to remove the Vermilion Knight's beautiful armor, but it will later be reinforced in a subtler form by Gornemant's advice. Indeed, Perceval's tendency to under-interpret becomes a major stumbling-block, as we shall see.

Equally unsatisfactory, however, is the tendency to over-interpret that Perceval has learned from his mother. She is not merely a source of misinformation, as Bloch asserts,[51] but suggests an entire theory of interpretation. In her own naive way, she is an allegorist in the neoplatonic tradition: she finds in physical appearances reliable signs of spiritual reality. Thus beauty, for her, signals goodness, ugliness evil. Moral and religious meanings are clearly indicated by literal reality, read metaphorically. But the romance itself demonstrates that her allegorical view is wrong. Beauty and ugliness can coexist in the same physical being, as in the knights' visual and aural signs, and have no necessary symbolic correspondence with good and evil. Indeed, the way to find meaning in any aspect of literal reality is not to translate it into spiritual terms but to situate it in a larger, and equally literal, context. Perceval's mother herself demonstrates this when she gives meaning to the concept "chivalry" by situating it in her own family's history, as do the knights by situating it in the practical context of their own lives.

These latter two examples of genuine, fruitful interpretation (that is, of interpretation that helps the interpreter understand the world and respond to it appropriately) suggest that two different perspectives on, and experiences of, chivalry will lead to two mutually exclusive interpretations of it, though both are purely literal. This ambiguity in its literal meaning should not be surprising after Hugh of St. Victor's demonstration that such disagreements are inherent in the literal level. In Biblical exegesis, as we have seen, only the spiritual level, attained through allegorical interpretation, brings them into harmonious accord; but in a romance that emphasizes the danger and absurdity of forcing a complex literal reality into any symbolic schema, these mutually exclusive readings of the same phenomenon can both be accepted as equally valid, according to the varying contexts that produce them. Perhaps it is this confusion that causes Perceval to reject literal contexts as the source of meaning. In any case, meaning can again be associated with context—by the reader if not by Perceval—in the next sequence. His mother's parting advice seems intended to initiate Perceval into proper chivalric codes of behavior. He should aid ladies without annoying them, accepting kisses or love-tokens if they are offered; he should seek the company of good men; he should attend Mass in churches and minsters, which she defines for him:

> Une maison bele et saintisme
> Ou il a cors sains et tresors. (lines 578–79)[52]

This new code will once more cause Perceval trouble.

Whereas he previously moved from over-interpreting the knights by referring to an irrelevant spiritual register, to under-interpreting them by referring exclusively to his sensory impressions of them, his mother's new advice now causes Perceval to oscillate back to over-interpretation (and this movement back and forth between the two inappropriate modes will characterize most of his future adventures).

It should be noted that the first minsters he encounters, at Belrepeire, do not conform to her description, with its emphasis on wealth and beauty, but oppose it:

> Deus mostiers en la vile avoit
> Qui ja furent deus abeïes:
> L'une de nonains esbahies,
> L'autre de moignes esgarez.
> Ne trova mie bien parez
> Ces mostiers ne bien portendus,
> Ainçois vit crevez et fendus
> Les murs et les tors descovertes. (lines 1756–63)[53]

Despite their appearances, these minsters are still functioning houses of God: the nuns and monks remain. Not so the first structure he finds that does match his mother's description: just as he earlier misperceived knights as angels because of their beauty, Perceval now misperceives as a church a pavilion shared by an absent knight and his mistress. What takes place in it is not the Mass but a comic parody of the Eucharist, caused by a movement back once more to under-interpretation: just as he was unable to comprehend the function of the knights' armor or his family's relations with the chivalric world, he now forgets the context of the social gestures recommended by his mother. Because the proper context is absent, the mere gestures themselves violate the chivalric code he thinks he is acting out:

> "Ains vos baiserai, par mon chief,"
> Fait li vallés, "cui qu'il soit grief,
> Que ma mere le m'ensaigna."
> "Je voir ne te baiserai ja,"
> Fait la pucele, "que je puisse,
> Fui! que mes amis ne te truisse;
> Que s'il te trove, tu es mors."

> Li vallés avoit les bras fors,
> Si l'embracha molt nichement,
> Car il nel sot faire autrement. (lines 693–702)[54]

The same is true of the love-token, a ring he takes by force. By separating action from context, Perceval also separates signifier from signified and thus disrupts the conventional, social semiology by which this woman lives: her lover cannot believe her truthful explanation of what has happened, precisely because Perceval's actions do not conform to that system. For the knight, a ring has meaning beyond the object itself:

> "Il i a plus, sire," dist ele.
> "Mes aniax est en la querele,
> Qu'il le m'a tolu, si l'en porte.
> Je volsisse mix estre morte
> Qu'il l'eüst ensi emporté."
> Ez vos celui desconforté
> Et angoisseus en son corage.
> "Par foi," fait il, "ci a outrage.
> Et des qu'il l'en porte, si l'ait;
> Mais je quit qu'il i ot plus fait." (lines 799–808)[55]

There is no need to continue this detailed analysis of Perceval's abuses of signification; the pattern outlined above, in which he learns a social code but is unable either to apply it in its proper context or to adapt it to new circumstances, and so disrupts the reigning semiology through his misinterpretations, is repeated several times in the course of his adventures. Much has been made of Perceval's development throughout the romance,[56] and it is certainly true that he becomes more sophisticated after his encounters with Gornemant de Goort and with Blanchefleur; he is even able to rectify some of his earlier errors, as when he meets the inhabitants of the tent again and proves the cruel knight wrong about his lover's fidelity (lines 3691–949). On the other hand, most of Perceval's triumphs can be attributed to his instinctive knightliness, a family trait latent in his character from the very beginning, and not to new codes he learns, most of which he continues to misapply through his final appearances in the *Conte del Graal*. Thus Gornemant's advice not to talk too much is, like his mother's earlier advice, applied without regard to context or circumstances and hence inappropriately, both at Belrepeire and at the Grail-castle.

At the Grail-castle, indeed, he continues to apply Gornemant's code of behavior in spite of his own better instincts, which usually provide a reliable guide. The Grail procession passes through the room:

> Li vallés voit cele merveille
> Qui la nuit ert laiens venus,
> Si s'est de demander tenus
> Coment ceste chose avenoit,
> Que del chasti li sovenoit
> Celui qui chevalier le fist,
> Qui li ensaigna et aprist
> Que de trop parler se gardast. (lines 3202–09)

> Mais plus se taist qu'il ne covient,
> Qu'a chascun mes que l'on servoit,
> Par devant lui trespasser voit
> Le graal trestot descovert,
> Ne ne set pas cui l'en en sert
> Et si le volroit il savoir.
> Mais il le demandera voir,
> Ce dist et pense, ains qu'il s'en tort,
> A un des vallés de la cort;
> Mais jusqu'al matin atendra,
> Que al seignor congié prendra
> Et a toute l'autre maisnie. (lines 3298–3309)[57]

If his mother's advice caused Perceval to misinterpret sensory phenomena through over-interpretation, Gornemant's prevents his instinctive desire for literal understanding from being expressed at all, at least at the moment when it would have been efficacious, and this reinforces the tendency toward under-interpretation. In his initial meeting with the knights his instinctive desire for understanding was freely expressed in his many questions, though he seemed to absorb little of the forthcoming information; at the Grail-castle that desire itself is inhibited, so that one might see his "development" with equal justice as a regression, at least in terms of interpretation-skills. In any case, Perceval's *lack* of development in his responses to the contextual meaning of his adventures, as opposed to their surface appearances, becomes evident after his departure from the Grail-castle. He meets his cousin and with her re-enacts the earlier scene with his mother. As in that encounter, in this one he hears a part of his family's history; just as his mother's narrative should have given literal, contextual meaning to his encounter with the knights, so his cousin's should give such meaning

to his experience at the Grail-castle. But Perceval appears to understand—
or even attend to—this version of the family history as little as the other.
She has explained what Perceval should have done during the Grail-procession, and why, and has also told him that he caused his mother's death:

> ". . . Felon conte m'avez conté.
> Et des que ele est mise en terre,
> Que iroie jou avant querre?
> Kar por rien nule n'i aloie
> Fors por li que veoir voloie;
> Autre voie m'estuet tenir.
> Et se vos volïez venir
> Avec moi, jel vold[r]oie bien;
> Que cis ne vos voldra mais rien
> Qui chi gist mors, jel vos plevis.
> Les mors as mors, les vis as vis;
> Alons ent moi et vos ensamble.
> De vos grant folie me samble,
> Qu'isi seule gaitiez cest mort;
> Mais sivons celui qui l'a mort,
> Et je vos pramet et creant:
> Ou il me fera recreant
> Ou je lui, se jel puis ataindre." (lines 3620–37)[58]

Perceval responds neither to the information about the Grail-castle, nor to
his own responsibility for his mother's death; in fact, he is concerned only
with what he should do next, with action itself rather than with the meaning
of his actions, part of which has just been revealed to him. As usual, he is
unable to respond to contextual meaning; he rejects his cousin's example
of fidelity to the memory of the dead in favor of further fatal action. This
constant pursuit of meaningless action corresponds to Perceval's earlier
fascination with sensory impressions: both responses to the world are
under-interpretations, refusals to situate immediate experience in any larger
context that might give it meaning. His later vow to seek the Grail is part of
the same pattern; having heard the ugly damsel's repetition of his cousin's
condemnation, Perceval vows to take action in order to find the meanings
that have so far eluded him:

> Et Perchevax redist tout el:
> Qu'il ne gerra en un hostel
> Deus nuis en trestot son eage,
> Ne n'orra d'estrange passage

> Noveles que passer n'i aille,
> Ne de chevalier qui miex vaille
> Qu'autres chevaliers ne que dui
> Qu'il ne s'aille combatre a lui,
> Tant que il del graal savra
> Cui l'en en sert, et qu'il avra
> La lance qui saine trovee
> Et que la veritez provee
> Li ert dite por qu'ele saine;
> Ja nel laira por nule paine. (lines 4727–40)[59]

Once again, however, he succeeds only in performing the actions, not in finding any meaning:

> Tot ensi cinc ans demora,
> Ne por che ne laissa il mie
> A requerre chevalerie;
> Et les estranges aventures,
> Les felenesses et les dures,
> Aloit querant, et s'en trova
> Tant que molt bien s'i esprova.
> Soissante chevaliers de pris
> A la cort le roi Artu pris
> Dedens cinc ans i envoia.
> Tot ensi cinc ans emploia
> N'onques de Dieu ne li sovint. (lines 6224–37)[60]

Chivalric action, it turns out, does not lead to meaning; in fact, the *Conte del Graal* presents action, at least of this kind, as a way of avoiding meaning,[61] and this detachment of action from meaning reinforces Chrétien's rejection of allegory. Each time Perceval is offered an explanation of his life, whether by his mother, his cousin, or the ugly damsel, he immediately rides off in search of adventures, without ever recognizing the meanings offered for what they are: descriptions of his flaws that require spiritual, not physical, change. As we have seen, he rejects meanings located outside himself as well as those within; given the chance to learn the meanings of the mysterious phenomena he encounters (a knight's armor, a lady's ring, a Grail-procession), Perceval single-mindedly applies an inappropriate system of signs learned in other circumstances and either misinterprets or refuses interpretation altogether.

This double pattern in Perceval's adventures can orient us toward two conclusions about how signification is thematized in his sections of the

Conte del Graal. First, it presents a world in which interpretation is always necessary and always problematic, as each new situation has its own semiology and renders earlier ones useless; and second, those necessary interpretations are never allegorical. Perceval's tendency to under-interpret, choosing to ignore contextual meaning in favor of pure action, while it is shown to be faulty in itself, also prevents the reader from over-interpreting. Action, I have argued, does not lead to meaning in this romance but away from it; the physical does not signify the spiritual, but distracts from it. This pattern is analogous to the relationship between sensory and spiritual experience, and both point to a view of signification that is not only non-allegorical but essentially opposed to allegory.

Allegory is precisely the mode of signification that relates action to meaning and sensory to spiritual experience; as we shall see, the *Queste del saint Graal* makes those connections explicit over and over again, giving abstract spiritual meaning to chivalric adventures and to the objects of their sense-impressions encountered by its heroes in their quest. Chrétien's exposure of action as a distraction from meaning thus confirms the rejection of allegory that we found in his presentation of Perceval's mother.

The Grail itself provides another confirmation of this rejection. Although Perceval fails to ask the essential question about it (whom does one serve with the Grail?), he does receive the answer, along with an explanation of its supernatural properties, from his uncle the hermit, in the episode which is Perceval's final appearance in the poem:

> Cil qui l'en en sert est mes frere,
> Ma suer et soe fu ta mere;
> Et del riche Pescheor croi
> Qu'il est fix a icelui roi
> Qu'en cel gr[a]al servir se fait.
> Mais ne quidiez pas que il ait
> Lus ne lamproie ne salmon;
> D'une sole oiste le sert on,
> Que l'en en cel graal li porte;
> Sa vie sostient et conforte,
> Tant sainte chose est li graals. (lines 6415–25)[62]

The Grail is so holy an object that it allows a single eucharistic wafer to provide physical as well as spiritual nourishment. The spiritual bread thus becomes physical bread, a process just the opposite of allegory or allegoresis: here a symbolic object acquires a literal meaning and function, rather than the other way around. If allegory is the location of a spiritual sense in literal reality then the Grail's function is to de-allegorize, to give a literal, physical function to the spiritual or symbolic object. Chrétien is careful not to associate religious meaning with allegory or symbolism: the Grail's holiness is demonstrated precisely by this anti-allegorical function. Spiritual meaning here exists on the literal level.[63]

This is true of all religious meaning in the *Conte del Graal*, and indeed of all meaning of any kind in the poem. When the hermit explains Perceval's failings to him, he does so (as both Perceval's mother and his cousin tried to do earlier) entirely in terms of his literal family history. This literal-mindedness does not exclude an important Christian component in his explanation; but it is stated directly and given meaning by the literal context:

> . . . "Frere, molt t'a neü
> Uns pechiez dont tu ne sez mot:
> Ce fu li doels que ta mere ot
> De toi quant departis de li,
> Que pasmee a terre chaï
> Al chief del pont devant la porte,
> Et de cel doel fu ele morte.
> Por le pechié que tu en as
> T'avient que rien n'en demandas
> De la lance ne del graal,
> Si t'en sont avenu maint mal." (lines 6392–402)[64]

Perceval's sin was a literal action that has been narrated directly, and its consequences were the literal facts of the romance's plot.

One of Perceval's few attempts at literal interpretation occurs simultaneously with one of the few misunderstandings of him by another character, in the famous episode of the three blood-drops on the snow, which is also the occasion for the narrative's focus to begin its shift to Gawain and his more successful manipulation of sign-systems. Grace Armstrong analyzes this scene in terms of Perceval's responses to sensory experience, which, as we have seen, are problematic throughout the romance. She notes the emphasis Chrétien places on the involvement of his senses at this point, and suggests that this comparison of the natural red and white colors he sees here to Blanchefleur's coloring is his first appropriate and creative response to sensory experience.[65] Although this is true, what Armstrong does not note is that this comparison is also the first example of Perceval's responding to a sensory experience neither with an under-interpretation, or simple fascination with surface appearances, nor with an inappropriate symbolic over-interpretation, but with a simple, literal comparison: the physical object before him, the drops of blood, reminds him of another physical object, Blanchefleur's complexion:

> En l'esgarder que il faisoit,
> Li ert avis, tant li plaisoit,
> Qu'il veïst la color novele
> De la face s'amie bele. (lines 4207–10)[66]

"Pleasing" interpretation does not find correspondences between different levels of reality but places a new experience in the literal context of previous ones.[67]

It is interesting that Perceval's ability to draw such imaginative comparisons renders him unreadable to others: the trance he falls into while contemplating the blood drops is read by the squires accompanying King Arthur as "someille" (line 4226), the result being Sagremor's and Kay's unfortunate attempts to bring Perceval to the king, first by a summons and then by force. Having temporarily abandoned chivalric action in favor of finding or creating literal meanings in the natural world (another example of Chrétien's opposition between action and meaning), Perceval cannot be interpreted correctly by those who are limited by the codes of action from perceiving meaning in other kinds of behavior. Sagremor and Kay thus ironically become images of Perceval's own previous inability to understand new circumstances. Kay's limited semiology is spelled out soon after his defeat, in his sarcastic reading of Gawain's successful attempt to bring Perceval to court:

> "Ore en a le pris et l'onor
> Mesire Gavains, vostre niez.
> Molt fu or perilleuse et griés
> La bataille, se je ne ment,
> Que tot ausi haitïement
> S'en retorne come il i mut,
> C'onques d'autrui cop n'i rechut,
> N'autres de lui cop n'i senti . . . ." (lines 4518–25)[68]

For Kay, wounds alone signify honorable action, which is to say that battle is the only possible honorable relationship between two knights. That such a method of interpretation is not appropriate to the new situation represented by Perceval's pensiveness is suggested by a more sophisticated interpreter, Gawain himself.

Signification as Theme in the Conte del Graal: *Perceval and Gawain*

His theory of signs is both more flexible and more successful, because he does not assume that he knows the single correct method of interpretation and indeed admits that reading the signs of others is difficult and often impossible:

> "Sire, sire, se Diex m'aït,
> Il n'est raison, bien le savez,
> Si com vos meïsmes l'avez
> Tos jors dit et jugié a droit,
> Que chevaliers autre ne doit
> Oster, si com cist dui ont fait,
> De son penser, quel que il l'ait.
> Et s'il en ont le tort eü,
> Ce ne sai jou, mais mescheü
> Lor en est il, c'est chose certe." (lines 4350–59)[69]

He does not presume to judge Sagremor and Kay but can see their lack of success. His own speculation, that Perceval is sorrowful because of "aucune perte" (line 4360), also proves incorrect, but in his own approach to Perceval he has already admitted that he cannot really read another's mind:

> . . . "Sire, je vos eüsse
> Salüé, s'autretel seüsse
> Vostre cuer com je sai le mien. . . ." (lines 4435–37)[70]

Gawain here implies that his judgment of Perceval cannot rest on external appearances but must take into account his internal state, or, given the difficulty of such internal understanding, must be deferred. His view is not too distant from Abelard's ethic of intentions, with its suggestion that actions can be judged only by the intentions that prompt them.[71] The internal, psychological state that Abelard and Gawain both take as their standard of judgment thus provides another kind of literal context that can give meaning to appearances, just as Perceval's family history has previously been shown to do.[72] It presents another way of steering between under- and over-interpretation.

Judgment on the basis of appearances alone, physical action or inaction, is a kind of under-interpretation whose inadequacy is demonstrated over and over again in the rest of Gawain's adventures. Such false judgments may arise because of conflicts among social contexts and among the codes they produce, like those that cause so many of Perceval's problems; they may also arise simply because of Gawain's chivalric superiority to other knights. The key to Gawain's success often lies in his willingness not to impose a given interpretive code in a new situation, as Perceval so often does, but to allow signs to retain their mysterious ambiguity or indeterminacy, at least until the circumstances become clear or the signs reveal their own meaning, as Perceval reveals the meaning of his trance when given the opportunity.

If Perceval is usually the one who cannot interpret and must always be taught new rules for doing so, Gawain is usually the one who cannot be interpreted and who must prove the truth about himself time and time again.[73] A conflict of two codes of behavior arises during the tournament in which Meliant de Liz does battle against Tiebaut de Tintaguel in order to win Tiebaut's eldest daughter. Gawain has already promised to meet Guinganbresil for a trial by battle in which he is to prove his innocence of a false accusation; in order to prevent an injury that might keep him from this battle, he decides against participating in the tournament. He has with him some spare armor, a sign of the esteem in which his fellow knights of Arthur's court hold him:

> Qui bon cheval et bone lance
> Ou bone elme ou bone espee ot,
> Presenta lui; mais lui ne plot
> Qu'il em portast rien de l'autrui.
> Set escuiers maine avec lui
> Et set chevax et deus escus. (lines 4800–05)[74]

Thus, his non-participation and the extra arms are signs of Gawain's truly chivalric nature, but their conflict with a more rigid code of chivalric behavior causes him to be misread, first as two knights (because of the two shields, lines 4932–35) and then by Tiebaut's daughters as a progressively lower- and lower-class professional. The scene illustrates the large number of possible misreadings of a given situation and is therefore worth quoting at length:

> "Diex!" dist l'une des damoiseles,
> "Cil chevaliers desoz cel charme,
> Que atent il que il ne s'arme?"
> Une autre plus desmesuree
> Lor dist: "Cist a le pais juree."

Et une autre redist aprés:
"Marcheans est. Nel dites mes
Qu'il doie a tornoier entendre;
Toz ces chevax maine il a vendre."
"Ains est changieres," dist la quarte;
"Il n'a talent que il departe
As povres bachelers anqui
Cel avoir qu'il porte avec l[u]i. . . ." (lines 5054–66)[75]

Despite the youngest sister's accurate perception ("Chevaliers est il, bien le samble," line 5079), the others continue their malicious misreadings:

Et les dames totes ensamble
Li dïent: "Por che, bele amie,
S'i[l] le samble, ne l'est il mie.
Mais il le se fait resambler
Por che que ensi quide embler
Les costumes et les paages.
Fols est et si quide estre sages,
Que de cesti sera il pris
Come lerre atains et repris
De larrecin vilain et fol,
Si en ara le hart el col." (lines 5080–90)[76]

Gawain descends in their estimation from knight to peacemonger to merchant to moneylender to thief, specifically in terms of his appearance (as is emphasized by the play on "samble" and "resambler"). Judgment without regard for the context provided by a knowledge of intentions thus produces as many contradictory readings as Hugh of St. Victor found in the literal level of Scripture, or Arnulf of Orléans found in Lucan. Tiebaut's elder daughters seem to subscribe to Kay's faulty belief that only violent action can signify chivalric honor, while Gawain's more flexible system (interpretable only by the child, perhaps because she is more innocent of her society's semiotic conventions than her sisters) disregards appearances in favor of an inner truth, as we saw in his reading of Perceval. Unlike Perceval, however, he can and does learn the semiology prevailing in this new context and adapts to it, agreeing to fight as the child's knight. But he can also adapt the system to his own needs, departing from the battle early—but still winning the prize. Gawain's flexibility where signification is concerned allows him both to learn a system unlike his own and to use it to reveal his true character.

Another series of misreadings of Gawain takes the form of false accusations: by Guinganbresil, by Greorreas, by Guiromelanz. These misinterpretations, too, are caused by the conflict of social codes: Gawain's chivalric justice opposed to Guinganbresil's family loyalty, for example (lines 4759–87), or to Greorreas' personal dignity (lines 7109–31). And his very superiority as a knight, the fact that he is not typical, prevents the recognition of his true character by those whose methods of interpretation are based on the typical and on the weight of tradition, of what has always been the case. Thus the ferryman, having described the dangers of the Castle of the Maidens, assumes that no knight could survive them and liberate the castle:

> ". . . Mais ainz ert mers trestote glace
> Que l'en un tel chevalier truisse,
> Qui el palais remanoir puisse
> Qu'il le covenroit a devise
> Bel et sage, sanz covoitise,
> Preu et hardi, franc et loial,
> Sanz vilonie et sanz tot mal . . . ." (lines 7590–96)[77]

This description of a knight too good to exist turns out, of course, to be a description of Gawain himself, who, knowing himself as others do not, is anxious to undergo the castle's wonders in spite of the ferryman's skepticism. We have seen Gawain's theory that one cannot know the mind of another like one's own; the corollary is that one can truly know oneself, despite the opinion of others (and despite appearances). His success at the castle proves that the ferryman was identifying and describing him without realizing it, but does not prevent similar misreadings by other characters, e.g., the castle's inhabitants' assumption that he must fail at the Perilous Ford, or Guiromelanz's skepticism regarding his adventures in the Wonder Bed (lines 8458–66; 8676–83).

The contrasts to be drawn between Perceval and Gawain should now be clear. Whereas Perceval consistently interprets other people's signs, or fails to interpret them, by applying to them inappropriate social codes learned in other circumstances, that is, by ignoring the context, Gawain himself is consistently misinterpreted by others, who inappropriately apply to him their own inflexible codes and semiologies; whereas Perceval's interpretive rigidity opens him to accurate and negative readings by those he encounters, Gawain learns to adapt and manipulate unfamiliar codes and is thus able to triumph in new situations. Both sections of the *Conte del Graal*, then, are to a great extent about problems of signification. Both present a world, especially a social world, in which signification is never immediate or transparent, in which all semiotic systems and codes of behavior are in a constant state of flux, and that therefore demands an alert flexibility in methods and theories of interpretation.

It is a world, in fact, very much like the newly literate twelfth-century Europe described by Stock in *The Implications of Literacy*. His description of the new, textually determined view of adolescence sounds remarkably like Chrétien's romance:

> The wandering between two periods of relative stability was also essential. It was, so to speak, every young man's personal *Bildungsroman*, through which he recreated, interpreted, and re-expressed his individual development for himself. It was a hermeneutic exercise whose text was life itself. . . . As a consequence, they were compelled to adapt older values to new circumstances.[78]

The world was thus a text requiring flexible interpretive skills, because each individual has different experiences of it. Perceval's failures are failures of interpretation, of sign-reading, as are those of the many inaccurate interpreters of Gawain, whereas Gawain's successes are due to his own willingness to learn and to transform unfamiliar semiotic and social systems. Perceval, as most criticism of the *Conte del Graal* attests, is the more interesting of the two because of the sequential nature of his adventures; although he continues to make errors throughout the romance, the errors become more sophisticated as he progresses, so that he can rectify earlier ones even while committing new ones. His new ability to produce creative, imaginative interpretations, signalled in the episode of the blood drops, and his acquisition of genuine familial and religious values in the hermit episode, suggest that he is on the right track at last, toward (and presumably beyond) the chivalric and interpretive perfection Gawain has already attained. Perceval's integration of spirituality into his own literal experience of the world, especially, demonstrates a potential superiority to Gawain (who is not, however, totally lacking in religious values; thus his success at the Castle of the Maidens, a parallel to Perceval's failure at the Grail castle, is "l'onor que Diex li a fait," line 7949, the honor God has done him).[79]

Neither hero's adventures are allegorical. We have seen, indeed, the Perceval section is even opposed to allegory in its mode of signification, resolutely separating action from meaning and sensory from spiritual experience rather than allowing one to represent the other. The Gawain section, too, refuses allegory (though without thematizing it as clearly): all meanings, when we learn them, are literal, and the frequent disjunctions between Gawain's appearance (as merchant, moneylender, thief, jongleur, or even typical knight) and his character must reinforce the opinion that sensory experience does not point the observer toward a hidden meaning but merely distracts from it.

We may find in the *Conte del Graal* support for Minnis's contention that the concentration of twelfth-century exegetes on the literal level of Scripture made possible a new theory of authorship applicable to secular literature.[80] Chrétien represents the realization of just such a theory: he takes the implications of this emphasis—the ambiguity inherent, for twelfth-century thinkers, in literal reality—as he takes the implications of twelfth-century textuality generally, making the world of his romance as mysterious and contradictory as the literal level of Scripture, or as the experience of twelfth-century adolescents. His fictional world recreates for the reader the experience of twelfth-century reality, physical as well as textual.

The "sense of baffled involvement in a mystery," the "semiotic breakdown"[81] that many critics have found in the *Conte del Graal* is, then, at least partly a result of its concern with problems of signification. The reader witnesses a world in which action, sensory evidence, and indeed any physical or social sign leads the interpreter away from meaning rather than toward it. If, as Quilligan suggests, allegory always teaches its readers how it is to be interpreted,[82] the *Conte del Graal* must be seen as radically non-allegorical: far from teaching us a reliable method of reading its signs, it constantly demonstrates the arbitrary nature of all such methods, showing how ineffective they must be in circumstances other than those that produced them. Interpretation is not, however, dismissed: Perceval in his failures and Gawain in his successes prove that however arbitrary a system of signs may be, it is also necessary to learn and relearn in each new situation how it is to be literally interpreted. Failure to do so leads to humiliation and disgrace.

Although the indeterminacy of literal signification is thematized in the *Conte del Graal*, the reader does not participate in it as fully as in many later romances—precisely because it is thematized. Thus while Tiebaut's daughters propose a wide variety of contradictory ways to interpret Gawain, reminiscent of the contradictions Hugh of St. Victor found in Scripture's literal level, the reader knows Gawain's true intentions (to use Abelard's terminology) in refusing to fight and has thus been given an authoritative reading of this scene.

But there are also aspects of the *Conte del Graal* that draw the reader into the hermeneutic circle without allowing any such definitive interpretations. It has been pointed out, for example, that one of Chrétien's innovations in the *Conte* is the weakening of his narrator's omniscience, the result being that the reader, deprived of narrative foreknowledge, is frequently placed in a position, with regard to the literal meaning of the poem's events, very similar to that of the two heroes.[83] We learn Perceval's name and the consequences of his failure at the Grail castle only when he does; the same is true of Gawain's knowledge of Greorreas' identity, or of the Haughty Maiden's reason for her cruelty. We share the heroes' slow interpretive processes (as is not true in, for example, the *Chanson de Roland*, in which we always know more than they do); thus, the romance itself to some extent becomes an event in the reader's life as mysterious to him or her as the events of Perceval's and Gawain's lives are to them. Though some of its mysteries are resolved (as when the hermit reveals the answer to Perceval's first unasked question of whom one serves with the Grail), others are not; and although answers might have been provided eventually had Chrétien completed his poem, its explorations of meaning suggest just as plausibly that they might never have been provided. Why does the lance bleed? Would Perceval's sword actually betray him as predicted by his cousin, and why? Who is the wealthy cripple Gawain sees outside the Castle of the Maidens, and who is never mentioned again? The reader learns to see the romance as Perceval must learn to see the world: as a mystery rather than an allegory, imbued with religious values, but concretely and literally, and always in need of an interpreter willing, in each new situation, to learn the rules of its own unique semiology rather than to impose others learned elsewhere.

Perhaps the modern allegorists like Holmes and Klenke who insist on imposing such an exegetical scheme upon Chrétien's poem cannot be blamed for their responses to it; as I suggested earlier, allegoresis is one genuinely medieval response to the many phenomenological "blanks," to use Iser's terminology,[84] in Chrétien's romance. Allegoresis is frequently the critic's reaction to a work that seems ideologically unsatisfactory or textually mysterious in itself; in a work like the *Conte del Graal*, which demands to such a great extent the reader's engagement with problems of signification, the temptation to answer those questions or fill in those blanks allegorically can apparently become irresistible. Chrétien himself presents the mysteries alone and merely asks the questions; the various medieval and modern allegorical responses must be seen only as reactions to Chrétien's work, not as an integral part of it.[85]

Nevertheless, the extent to which more determinate modes of thought remained powerful in the twelfth century is suggested by the very thematization of these concerns that I have traced in Chrétien's romance. The presence of such a theme paradoxically implies that the work's textual signs do have something to communicate to the reader; despite Chrétien's interest in the problems of signification when divine guarantees of language are bracketed, his romances are still heavily influenced by the neoplatonic union between words and things. As Bloch notes, "Chrétien, like Perceval, himself seeks a poetic rectitude that is, in the telling of the tale, constantly disseminated—scattered and partial; and that accounts, ultimately, for the increasing incoherence of a bifurcated romance which cannot end."[86] I have tried to suggest some ways in which this bifurcated romance is, in fact, coherent; it is precisely the thematized concern with signification that unites the two sections. It is this concern that provides the poetic rectitude whose existence Bloch denies. Our experience of this romance, then, is both directed and undirected; it tends to destabilize meaning on the one hand, but on the other hand it also tends to turn that destabilization into a new (and stable) meaning to be communicated. In Chrétien, we find a writer responding to the new ways of thinking about texts and meaning outlined in chapter 1, but in whose work those new ways are still competing with older, more determinate ones.

The Queste: *Allegory and the Search for Meaning*

The allegorizing textual interventions of later writers are, as we have seen, an important aspect of the work of the literary community of readers/ writers that tends to form around any "original" medieval text. We may thus see the allegorizing tendencies of a prose romance like the *Queste del saint Graal* as one more example of the fact that "the act of adding to a text is also the act of eliciting from it that which remains unspoken."[87] We have seen how Chrétien's romance embodies the high medieval competition between determinate and indeterminate modes of signification; I would now like to examine briefly the *Queste del saint Graal*'s allegorical mode, in order to distinguish it from Chrétien's non-allegorical mode and to suggest some differences between the reader's role in allegory and in the kind of literally interpretable work I shall discuss in the remainder of this book. Even in a period when, as Bursill-Hall and other recent scholars have suggested, the relation between signs and meanings, or between words and reality, was being radically questioned by such thinkers as the speculative grammarians (or had already been questioned, in the case of a thinker such as Abelard), allegory still suggests the existence of a neoplatonic hierarchy linking human sign-making activities to divinely controlled meanings.[88] Since allegory is not my main concern, I shall limit my discussion of the *Queste* only to those points most relevant to these issues, and to those that demonstrate most clearly how these other texts do *not* signify.

The *Queste del saint Graal*, like the *Conte*, suggests that various ways of responding to the world's signs are possible. But as we have just seen, the earlier romance rejects both meaningless under-interpretation and allegorical over-interpretation in favor of a literal interpretive mode, one that finds meaning in phenomena by situating them in a context; different contexts suggest different meanings. The *Queste*, on the other hand, while accepting the necessity of finding literal meaning in an historical context also presents as valid the possibility of reading literal reality as a metaphor, and thus of moving from it to various symbolic, spiritual levels of meaning. This method is precisely the kind of allegoresis that Perceval's mother teaches her son, with such disastrous results, in Chrétien's romance. In the *Queste* it is not only a valid way to read the world but the preferred method of arriving at authoritative, divine Truth.

The *Queste*'s allegorical method is a variation on the venerable fourfold one derived from St. John Cassian.[89] History is the record of actual, literal events; if it is read as a metaphor for the life of Christ or the Church, the interpretation is allegory proper (which I shall henceforth call "allegory in the strict sense" to distinguish it from the generic meaning of "allegory," which has previously been my concern). If the historical level is read as a metaphor for the moral life of the individual soul, the interpretation is tropological; if it is read as a metaphor for the afterlife, the interpretation is anagogical. Each of the different knights pursuing the Grail experiences his quest on one of these different levels of meaning, as we shall see; and each has his adventures interpreted for him, on the appropriate level, by the holy interpreters he encounters. The Grail itself also encompasses all four levels and functions differently in the life of each knight, according to his own spiritual state. Although the literal or historical level thus plays an important role in the *Queste* and figures as one level of interpretation in its allegorical method, it is clearly the least important kind of meaning, as it was for Hugh of St. Victor in his Scriptural exegesis;[90] indeed, those who live on this level alone are repeatedly condemned (just as the attempts at allegorical reading are, less directly, condemned in the literal *Conte*).

Thinkers like Hugh, as we saw at the beginning of this chapter, held a variety of opinions on the possibility of allegory in secular literature; none of them were enthusiastic about it, usually preferring to reserve allegorical interpretation for Scripture. Might it not seem presumptuous for the author of the *Queste*, then, to give his work such clearly allegorical meanings? Like Dante, he solved this problem by placing his work squarely in a Biblical tradition, as well as in the Arthurian romance tradition; if, as Pauphilet suggests, it is "l'Evangile de Galaad" or "l'Evangile de la Table Ronde," and if its use of Scriptural allegory is as unusual as Pauline Matarasso believes,[91] the *Queste* may actually prove Bloomfield's rule that merely human literature would not aspire to divine allegory in the Middle Ages. At least one of its medieval readers placed it in the divine rather than the human realm: the author of the *Estoire del saint Graal*, a work composed after the prose *Lancelot* (of which the *Queste* is one section), to serve as an introduction to it, claims that the book is a transcription of a divine book given to him by Christ.[92] In this case, and perhaps only in such cases, the author could not be accused of trying to take on Godlike powers in providing allegorical interpretations within the text.

Sir Bors in the course of his adventures sees a great bird that kills itself in order to revive its children with its own blood.[93] This phenomenon is soon interpreted for him by a Cistercian abbot:

> "Li oisiax senefie nostre Creator, qui forma a sa semblance home. Et quant il fu boutez de paradis fors par son meffet, il vint en terre ou il trova la mort, car de vie n'i avoit point. Li arbres sanz foille et sanz fruit senefie apertement le monde, ou il n'avoit alors se male aventure non et povreté et soufreté. Li poucin senefient l'umain lignage, qui alors ert si perduz qu'il aloient tuit en enfer, ausi li bon come li mauvés, et estoient tuit egal en merite. Quant li filz Dieu vit ce, si monta en l'arbre, ce fu en la Croiz." (184)[94]

The interpretations provided by such monks, hermits, recluses, and divine visions are obviously very different from the explanations offered to Perceval by his various family members in the *Conte del Graal:* whereas in the *Conte*, literal events receive literal explanations, in the *Queste* interpretation erases the surface narrative and substitutes a spiritual truth from another level of reality, as Christ's sacrifice is substituted for the great bird's in Bors's adventures. Perceval's adventure at the Grail castle in Chrétien's romance, for example, is later explained by his uncle, the hermit, in purely literal, historical terms (those of family connections, in particular), with no metaphorical substitutions of one narrative for the other. The Fisher King is simply the hermit's brother and Perceval's other uncle; he does not symbolically stand for anything other than himself. The hermit's narrative completes Perceval's adventure by adding to it literal information of which Perceval and the reader were previously unaware; it does not substitute a metaphorical meaning with no literal connections to the adventure, as the decoding of "bird" into "Christ" does in the *Queste*.

It might be objected that these two examples are not really comparable: the *Queste*'s wounded king, Mordrain, also receives a purely historical explanation like that of the Fisher King in the *Conte*.[95] The point, however, is that the *Conte* provides no example comparable to the symbolic bird: all its explanations are equally literal and "historical," while, as I have suggested, the *Queste* follows medieval theorists of allegory in recognizing several levels of true meaning, of which the historical is only one.[96] Allegory in the strict sense is also common, as in the example of the bird's sacrifice; so is tropology (referring to human moral conduct), as in the interpretation of Lancelot's dream:

> "Je t'ai mostré que en toi est toute durtez, et la ou si granz durtez est herbergiee ne puet nule douçors repairier, ne nos ne devons pas cuidier qu'il i remaigne riens fors amertume; et amertume est donc en toi si grans come la douçors i deust estre. Donc tu es semblables au fust mort et porri ou nule douçor n'est remese, fors amertume. Or t'ai mostré coment tu es plus durs que pierre et plus amers que fust." (69)[97]

Although historical explanations are present in the *Queste*, then, the danger of a life lived only on the literal and historical level is constantly emphasized: "Car cist servises ou vos estes entrez n'apartient de riens as terrianes choses, mes as celestiex" (116).[98]

Chivalric adventure here receives a certain dignity because it can represent spiritual truths; but it is redeemed only in so far as it does so. The knights like Gawain and Hector who live only on the literal level of romance adventures are condemned: "Les aventures qui ore avienent sont les senefiances et les demostrances dou Saint Graal ne li signe dou Saint Graal n'aparront ja a pecheor ne a home envelopé de pechié. Dont il ne vos aparront ja; car vos estes trop desloial pecheor. Si ne devez mie cuidier que ces aventures qui ore avienent soient d'omes tuer ne de chevaliers ocirre; ainz sont des choses esperituex, qui sont graindres et mielz vaillanz assez" (160–61).[99]

The different knights, in fact, experience the quest on different levels of meaning; similar adventures reveal different truths to Gawain than they do to Galahad, because of the two knights' very different spiritual values. At the Castle of Maidens, for example, Galahad defeats the seven knights who hold its inhabitants captive; the seven flee and later encounter Gawain and two companions, who kill them. This adventure receives two different readings from the same monk to whom Gawain confesses. Gawain himself receives a literal explanation: "Se vos ne fussiez si pechierres come vos estes, ja li set frere ne fussent ocis par vos ne par vostre aide, ainz feissent encore lor penitance de la mauvese costume que il avoient tant maintenue ou Chastel as Puceles, et s'acordassent a Dieu. Et einsi n'esploita mie Galaad, li Bons Chevaliers, cil que vos alez querant: car il les conquist sanz ocirre" (54).[100] For the more spiritual Galahad, the interpretation is, in the strict sense, allegorical (with anagogical overtones):

> "Par le Chastel as Puceles doiz tu entendre enfer et par les puceles les bones ames qui a tort i estoient enserrees devant la Passion Jhesucrist; et par les set chevaliers doiz tu entendre les set pechiez principaus . . . . Mes quant li Peres del ciel vit que ce qu'il avoit formé aloit si a mal, il envoia son filz en terre por delivrer les bones puceles, ce sont les bones ames. Et tot ausi come il envoia son filz qu'il avoit devant le comencement dou monde, tout einsi envoia il Galaad." (55)[101]

One might ask why, if the seven knights must be understood as the seven deadly sins, it was wrong to kill them; but they are symbolic of sins only for the knight who lives on the spiritual, symbolic level, in this case, the one who is himself an allegory of Christ. For the exclusively literal and sinful Gawain, the knights are only knights.[102] If the sinful Gawain's experiences are literal while the perfect Galahad's are allegorical in the strict sense, Lancelot's are largely tropological: since he is the sinful knight who, unlike Gawain, nevertheless tries to attain Galahad's spiritual perfection, the level referring to human moral conduct is most appropriate to him, as in the dream interpretation cited above. Note that whereas Chrétien, in showing Gawain to defer his interpretation of Perceval's behavior until he should better understand the latter's internal state, appears to understand and accept the implications of Abelard's ethic of intentions for purely human understanding, the author of the *Queste* views those implications from a different perspective. Here, the holy interpreters understand the knights' motives better than the knights understand themselves and are thus able to judge them with authority. Chrétien chooses to emphasize how Abelard's ethic affects human interaction in a world deprived of divine immanence, where no individual can validly assume knowledge of another's spiritual state; but the *Queste*'s author shows a world in which God is indeed immanent, in which holy men and women, presumably under divine inspiration, can see through their interlocutors' literal reality to its symbolic spiritual meaning. For Chrétien, literal appearances conceal an equally literal reality; in the *Queste,* the entire literal level, though illusory in itself, can metaphorically reveal a higher reality.

The various knights' experiences of the Grail itself also accord with their spiritual states, as Emmanuèle Baumgartner has suggested; for her, the Grail "se donne à voir sous la 'semblance' la mieux adaptée à chaque destinataire," and she asks if it is "finalement rien d'autre que la représentation, l'image que chacun des compagnons de la quête peut susciter en lui et projeter sur l'univers sensible lorsqu'il tente d'évoquer Dieu et Ses mystères?" Thus it provides literal nourishment for the court as a whole (as it did in the *Conte del Graal*), appears as a healing vessel to Lancelot, and produces mystical visions for the chosen three who attain it.[103] Once again, we may see here the multiple levels of medieval Scriptural interpretation: literal for the court, tropological for Lancelot, allegorical for the three companions; and perhaps anagogical for Galahad alone, who is apparently translated, immediately following his ineffable vision, from earthly life to the afterlife.[104]

The *Queste del saint Graal* is thus a clearly allegorical work, one that operates now on one, now on another of the levels of meaning recognized by medieval theorists of interpretation. It is not, however, only the work's constant inserted self-interpretations spoken by monks and hermits that signal its allegorical status. As we have seen, Maureen Quilligan, like other readers of allegory, suggests that "the real 'action' of any allegory is the reader's learning to read the text properly,"[105] and the *Queste* is no exception. Though it might be tempting to regard the *Queste*'s reader simply as a passive receiver of the didactic doctrinal information provided by the many interpreters within the romance, it is more plausible to view these self-interpreting sections as teaching the reader how to interpret the romance adventures generally, as well as teaching him or her the meaning of the specific adventure under discussion. The symbolic clues to spiritual meanings are frequently quite conventional (as are iconographic details such as the bird's self-sacrifice). Once the color black has been associated with the devil and white with God, as in Perceval's adventures with the black horse and the angelic figure in the white ship, for instance, the reader can easily and correctly assess the diabolical nature of the black ship that Perceval encounters next.[106] Even when the connotations of black and white are reversed, as in Bors's vision of the black and white birds, another clear clue to their meaning is provided to prevent misunderstanding, in this case a reference to the black bride of the Song of Songs: "ne m'aies mie en despit por ce se je sui noire. Saches que mielz viaut ma nerté qu'autrui blanchor ne fait" (171).[107] The reader's assessment in all these cases is quickly confirmed by one of the romance's holy men or women, but the single correct reading of such episodes would be clear even without them.

And not all the romance episodes are interpreted within the text; in some cases, the reader must exercise the interpretive skills learned elsewhere in the *Queste* without the assistance of a monk or hermit. One such episode is the self-sacrifice of Perceval's sister (similar to that of the bird seen by Bors); she gives her blood to cure a leper and dies as a result: "Celui jor meismes fu la dame garie. Car si tost come ele fu lavee dou sanc a la sainte pucele, fu ele netoiee et garie de la meselerie, et revint en grant biauté sa char, qui devant estoit noire et orible a veoir" (242).[108] This adventure is never interpreted within the text, but a commentator like Pauline Matarasso, by invoking similar allegorical patterns that have been authoritatively interpreted earlier, can arrive at a reading that is clearly correct:

> Leprosy is a traditional symbol of sin, and the *Quest* alludes more than once to the external manifestations of grace or sin in the soul; first in the repeated insistence on Galahad's physical beauty, and secondly in Gawain's vision, where the companions of the Round Table appear as bulls, dappled and spotted, because "their guilt could not stay hidden in the inner man but must affect the outer" (p. 170). Perceval's sister, through her offering of her life-blood, freely made, redeems the figure of sinful Eve.[109]

Note that here, a physical, sensory fact, leprosy, clearly (and conventionally) represents a spiritual condition, as never happens in Chrétien's romances. The two conditions correspond adequately to each other, each on its own level. And even without any knowledge of the conventional association between leprosy and sin, the reader has already read the interpretation of a similar sacrifice of life-blood in the passage on the great bird, cited above, whose death symbolized Christ's redemption of humanity from original sin. The obvious iconographic parallels in this second sacrifice signal a meaning also parallel to that of the first; the *Queste* itself has already shown the reader how such signs are to be interpreted, so that the reader can now confidently provide correct interpretations without the work's direct assistance. To this extent, one might say that romance as a genre, including even such a didactic romance, tends to activate the reader, who must still fill in the "blanks," though in this case with an unusual confidence in being able to do so correctly.

Perhaps the most important element of the *Queste* that is not fully interpreted within the text is the Holy Grail itself. The lack of an authoritative reading for the central goal of the quest is not due to any lack of meaning for the Grail but to the fact that its meaning is ineffable. That its meaning cannot be simply expressed is no sign of multiplicity or indeterminacy, either; indeed, those critics who have addressed this question have added nuances to one another's discussions rather than opposing them with mutually exclusive readings, as has been the case with critics writing on Chrétien's Grail. Thus for Pauphilet, the Grail represents God,[110] while Gilson finds in it an image of grace (this latter reading is the one most directly supported by the text: "ce est li Saint Graax, ce est la grace del Saint Esperit").[111] Myrrha Lot-Borodine has attempted to reconcile these two views, suggesting that Galahad's Grail-vision is of "la Face même du Dieu trine," that is, the uncreated grace that is God.[112] W. E. M. C. Hamilton sees in the Grail a symbol of the Eucharistic mysteries.[113] These are mysteries that transcend language; nevertheless, the clear Cistercian influence on the *Queste* has oriented all these critics to similar and reconcilable readings unlike the conflicting and mutually exclusive allegories imposed upon Chrétien's *Conte del Graal*. Matarasso, in fact, has demonstrated just how reconcilable these readings are, finding that they "complete one another more than they contradict."[114] Like Hugh of St. Victor in his reading of the Bible, Matarasso can thus find no disagreements or conflicting readings on the spiritual level. Arnulf of Orléans' multiple interpretive possibilities, which provide a helpful model for interpretation in the *Conte*, simply cannot be applied to an allegory like the *Queste*.

Several critics have seen the Grail-quest as "a search for meaning";[115] almost all agree that this search is oriented in a specifically allegorical way. A brief comparison of the manner in which the Grail signifies in the *Queste* and in Chrétien's *Conte* should cast some further light on the nature of each work. We have seen that for Chrétien, the Grail points away from allegory: the Host it contains is, for twelfth- and thirteenth-century theologians, literally Christ's body; it does not provide physical nourishment. It is bread only in outward appearance or "accidents."[116] But in the *Conte del Graal*, this spiritual food is transformed into literal nourishment, apparently by the action of the Grail itself, which thus takes a spiritual object and invests it with a literal, physical meaning. The opposite is true of the Grail as it appears in the *Queste:* as has been noted, its first apparition provides literal nourishment, but it gradually loses this physical function and becomes more and more completely spiritual, until it finally provides Galahad's vision of God.[117] The physical object takes on spiritual meaning, whereas the reverse was true of Chrétien's Grail. The *Queste*'s Grail is virtually a definition of fourfold allegory, where Chrétien's refuses that mode of signification. The Grail can therefore be seen as an image of each work's fictional mode: allegorical for the *Queste*, non- or even anti-allegorical for Chrétien.

The attitude toward the relationship between abstract and concrete, or spiritual and physical, that the image of the Grail sums up, is also evident throughout the *Queste del saint Graal*'s entire narrative, just as the opposite attitude can be traced throughout Chrétien's romance. Whereas the *Conte del Graal* emphasizes the danger of regarding the physical world as a sign of the spiritual and indeed creates important disjunctions between the two, the *Queste* demonstrates a much greater coherence between them. This relation of physical to spiritual may well be rooted, at least for the *Queste*, in the doctrine of transubstantiation, that is, of the real presence of Christ in the Eucharist, which was established as dogma at the Fourth Lateran Council of 1215, after the composition of Chrétien's works and just before the writing of the *Queste*.[118] Here physical signs are trustworthy images of spiritual realities and must be read as such if proper behavior in the physical world is to be insured, as we have seen in the contrast between Gawain and Galahad. Hence the ease with which the reader can decode the romance's conventional signs (black and white, for example), and the promptness with which such readings are usually confirmed in the text. As in the *Chanson de Roland*, it is only the evil characters (including the devil himself in his various guises) who violate this correspondence between sensory and spiritual experience. Even when the knights are fooled by such violations, the reader is not: "Et il cuide bien que ce soit fame a qui il parole, mes non est, ainz est li anemis qui le bee a decevoir et a metre en tel point que s'ame soit perdue a toz jorz mes" (91).[119] Our perception of the true relation between sensory and spiritual is not allowed to be clouded even momentarily; we do not share the knights' temptations (and note the contrast with the reader's frequent limitation to Perceval's point of view in Chrétien's poem). The devil's defeats are always signalled by the restoration of that clear relationship. His true form reveals the spiritual reality:

> Lors lieve sa main et fet le signe de la croiz en son front. Quant li anemis se senti chargiez dou fessel de la croiz, qui trop li ert pesanz et griés, si s'escout et desvelope de Perceval, et se fiert en l'eve ullant et criant et fesant la plus male fin dou monde. Si avint maintenant que l'eve fu esprise en plusors leus de feu et de flamme clere, si qu'il sembloit que l'eve arsist.

> Et quant Perceval voit ceste aventure, si s'aperçoit bien tantost que
> ce est li anemis qui ça l'avoit aporté. (92)[120]

In the normal course, then, appearances are to be trusted in the *Queste*,
and spiritual significance can be deduced from sensory experience. There
is never any sign that the monks, angels, and recluses who specify these
deductions are not reliable, except in the case of the false priest whom Bors
encounters, and even he is riding a tell-tale black horse.[121] The tale can even
dispense with the interpreters within the text and provide the truth directly,
as in the "Tree of Life" section: "Li contes" itself becomes the speaker of
authoritative truths.[122]

The truth about all characters, on the literal as well as the allegorical level,
is quickly revealed in the *Queste*. Here we find no concealed identities like
Lancelot's or Perceval's in Chrétien's works, and no unasked or unanswered questions such as are central to the *Conte del Graal*. The difference
in Perceval's character between the two works is striking; far from the
ignorant boy to whom it never occurred that an event could have a meaning
he did not understand, or who refused to ask the meaning of such an event,
the *Queste*'s Perceval, as one of the three chosen knights who will succeed
in their quest, perceives hidden significance everywhere and eagerly asks
that it be revealed to him: "Biau sire, ce me semble que ce soit mout grant
senefiance; si le voldroie molt savoir s'il pooit estre; et por ce vos pri je
que vos le me dioiz" (83).[123] In fact, the incidents left most mysterious in
Chrétien's romance (Perceval's sword, the nature of the wounded king's
injuries) are here rationalized with historical explanations: "Quant [Parlan]
ot trovee ceste espee, si la trest del fuerre tant com vos poez veoir, car
devant ce ne paroit il point de l'alemele. Et toute l'eust il trete sanz targier;
mes maintenant entra laienz une lance, dont il fu feruz par mi oultre les
deus cuisses, si durement qu'il en remest mehaigniez si com il apert encore,
ne onques puis n'en pot garir, ne ne fera devant que vos vendroiz a lui"
(209).[124] (Recall once more that the use of such historical explanations does
not necessarily signal any rejection of allegory; history, as the bottom level
of meaning in the fourfold method of allegorical interpretation, is simply
absorbed into the *Queste*'s overall allegorical scheme.) This authoritative
explanation of literal details whose interpretation Chrétien left to the reader
is quite appropriate to the allegory, which by its very nature directs its
readers to a predetermined meaning as their single goal.

The more admirable the knight, the more transparent his character; in this
allegory, virtue reveals itself almost automatically. Thus the most perfect
knight, Galahad, is also the one whose virtue is most apparent: all the

others consistently agree that he is the one for whom the most difficult and prestigious adventures are reserved. He achieves them all with ease, as in the episode of the sword in the stone:

> Et li rois dist a Galaad: "Sire, veez ci l'aventure dont je vos parlai. A ceste espee trere fors de cest perron ont hui failli des plus proisiez chevaliers de mon ostel, qui onques ne l'em porent trere." "Sire," fet Galaad, "ce n'est mie de merveille, car l'aventure estoit moie, si n'ert pas lor. Et por la grant seurté que je avoie de ceste espee avoir n'en aportai je point a cort, si com vos poïstes veoir." Et lors met la main a l'espee et la trest fors dou perron autresi legierement come se ele n'i tenist pas; puis prent le fuerre et la met dedenz. (12)[125]

Hence the ritual nature of Galahad's actions: because of his perfection, his adventures need not prove what is obvious to all but simply serve as rituals to be performed by the chosen one.[126] Despite the disclaimer preserving his free-will—"sachiez de voir que s'il se menoit jusqu'a pechié mortel,—dont Nostre Sires le gart par sa pitié,—il ne feroit en ceste Queste nes que uns autres simples chevaliers" (116)[127]—Galahad's single-minded ritual actions go far toward justifying Angus Fletcher's association of allegory with obsession.[128] It is also true that Galahad is not an interpreter but must have the significance of his adventures explained to him, as do all his companions. As a ritual figure, he has no need to understand the spiritual plane intellectually, because he instinctively lives on that plane; Galahad unconsciously suits his actions on the literal level to the meaning they must have on the spiritual level and has no need of prior interpretation to do so. Interpreted after the fact, his actions can lead others, both his fellow knights and the *Queste*'s readers, to the singular goal of authoritative truth.

Authoritative truth, in fact, whether specified in the text or not, and even when ineffable, is inevitably a by-product of this particular allegorical mode of perception. If sensory experience of the physical world is, properly perceived, a reliable guide to a higher plane of reality, the reader, like the tale's characters, has no interpretive option but to follow these signs to their singular and definitive goal. Whereas Chrétien's works, especially the *Conte del Graal*, show signification to be problematic and refuse to direct the reader to a given interpretation, and even, in demonstrating the effects of Perceval's mother's allegoresis, ridicule allegory, the *Queste* responds to an earlier and still powerful neoplatonic and Augustinian world-view, the same that produced the "directed vision" of the *chansons de geste*.[129]

This contrast can be pursued even on a stylistic level. Mary Hynes-Berry, contrasting the *Queste*'s style with Malory's (in his adaptation of it) suggests that "the *Queste*'s invitation to see the meaning and the manner in which things happened is replaced by a less detailed paratactic account of events."[130] Allegory is an essentially metaphorical style in which events on one level are explained by substituting for them events on another, while the texts I examine elsewhere in this book, including both Chrétien's works and Malory's, use metonymic explanations, adding more information on the *same* level of experience and thus creating an explanatory context, or, by withholding such information, creating mysteries for the reader to solve.

Medieval religious allegory, whatever its other virtues, limits the reader's freedom of interpretation. Many earlier critics have seen all medieval literature as limiting this freedom, whether because it was all seen as allegory or because medieval Christianity was perceived as monolithically controlling even secular literature. In these first two chapters, I have tried to show the existence of two competing ways of thinking about signification in medieval thought, and two methods of writing literary narrative that reflect this competition in different ways. Thus St. Augustine, for example, can be seen as a source for both ways of thinking in the earlier Middle Ages, just as Chrétien reflects both traditions in his *Conte del Graal*. In the remaining chapters, I shall examine a number of literary narratives more like the *Conte* than the *Queste*, in that they reflect this competition rather than simply adopting the neoplatonic view, and do so with a greater and greater emphasis on the indeterminate modes of thought and signification. More and more, these works free the reader's interpretations from predetermined goals, even as they engage him or her in the act of interpreting.

3

Marie de France and Guillaume de Machaut: Love and Reading in the Twelfth and Fourteenth Centuries

In chapter 2, I drew a distinction between two kinds of high medieval romance, which I associate with the two different ways of reading the world (and literary works) described in chapter 1. Traditional neoplatonic theology produces works like the *Queste del saint Graal* that show the visible universe to consist of signs directing our attention toward singular and authoritative spiritual realities, on various symbolic levels, by means of metaphor and allegory. The newer *mentalité* emphasizes this visible universe alone, in a world in which divine immanence is bracketed, and Chrétien de Troyes reflects on how the world can best be understood under these conditions, rejecting symbolic meanings in his *Conte del Graal* in favor of finding meaning for the world's signs by placing them in literal contexts, each of which produces a different meaning for the sign thus understood. Nevertheless, these reflections themselves become a determinate theme to be communicated, suggesting a continuing competition between the two modes rather than the triumph of the newer one.

I also suggested that in each work the reader is encouraged to imitate the most successful interpreters represented there. The *Queste* teaches us to decode it allegorically, with confidence of finding a single correct meaning for each of its signs, while Chrétien demonstrates that we must accept the multiplicity of possible interpretations on the literal level, or even accept that certain mysteries must remain completely mysterious. In the *Conte*, however, the strongest emphasis is on showing the reader examples of successful and unsuccessful interpretation, rather than on directly involving him or her in the interpretive process—another aspect of the work's thematization of signification. Despite certain phenomenological "blanks" inviting the reader's participation, the *Conte* is most interesting in its thematization of that process, rather than in its activation of the reader.

In this chapter, I will move beyond interpretation as theme in order to investigate two works that invite the reader much more directly into the hermeneutic circle. Signification and interpretation remain important themes for Marie de France, who, as a contemporary of Chrétien's, still does not free her works from this kind of determinate communication. Nevertheless, her *Lais* use those themes to activate the reader much more directly and consistently than Chrétien's works do. Whereas Chrétien is concerned mostly with semantic indeterminacy in itself, Marie is also concerned with the effect of the indeterminacy on her readers. She draws parallels between her characters' erotic activity and her readers' interpretation of the book and is concerned also with the tension between the private and the public aspects of love and of reading, as well as with the ambiguity or indeterminacy of meaning in each activity.

Machaut's *Livre du Voir-Dit* shares these concerns and uses some of the same techniques, but the differences between his work and Marie's are as telling as their similarities and reflect the changing cultural context as the high Middle Ages become the late Middle Ages. Marie de France, reflecting twelfth-century rhetorical concerns, demonstrates a very specific interest in the creation and interpretation of concrete artifacts, including, though not limited to, written texts of various kinds. Such texts, including her own compositions, are shown to share the ambiguity that twelfth-century scholars and exegetes found in the literal level of Scripture and in the classics; and rather than simply observing this fact, the reader, much more consistently than in Chrétien's works, is urged to emulate such literary scholars, actively seeking and even creating new meanings for these narratives of old events. The same interpretive models are relevant in the *Lais* as in Chrétien's works, but now they are models for the reader as fully as for the characters.

Guillaume de Machaut, on the other hand, reflects later developments in philosophy, as well as the linguistic concerns of the earlier period. He presents semantic ambiguity and indeterminacy not in an exclusively linguistic and literary context but above all as epistemological problems, as problems about what we can truly know about the world outside our own minds, as well as about how we can communicate it to another. This question about the certainty of knowledge is to some extent anticipated by Abelard's ethic of intentions, but it is addressed most directly and completely by William of Ockham and the post-Ockhamist philosophers, just before Machaut's active period. The issues they raise give semantic indeterminacy much wider implications than it had in Marie's period, and this extension of the problem beyond textual concerns is reflected in the *Voir-Dit*.

One way it is reflected is in this work's more radical questioning of knowledge, not only the characters' knowledge of their world but the reader's knowledge of the text as well. Signification is not a theme for Machaut as it is for the twelfth-century writers, because communication of such a theme between text and reader is much more problematic in a period that questions the validity of knowledge. His work is thus more playful than Marie's in its ambiguous relations with the reader, balancing literary convention with potential "truth" and inviting the reader's ironic participation in the literary work as game, rather than communicating these issues as themes. By the fourteenth century, at least for Machaut's sophisticated audience, such indeterminacy of meaning had become enjoyably conventional. A comparison of the earlier and the later works thus demonstrates a changing attitude toward these problems.

Self-conscious Textuality in Marie de France's Lais

Although criticism in recent years of the *Lais* of Marie de France has done much to enhance the understanding of each of her individual tales, little attention has been devoted to the common themes and structures that unite them. Judith Rice Rothschild in her study *Narrative Technique in the Lais of Marie de France*[1] has pointed out a number of themes reappearing in several tales; she believes that these common themes point toward an "artistic unity for the ensemble."[2] As a point of departure for my own investigation of the *Lais*, to Rothschild's list of themes I would like to add the complementary themes of signification and interpretation that we have already found in the works of Marie's near-contemporary, Chrétien de Troyes. But whereas Chrétien de Troyes is concerned with the characters' responses to a variety of mysterious signs occurring in the natural and social worlds, Marie is much more directly concerned with textuality, that is, with the creation by one individual of a "work" (not necessarily linguistic) designed to be interpreted by someone else, and with the successes and failures of interpretation to which these "works" give rise. As I have suggested, Marie includes her own *Lais* in this category of interpretable artifacts, signaling their need for interpretation in her direct addresses to the reader. Many of the *Lais* present figures who act as readers or interpreters analogous to the reader of the *Lais* themselves. Since the interpreting figures within the *Lais* are invariably lovers, a further analogy, between the activities of love and of reading, is also suggested. Some of the *Lais* pose problems raised by these analogies, while others suggest solutions.

Marie's book, considered as a whole, presents the reader with a variety of fictional worlds, some of which seem faithfully mimetic (the world of "Laüstic," for example, or of "Chaitivel"), while others are more overtly fabulous (such as "Bisclavret," whose hero is a werewolf, or "Lanval," with its population of fairies).[3] The mimetic worlds seldom come into contact with the fabulous worlds, and therefore neither of these two basic types calls the other's reality into question. There is, however, an ever-present tension between the apparent reality of whatever kind of world is being presented, and this self-conscious textuality of the *lai* itself. Each *lai* continually acknowledges, even emphasizes, the fact that it is a verbal, fictional creation, a text; self-reflexive details subvert any impression the reader may have gained of a reality other than a purely textual one, the reality that words alone, and not a world, are present in the work. In this, Marie can be associated with the rhetoricians, who were composing the first *artes poeticae* at about the same time that she wrote the *Lais*. We have already seen the extent to which they emphasized language itself and the meanings to be derived from purely linguistic procedures (the tropes and "colors of rhetoric"), rather than from the representation of the world;[4] and Marie herself, to some extent, explores the possibility that life can imitate linguistic structures—stories—as well as the reverse.

Perhaps the clearest example of the *Lais'* self-reflexiveness is to be found in the *lai* of "Yonec." The unnamed heroine, locked in a tower by her jealous husband, wishes that she might gain her freedom by becoming what the author and the reader know her to be: the heroine of a *lai*. At the end of her first speech, she expresses her desire for liberation in terms strongly reminiscent of those in which Marie de France herself, speaking in her own authorial voice in the "Prologue" to her book, describes how she came to write it. The heroine says:

> Mut ai sovent oï cunter
> Que l'em suleit jadis trover
> Aventures en cest païs
> Ki rehaitouent les pensis.
> Chevalier trovoent puceles
> A lur talent, gentes e beles,
> E dames truvoent amanz
> Beaus e curteis, pruz e vaillanz,
> Si que blasmees n'en esteient
> Ne nul fors eles nes veeient.
> Si ceo peot estrë e ceo fu,
> Si unc a nul est avenu,

Deus, ki de tut ad poësté,
Il en face ma volenté! (lines 91–104)[5]

She wishes, in other words, for her life to become like one of the stories
she has heard. Her words, especially the first four lines of the quotation
above, inevitably recall what Marie has to say about similar stories:

Des lais pensai, k'oïz aveie.
Ne dutai pas, bien le saveie,
Ke pur remambrance les firent
Des aventures k'il oïrent
Cil ki primes les comencierent
E ki avant les enveierent.
Plusurs en ai oï conter,
Nes voil laissier ne oblier. ("Prologue," lines 33–40)[6]

This heroine, then, does not simply desire sexual freedom and adventure;
her speech makes it clear to the reader that, whether she realizes it or not,
the attainment of what she desires involves entering a story, or becoming
like a text. She wants to be like a fictional character, and the fictions she
wants to emulate correspond closely to this very collection of *lais*. When in
the following lines her wish is granted in a particularly extravagant manner
(a bird flies in through her window and magically becomes just such a lover
as she dreamed of), the reader is made aware that the *lai* is, indeed, exactly
parallel to the tales the heroine has heard; it does not present a purely
mimetic reality but a fictional text conscious that it is like other fictional
texts. Whatever suspension of disbelief the reader may have experienced
is here subverted, not by the tale's fantastic elements but by its textuality.
The lady's passage from a presumed reality into fictionality can only emphasize the *lai*'s rhetorical self-consciousness as a text.

The heroine's situation at this point is, in one way, similar to the reader's.
She is an audience to ancient tales of love and adventure, just as the reader
is an audience to Marie de France's similar tales; Marie from time to time
(ironically or paradoxically, considering her simultaneous emphasis on the
work's fictionality) even tells her readers that her *lais* are historically true,
as the heroine of "Yonec" believes the tales she has heard to be true (in
Marie's straight-faced conclusion to "Bisclavret," for instance, she assures
us that this tale of a werewolf was true, "veraie fu," line 316; I shall explore
this tension between history and fiction in greater detail in chapter 5). The
lady, however, is a far more naive reader than Marie allows her readers to

be; the heroine wishes only for the reality recounted in those tales to become her own reality. She believes them to be faithful representations of what life could be like (as, within the tale, they are). This justifiable naiveté on her part makes it impossible for "Yonec"'s reader to be similarly naive: her desire to be like a character in a tale emphasizes the fact that she is indeed only a character in a tale, a verbal creation and not a possible model for the reader to emulate as this character emulates fictional heroines. The reader, unlike this lady, remains highly conscious of the tension between the *lai*'s representational and purely textual aspects.

If we become aware of the lady's textuality because of the resemblance between the tales she wishes to imitate and the text we are reading, the *lai*'s resemblance to a somewhat different kind of text-within-the-text makes it clear that her lover, Muldumarec, also contributes to the tale's self-consciousness. Fatally wounded by the suspicious husband, Muldumarec prophesies that his son Yonec will avenge him when the boy learns his father's story:

> Par une tumbe k'il verrunt
> Orrunt renoveler sa mort
> E cum il fu ocis a tort.
> Ileoc li baillerat s'espeie.
> L'aventure li seit cuntee
> Cum il fu nez, ki l'engendra:
> Asez verrunt k'il en fera. (lines 430–36)[7]

The "aventure" whose narration will be prompted by the sight of Muldumarec's tomb is, of course, the plot of this very *lai* of "Yonec." When Yonec, along with his mother and her husband, finally does see his father's tomb, the story we have just read is pieced together for him by the tomb's guardians and by the heroine, who also reveals its relevance to her son by contextualizing it, like Perceval's family members recounting their history:

> Cil comencierent a plurer
> E en plurant a recunter
> Que c'iert li mieudre chevaliers
> E li plus forz e li plus fiers,
> Li plu beaus e li plus amez
> Ki jamés seit el siecle nez.
> De ceste tere ot esté reis,
> Unques ne fu nuls si curteis.

A Carẅent fu entrepris,
Pur l'amur d'une dame ocis.
"Unques puis n'eümes seignur,
Ainz avum atendu meint jur
Un fiz qu'en la dame engendra,
Si cum il dist e cumanda."
Quant la dame oï la novele,
A haute voiz sun fiz apele:
"Beaus fiz," fet ele, "avez oï
Cum Deus nus ad menez ici?
C'est vostre pere ki ci gist,
Que cist villarz a tort ocist.
Or vus comant e rent s'espee,
Jeo l'ai asez lung tens gardee."
Oiant tuz li ad coneü
Qu'il l'engendrat e sis fiz fu;
Cum il suleit venir a li
E cum sis sires le trahi,
La verité li ad cuntee. (lines 513–39)[8]

The heroine wished to be like a character in a story; Muldumarec ends as
the main character in this story told to his son. She projected herself into
a tale of the past by means of her memory, while he projects himself into
a future tale by means of his prophecy. Both of these texts, remembered
tale and predicted narration, are reflections in miniature of the *lai* of "Yonec"
itself: the heroine's ideal stories are very much like this *lai*, and Muldumarec's projected narrative turns out to be an exact recapitulation of it. In this
way, both of the tale's main characters demonstrate their own textuality:
by projecting themselves into texts which are reflections of the *lai* itself,
they insure the reader's consciousness of the tale as text.

Textual Signs: Interpretation as Creation

Self-consciousness is not, however, an end in itself for Marie's *Lais*. These
tales do not point out their own fictionality simply in order to demonstrate
the lack of genuine human contact between tale and reader that such self-
reflexiveness might imply. The *Lais'* emphasis on their own textuality is
only the first step toward engaging the reader's awareness of, and responses
to, a thematic concern central to all of them: the problem of interpretation,
which is first approached by Marie herself in her "Prologue":

> Custume fu as anciens,
> Ceo testimoine Preciens,
> Es livres ke jadis feseient,
> Assez oscurement diseient
> Pur ceus ki a venir esteient
> E ki aprendre les deveient,
> K'i peüssent gloser la lettre
> E de lur sen le surplus mettre. (lines 9–16)[9]

These lines have sparked an ongoing critical debate. Leo Spitzer and D. W. Robertson, Jr.,[10] have argued that the *sen* or *surplus* to be added by the reader "is obviously the 'Christian' attitude"[11] or *sententia*. This is not what Marie's words (*"lur* sen") say, however; and Tony Hunt has provided a much more convincing reading of these lines with greater fidelity both to the text as it stands and to certain theories of interpretation current in Marie's period.[12] He paraphrases the lines in question (lines 15–16) thus: "they might construe their writing and through their wits add the rest (that was necessary to complete elucidation)."[13] The *sen* to be added, then, is not a predetermined Christian doctrine but something readers bring to the text themselves. This point is necessary to an understanding of how signification and interpretation work in the *Lais*. Marie sees herself as an emulator of the ancient writers, that is, as one who writes obscurely so that later readers might gloss her text and add (as Marie added to the *aventures* she remembered hearing) their own interpretations to the work. Note how closely related are the functions of audience and author: Marie's authorship is the result of her having been an audience to earlier versions of these tales. A good audience adds new understanding to the old works, thus recreating them, that is, becoming an author. And this chain of creation and interpretation, in which the interpretation becomes a new creation, is endless: Marie's own readers, with their own new understandings, are at least potential re-creators of her tales, which were in turn interpretations/recreations of others. The "grevose ovre" referred to in line 25 is presumably the work the reader is now beginning, the *Lais* themselves, as well as Marie's work in creating them; Marie has provided her readers with an especially difficult text so that they, too, might fully experience the joys of interpretation. Since she made it clear in the earlier lines that the addition of the reader's own *sen* or meaning to the work is an important aspect of the interpretive act, Marie de France seems to invite the reader's interpretation as a valid expansion of her work. What she desires is not simply that he or she understand the story, if by "understanding" is meant only an acceptance of her own point of view toward it; equally necessary is the reader's very act of engagement with the text, the process itself of interpretation.[14]

The heroine of "Yonec" is not the only figure of the reader, naive or otherwise, to be found in the *Lais*. The plot of each of the *lais* depends at one point or another upon the interpretation by one character of a sign of some kind made by another character. These signs range from complex verbal narratives and expressions of emotion to simple love-tokens, but all are made specifically to be interpreted. Characters in these tales spend an inordinate amount of time "reading" each other by means of these texts and tokens, and if the making of signs self-consciously reflects the making of the *lais* themselves, the reading of them necessarily projects a far more active role for the readers than the simple contemplation of a self-reflexive work having no relevance to their own reality. The reader's awareness that the text is a text is only the preparation for a more important realization: that the text, even the self-conscious text, is interpretable, that it requires the reader's participation if meaning is to emerge from it. By signaling their own status as texts, the *Lais* are able to move beyond that mere static textuality into a kind of dialogue with the reader.

An example of the history of one tale's creation and interpretation/re-creation occurs in "Chievrefoil," the shortest and perhaps best known of Marie de France's *Lais*, most of whose action is concerned with the making of a text by one character, Tristan, for the benefit of another, Iseut. This *lai* makes no secret of the fact that it is about the making of a *lai*, that it records the history of its own composition; its four-line prologue and twelve-line conclusion tell the reader directly that such is its subject-matter:

> Asez me plest e bien le voil,
> Del lai qu'hum nume *Chievrefoil*,
> Que la verité vus en cunt
> Pur quei fu fez, coment e dunt. (lines 1–4)

> Pur la joie qu'il ot eüe
> De s'amie qu'il ot veüe
> E pur ceo k'il aveit escrit
> Si cum la reïne l'ot dit,
> Pur les paroles remembrer,
> Tristram, ki bien saveit harper,
> En aveit fet un nuvel lai. (lines 107–13)[15]

Between its beginning and its ending, however, "Chievrefoil" presents a more subtle consideration of the creation and interpretation of written signs, of the relationship between a writer of words and an interpreter of writing. The plot of this tale is simple: Tristan, exiled from King Mark's court, learns that Iseut is about to undertake a journey. He hides in a wood through which she must pass and leaves a message of some kind written on a piece of wood for her to see. When Iseut sees and understands the message, she joins Tristan in the woods for a brief encounter before continuing on her way. Tristan composes a *lai* on the subject of the message and their meeting; Marie de France herself composes a *lai* on the subject of the composition of Tristan's *lai*.

The brevity of this *lai* causes Marie to be somewhat elliptical; the longest continuing debate among scholars writing on Marie's work concerns the exact nature of Tristan's message in "Chievrefoil."[16] It is interesting to note that, although none of them mentions the problem specifically, all of these critics are mainly concerned with just how much interpreting Iseut has to do. Their own interpretations are many: did Tristan write only his name on the famous piece of wood, leaving Iseut to supply the interpretation that occupies lines 63–78? Did he write out the entire message himself? Was the piece of wood an ogam and was Iseut versed in the interpretation of ogamic characters? Had he written her a letter beforehand containing the interpretation? There is no way of knowing what Marie intended; line 53 states that Tristan carved his name, while lines 61–62, referring to the long interpretation that follows, say: "Ceo fu la summe de l'escrit / Qu'il li aveit mandé e dit."[17] "Summe" is defined by Greimas as either "résumé" or "l'essentiel," and whether this gist or meaning was written out or meant to be divined by Iseut from the sight of Tristan's name alone is impossible to determine.

What is certain is Tristan's intention, for he, like Marie, is an artist, as the *lai*'s conclusion on his abilities as a harpist and composer of *lais* informs us. Whether or not he wrote in ogamic characters, he is, as an artist, well-versed in the creation of other kinds of sign, and what he intends is for Iseut, his reader, to interpret them. Whether lines 63–78 represent what Tristan actually wrote or what was to be divined by Iseut, at the heart of this message lies a sign created by Tristan to be read by Iseut:

> D'euls deus fu il tut autresi
> Cume del chievrefoil esteit
> Ki a la codre se perneit:
> Quant il s'i est laciez e pris
> E tut entur le fust s'est mis,
> Ensemble poënt bien durer,

Mes ki puis les voelt desevrer,
Li codres muert hastivement
E li chievrefoilz ensement.
"Bele amie, si est de nus:
Ne vus sanz mei, ne jeo sanz vus." (lines 68–78)[18]

The medium here is clearly the message: the branch on which the message is carved is of "codre" (line 51), probably hazel, and presumably the "codre" entwined with honeysuckle ("chievrefoil") mentioned in line 70. Tristan has combined a written text with a physical signifier demanding and encouraging interpretation from the audience for whom it was intended. He winds up composing a *lai*[19] about that very process (line 109), and Marie herself ends the tale with the information that she, an audience to his composition, has created a similar composition about Tristan's *lai*:

Dit vus en ai la verité
Del lai que j'ai ici cunté. (lines 117–18)[20]

"Chievrefoil," then, is a poem about the creation of a *lai* about the creation of a poetic, or at least verbal and interpretable, symbol. It seems likely, therefore, that these three creations are to be seen as parallels, and at the basis of all three there lies the demand for a reading, for interpretation. Just as Iseut's reading of Tristan's wooden sign prompts the composition of his *lai* (whose subject is, in part, her response to the original sign), so Marie's "reading" of that *lai* prompts her own composition aimed, in turn, at readers who will necessarily occupy a position similar to Iseut's and Marie's: that of responsive audience to an artistic performance. "Chievrefoil" presents a chain of compositions and their audiences leading to itself and its own audience; implicit is the likelihood that the active reader, seeing himself or herself reflected in the images of previous readers in the chain, Iseut and Marie, might emulate their responses and, by means of his or her own interpretive reading, also join in this creative process. By providing characters who perform functions corresponding to the reader's, Marie draws her own readers into an active involvement with her creation.[21]

Public and Private Interpretation

Marie de France also demonstrates an interest in entirely non-verbal signs whose need to be interpreted by an engaged reader is emphasized. She provides a number of examples; the best are to be found in her collection's first *lai*, "Guigemar." This tale's self-conscious textuality is demonstrated, at certain points, in the same way as that of "Yonec": the lovers recapitulate to each other the stories of their lives that the reader already knows, much as Yonec's mother recapitulates Muldumarec's story; each of the lovers thus makes the other a reader and himself or herself a narrative to be read (as in lines 311–58, for example). The necessity of interpretation, however, is given greater emphasis in the episode of their exchange of love-tokens. Fearing that they might be separated (as they soon will be), each devises an ingenious method of assuring the other's fidelity:

> "Amis, de ceo m'aseürez!
> Vostre chemise me livrez;
> El pan desuz ferai un plait:
> Cungié vus doins, u ke ceo seit,
> D'amer cele kil defferat
> E ki despleier le savrat."
> Il li baile, si l'aseüre.
> Le plet i fet en teu mesure,
> Nule femme nel deffereit,
> Si force u cutel n'i meteit.
> La chemise li dune e rent.
> Il la receit par tel covent
> Qu'el le face seür de li;
> Par une ceinture autresi,
> Dunt a sa char nue la ceint,
> Par mi le flanc aukes l'estreint:
> Ki la bucle purrat ovrir
> Sanz depescier e sanz partir,
> Il li prie que celui aint. (lines 557–75)[22]

Untying the knot and unbuckling the belt are forceful images of the interpretive process; it is an essential feature of these devices that they are not simply a means of preserving the beloved for the lover but are also a means by which the beloved can identify the lover, that is, a way of recognizing or of reading the other's identity. The correct interpretation of these signs would lead to the recognition of the lover. It seems, curiously enough, that without them the lovers would not know each other; when they meet again after having been separated, the sight of his beloved is not apparently enough to convince Guigemar of her identity:

"Est ceo," fet il, "ma duce amie,
M'esperaunce, mun quor, ma vie,
Ma bele dame ki m'ama?
Dunt vient ele? Ki l'amena?
Ore ai pensé mut grant folie;
Bien sai que ceo n'est ele mie:
Femmes se resemblent asez,
Pur nïent change mis pensez." (lines 773–80)[23]

Even verbal communication is not enough proof; only when they have formally solved the puzzles posed by the knot and the buckle does recognition take place:

Quant ele ot le comandement,
Le pan de la chemise prent,
Legierement le despleiat.
Li chevaliers s'esmerveillat;
Bien la conut, mes nequedent
Nel poeit creire fermement.
A li parlat en teu mesure:
"Amie, duce creature,
Estes vus ceo? Dites mei veir!
Lessiez mei vostre cors veeir,
La ceinture dunt jeo vus ceins." (lines 809–19)[24]

Direct apprehension of each other cannot take place between these lovers; they require the assistance of interpretable signs, both the puzzle-devices themselves and the process of solving or undoing them serving as signs whose correct reading will lead to union with the other. It is possible to find reflected here another implication of Abelard's ethic of intentions, whose influence we have already explored in chapters 1 and 2. If, as I have suggested, that ethic inevitably emphasizes the impossibility of knowing another's internal state by means of his or her external signs, Marie de France here takes this problem a step further and proposes a solution. The other's external appearance may now even conceal identity itself; but the corollary to this difficulty is that one does know one's own intentions and can therefore read one's own signs. Guigemar can interpret the buckle's meaning because he himself created it as a sign, and it reflects his own intentions; the same is true of his lover's "reading" of the knot. What each of them recognizes is her or his own sign, not the other's; but in this case, one's own sign can identify the other.

Correct interpretation, however, is not the sole purpose of these signs; instead, the making of signs and texts that require a reader's interpretation serves a double purpose in each of these *lais*. It serves to reveal the lovers to each other and to conceal their relationship from the world at large. (We will find a similar process in Machaut's *Voir-Dit*.) This point is made most specifically in "Yonec"; Muldumarec's dying gifts to his mistress are a ring whose magical properties cause the jealous husband to forget what he knows of the lady's infidelity, and a sword that is to serve as a reminder of their love, a sign to be used when revealing the truth to their son, Yonec:

> Un anelet li ad baillé,
> Si li ad dit e enseigné,
> Ja tant cum el le gardera,
> A sun seignur n'en membera
> De nule rien ki fete seit,
> Ne ne l'en tendrat en destreit.
> S'espee li cumande e rent,
> Puis la conjurë e defent
> Que ja nuls hum n'en seit saisiz,
> Mes bien la gart a oés sun fiz. (lines 415–24)[25]

These signs are meant to be interpreted only by those characters actually involved in the love-relationship, Muldumarec, his mistress, and their child; in the relationship between that group and the rest of the world, the signs serve precisely the opposite function: they actually prevent interpretation, concealing, by their very existence, their true meaning, and preventing any reading on the part of others. The same functions are served by Tristan's text in "Chievrefoil"; although Iseut interprets it correctly,

> Le bastun vit, bien l'aparceut,
> Tutes les lettres i conut (lines 81–82),[26]

its meaning and even, apparently, the very fact that it is a sign demanding that someone read it, is lost on her companions:

> Les chevaliers ki la menoent
> E ki ensemble od li erroent
> Cumanda tuz a arester:
> Descendre voet e reposer.
> Cil unt fait sun commandement.
> Ele s'en vet luinz de sa gent. (lines 83–88)[27]

Again, in "Guigemar," the love-tokens both identify the members of the love-relationship and prevent others from joining in that relationship:

> Le plet i fet en teu mesure,
> Nule femme nel deffereit,
> Si force u cutel n'i meteit. (lines 564–66)[28]

Numerous other examples of the sign or text interpretable by the lovers but preventing interpretation by the world outside the relationship might be cited from Marie de France's *Lais;* the swan-messenger in "Milun" comes to mind, or the nightingale in "Laüstic."

The point here is that in any love-relationship presented in the *Lais* the lover is always an interpreter, and also that interpretation, or at least correct interpretation, is a function only of the lover. To love, for Marie de France, is to interpret the signs and texts that identify the beloved, and to interpret those signs and texts correctly is to achieve the union or reunion of lovers. In a sense, the active participation in the creative process allowed the reader by Marie's *Lais* might be perceived as an activity parallel to that which unites the lovers within the text: to read or interpret the text correctly is to enter into an erotic relationship with it.[29] Love and interpretation are metaphors for each other.

Love and Reading

Marie suggests this relationship subtly, but more directly than might at first be imagined, in the interplay between a passage in her "Prologue" to the whole book of *Lais* and several suggestive passages in the individual *lais* themselves. Near the end of the "Prologue," Marie, speaking as the author of her book directly to her readers, describes her method of composition:

> Rimé en ai e fait ditié,
> Soventes fiez en ai veillié! (lines 41–42)[30]

The problem of composition, that is, of interpreting her predecessors and of creating a work obscure enough to allow interpretation by her readers (as discussed above), often kept Marie awake at night. This issue of someone's inability to sleep at night because he or she is beset by problems of interpretation is one that comes up often throughout the *Lais*, but only here in the "Prologue" is it applied to an author's attempt at literary creation. Every time this problem is raised in the *lais* themselves, the victim of sleeplessness is not a reader/author figure like the "Prologue"'s authorial voice but a lover trying to interpret the behavior of his or her beloved.

Several examples can be cited from the various tales. In "Guigemar," the man and the woman each pass a sleepless night wondering how the other feels. Of Guigemar himself the author says:

> Tute la nuit ad si veillé
> E suspiré e travaillé (lines 411–12),[31]

and his work consists of attempts to determine whether or not the lady will prove "orgoilluse e fiere" (line 404) and refuse him. The lady, meanwhile, experiences the same difficulty:

> Veillé aveit, de ceo se pleint;
> Ceo fet Amur, ki la destreint (lines 429–30),[32]

the problem being her lack of knowledge of Guigemar's feelings, "s'il l'eime u nun" (line 436). In a similar fashion, the king in "Equitan" "veilla tant que jur fu" (line 101) because, as he says,

> Uncor ne sai ne n'ai seü
> S'ele fereit de mei sun dru. (lines 93–94)[33]

Again, the young lady in "Eliduc"

> Tute la nuit veillat issi,
> Ne resposa ne ne dormi (lines 331–32),[34]

and for the same reason.

Finally, and most strikingly, the entire plot of "Laüstic" revolves around the problem of being kept awake by love. The lovers in this tale, already aware that their feelings are reciprocated, stay awake because only at night are they sure of the privacy necessary for their secret communication. The lady's excuse to her husband for staying awake, that she is listening to the nightingale's song, thus becomes a doubly meaningful symbol like the ring in "Yonec": to the lovers it is a sign of their love, while it conceals that love from the rest of the world. Ultimately, when the jealous husband kills the nightingale to remove the lady's excuse for staying awake, the symbol of a living bird becomes an ornate but lifeless text substituted for the lovers' oral communication:

"Lasse," fet ele, "mal m'estait!
Ne purrai mes la nuit lever
N'aler a la fenestre ester." (lines 126–28)

En une piece de samit
A or brusdé et tut escrit
Ad l'oiselet envolupé;
Un suen vaslet ad apelé,
Sun message li ad chargié,
A sun ami l'ad enveié. (lines 135–40)[35]

Their relationship destroyed by the destruction of its symbol, all that re-mains is this text created by the lady for her lover.

In her "Prologue," then, Marie de France chooses to speak of the activity of literary interpretation in terms otherwise reserved for her characters' interpretations of their lovers' emotions. That these activities might be regarded as parallels is suggested by the similarity of the situations in which the literary interpreter of the "Prologue" and the lovers in "Guigemar," "Equitan," "and "Eliduc" find themselves, kept awake by problems of interpretation. The parallel can only be strengthened by reference to "Laüs-tic," whose heroine substitutes the creation of a text for the love that had kept her awake. All these tales suggest that love is related metaphorically to literary creation and interpretation; in "Laüstic," the reader of the lady's text is her former lover, who responds to her message by creating his own work of art as a commemoration of their love:

Quant tut li ad dit e mustré
E il l'aveit bien escuté,
De l'aventure esteit dolenz;
Mes ne fu pas vileins ne lenz.
Un vaisselet ad fet forgier;
Unques n'i ot fer ne acier,
Tuz fu d'or fin od bones pieres,
Mut precïuses e mut chieres;
Covercle i ot tres bien asis.
Le laüstic ad dedenz mis. (lines 145–54)[36]

To love is to interpret, that is, to read the beloved's text and react to it;[37] thus the reader of Marie's *Lais* is to the text as a lover within the text is to his beloved. Text and reader form an erotic alliance.

Once again we may find here a relation between Marie de France's works and the rhetorical tradition. As we have seen, Christian opponents of secular literature considered it a seductive trap for the reader, and indeed Alain de Lille, extending the venerable tradition which used grammatical terminology to describe sexual activity, condemns aesthetic pleasure in fiction in clearly sexual terms.[38] In drawing the parallel between love and reading, Marie accepts this traditional perception but refuses the negative judgment that accompanies it. She aligns herself instead with the rhetoricians, for whom the reader's aesthetic pleasure was a valid goal.[39]

To develop this parallel: the text reveals itself gradually to the reader, as characters in the tales slowly reveal themselves to each other. In "Eliduc," for example, we glean as little information from observing the hero as the heroine does, even though we have heard two fairly complex theories of interpretation from the lady and from her chamberlain. Before hearing them, the reader has been made aware that Eliduc, though still faithful to his wife, Guildeluëc, also feels a strong attachment to a second lady, Guilliadun; suspense as to whether or not he will, in fact, love Guilliadun is maintained as the poet documents Eliduc's vacillations:

> Tuz est murnes e trespensez,
> Pur la belë est en effrei,
> La fille sun seignur le rei,
> Ki tant ducement l'apela
> E de ceo k'ele suspira. (lines 314–18)

> De sa femme li remembra
> E cum il li asseüra
> Que bone fei li portereit
> E lëaument se cuntendreit. (lines 323–26)[40]

At this point the narrative leaves Eliduc in a state of indecision and turns to Guilliadun, who has already fallen in love with him, and to her chamberlain; these two share the reader's suspense about Eliduc's feelings toward the lady and discuss the possibility of arriving at a correct interpretation of them:

> "Dame," fet il, "quant vus l'amez,
> Enveiez i, si li mandez;
> Ceinturë u laz u anel
> Enveiez li, si li ert bel.
> Si il le receit bonement
> E joius seit del mandement,
> Seüre seiez de s'amur." (lines 355–61)

La dameisele respundi,
Quant le cunseil de lui oï:
"Coment savrai par mun present
S'il ad de mei amer talent?
Jeo ne vi unques chevalier
Ki se feïst de ceo preier,
Si il amast u il haïst,
Que volentiers ne retenist
Cel present k'hum li enveast." (lines 365–73)[41]

The chamberlain believes that Eliduc's reaction to a token sent by Guilliadun will serve as an interpretable sign of whether or not he loves her, while Guilliadun herself maintains that appearances might be deceiving, without proposing any more effective plan. These attempts to read Eliduc's emotions emphasize the closeness of the parallel between the reader's situation with regard to the text, and the lover's, Guilliadun's, situation with regard to the beloved, Eliduc: each is in suspense about the outcome of events, looking forward to a sign (whether from the author or from the beloved) that will allow a correct interpretation of the mystery.

Guilliadun at last consents to the chamberlain's plan; the reader then witnesses a scene that, according to the theory of interpretation proposed by the chamberlain, should provide such an interpretable sign, a clue to Eliduc's feelings:

Li chamberlencs mut se hasta.
A Eliduc esteit venuz.
A cunseil li ad dit saluz
Que la pucele li mandot,
E l'anelet li presentot;
La ceinture li ad donee.
Li chevaliers l'ad mercïee,
L'anelet d'or mist en sun dei,
La ceinture ceinst entur sei;
Ne li vadlez plus ne li dist
Ne il nïent ne li requist
Fors tant que del suen li offri.
Cil n'en prist rien, si est parti. (lines 402–14)[42]

The surprise, of course, is that we learn nothing from this anxiously awaited interview; Guilliadun's suspicion that appearances might be deceiving proves disappointingly accurate. Eliduc remains opaque even to the watchfulness of the chamberlain, and of the reader as well, who learns that Eliduc is willing to give his love to Guilliadun only when she herself learns it. In this way, Marie de France develops a technique already familiar from Chrétien's *Conte del Graal:* the withdrawal of omniscience from the reader. This text teases the reader into involvement, giving him or her in Guilliadun a representative within the tale who demonstrates the process of interpretation and who eventually allows the reader to become a party to the lovers' secret. If the purpose of signs and texts is to reveal lovers to one another while concealing their relationship from the rest of the world (and Guilliadun's gifts of a ring and a belt remind us that the same gifts served just this double purpose in "Yonec" and "Guigemar"), then the reader interpreting the text becomes a member of that relationship, as it is revealed.

Love and Ambiguity

The very nature of literature, however, and especially the nature of these *lais*, as Marie seems to conceive of them, complicates this seemingly private, erotic encounter between reader and text. Marie continually emphasizes in the brief prologues and epilogues to her various tales the public nature of literature, the fact that she is giving the secret away by writing about it. "Laüstic," for example, whose plot's major concern is with the attempt to conceal a love-affair from the outside world, ends with an admission that the attempt failed precisely because it was turned into a *lai:*

> Cele aventure fu cuntee,
> Ne pot estre lunges celee.
> Un lai en firent li Bretun:
> Le Laüstic l'apelë hum. (lines 157–60)[43]

Marie de France is clearly contributing to this public knowledge of the lovers' relationship by writing her own version of the *lai;* if the individual reader can be seen as a participant in the private encounter of lovers, it is also true that he or she can be seen as a member of the public to whom that relationship is revealed against the lovers' will. Publicity, we learn over and over again in the tales themselves, can destroy the love-relationship; this is the reason for using symbols interpretable only by the lovers themselves in "Guigemar," "Yonec," "Milun," "Chievrefoil," and others. This is as true of the reader-text relationship as of the lovers' relationship within the text. If we become engaged in the text through the private interpretation of signs, the public revelation of those signs must vitiate our engagement, making us members of the outside world rather than the love-relationship. And yet publicity is the very reason for making a *lai*, the point being to bring a private story to the attention of others "pur remambrance," as Marie says in her "Prologue" (line 35). The encounter between reader and text cannot be hidden from the rest of the world, because the reader is part of that world. The problem lies in the definitive nature of the interpretations we have considered thus far: in each case, the "blanks" in the plot-line are eventually filled in when the reader learns the singular correct interpretation.

Several of Marie's *Lais* propose solutions to this paradox of the reader's position as a member both of a private love-relationship and of the public whose knowledge destroys love. What is needed are texts that allow the reader to enter into the erotic, interpreting relationship with them without wholly exposing their secrets to the public knowledge, texts that engage each reader as an individual without imposing any single solution to their mysteries.[44] Marie's description in the "Prologue" of how a reader should approach a text—"de lur sen le surplus mettre" (line 16)—can, then, be seen as an invitation to personal interpretation, to the private solution of problems or mysteries that the text itself refuses to solve.

One such text that invites the reader's active interpretation is the well-known *lai* of "Lanval." The major emphasis of this tale's plot is entirely upon the maintenance of secrecy, specifically Lanval's maintenance of the secret of his fairy-mistress's identity. The danger of publicity to the love-relationship is spelled out even more specifically than usual in this *lai*; the lady, speaking with the authority of the supernatural, tells Lanval:

> ". . . Ne vus descovrez a nul humme!
> De ceo vus dirai ja la summe:
> A tuz jurs m'avrïez perdue,
> Si ceste amur esteit seüe;
> Jamés nem purrïez veeir
> Ne de mun cors seisine aveir." (lines 145–50)[45]

Love here clearly depends upon mystery; and the lady is as mysterious to the reader as she is to Lanval and, later, to the members of King Arthur's court. Emphasis is placed on the enigmatic nature of this lady from the first moment she appears; her handmaidens carry ritual objects whose significance is never explained,[46] and she herself explains her presence without ever mentioning her origins or identity:

> "Lanval," fet ele, "beus amis,
> Pur vus vinc jeo fors de ma tere:
> De luinz vus sui venue quere! . . ." (lines 110–12)[47]

Her parting words to Lanval remind him that she must remain a mystery to all:

> ". . . Nuls hum fors vus ne me verra
> Ne ma parole nen orra." (lines 169–70)[48]

The question of who this lady is remains unanswered in the text, even though Lanval disobeys her command and reveals the existence of their relationship to the queen when she mocks him for refusing her love. Indeed, the point is made more forcefully here than in any other *lai* that the lady's existence is revealed, as is her beauty, directly to a public gathering of people outside the relationship. Lanval having been condemned because of his boast that his lady's beauty exceeds the queen's, the lady refuses at first to appear and thus justify him, because he has broken her rule of secrecy. She finally relents in order to save him by proving that his boast was true:

> Devant le rei est descendue,
> Si que de tuz iert bien veüe.
> Sun mantel ad laissié cheeir,
> Que mieuz la peüssent veeir. (lines 603–06)[49]

This emphasis on the extremes of secrecy and publicity suggests that they are of special importance in "Lanval"; and in spite of the publicity, this lady remains a tantalizing enigma: although often called the "fairy-mistress"[50] by critics, nowhere is the reader given direct information on her nature. In fact, when her handmaidens appear to announce her arrival, even Lanval must admit that

> ". . . ne seit ki sunt
> Ne dunt vienent n'u eles vunt." (lines 483–84)[51]

Although we learn that she takes Lanval away to Avalon, we also learn that that information comes second-hand ("Ceo nus recuntent li Bretun," line 642); Marie in this line joins the puzzled audience as one who knows only what she has heard but cannot tell if it is the true story. She prefers to end on a note of mystery:

> Nuls hum n'en oï plus parler
> Ne jeo n'en sai avant cunter. (lines 645–46)[52]

Although Lanval may have violated the lady's secrecy, the text refuses to do so. It presents the reader with an enigmatic character and refuses to explain her. It does, however, try to tempt its readers into explaining her on their own; clues like the unexplained ritual objects and the second-hand Breton speculation about the isle of Avalon invite the reader to provide an interpretation. Lanval's ignorance about her identity points out that we are in the presence of a mystery waiting to be solved. As readers, we must interpret without the author's assurance that any one reading will be correct; we must be willing to find a *sen* on our own. In this way we find ourselves engaged with the text without violating it; our reading remains a private, erotic encounter rather than a public one with meaning imposed by the author. The act of interpretation will not be vitiated by public explanation of this tale, because no explanation is forthcoming. The reader thus remains a full participant in the tale to the end.

The love-relationship, as well as the relationship between reader and text, is presented more poignantly in the *lai* of "Chaitivel," which returns us to Marie's direct thematic concern with literature. This tale's consciousness of its own textuality is as pronounced as that of "Chievrefoil": almost one-fifth of the entire *lai* concerns the manner in which the heroine made her experiences into a *lai*, and the problem of choosing a correct title for it. Four knights love the same lady, who is unable to choose among them; all fight in a tournament to prove their worth, and three are killed while the fourth is badly wounded. The lady is unable to love the survivor because of her memories of the others; she decides to compose a *lai* about them to be called *Quatre Dols* ("Four Sorrows"). The surviving knight protests that *Chaitivel* ("Wretched One") is a better title. Marie ends by saying that either title would do.[53]

The problem confronted in the final section of this *lai* is the difficulty of reconciling two different perceptions of an event, of bringing two points of view into harmony. The lady and the knight experience that inability to know another's mind implied in Abelard's ethics. Indeed, each of them finds a different meaning in this story because each situates it in a different context, as Perceval's mother and the knights do with the concept of chivalry in the *Conte del Graal*. Their own experiences of the events it recounts provide two different contexts, and hence two irreconcilable meanings. The lady's preferred title, "Quatre Dols," refers to her own perspective on the events just recounted: she alone experiences them as four separate sorrows, one for each dead or wounded suitor. Her reasons for preferring that title take the form of an explanation of her own state of mind:

> ". . . Pur ceo que tant vus ai amez,
> Voil que mis doels seit remembrez:
> De vus quatre ferai un lai
> E *Quatre Dols* le numerai." (lines 201–04)[54]

The surviving knight, on the other hand, does not seem to recognize her point of view at all; his explanation of his own title takes into account the sufferings of the other knights, which ended in their deaths, but not the lady's sorrow. His sorrow alone, he implies, is worthy of mention in the *lai*'s title:

> ". . . Mes jeo, ki sui eschapez vifs,
> Tuz esgarez e tuz cheitifs,
> Ceo qu'el siecle puis plus amer
> Vei sovent venir e aler,
> Parler od mei matin e seir,
> Si n'en puis nule joie aveir
> Ne de baisier ne d'acoler
> Ne d'autre bien fors de parler.
> Teus cent maus me fetes suffrir!
> Mieuz me vaudreit la mort tenir!
> Pur c'ert li lais de meiz nomez:
> *Le Chaitivel* iert apelez." (lines 215–26)[55]

The lady finally agrees to use his title, but it is clear that he has not understood her point of view at all, perhaps believing that "Quatre Dols" refers not to her own sorrows but to those of the dead knights and himself. Marie's brief epilogue to the tale proper emphasizes, not the fact that her own version bears the title "Chaitivel," but the unresolved tension that remains between the two points of view as represented by the two titles, the difficulty or even impossibility of choosing one as more appropriate than the other:

> Issi fu li lais comenciez
> E puis parfaiz e anunciez.
> Icil kil porterent avant,
> *Quatre Dols* l'apelent alquant;
> Chescuns des nuns bien i afiert,
> Kar la matire le requiert;
> *Le Chaitivel* ad nun en us. (lines 231–37)[56]

In the final lines, in fact, the narrator specifically says that no more satisfactory conclusion could be reached:

> Ici finist, nen i ad plus,
> Plus n'en oï ne plus n'en sai
> Ne plus ne vus en cunterai. (lines 238–40)[57]

This disclaimer, the narrator's inability to give any more information or provide a solution, is reminiscent of the similar conclusion to "Lanval." In each case, the narrator leaves the reader with a problem or mystery requiring resolution, refusing to speculate any further or even to provide more information. Like Perceval learning about chivalry at the beginning of the *Conte del Graal*, we are presented with two contexts suggesting mutually exclusive meanings; but because Marie, in addressing us directly, insists on the disjunction between them, we cannot ignore the problem as Perceval does. Although "Chaitivel"'s problem is more concrete and presents a more limited number of possible solutions than the mystery of the lady's identity in "Lanval," the two tales do have in common the narrator's final withdrawal into silence. Both present a situation requiring interpretation, and clues or possible points of view that tempt the reader to try and provide that interpretation; neither imposes an authoritative reading. They allow the engaged reader to supply the tale's meaning.[58]

In order to situate Marie's work in its context, it is worth recalling at this point that her near-contemporary Arnulf of Orléans (whose active period has been dated in "the latter part of the twelfth century"), in his commentary on Lucan, frequently juxtaposed several interpretations of a given passage without expressing a preference for any one and even defined poetry, as distinct from history or philosophy, by its refusal to affirm any single explanation.[59] If Marie de France's secular works were to be interpreted like Scripture, an exegete like Hugh of St. Victor might have retreated to an allegorical level in order to resolve her contradictions; but Marie's own technique in "Lanval," and especially in "Chaitivel," is more similar to Arnulf's: rather than affirming one interpretation as a true and adequate explanation of the events the tale recounts, she juxtaposes two different readings of her own tale and suggests that they are equally valid. Poetry, in Marie's practice as in Arnulf's theory, presents a multiplicity of potential meanings rather than absolute truth.

The reader is free, at the end of "Chaitivel," to find its meaning not in either the lady's point of view or the knight's but in the remaining tension between the two, in the Abelardian knowledge that one consciousness is inevitably isolated from another, that direct apprehension of one mind by another is impossible. What can be accomplished, however, is mutual contact through interpretation. Lovers can read each other's signs even when, as in "Guigemar," they cannot recognize each other; and readers can participate in the chain of creation and interpretation best when meaning is not imposed upon them, because Marie's texts allow it. When, as in "Milun," whose characters communicate secretly for years without coming together, love is exclusively a matter of signs and texts that substitute for contact, it becomes clear just how closely the activities are linked. For Marie, both love and literature involve a frustrated desire for communication, and both try to deal with frustration through sign-making and interpretation; if her lovers are like readers and her readers are like lovers, it is because these functions are analogous means of engaging another by inviting his or her participation in the creation of meaning through interpretation.

As in Chrétien's case, however, signification and interpretation themselves become themes in Marie's works, to be communicated to the reader. Like her contemporary, Marie de France paradoxically suggests an indeterminacy of meaning by a determinate thematization of these issues. For both twelfth-century writers, determinate and indeterminate modes remain in competition with each other. But by the fourteenth century, the separation of language from reality by Abelard and the speculative grammarians had been more fully assimilated by imaginative writers, and a more radical questioning of knowledge had been undertaken by the Ockhamist philosophers. Since thematization suggests determinate communication, indeterminacy could no longer be thematized. Writers concerned with these issues in the late Middle Ages were influenced by these developments in ways that go far beyond thematization; indeterminacy left its mark in the very structure of certain literary narratives by Guillaume de Machaut and Geoffrey Chaucer. I now turn to a text very similar in many ways to Marie de France's, but whose differences demonstrate just how far-reaching these developments become by the fourteenth century.

Public and Private Knowledge in the Livre du Voir-Dit

Guillaume de Machaut's *Livre du Voir-Dit* has in recent years finally begun to gain the recognition it deserves. After years of neglect Machaut's narrative poetry has, since the publication of William Calin's full-length study in 1974, ceased to be overshadowed by his musical compositions and his lyrics, and the *Voir-Dit* has deservedly received the most attention.[60] It is, perhaps, not surprising that it is this work that has the most appeal for scholars, especially in the past fifteen years: as purported autobiography, it has been useful to those engaged in the current debate on literary constructions of the self, while its form, a combination of direct octosyllabic narrative with inserted lyrics and prose letters supposedly sent between the narrator and his lover, "Toute-belle," during the separations which comprise most of their relationship, has provided material for the discussions of writing and absence provoked by the works of Jacques Derrida (a discussion I take up in chapter 4).[61] Most of these discussions have centered on the work itself as an object or, still, on the degree of actual autobiographical truth this self-declared "true story" contains;[62] few scholars have discussed to any extent the relationship the *Voir-Dit* establishes with its readers.[63] The remainder of this chapter, then, outlines the manner in which Machaut's poem engages the reader in active interpretation.

As I suggested at the beginning of this chapter, the *Voir-Dit* has much in common with Marie's *Lais*, but the way it uses their shared concerns to draw the reader into the hermeneutic circle is very different, reflecting not only philosophical developments between the twelfth and fourteenth centuries but also the differences between the two poets' professional status and generic differences between the two works themselves. Despite these important distinctions, however, both works allow their audiences a high degree of interpretive freedom by stressing the need for the reader's active participation in filling in their phenomenological blanks.

To start with the similarities: like the *Lais*, the *Voir-Dit* suggests a parallel between the characters' activities of love and of reading. In fact, the gradual displacement for them of erotic by literary contact has been shown in a recent study to structure the work as a whole.[64] This parallel within the work suggests another possible comparison with Marie's *Lais*: the reader's act of interpreting the work comes to resemble the lovers' acts of interpreting each other. Machaut also demonstrates a concern with the potential danger to the love-relationship resulting from its public revelation, as literature, to an audience, again echoing Marie's similar concern.

But the *Voir-Dit*'s relationship with its audience is complicated by the historical and generic developments mentioned above. The first of these is Machaut's status as a professional court-poet, a man of lower social standing much more clearly dependent upon his noble patrons than was Marie, who seems to have been of noble birth herself.[65] The court poet's role was an explicitly public one; though his subject was love, his function was to offer advice, comfort, and celebration to his patrons rather than to explore his own experience. Daniel Poirion has examined the professional disjunction

between private emotion and public expression, "la tension entre le senti-
ment personnel et le ton officiel, la contradiction qui se dessine dans la
situation de l'écrivain."[66] Thus the *Voir-Dit*, though ostensibly about a personal experience of the poet's, is necessarily a public declaration, written
for the noble audience that is, in fact, inscribed as a series of reader-figures
within the text. This exposure of a private relationship to public knowledge
creates difficulties for these lovers as it did for Marie's in the *Lais*; but unlike
Marie, Machaut begins with the assumption that his audience's awareness
is necessary.

As we shall see, however, this apparent openness of the "love-affair"
(and the book that supposedly recounts its progress) to its audience's
definitive knowledge is less complete than first appears. The text at certain
points is revealed to be merely a pretext concealing a "reality" outside its
scope, just as some of Marie's tales (e.g. "Lanval") hint at further developments that they cannot recount. This supposed extra-textual "reality" may
simply be a further literary construct in Machaut's case, as it is in Marie's:
we know that her stories of werewolves and fairies are not historically true,
and we may suspect the same of the *Voir-Dit*'s love-affair. However, the
generic distinction between the two works complicates matters further:
whereas the Breton *lai*, like the romance, is an overtly fabulous genre, the
Voir-Dit purports to be an autobiography. Machaut's continual claims to be
telling the truth, and his inclusion of seemingly authentic details, make it
much more difficult to be certain that his work is purely fictional, as is
suggested by the continuing debate on this topic among critics. The very
structure of this text thus frustrates communication.

The *Voir-Dit* ("true story") can, in fact, be seen as an ironic game, whose
"truth" may refer to an historically real experience (that in turn may be
either revealed or concealed by the literary work itself), or in which "truth"
may instead be redefined, while the *Voir-Dit* is being read, as whatever is
contained in the book (in other words, as the same kind of "poetic truth"
found in other works of fiction).[67] Rather than choosing the "correct" answer
among these possibilities, the reader is encouraged to participate by playing
the game. This game may be even more inviting to a modern reader than
to Machaut's original audience: whereas they may have had evidence from
outside the text to authenticate one or another of its versions of the truth,
we have only the text itself. Thus the historical disjunction between an
event and the recounting of it, of which Marie took note in her "Prologue,"[68]
and that is mentioned explicitly in the works I discuss in chapter 5, is
experienced directly by the *Voir-Dit*'s modern reader. This difference be-

tween experiencing indeterminacy and understanding it as a theme is the difference between the late and high medieval works that deal with it.

Marie's concern with the tension between private experience and public knowledge is thus carried much further in Machaut's poem. In addition, personal, individual knowledge now becomes more problematic as well, reflecting an epistemology of indeterminacy developed shortly before Machaut's period by Ockham, and especially by his followers. The *Voir-Dit*'s presentation and representation of both kinds of knowledge function like the withholding of information from the reader in Marie's *Lais:* both draw the reader into an erotic/interpreting relationship with the literary work.

Texts Within the Text

The *Voir-Dit* is made up very largely of texts-within-the-text, formal verbal constructs of one kind or another made by one character to be read by another, often absent, character. This emphasis on verbal and even written texts, on the formal, literary nature of many of these texts-within-the-text (or, more simply, inserted texts) and on the interpretive response they call forth from a reader-within-the-text, brings the experience of the characters much closer to that of the reader in his role *as* reader of a written, literary text and turns the *Voir-Dit* into a book whose subject is very much language rather than the love-affair whose story it recounts.

The amount of space devoted to texts-within-the-text also allows this book to present perhaps the most extreme example to be found in a medieval work of a process evident in much modern literature: the reduction of human relationships almost entirely to a matter of texts. The written texts, of course, are always intended to communicate some truth beyond themselves (though how successful they are may be open to question) and are perceived by the book's two lovers simply as a means by which their human reality may be revealed; and yet in one sense, the *Voir-Dit* as a whole is ultimately more about itself than about any of the subjects its characters discuss. As Sarah Jane Williams points out, "to the extent that in the *Voir dit* the writing of the book becomes the subject of the book itself, it may not be entirely fanciful to think of it as a remote ancestor of such works as *Les Faux Monnayeurs* or *Point Counterpoint.*"[69] William Calin, too, has noted the *Voir-Dit*'s self-reflexiveness.[70]

The *Voir-Dit* as a whole might be regarded as a text-within-itself. Scattered throughout the book are references to the fact that it is in the process of being written; at every stage of its composition, the narrator reminds his lady that it is being written for her, sometimes sending her a recently completed section for her approval or complaining that the work is going slowly because he has nothing to write about. The work continually reflects on its own progress and presents itself as a series of stages always approaching completion. Since these stages are always being read by other characters in the book, all that has been written at any one point can be seen as an inserted text, a text-within-the-larger-text, within the always unfinished book itself. The work as a whole is thus analogous to any of the smaller texts it contains; the reader is challenged to respond to the larger text as its characters respond to the texts within it, and since the texts within it often include the entire work up to that point, the parallel between actual reader and reading character can become extremely close.

The characters' awareness of their own textuality should be noted here; both lovers are aware as the book is being made that they are, of course, literary characters in it, and that they will in the future be read as such. (We will find a similar development in Malory). This textuality is emphasized by their frequent references to previous fictional characters: "Et si, vous jure & promet, que a mon povoir onques Lancelos n'aima Genevre, Paris Helaine, ne Tristan Yseult plus léaument que vous serez de moi amée & servie" (21).[71]

As has been noted, the *Voir-Dit* contains a minimal amount of direct narration; the narrator spends comparatively little time recounting the plot directly to the reader. The inserted texts that constantly interrupt the narrative (or at least slow it down) are of several different kinds. Some of them are clearly intended by the narrator to be perceived as such, as smaller, formal works created outside the narrative and existing independently of it but included because of their bearing on the plot; these are the forty-six letters sent by the narrator to his lady, or vice versa, as well as the numerous rondeaux, ballades, virelais, and other poems composed by each of the lovers for the other.[72] In such cases, the two lovers can simply be regarded as author and reader figures, one providing a formal, written text, and the other reading and responding to it (usually with another formal, written text, whether letter or poem or both). Thus, early in their epistolary relationship, before they have ever seen each other, the narrator responds to a chance remark of the lady's, made in an earlier letter, with a somewhat defensive interpretation: "Et quant ad ce que vous me mandés que se vous estiés uns homs, vous me verriés bien souvent, je vous pri pour Dieu, & sur toute l'amour que vous avés a moi, que vous me vueilliés tenir pour excusé, se je ne vois & suis alés devers vous; car, par m'ame, Dieus scet que ce n'a mie esté par deffaute d'amour ne de bonne volenté" (52–53).[73] The lady in turn responds with a reinterpretation of her original statement, assuring him that his interpretation is incorrect: "Et se je vous ay escript que se je fuisse uns homs, je vous véysse bien souvent, par ma foy j'ay dit voir; mais pur ce, n'est-ce mie que je vueille que vous veniés vers moi, se n'est a l'aise & santé de vostre corps" (58).[74] In this way, texts generate more inserted texts, and interpretations generate further interpretations as the lovers continually exchange the roles of author and reader.

In the case of some other kinds of inserted text, the author-reader relationship is not quite as clear-cut. These texts-within-the-text are not set off from the main text as the letters and poems are, nor does the narrator always seem to intend that they be perceived as separate from it. Nevertheless, certain sections of the main text are indeed separable set-pieces read or interpreted by characters in the book as well as by the actual reader and can therefore be considered inserted texts (although the whole work, read as a text-within-itself, is read by the characters within it as well; the set-pieces, then, may be seen as texts-within-the-text-within-itself). These inserted texts include dreams, retellings of myths, and reports or gossip conveyed to the narrator by third parties. The narrator himself is the character who reads and interprets these inserted texts, whether they are provided by other characters, generated, in the case of dreams, by his own mind, or told to him, as in the case of certain texts-within-the-dream-within-the-text, by characters in his dreams. Thus in the course of one of his dreams (pp. 315–30), the lady's portrait tells the narrator the story of Phoebus and the crow, in the course of which the crow is told another story. The narrator in this instance is the reader of a text, his dream, made up largely of inserted texts; that is, his position is to some extent analogous to the reader's, while the dream is to some extent analogous to the entire *Voir-Dit* itself. This parallel between narrator and actual reader is, of course, only partial: although both are reading and interpreting the same material, they are separated by the ironic distance between text and world. Although his dreams have serious and potentially even tragic meanings for the narrator, for the reader (especially for Machaut's original, socially superior patrons) the dreams are part of the real poet's "performance" as the narrator, part of the game that holds various ambiguous perspectives on reality and illusion in tension with one another. The activity of reading itself as represented in the text can thus be similar to that experienced by the actual reader; but the effect of that reading may be very different in each case. I return to this dream at the end of the chapter.

The Narrator as Interpreter

The result of all this reading and interpretation of inserted texts is that even in those sections of the book that might be labelled the "main text," that is, in those sections in which the narrator tells his own story directly to the reader without mediating inserted texts or reader-figures within the book, there is little reporting on events actually happening in the "real" world supposedly recorded in the work. There has been much scholarly debate on how realistic the *Voir-Dit* is, both on the question of its value as autobiography and on the question of how naturalistic are Machaut's senses of time and place.[75] But whether the world of the *Voir-Dit* is verifiably fourteenth-century France and is peopled by such historical figures as Guillaume de Machaut and Péronne d'Armentières,[76] or whether it is a conventional landscape populated with literary types, the reader learns less about it than he or she learns about the narrator's state of mind. Even when the subject of the narrative is the love-affair he is supposedly chronicling, information on the progress of the affair itself is often replaced by information on the narrator's beliefs about it.

His highly conventional speculations tend to replace the book's "real" world, especially the reality of the love-affair, because of the lack of direct contact between the lovers. In the Paulin Paris edition, their first meeting does not occur until page 79, and their last ends on page 162 of the 371-page volume. Counting the intervals between visits, the lovers are together for only about one-fifth of the poem and are separated throughout the entire second half. Indeed, even the time they spend together is, as Brownlee has demonstrated, marked by Machaut's overt employment of literary conventions;[77] but we return to these visits below. In any case the poems and letters that take up so much of the text exist only because the lovers are usually separated and have no other means of communicating; since the affair is conducted largely by means of these inserted texts, they are often the only "reality" it has to offer. Once they have been faithfully reproduced as texts-within-the-text, the main text can say nothing more about the affair, because for the most part nothing else, nothing besides the exchange of written words, has happened. All it can talk about is the narrator's reaction to this exchange, a reaction that generally takes the form of fiction-making. Early in their relationship, when the narrator knows of the lady only what he has heard of her and what he can glean from the rondeau she has sent him (which, indeed, gives him his first inkling of her existence), he signals the very literary, even fictional, nature of his love for her by use of *amor de lonh*'s stock literary conventions:

> . . . Douls-pensers adoucissoit
> Mes douleurs & Les garissoit,
> Sans avoir d'elle la véue.
> Onques ne l'avoie véue;
> Mais Souvenirs la figuroit
> En mon cuer. . . .
>
> . . . .
>
> Ainsi sui-je fais amoureus,
> Par ces dous pensers savoureus. (13)[78]

The same may well be true of the lady's love for him; although she credits his good reputation rather than her own "dous pensers" as the cause of her love, her original lyric is about the existence of that love well before first sight:

> Celle qui onques ne vous vit,
> Et qui vous aime loiaument,
> De tout son cuer vous fait present. (7)[79]

The reader, however, learns little of the lady's state of mind, while the narrator's is chronicled in exhaustive detail. Each new advance in their epistolary affair is interpreted and reported to the reader, and the narrator's interpretations are not always as positive as they were at first; thus when the lady mentions in one of her poems that she would like to see him, he is plunged into melancholy:

> Mais quant Amours .I. amant point,
> Il n'est pas toujours en .I. point;
> Ains a des pensées diverses
> Et des douces et des parverses.
> Si pris une merencolie
> Contre moi, dont ce fu folie;
> Car de ma dame à la hautesce
> Pensoie, et à ma petitesce.
> Et en mon cuer imaginoie
> Que riens encontre li n'estoie,
> Et que c'estoit grant cornardie
> De penser qu'elle fust ma mie;
> Et qu'elle en véoit tous les jours,
> A lieu où estoit ses sejours,
> De milleurs une quarantainne,
> Voire, par Dieu, une centaine;

> Et que l'ueil moult souvent contraint
> Un cuer, & maistrie & destraint,
> Par plaisance qui le doctrine;
> Si qu'il aime d'amour très-fine. (50)[80]

Again, the conventionality of this melancholy emphasizes, especially to a courtly fourteenth-century audience, the fictional nature of the narrator's interpretations which, as far as the reader or the narrator can tell, have no basis in the language of the lady's poem, with its expressions of enthusiasm for meeting him:

> Car vos dolours mueray,
>   Par bien amer,
> Et par doucement parler,
>   Quant vous verray. (49)[81]

The narrator, then, in his role as reader and interpreter of the lady's texts, reacts to them by making fictions. Whereas some genuine contact between the lovers might reveal the truth about their respective personalities and motives to each other, which truth could then be directly related to the reader, this indirect contact, mediated by written texts, leads only to interpretive fantasies by the readers of those texts, fantasies that fictionalize the affair to the point where no tangible reality can be discerned. Extra-textual reality is displaced by the creation of more and more elaborate fictions as the text's reader-figures try to interpret the inserted texts. As Calin notes, "The *Voir-Dit* is a tale of language—speech, poetry, prose correspondence— in which words and the poetic art impede rather than encourage physical action."[82]

The narrator's descents into melancholy and suspicion, always apparently without reason, occur periodically throughout the *Voir-Dit*, forming a kind of emotional refrain to the work. Yet they do not remain always at the same emotional pitch but rather increase in intensity. Near the middle of the affair, one of his most complex reactions occurs in response to a single sentence in one of the lady's letters, a simple (but unexplained) request that he not write to her while she is travelling: "Si ne m'escrivés rien jusques à tant que vous orrés nouvelles de moy." (206)[83] This request is the occasion of his usual fears:

> Si que je ne savoie s'elle
> Faisoit d'escrire ce demour
> Par ruse ou par deffaut d'amour. (212)[84]

It also occasions a more elaborate interpretation as well, in the form of a dream:

> Qu'en dormant un songe sonjay,
> Et véu dedens mon songe ay,
> Qu'en aourant ma douce ymage,
> Son chief tournoit & son visage;
> Ne regarder ne me daignoit,
> Dont mes cuers trop fort se plaingnoit;
> Et tout estoit de vert vestie,
> Qui nouvelleté signifie. (213)[85]

This dream at first suggests the possibility that the lady is unfaithful to him, by showing his portrait of her dressed in green; but it is also the dream itself that finally demonstrates to the narrator that this interpretation is entirely fictional. Most of the dream concerns advice given by the dreamer/narrator to a king, "le Roi qui ne ment" (p. 215), named for the popular parlor-game. When he in turn asks the king's advice, the king lives up to his name ("the king who does not lie") by assuring him that he is only dreaming, and that dreams may not be true:

> "Biaus amis, c'est grant niceté
> Dou penser; car il le te semble,
> Tu dors & paroles ensemble,
> Et si m'est avis que tu songes.
> On ne doit pas croire les songes." (225)[86]

Without stating exactly what the real situation is, or suggesting why the lady asked the narrator not to write, the text here emphasizes the fictionality of the narrator's response to that request. Both the reader and the narrator as reader of an inserted text are left aware that this interpretation was only an exercise in fiction-making, without having any extra-textual reality substituted for the fiction.

This last point needs to be emphasized: although the dream might be taken as a warning against fiction-making as a form of interpretation, the *Voir-Dit* also makes it very clear that the dream itself is fictional. Indeed, as a product of the narrator's own mind, it is no more authoritative than his waking suspicions. Once again Brownlee has demonstrated that Machaut's use of literary conventions places the dream self-consciously in the tradition of earlier literary dream-visions, and specifically in that of the *Roman de la Rose*.[87] In addition, the "king"'s advice occurs in the context of a parlor-game in which a player takes the role of king (in this case, that player is actually the dauphin, duke of Normandy). The dream is thus not only a dream and a literary convention but a game as well: all are self-contained events or constructs set off from the "real world" of the *Voir-Dit*, which in turn is a text set off from our own real world—and a text that, as we have seen, functions to some extent as a game. The "king's" advice thus subverts the apparent meaning of the earlier part of the dream but is itself subverted by its own reflection both of the ambiguous, ludic main text and of several other constructs at various removes from the world outside the text. The lady's fidelity is never either definitively established or definitively denied; the text presents a variety of opinions on this matter, and rather than suggesting what the "truth" might be, suggests instead what attitudes the reader might take toward such a problematic and ambiguous notion of truth.[88]

It is interesting to note that during the same period of his response to her request, the narrator's suspicions are exacerbated by the fact that, aside from asking him not to write to her, the lady also does not write to him. The request that upsets him so is only the initial cause of his fearful speculations; what keeps him in a state of panic and melancholy is his lack of communication from her. As he says in his dream,

> Et Fortune m'i est contraire:
> "Car il ha près de .IX. semaines
> Que de li nouvelles certaines
> N'oÿ, dont je suis en doubtance
> Qu'elle n'ait aucune grevance,
> Ou que son cuer ne soit ailleurs." (221)[89]

This interpretation is in part based not on a written text but precisely on the absence of writing. Rather than simply accepting what the lady has written, the narrator first subjects her text to a fictionalizing interpretation and then, lacking further written texts to fictionalize, continues to speculate about what is unwritten. Once provoked by an interpretable text, the processes of interpretation and fiction-making continue, even in the absence of a text, and are all the more clearly fictional when based on no written evidence.

As in Marie de France's *Lais*, to read someone else's text in the *Voir-Dit* is to rewrite it; to interpret is to create a new and equally interpretable fiction that can be read and re-created in its turn. But for Machaut, this is a more problematic activity than it is for Marie: to some extent, this fictionalization can be destructive. It can be a "bad reading" (and I examine just what constitutes "good" and "bad" readings more fully at the end of this chapter). The narrator, in these instances, is trapped in his own limited consciousness even more completely than the knight in "Chaitivel."

A philosophical analogue to this state of affairs may be found in the thought of the post-Ockhamist philosopher Nicholas of Autrecourt, who was active in the 1330's, that is, just before Machaut's active period. For Nicholas, only the principle of non-contradiction provides certitude. Among the few kinds of knowledge that always conform to this principle are what Weinberg has called "data of consciousness": "The examination of the data of consciousness shows that, *qua* data, their existence is not open to question."[90] That is to say, we know what is in our minds; we know that we perceive what we perceive. Whether what we perceive is *real*, is another question, and for Nicholas a strictly unanswerable one: it is a question that cannot be reduced to the principle of non-contradiction.

Machaut's narrator has just this problem: he can assemble various perceptions and data in his mind and know that he perceives them, but he is unable to ascertain what relation they may bear to reality. He is trapped in his own internal speculations, painfully aware that they may or may not be true, and that he has no reliable way to authenticate them. In the twelfth century, Chrétien's character Gawain suggested that, although one may not be able to know others truly, one can truly know oneself. By the fourteenth, Machaut has shifted the emphasis to the problems created by not knowing others.

Publicity and the Inscribed Readers

As I suggested earlier, the *Voir-Dit* as a whole, because it is continuously read by the characters who appear in it, can be regarded as a constantly unfolding text-within-itself. The characters who read it, including both "Toute-belle" and a number of anonymous friends of the narrator (and perhaps of the lady as well), are in almost the same situation with regard to the text as the reader who exists outside it: the narrator apparently shows each section of the book to his noble friends as it is completed, so that they have always read to the same point the reader has (and since the writing of the text eventually catches up with the events it records, all the readers, both inside and outside the text, come to know approximately as much as the narrator does). This anonymous crowd of readers within the text are thus even more direct figures of the actual reader than are the narrator and his lady as readers of inserted texts. Not only do they read the same work we do, and at the same rate; reading and reacting to what they have read are their only functions in the book, the only activities in which we see them engaged. They are exact mirrors of the reader, and nothing else.[91] They would have been even more exact mirrors of the original audience than they are of the modern reader: as "pluseurs grans signeurs," at least some of these reader-figures must correspond to Machaut's real patrons. This correspondence helps to explain their detachment from the narrator's problems, and indeed their ridicule of him: as Poirion points out, the court-poet's function is to interpret his patrons' love-experiences, not to take on the inappropriate role of lover himself.[92]

The existence of these reader-figures raises one of the most important recurring issues in the *Voir-Dit*: the problem of publicity, or of openness as opposed to secrecy. The publication of the narrator's book and the reader-figures' status as patrons imply the necessity of accepting openness in conducting his affair, while courtly conventions regarding love argue for secrecy, as in Marie's *Lais*. The two lovers, and especially the narrator, vacillate between the desire for secrecy and the desire for publicity.[93] Initially, the narrator seems to be in favor of the latter, as when he first reveals the contents of the lady's first communication:

> Et pour ce que si noble chose
> Ne doit celée estre n'enclose,
> Vous diray, sans oster ne mettre,
> Ce qu'il y avoit en la lettre. (7)[94]

Soon, however, he is advocating discretion to his confidant:

> "Mais vous, serez mon secretaire
> Pour parler a point & pour taire," (12)[95]

while later still, in a letter to the lady, he says proudly that he has revealed the book, and thus the affair, to his patrons:

> Pluseurs grans signeurs scèvent les amours de vous & de mi, & ont envoié par devers moy un chapellain qui est moult mes amis, & m'ont mandé que par li je leur envoie de vos choses & les responses que je vous ay fait: especialment: Celle qui onques ne vous vit; si ay obéy à leur commandement. Car je leur ay envoyé pluseurs de vos choses & des miennes, & ont voulu savoir se il est verité que je aie vostre ymage, & je l'ay monstré a leur message, bien & richment parée & mise haut

au chevés de mon lit; si que chascuns se merveille que ce puet estre.
Et sachiez qu'il scèvent comment vous m'avez resuscité, & rendu joie
& santé sans ce que vous m'eussiez véu. (189)[96]

This, again, despite earlier enjoinders to secrecy:

Mais, pour Dieu, ne faites chose pour ma plaisance dont on puisse
parler; car, par ycelui dieu qui me fist, j'ameroie mieus morir ou que
jamais je ne vous véisse, dont Dieus me gart! car s'il advenoit, je seroie
bien mors. (134)[97]

The lady, too, wants both secrecy and openness at different points in the
course of the affair. Often an advocate of openness and publicity in their
relationship, it is at her command that the book is written at all, and that
it contains only the truth:

Et, ma douce dame jolie,
Ce n'est pas trop grant villenie,
S'en ce livre riens mettre n'ose
Qu'ainsi comme il est, & sans glose.
Car contre son commandement
Feroie du faire autrement:
Et, puisqu'il li plaist, il m'agrée,
S'obéiray à sa pensée. (84–85)[98]

She also wants everyone to know of their love simply because it would
make things easier for them:

"Et de ce qu'amy vous appelle
Devant la gent, cest à cautelle;
Que je puisse à vous mieus parler,
Et vers vous venir & aler." (106–07)[99]

By the end of the book, however, when excessive publicity threatens to
destroy the relationship through the narrator's jealousy and suspicion, she
claims that she is innocent of indiscretion: "'Et, par Dieu, je ne fis onques
chose que nuls peust savoir l'amour que j'avoie à vous'" (346).[100]

Since both lovers seem to perceive simultaneous dangers and benefits in
a wide audience of readers and patrons who know their story, it is interesting to examine the kinds of reading and interpretation that the book actually
provokes in this group of reader-figures within the text, especially given
the fictional, speculative interpretations provoked by inserted texts on the

part of the narrator in his role as a more involved reader-figure. Does the text as a whole give rise to similar fictional interpretations in the minds of those who read it? At first, it would seem not; these readers are initially led to seek out the concrete reality behind the written text. In the passage quoted above, when the narrator reveals that he has shown the book to them, he also says that they sent a messenger to look at the portrait they have read about, to verify its reality; and further, "Si tiennent si grant bien de vous, de vostre douceur & de vostre humilité, comme de dame dont il oyssent onques parler" (189).[101] They are detached enough not to fictionalize the relationship as the narrator does when confronted with a text; instead they check on the reality of the text's details and finally arrive at the precise interpretation intended by its author: belief in the lady's "douceur," "humilité," and other virtues. It seems like an instance of totally successful communication by means of a verbal text.

And yet it is not the "grans signeurs" themselves who come to look at the picture but their messenger; and it is not the real lady that the messenger sees but her portrait, another artistic creation like the book itself. These readers' knowledge of reality is thus doubly mediated even when they seem to be searching for truth unmediated by texts: the notion that a sense of extra-textual reality has been communicated in this exchange is seriously undercut, even if no actual fictionalization has taken place.

This type of reader's apparent freedom from fictional interpretation and from the kind of negative fantasies indulged in by the narrator is denied even more completely in the final section of the *Voir-Dit*. Their own fictional interpretations of the book as a whole are remarkably similar to the narrator's interpretations of the lady's inserted texts, in that they consist of speculations on the lady's attitude toward the narrator; as one of the "grans signeurs" says to the narrator,

"Amis, par Dieu, c'est chose voire,
Qu'il a plus d'un asne a la foire.
Car vo dame a pluseurs acointes,
Juenes, jolis, appers & cointes,
Qui la vont viseter souvent.
Et encor vous ay-je en convent
Que par tout vos lettres flajolle
Et monstre, nés à la carole.
Dont ce n'est qu'une moquerie,
Et po y a qui ne s'en rie . . . ." (302)[102]

The noble audience publicly embarrasses the narrator for playing the role of lover, apparently indulging in their own game at his expense. The very fact that the book is known to a wide audience, as the lady, at least, always intended (as in the passages quoted above), is here taken as evidence both of her lack of seriousness and of her lack of love:

> "Et cuidiez-vous qu'elle vous aime,
> Pour ce que son amy vous claime?
> Aussi amy clameroit-elle
> Le plus estrange de Castelle . . . ." (302)[103]

From this point on, the rumors multiply at a rate distressing to the narrator but comical to the reader; everyone seems to be laughing about the lady's seriousness and fidelity:

> Ainsi chascuns me rapportoit
> Chose qui mon cuer enortoit
> D'oublier ma dame de pris,
> Que j'aim, criem, fers, & loe, & pris.
> Nés, en alant parmi la rue,
> Chascuns un escrabot m'en rue,
> En disant, & par moquerie,
> "Je voy tel qui a bel amie." (307)[104]

It should be emphasized that no words pass between the lovers on this point for some time; the reader, along with the narrator, has only unsubstantiated rumors to deal with. These rumors become for the narrator another kind of inserted text to which he responds as he responds to the others: he incorporates them into the *Voir-Dit* and uses them to create yet more fictional interpretations. One of his most elaborate responses comes in the form of a cycle of poems comparing the lady to the goddess Fortune (336–39); as a formal set-piece, this association of the lady with an allegorical figure is perhaps the clearest example of the fictionality of the narrator's interpretations, and also of the manner in which one text, the entire work as read by the narrator's friends, produces a fictional interpretation in the form of an inserted text, their reports to the narrator on the lady's behavior, that in turn produces the narrator's own fictional interpretation in the form of another inserted text. No truth is communicated in all this reading, writing, and telling; no one arrives at any sense of extra-textual reality. The attempt to create a work that tells the truth, a "voir dit," leads only to negative and fictional interpretations. It is also interesting to note that the lady, though more sinned against than sinning at this point, herself indulges in speculative interpretation; her letter in the midst of the narrator's crisis provides an entirely different perspective on the matter: "Il me semble pour certain que vous m'avez de tous point guerpie & mise en nonchaloir, & que vous n'avez mais nulle amour à moi. . . . Vous savez que les amours de vous & de moy ont esté scéues de pluseurs bonnes personnes; que, se il savoient que elles fussent departies, il cuideroient que je vous éusse fait faussité, ou que vous éussiez trouvé en moy aucune mauvaistié ou folie, pourquoy vous l'éussiez fait" (310–11).[105] She interprets the fact that he has not written to her as evidence of a lack of love, caused by some fault of hers. Since the narrator says that at this point she is ignorant of the rumors ("riens ne li manderoie / De ce qu'on dit tout en appert," 313),[106] it is clear that the lady's letter is another example of fictional interpretation; she, however, seems to understand only too well the process by which such fictions are made, fearing as she does (justifiably, we know) the negative and fictional interpretations of others.

The anonymous readers of the *Voir-Dit*, then, become "médisants," rumor mongers, unsympathetic and inaccurate reporters. The narrator finally confronts the lady, by letter, with these rumors: "Ma tres-chiere & seule dame, se je vous escri ce qu'on m'a dit, je vous pri qu'il ne vous desplaise. Vueillez savoir que uns riches homs, qui est tres-bien mes sire & mes amis, m'a dit pour certain que vous monstrez à chascun ce que je vous envoie, dont il semble a pluseurs que ce soit une moquerie" (342).[107] The lady, as was noted above, protests her innocence; the rumors were, she claims, untrue. Neither position is established as true. The book ends ambiguously; it seems that the lovers have been reconciled at last:

> Ainsi fusmes nous racordé,
> Com je vous ay ci recordé,
> Par tresamiable concorde.
> Grant joie ay quant je m'en recorde,
> Et grant bien est dou recorder,
> Quant on voit gens bien acorder,
> Et plus grant bien de mettre acort
> Entre gens où il a descort,
> Et, por ce, encor recorderay
> Briefment ce qu'à recorder ay:
> Comment Toute-belle encorda
> Mon cuer, quant a moy s'acorda.[108]

They agree, however, that the book should end: "Si vous pri, si tres-chierement & humblement come je puis, que tous rappors, toutes chose faites, dites ou escriptes entre vous & moy, soient oubliées & pardonnées de tres-vray cuer d'amie & d'amy; & que jamais n'en souveigne" (362).[109] It seems to me that the desire to forget "all that has been done, said, and written" suggests that more than just their quarrel is to be forgotten, especially since the book does, in fact, draw to a close shortly hereafter. The price of continuing the relationship may well be the rejection of public writing, the end of that attempt "to tell the truth" which led only to so many false suspicions and outright lies; clearly, it was a mistake to reveal their love to public knowledge by means of a text. The anonymous readers in the text are obviously not desirable readers; it is therefore interesting in this context to consider who might be a good reader of the *Voir-Dit*.

Good and Bad Readers

I suggested earlier that much of the *Voir-Dit* is taken up with inserted texts rather than with the main narrative, and further, that even the main narrative gives little information on real events ("real" in the context of the book, at least) but tells the reader more about the fictional speculations and interpretations of the narrator and the other characters, made necessary because there is so little direct contact between the two lovers. There are passages, however, that do record moments of direct contact: early portions of the book do report on several meetings between the narrator and his lady. Such passages are directed specifically at the *Voir-Dit*'s actual readers, unlike the letters and poems directed first at characters within the book. Since the problem of publicity as opposed to secrecy is raised with regard to the reader-figures within the text, it should be of interest to examine how these passages of direct narration deal with this problem with regard to the real reader.

In some ways, the reader of the *Voir-Dit* seems to experience the book like the reader of certain *lais*, in the same way that the lover/narrator experiences the love-affair it recounts. As I noted earlier, because the narrator comes to record each stage of the affair as it occurs, the reader eventually knows approximately as much about this relationship as he does. In addition, except for the lady's letters and poems and an occasional messenger sent by her, the reader is exposed exclusively to the narrator's point of view, to his interpretations of events rather than hers. The reader of the

Voir-Dit's later episodes seems to be in the position of knowing exactly what the narrator of the book he is reading knows, no more and no less; even the lady's texts come to the reader's attention only at the moment when the narrator reads them. The narrator thus finally seems to expose himself fully to the reader.

This exposure, however, proves to be less complete than it first appears, especially in the passages of direct narration. For example, this apparently realistic story, full of naturalistic (though, perhaps, irrelevant) descriptions of the weather and of the dangers of fourteenth-century travel (as on p. 285), turns out upon closer examination to yield a surprisingly small number of details about the events it supposedly records. The lady's name, for instance, is not revealed, nor are any of the names of the towns where she stays in her apparently extensive travels.[110] This lack of detail might be attributed to Machaut's discretion if one assumes that the book chronicles an actual relationship; it is surprising only in the context of the work's many claims to tell the whole truth:

> Car celle pour qui Amours veille,
> Vuet que je mete en ce *Voir-dit*
> Tout ce qu'ay pour li fait & dit,
> Et tout ce qu'elle a pour moy fait,
> Sans rien celer qui face au fait. (17)[111]

What is even more confusing to the modern reader, and what denies both the narrator's seeming exposure of himself and the text's claims to total honesty, is the use of allegory. This mode completely overwhelms the mimetic mode in the book's most crucial scene for understanding the real nature of this love-relationship. It is a scene narrated directly to the reader, without mediating texts, and concerns a meeting between the lovers; in fact, it is probably the moment of closest and most direct contact between the two in the entire work. And yet it is impossible to discover exactly what this scene means: there is no way of knowing just what takes place in it. (We shall find a similar scene in Malory.)

The scene is set in the lady's bedroom at the end of several days the two have spent together; the narrator comes to say goodbye in private. As usual, he is afraid of displeasing the lady and so prays to Venus for the courage to touch her. The goddess hears his prayer:

> Si fu tost la déesse preste,
> Car tout en l'eure est descendue,
> Couverte d'une oscure nue,

Pleine de manne & de fin baume
Qui la chambre encense & embaume.
Est là fist miracles ouvertes,
Si clerement & si appertes
Que de joie fui raemplis,
Et mes desire fu acomplis;
Si bien que plus ne demandeie
Ne riens plus je ne desiroie. (157)[112]

This declaration may seem like a more or less straightforward announce-
ment of sexual satisfaction, but it presents certain apparently insoluble
problems of interpretation; the "obscure cloud" that covers Venus covers
the meaning of this passage as well. Is it in fact an allegorical representation
of sexual consummation? Calin thinks not and reviews several possible
alternative interpretations:

> Some scholars assume that, having given herself to the Narrator, from
> that moment Toute-belle ceases to be a maiden. However, the Narrator
> protests at length that Toute-belle's honor has not been sullied and
> that only people with dirty minds will accuse them of sin. Perhaps
> Machaut believes that the last of the *quinque lineae amoris* is praiseworthy
> or that Toute-belle's honor will be preserved if tale-bearers do not catch
> them in the act, that her reputation remains untarnished regardless of
> the state of her virtue. Or perhaps the Narrator's paean of satisfied
> desire should not be taken as literally as in a contemporary novel. He
> says that his soul became satisfied by Toute-belle's fruit (p. 159), but
> we are then informed that *Pité* plucked this fruit from Toute-belle's
> "colored" face. The fruit may then be nothing more than a silent avowal
> of passion (Toute-belle's blushing countenance), rather than more con-
> crete sexual favors.[113]

This final interpretation is basically in agreement with Paris: "Je suis du
parti de ceux qui n'y découvriront rien qui ne soit de bon exemple, à
l'honneur des dames & des gens de bien."[114]

What at first seems straightforward is in fact indecipherable: the impression to be gained from scholars writing on this passage is less one of
confident elucidation than one of hesitant speculation, admittedly not authoritative. Their unwillingness to conclude that consummation has taken
place in this scene stems from claims made by the narrator himself. Soon
after this episode, he says that "il n'i ha vice ne tache" (163),[115] and elsewhere
in the text, as Calin notes, he makes similar statements regarding the
preservation of the lady's honor; and yet something certainly happened in

that bedroom. The narrator even seems aware of the manner in which the reader is being teased, or frustrated:

> Et se j'ay dit ou trop ou pau,
> Pas ne mespren, car, par saint Pau,
> Ma dame vuelt qu'ainsi le face,
> Sus peine de perdre sa grace. (163)[116]

He says here that he may have revealed too much but also admits that he may have revealed too little ("ou trop ou pau"), that something has, at the lady's command, been kept back from the reader. Despite her overt desire for publicity, here at least "Toute-belle" and the narrator agree to refrain from a full revelation, even in the book's own terms. Thus in the most important love-scene, the one that might have revealed the true nature of this relationship and given the reader some sense of its reality, the reader is consciously denied essential information: the narrator's claimed honesty gives way to a fiction, an allegory that conceals more than it reveals, and leads to ambiguity rather than truth. The only possible response to this situation—an obvious allegory demanding interpretation, but denying the information needed to interpret correctly—is the kind of speculative interpretation exhibited by Calin and Paris. Like the narrator in his fictionalizing interpretations of the lady's texts, the reader must respond to this main text with speculations that are themselves fictional. We too must speculate on what is unsaid, on information withheld.

Machaut's use of allegory is thus perhaps the medieval example closest to the indeterminate allegory theorized by Paul de Man; the bedroom scene is only the most noteworthy example of allegory used to withhold rather than to communicate information.[117] And the withholding of information is, in fact, a common phenomenon in the *Voir-Dit* as a whole, not limited to the allegorical passages. By the end of the book, especially, the lovers' letters to each other have become consciously wary of revealing any information about themselves too openly: "Et vorroie bien que vous ne me escrisissiez point, si ce n'esteit chansons, ou se ce n'estoit par vostre vallet qui autrefois y a esté, & qui scet la maniere. Et si m'est advis que c'est le meilleur" (368).[118] The reader here is warned quite explicitly that he or she is no longer being told the whole truth, if indeed that were ever the case; their texts are now not a means of revealing reality but of concealing it from the reader.

Indeed, it finally transpires that we have been excluded from true knowledge all along. The lady is writing her last letter: "Et comment que je vous aie toujours acoustumé à escrire ouvertement, & que pluseurs scèvent les amours de vous & de moi, n'est-il nuls qui en saiche parfaitement la verité, fors une & moi & vostre secretaire" (368).[119] She says that only those actually involved in the love-affair, the two lovers and their confidants, really know the truth about it, no matter what others, those who have read the text, think they know. Calin takes note of this problem, and blames the narrator's restricted vision:

> The "I" is not necessarily reliable nor are we obliged to accept without question his interpretation of the events he recounts. We have the right to disagree with him. We know the Narrator's interpretation of events but not that of Guillaume de Machaut the poet, for whom the "I" is a literary character the same as *Toute-belle*. . . . Ironically, in VD, The True Story, neither protagonist knows the truth, nor do we, the readers.[120]

The narrator's limited perspective is certainly part of the problem but so is the manner in which he has problematized the very notion of "truth," as we shall see.

The book's final anagram is, in a sense, emblematic of the work as a whole. The narrator gives instructions on how to derive the lovers' names from the eighth and ninth lines from the end of the poem. He does not give the lady's name directly, concealing it to the end as "Toute-belle" (as on p. 371), but he does encourage the reader to find it for himself or herself. And yet, as Paris notes,[121] the lines as they stand in all the manuscripts do not provide an identification: Paris resorts to an emendation (though the manuscripts are apparently unanimous in their wordings) in order to arrive at one. As is common in this work, the reader is teased into interpretation only to be frustrated by the lack of information: ultimately, the book itself is a fiction concealing rather than revealing its own reality.

Given this concealment, it may seem as if the reader's only possible response, again, must be to speculate on what it is that is not being told. Fantasy and fictional interpretation may be the only alternatives when truth is concealed, especially when it is so ostentatiously concealed as to demand interpretation. The narrator frequently seems aware that his readers must be reacting in just this way, with fictional and even negative interpretations:

> Je ne say qui en parlera,
> Mais, por ce, autrement ne sera. (17)[122]

> Et cils qui mal y penseroit,
> Traitres et mauvais seroit. (125)[123]

> Taire me veuil d'or en avant,
> De ce qu'ay parlé cy devant;
> Car bien say que tele matiere
> Li mauvais ne l'ont mie chiere,
> Pour ce qu'il vuelent leur malice
> Celer, s'il puelent, & leur vice. (128)[124]

This kind of passage seems to recognize that the reader risks becoming a "médisant"; like the anonymous reader-figures within the book, the real reader is often in the position of fictionalizing the text, of providing interpretations that the narrator himself might not approve. Machaut successfully recreates in the reader that same state of consciousness, reflecting Nicholas of Autrecourt's and similar epistemologies, that we found in the narrator. We know what we perceive in the text; but its relation to any reality outside the text is unknowable. The danger Marie de France recognized in the literary revelation of a secret love is potentially realized here as well: it is the risk run by the text of finding only "bad readers."

Machaut thus takes us a step beyond Marie's more ambiguous *lais* and inquires what happens to the reader's response if the text does not violate the erotic secrecy of the events it recounts. As we have seen, several of the *lais* allow the reader to engage in free interpretation by refusing to reveal an authoritative truth; but the *Voir-Dit* also recognizes the potential danger of such freedom, in its models of "bad readers" within the text and in its narrator's concern with potential negative interpretations by its actual readers. It seems appropriate at this point to ask whether Machaut also suggests what might constitute a "good reading" of the *Voir-Dit*.

Such a reading would have to take into account the narrator's playful redefinition of "truth." We have seen that the *Voir-Dit* violates mimetic, extra-textual reality at several points (as in the allegorical scenes), and that it presents itself as having deceived the reader about the love-affair it supposedly recounts; but we have also seen that it consistently proclaims its own truth. Can these two perspectives be reconciled? If the claims of truth are to be believed, the reader must first accept a new definition of "truth": it is whatever the narrator chooses to include in the text, no more and no less. "Truth" can no longer refer to our own reality outside the text, but, as Brownlee points out, it does include matters such as literary conventions and allegory (and the function of the allegorical scenes is thus precisely to emphasize this tension).[125] More significant for my purposes, though, is that "truth" in this context loses its ordinary connotations of authority, singularity, and definitiveness. This redefined, textual truth includes ambiguity and even concealment: in the game Machaut plays with his readers, the truth is a fiction emphasizing its fictionality. A lie that tells us it is a lie is, paradoxically, true.

In short, whereas Marie de France's narrative voice admits the existence outside the literary work of a reality about whose true nature she is as puzzled as the reader, the *Voir-Dit* insists that as long as we are engaged in reading it, reality outside the text is not our concern and may, in fact, prove destructive. This point can be clarified by a brief consideration of one final inserted text, a story told in another of the narrator's dreams and prompted by the *médisants'* rumors. It is the Ovidian tale of Phoebus and the crow: the crow is punished (its feathers become black) because it told Phoebus the truth about his lover's adultery. Phoebus kills his lover but immediately regrets his action and blames the crow for having told him the truth. The moral drawn in the dream itself is that the narrator should refuse to believe the rumors of his lady's infidelity, as Phoebus should have refused to believe the crow. That the crow's story was true is irrelevant, as is the "truth," whatever it may be, about "Toute-belle"'s fidelity; what is important is the resumption of the narrator's love:

> "Et c'est pechié contre noblesce,
> De croire chose qui tant blesce
> Qu'on en pert l'onnour & la vie,
> Et l'amour de sa douce amie." (329)[126]

The narrator himself has a double response to his dream, and to his suspicions. First, he accepts the dream's stated moral, regretting his suspicion:

> Ainsi pensoie & repensoie:
> Et, en la pensée ou j'estoie,
> Je pensay que j'avoie tort. (331)[127]

But then he recalls that the crow's story was true and fears once more that the *médisants'* rumors may also be true:

> Par icellui Dieu qui me fist,
> Cuer avoie si desconfist,
> Et si fort de desconfortoit
> Qu'à pou qu'en .II. pars ne partoit. (332)[128]

Eventually, however, he chooses to believe the lady.

In both cases, then, those of Phoebus and of the narrator, two points are emphasized: first, that a fiction may be preferable to the truth, especially when the truth can be destructive; and second, that as long as the truth is not known, the fictions one creates in its place can be benign as easily as they can be malicious. The benign ones allow the relationship to continue (hence the narrator's eventual choice to believe his lady rather than the *médisants*, though neither interpretation is definitely established as true). The reader can heed this lesson in his or her own relationship with the text: we need not imitate the *médisants* in our engagement with it, nor even imitate the crow in pursuing a potentially destructive truth. Instead, we can produce interpretations—necessarily fictional, as we have seen—that allow our engagement with the text, our participation in the game, to continue, just as the narrator's choice of "Toute-belle"'s (fictional?) version of the truth, rather than either the *médisants'* version or a definitive truth, allows their love to continue. Most important is that the reader's interpreting, fiction-making relationship with the text continue, like the narrator's relationship with "Toute-belle." This may include a recognition, with Nicholas of Autrecourt, that the only truth we can know is that we perceive what we perceive; not that it is true, but that we perceive it.

The audience thus participates in Machaut's indeterminacy more fully than in Chrétien's or Marie's, where it is understood rather than experienced. But is this fictionalized view of the truth merely frivolous? Does it imply that art is irrelevant to life as we really experience it? Is there not a problem in suggesting, as both Marie's and Machaut's works do, that a knowledge of reality is dangerous, or that the communication of a definite truth is undesirable? The next step in my argument is to examine how another late medieval writer answers these questions. Geoffrey Chaucer, late in the fourteenth century, undergoes in the space of his own career the same development in dealing with these issues that we have observed in moving from the twelfth to the fourteenth century. Beginning with an early work that thematizes and rejects indeterminacy, and moving on to one that tragically accepts it, Chaucer concludes his career with a work that, like the *Voir-Dit*, incorporates indeterminacy in its very structure.

4

Communication and Interpretation: Three Stages in Chaucer's Career

To review my argument thus far: in chapter 1, I discussed the growing competition, throughout the Middle Ages but especially prominent beginning in the twelfth century, between the intellectual tradition that inherited from neoplatonism a belief in a divinely guaranteed, determinate signification, and one in which the divine determination of meaning is bracketed, with attention directed to the inevitable indeterminacy of signification on a purely human level, where the divine guarantees become problematic. I also outlined some ways in which this competition appears in literary works. Since the medieval view of allegory is that it tends to orient the reader toward a single, correct, determinate meaning, writers in the older neoplatonic tradition were more comfortable with allegory than those who followed more recent trends in questioning such meanings. Chapter 2 therefore demonstrated, first, the awareness, apparent in Chrétien's *Conte del Graal*, of certain of the developments in twelfth-century methods of interpretation discussed in chapter 1, and second, Chrétien's rejection of allegory as a fruitful method in favor of a literal method in which meaning, arising differently from the context of each individual's experience, remains ambiguous. Paradoxically, however, Chrétien, writing in a period when the rejection of determinate signification was a new phenomenon, thematizes his rejection of allegory, making it a new, determinate meaning to be communicated to the reader; thus the competition between the two modes is visible even in a single romance. A comparison with the allegorical *Queste del saint Graal* confirmed the distinction between works belonging to the older, neoplatonic tradition, with its emphasis on the accessibility of singular truths, and works like Chrétien's that emphasize the multiplicity of potential meanings discovered by the more recent tradition.

Chapter 3 concentrated on the effect such ambiguity of meaning has on the reader in a twelfth-century and a fourteenth-century work. Marie de France and Guillaume de Machaut both compare textual interpretation with erotic activity; but whereas Marie emphasizes the role that texts play as mediators inviting the reader to interpret mysteries or puzzles outside their scope, Machaut presents his text as a self-contained game, emphasizing the isolation of the individual consciousness from any reality outside it. As a late medieval writer, following the radical questioning of human knowledge that took place in the earlier fourteenth century, Machaut is also unable to thematize these problems as further meanings to be communicated, as Marie still does, incorporating them instead into the very structure of his *Voir-Dit*. As I suggested at the end of that chapter, this emphasis might be considered disturbing rather than amusing; indeed, Machaut, in his refusal to impose any authoritative meaning on the reader, might be accused of denying the possibility of communication.

In this chapter, I examine three works by a late medieval writer who was influenced by Machaut and who, at least at the beginning of his career, appears to find this indeterminacy of textual meaning problematic rather than valuable. Geoffrey Chaucer, like Machaut, lived and wrote after William of Ockham and his followers had demonstrated the impossibility of certain knowledge, especially knowledge of the relations among individual beings.[1] Throughout his narrative works, Chaucer explores the difficulties of communication as enunciated in this intellectual tradition. His works demonstrate within a single career a development similar to that we have observed as we move from the twelfth to the fourteenth centuries: from a distrust of indeterminacy and a nostalgia for a fully present communication, Chaucer gradually moves to an acceptance of the value of indeterminate interpretation rather than of communication. His career as a whole thus sums up the competition between the two modes of thought that we have been tracing and, by confronting the dangers of the denial of communication, moves it to a new stage.

Perhaps the largest body of older Chaucer criticism (as distinct from textual and philological scholarship) is concerned with his representation of human interaction, of how people succeed or fail in their attempts to understand one another, and of how they behave in either situation. Hence the preponderance of books and articles on the "drama" of *The Canterbury Tales*, the "therapeutic" interaction of the two principals in *The Book of the Duchess*, or the emotional interplay of *Troilus and Criseyde*'s characters.[2] In this chapter, I examine these three narratives in the somewhat more elementary terms of two basic modes of verbal communication: speech and writing. Along with the related terms of presence and absence, as well as interpretation and communication, or referentiality, these modes have been emphasized in a growing body of more recent criticism of Chaucer's poetry. The work of such critics as Gellrich, Ferster, Shoaf, Leicester, and Vance in analyzing individual works in these terms makes possible a study of the overall development of Chaucer's attitudes throughout his career.[3] This chapter can only begin to outline this development by examining three poems, from the beginning, middle, and end of Chaucer's working life.

I begin with the very early *Book of the Duchess* (probably 1369),[4] with its many represented texts and readers, and explore how it opposes interpretation to communication, favoring the latter. Its characters' various failures and successes of communication also have implications for the actual reader's interaction with the poem itself. Next, Chaucer's masterpiece from the middle of his career, *Troilus and Criseyde* (1380–86), will appear as a transitional work in his presentation of these problems: communication rather than interpretation is still regarded as the ideal, but the more active role this work posits for the reader also suggests the possibility of transcending the failures of communication represented in *The Book of the Duchess*. This possibility achieves its fullest realization in *The Canterbury Tales*, and a comparison of that work's *Wife of Bath's Prologue* (after 1393) with one of its sources will allow me to speculate about Chaucer's final acceptance of interpretation at the end of his career.

Speech and Writing in **The Book of the Duchess**

The Book of the Duchess, like Machaut's *Voir-Dit*, deals with the textualization of experience. Chaucer's poem, more specifically, examines the tension between, on the one hand, speech, or oral communication where both parties are present, and, on the other, the way speech becomes formalized, reified, textualized. This formalization is the process of speech becoming more and more like writing, or becoming writing itself, that is, verbal interchange in which one party is absent and represented by a text.

The Book of the Duchess includes representations of many different kinds of language that vary in the degree to which they might be called textual: there is the actual written text read by the narrator to help himself fall asleep (the Ovidian tale of Ceyx and Alcione), his address to Morpheus and Juno, the stained glass of his dream, with its iconographic representations of myth and literature, the Black Knight's poem of "compleynte" (line 464),[5] his conversation with the dreamer (including his allegorical and metaphorical description's of the lady's death), the direct question and answer that end the conversation, the narrator's written record of his dream (that is, *The Book of the Duchess* itself), and so on. The entire poem might, in fact, be regarded as a series of tests of these different forms of language, according to where each might be located on a continuum between spontaneous speech and formal text.[6] They are being tested for their varying degrees of efficiency in communication: the poem asks how well each linguistic form succeeds in communicating a clear message, as opposed to how much ambiguity of meaning each allows. Ambiguity is very much a problem in *The Book of the Duchess*, especially in the conversation between the dreamer and the Black Knight: the dreamer must continually force the knight to make his language less literary and more direct in order for the essential fact, "She ys ded!" (line 1309), to be communicated. Ambiguity or obscurity is perceived here above all as a failure of communication and is consistently associated with the literary or textual aspects of language.

Because of the sequential nature of these tests, a brief examination of each one as it occurs in the poem will provide the most productive kind of reading. *The Book of the Duchess* opens with the narrator's famous complaint about his inability to sleep due to a mysterious illness, presumably love-sickness[7] (I will follow the critical convention of referring to this character as "the narrator" when he is not describing the central dream, and as "the dreamer" when he is).[8] To distract himself, he takes up the first of the texts-within-the-text, a volume of "fables" (line 52) including Ovid's tale of Ceyx and Alcione, which he retells (in part) in the following lines (62–114). The important point about this text is the inappropriateness of the narrator's response to it: although the point of the tale is that Alcione's grief for her husband is excessive (he comes to her in a dream telling her to stop grieving, that "in your sorwe there lyth no red," line 203), the narrator is distracted from this message in two ways. First, he empathizes with Alcione to the point that his own already excessive sorrow is increased:

> Such sorowe this lady to her tok
> That trewly I, which made this book,
> Had such pittee and such rowthe
> To rede hir sorwe, that, by my trowthe,
> I ferde the worse al the morwe
> Aftir, to thenken on hir sorwe. (lines 95–100)

Second, he is distracted from the tale's point by another text within it, Alcione's prayer to Juno that she be allowed to sleep and to dream of her husband. Just as he imitates Alcione's grief, so too he imitates her prayer, making his vow to Juno and Morpheus that he will repay them if they cure his insomnia. Once again he has missed the point: the dream, not sleep itself, was Alcione's object. Like her, however, he is granted both sleep and a dream that, correctly interpreted, could alleviate his sorrow; but also like her, he fails to understand his dream.

> Y fil aslepe, and therwith even
> Me mette so ynly swete a sweven,
> So wonderful, that never yit
> Y trowe no man had the wyt
> To konne wel my sweven rede. (lines 275–79)

We already know, from the present tense of the poem's opening lines, that even after the experience of the dream he remains uncomforted, sorrowful, and insomniac:

> I have gret wonder, be this lyght,
> How that I lyve, for day ne nyght
> I may nat slepe wel nygh noght. (lines 1–3)

Alcione's misinterpretation of her dream is not entirely her fault; although the surrounding lines, like those cited above, suggest that it is intended to advise her to stop sorrowing and regain her peace of mind, its most direct command is ambiguous: "Awake! let be your sorwful lyf!" (line 202). Alcione apparently takes this to mean that she should leave behind not only her sorrow but life itself; she dies "within the thridde morwe" (line 214). It is no wonder, then, that the narrator in turn misinterprets the tale and imitates Alcione rather than judging her. Textual ambiguity is thus presented as problematic from the start and is also associated with sorrow and with death.

The poem's exploration of textuality continues in the narrator's dream. He finds himself in a room whose stained-glass windows represent scenes from classical mythology, and whose walls are painted with "al the Romaunce of the Rose" (line 334). He has moved from written texts to visual, iconographic ones, perhaps because this is his first step away from pure textuality and toward the reality that his conversation with the Black Knight will eventually reveal. This passage also suggests that the dreamer is literally surrounded by texts, enclosed within them; he begins the process of moving beyond them when he leaves the room and enters the natural world, as his questions will later enable the knight to move beyond textuality in his language and toward an acceptance of reality. That textuality is still a force to be reckoned with, however, is indicated by the conventionality of the natural world's description, which is nevertheless quite beautiful.

In the midst of this vibrantly described world of birds, trees, flowers, animals, and the hunt, the dreamer comes upon a man in black, whose sorrowful costume and posture are clearly at odds with his colorful surroundings. Inevitably, he is a poet: in a setting teeming with life, he produces a text that, like the earlier Ovidian text, is about death:

> "I have of sorwe so gret won
> That joye gete I never non,
> Now that I see my lady bryght,
> Which I have loved with al my myght,
> Is fro me ded and ys agoon.
>   Allas, deth, what ayleth the,
> That thou noldest have taken me,
> Whan thou toke my lady swete,
> That was so fair, so fresh, so fre,
> So good, that men may wel se
> Of al goodnesse she had no mete!" (lines 475–86)

The longest ongoing critical debate about *The Book of the Duchess* concerns the dreamer's response to this "compleynte" (line 487): is he so stupid as not to understand its direct references to death? This reading is suggested by his continual efforts throughout the rest of the poem to make the knight explain what is troubling him. The other alternative assumes that he must understand those references, and therefore critics who subscribe to it regard his later questions as a subtle and tactful attempt to provide therapy by getting the knight to express his feelings directly.[9] More recent critics have begun to explore reasons other than stupidity for the dreamer's incomprehension, and these explorations have focused on the problematic nature of the Black Knight's language: Philip C. Boardman has located the problem in its "courtliness," which may suggest to the dreamer that the knight is merely playing verbal games (like those we observed in Machaut?), while Ruth Morse emphasizes the ambiguity of its reference.[10] Neither critic, however, has pinpointed the larger reason for such ambiguity, or the essential characteristic of the courtliness that creates it.

This characteristic can best be described as its textuality. As we have already seen, the written text as it appears at the beginning of *The Book of the Duchess* is associated with death and with the failure of communication; such a failure is precisely what occurs between the dreamer and the knight in the former's initial attempts to understand the latter. It is no accident that the dreamer's first contact with the knight occurs through a formal and conventional verbal text, set off by its rhyme-scheme from the surrounding narrative and given a generic identification, complaint, by the dreamer. He fails to understand it as communicating something true precisely because it is a text, made according to certain textual conventions; as Aers points out, "in the art of love poetry it has been utterly commonplace to view lovers' partings as deaths."[11] Thus the knight does not say in his poem that the lady is dead, but that she is dead *from him,* and gone. Although it is literally true that she is dead, his language makes that fact sound like a metaphor for the end of love, not of life. Such ambiguity is the same kind as that which caused Alcione's suicidal indulgence in grief, and the narrator's misguided empathy with her.

A step has, however, been taken away from the purely textual situation of the poem's opening. The dreamer is now not dealing with a book but with a man who can be questioned further. Though the complaint itself might as well be a written text, direct oral communication is possible in this situation as it was not in the act of reading. The knight's accounts of his lady's death now become gradually more conversational and less textual, more spontaneous and less conventional.

That transformation of the knight's language does not happen immediately. The conversation itself in which the dreamer engages the Black Knight because he does not understand the complaint is at first equally unsatisfactory because it remains textual: the knight's second description of his lady's death is not a formal poem, but it is, nevertheless, textual to the extent that it is a little allegory in which he plays a game of chess with the goddess Fortune. It is worth quoting at some length, in order to demonstrate the extended nature of this metaphor:

"At the ches with me she gan to pleye;
With hir false draughtes dyvers
She staal on me, and tok my fers.
And whan I sawgh my fers awaye,
Allas! I kouthe no lenger playe,
But sayde, 'Farewel, swete, ywys,
And farewel al that ever ys!'
Therwith Fortune seyde 'Chek her!'
And 'Mat!' in myd poynt of the chekker,
With a poun errant, allas!
Ful craftier to pley she was
Than Athalus, that made the game
First of the ches, so was hys name.
But God wolde I had oones or twyes
Ykoud and knowe the jeupardyes
That kowde the Greke Pithagores!
I shulde have pleyd the bet at ches,
And kept my fers the bet therby." (lines 652–69)

These lines form another formal set-piece, closer to a written text like the *Roman de la Rose* than to direct, conversational communication. The two characters' entire conversation, in fact, places us squarely in the textualized world of the *Rose:* personified in turn are death, fortune, love, youth, nature, dullness, and truth; thus, even after the extended allegory of the chess game has once again failed to communicate anything to the dreamer, the knight is unable to break out of the textual conventions that govern his language. As in the *Conte del Graal*, allegory is here rejected as misleading: its literal level has no necessary connection with what it is supposed to symbolize. Communication, if it is to take place, must be direct and literal.

It should be pointed out that the knight does seem to desire communication; he wants the dreamer to understand and even tells him that the listener bears some responsibility for successful communication:

> "Blythely," quod he; "com sytte adoun!
> I telle the upon a condicioun
> That thou shalt hooly, with all thy wyt,
> Doo thyn entent to herkene hit."
> "Yis, syr." "Swere thy trouthe therto."
> "Gladly." "Do thanne holde hereto!" (lines 749–54)

Nevertheless, having twice turned his experience into texts that fail to communicate it, the knight makes a third attempt that still remains textual. He has moved from a formal lyric to an allegorical narrative; now, in lines 758–1297, he tries another linguistic structure even less formalized, but still identifiable as a text: he tells an autobiographical story in the form of a romance, including such conventional romance elements as the golden-haired, white-skinned lady, the love-sick hero, his love-songs, the initial rejection, and the eventual reconciliation. Indeed, these lines might be seen as conventionalized autobiography in the generic context of the *Voir-Dit*. In addition to these common plot-elements and characterizations, and to the personifications listed above, the knight now makes use of rhetorical flourishes (such as the digression on music in lines 1162–70) and of many Biblical, mythological, and literary allusions.[12]

Once again, such textual devices are found wanting if communication is the goal; the romance/autobiography/*dit* tells the dreamer as little as the lyric and the allegory:

> "What los ys that?" quod I thoo;
> "Nyl she not love yow? ys hyt soo?

Or have ye oght doon amys,
That she hath left yow? ys hyt this?
For Goddes love, telle me al"; (lines 1139–43)

"Sir," quod I, "where is she now?" (line 1298)

Only the baldest statement, free of rhetorical devices, allusions, allegories, metaphors, and literary structure—free, in short, of textuality—can communicate the essential fact:

"She ys ded!" "Nay!" "Yis, be my trouthe!"
"Is that youre los? Be God, hyt ys routhe!" (lines 1309–10)

The knight has moved from a formal, "written" lyric, to an allegorical narrative, to a romance-autobiography full of rhetorical devices, to a final direct statement. All except the last are highly textual set-pieces, though the "written" elements become less prominent as he moves from one to the next; and all except the last prove unsatisfactory as modes of communication. Why?

The answer may lie in the opposed natures of textuality and oral communication. Jacques Derrida, in his attempt to deconstruct that opposition, first defines it and points out its dominance in earlier theories of language. It should be pointed out that in his own theory, "voix" and "écriture" cannot be equated with "speech" and "writing" in the medieval sense; nevertheless, his description of the projects of language theories earlier than his own makes the distinction very usefully:

> The privilege of the *phonè* does not depend upon a choice that could have been avoided. It responds to a moment of *economy* (let us say of the "life" of "history" or of "being as self-relationship"). The system of "hearing (understanding)-oneself-speak" through the phonic substance—which *presents itself* as the nonexterior, nonmundane, therefore nonempirical or noncontingent signifier—has necessarily dominated the history of the world during an entire epoch. . . .
>
> With an irregular and essentially precarious success, the movement would apparently have tended, as toward its *telos*, to confine writing to a secondary and instrumental function: translator of a full speech that was fully *present* (present to itself, to its signified, to the other, the very condition of the theme of presence in general), technics in the service of language, *spokesman*, interpreter of an originary speech itself shielded from interpretation [italics in the text].[13]

Thus (still describing earlier language theories), "writing is that forgetting of the self, that exteriorization, the contrary of the interiorizing memory, of the *Erinnerung* that opens the history of the spirit."[14] Derrida also suggests that "reading and writing, the production or interpretation of signs, allow themselves to be confined within secondariness," and that although this has been the case throughout history, it was so "especially in the Middle Ages."[15]

This is to say that the traditional (and particularly the medieval) view of textuality, of human writing (as distinct from, or even opposed to, the divine writing found in nature and the Bible) defines itself by the absence of its producer: writing preserves a speaker's language without preserving the speaker. Although this seems like a beneficial effect of writing, the dangers of such a preservation are made clear in *The Book of the Duchess*: the narrator can misunderstand the Ovidian tale he reads because its interpretation is entirely up to him; he cannot question the absent author about his intentions or about the truth that the book ought to communicate. Therefore the narrator sees in the book only a reflection of his own disordered and sorrowful state of mind and allows it to reinforce his distress rather than curing it, as differently interpreted it might have done. That this textual quality of language can defeat communication even in the presence of its producer is suggested by Alcione's similar reaction within the tale to the news of her husband's death: she cannot question the dream-messenger about the meaning of his ambiguous speech because he is present only while delivering it. The lack of interaction between Alcione and the messenger thus turns his oral message into a text, and like the narrator, Alcione interprets it according to her own state of mind, reinforcing rather than assuaging her self-destructive grief. The reader of *The Book of the Duchess* is thus left with the same ambiguity: "let be your sorwful lyf" (line 202) might be either an injunction to commit suicide or a request that Alcione cheer herself up.

Interpretation arises from the ambiguity that necessarily accompanies the absence of a speaker whose meaning could have been more clearly ascertained orally, and is therefore the opposite of communication, which can take place only when both the speaker and the receiver of a message are present. Interpretation is associated with written texts, or with any language that functions like a text in this manner, while communication is associated with oral conversation. Recall the similar difficulties caused by the "interlocutor"'s absence in the *Voir-Dit*. As in that earlier work, these difficulties in *The Book of the Duchess* can be associated with post-Ockhamist concerns over the inability of the individual consciousness to verify its own impressions. Textuality demonstrates that inability in a particularly overt manner: the interlocutor's absence makes the lack of verification, and the resulting ambiguity, unusually clear. But whereas Machaut's text responds to this situation by inviting the reader to enjoy its paradoxical redefinition of "truth" as purely textual, Chaucer's explores the (perhaps doomed) possibilities of breaking through textual ambiguity to an extra-textual reality, and of moving outside the isolated consciousness. It is, after all, a poem of consolation on the death of John of Gaunt's wife, that is, a poem written to have an effect in the world outside itself. The achievement of such an effect is, as I have suggested, thematized in the dream.

It is precisely verbal interaction with a speaker who is present that the dreamer tries to achieve in his dream of the Black Knight (which may suggest that he has unconsciously learned something about the dangers of textuality from his encounter with Alcione's story). Unlike Alcione, who does not question her dream-messenger about his true meaning, thus treating him as a text, the dreamer continually questions the knight, trying to make his interlocutor fully present in their conversation:

> "And telleth me of your sorwes smerte;
> Paraunter hyt may ese youre herte,
> That semeth ful sek under your syde"; (lines 555–57)

> "Loo, [sey] how that may be?" quod y;
> "Good sir, telle me al hooly
> In what wyse, how, why, and wherfore
> That ye have thus your blysse lore"; (lines 745–48)

> "And telleth me eke what ye have lore,
> I herde yow telle herebefore"; (lines 1135–36)

> "What los ys that?" quod I thoo;
> "Nyl she not love yow? ys hyt soo?
> Or have ye oght doon amys,
> That she hath left yow? ys hyt this?
> For Goddes love, telle me al"; (lines 1139–43)

> "Sir," quod I, "where is she now?"; (line 1298)

> "Allas, sir, how? what may that be?" (line 1308)

Yet the Black Knight refuses the conversational mode in favor of the textual, continually absenting himself as a source of direct communication and even emphasizing the fact that his texts cannot be understood by the dreamer, despite his paradoxical eagerness for the dreamer's attention and comprehension. His refrain throughout the dream is, "Thou wost ful lytel what thou menest; / I have lost more than thou wenest" (lines 743–44, and compare lines 1137–38 and 1305–06). He insists that he is to be interpreted rather than understood, that the dreamer must treat him as a text rather than as an interlocutor. In the dreamer's first sight of the knight, he is declaiming a formal text to an audience consisting of no one (he does not perceive the dreamer at first), thus emphasizing the absence of speaker and hearer from each other; and indeed his initial response to the dreamer is a refusal or an inability to acknowledge their mutual presence:

> Anoon therwith whan y sawgh this,
> He ferde thus evel there he set,
> I went and stood ryght at his fet,
> And grette hym, but he spak noght,
> But argued with his owne thoght. (lines 500–04)

The knight even turns himself into an allegorical figure representing sorrow, putting himself onto an equally textual footing with the personifications discussed above:

> "For whoso seeth me first on morwe
> May seyn he hath met with sorwe,
> For y am sorwe, and sorwe ys y." (lines 595–97)

In lines like these he actually becomes a text; he withdraws from the scene in his own being and substitutes an allegorical figure to be interpreted.[16]

All of the Black Knight's speeches, in fact, except the final direct statement of his lady's death, are to some degree textual and "written" within this definition of writing. They do not successfully communicate anything to the dreamer, who can respond only with bewildered questions and possible interpretations ("Nyl she not love yow?"). The knight does not respond to these questions either, because he refuses to be present in the conversation to the extent of answering the dreamer but only produces text after unsatisfactory text.

The dreamer's ignorance and persistence, however, do ultimately force the knight into presence, both to the dreamer and to the fact of death. In the poem's only successful act of communication (lines 1309–10, cited above), the dreamer is able to do what neither his own waking persona (the narrator) nor Alcione can accomplish: he moves beyond mere unsatisfactory interpretation of a text to direct communication with, and understanding of, another human being. He forces the knight to de-textualize his experience, to make of it neither lyric nor allegory nor rhetorical device nor romance, but a true response to another's interest, and a direct statement of the truth. The dreamer forces the knight to communicate, and thus to make further interpretation unnecessary. This accomplishment is possible because the knight, despite his reluctance, actually is there talking to him; despite his efforts to absent himself in textuality, he is, after all, present and available to the dreamer's direct questioning.

The end of the dream, however, is not the end of the poem: its conclusion returns to the frustrated narrator (who, as we know from the present tense of the poem's opening lines, is still frustrated after dreaming his dream), to the written text that inspired the dream, and to a new act, not of communication but of writing that denies communication:

> Therwyth I awook myselve
> And fond me lyinge in my bed;
> And the book that I hadde red,
> Of Alcione and Seys the kyng,
> And of the godes of slepyng,
> I fond hyt in myn hond ful even.
> Thoghte I, "Thys ys so queynt a sweven
> That I wol, be processe of tyme,
> Fonde to put this sweven in ryme
> As I kan best, and that anoon."
> This was my sweven; now hit ys doon. (lines 1324–34)

The dream's moment of successful communication is framed in a poem that, almost by definition, denies the possibility that it can achieve communication as well. We know already that the narrator cannot understand his dream and does not expect any reader to understand it either:

> Me mette so ynly swete a sweven,
> So wonderful, that never yit
> Y trowe no man had the wyt
> To konne well my sweven rede. (lines 276–79)

The dream cannot be "read"; it is an incomprehensible text. Not even Joseph or Macrobius, he goes on to assure us, could interpret it correctly. In addition to this incomprehension of the dream, there is the ominous fact that concludes the poem: he will now textualize it even further, and in fact has done so by the time we read it. He has not only written it down but has formalized it, put it into rhyme like the Black Knight's unreadable lyric. The danger of textuality to communication has been so strongly emphasized throughout *The Book of the Duchess* that its final reference must be seen as a return to the unresolved problem of its opening. Geoffrey Chaucer (not to mention his fictional narrator) is absent from us later readers; we cannot hope for communication from a text but must resign ourselves to that interpretation whose unsatisfactory nature has just been demonstrated. The reader of a text runs the risk, above all, of solipsism, of imposing his or her own state of mind on the writing whose producer is not present to elucidate it. *The Book of the Duchess*, having shown us that such solipsism can be overcome only through presence, leaves us with absence.[17]

This textualization of experience, the way human beings come to see themselves and others in conventional, textual forms and thus condemn one another to interpretation rather than communication, remains a problem in Chaucer's works throughout his career. He returns to it over and over, and his presentation of the problem both as theme and as structure of his various works is perhaps what has given rise to two diametrically opposed views of his poetry among twentieth-century scholars. On the one hand, Chaucer has been seen, especially early in this century, as a master realist, as one who broke through the courtly conventions of late medieval literature in order to put a fresher and more direct view of humanity into poetic form than had any other medieval poet. On the other hand, he has also been perceived, especially in the middle decades of this century, as a highly conventional poet, as one who manipulates existing forms in interesting ways, to be sure, but without ever leaving them behind.[18] One view emphasizes his differences with medieval literary tradition, while the other emphasizes its continued presence in his works. Both views can find (and have found) justification in a poem like *The Book of the Duchess*: it can easily be read as a rejection of the literary conventions that the Black Knight uses, but that must be discarded in favor of plain, "realistic" speech; yet at the same time, the knight's conventional language takes up most of the central dream-vision, which itself is a typical example of the venerable dream-vision tradition.

Perhaps we may now see these two tendencies in Chaucer's poetry not as an opposition or as a choice that must be made but in a dialectic in which they together produce a third possibility. Or perhaps we might see them as held in tension, or in balance, with each other. In any case, the relationship of convention to realism, or of "auctoritee" to experience, continues to be played out in Chaucer's works in terms of speech and writing, or conversation and text, or communication and interpretation.

Recent scholars have worked out some of these issues as they appear in the poetry intervening between *The Book of the Duchess* and *Troilus and Criseyde*. Ferster has discerned a relationship between communication and interpretation in *The Parliament of Fowls* similar to the one I have discussed in *The Book of the Duchess*, but with a more positive emphasis on interpretation. Gellrich's discussion of *The House of Fame* takes up the problem of knowledge and authority, specifically the difficulty of finding either outside the text itself; we may be reminded of Machaut's similar approach.[19] Turning to *Troilus and Criseyde*, we find Chaucer still wrestling with these issues.

Troilus and Criseyde: *Sexuality as Textuality*

In *Troilus and Criseyde*, communication is still presented as a rarely attainable ideal, while the textualization and interpretation of experience remain problematic and even dangerous. This poem's narrative voice is actively engaged in the interpretation of his "auctoritee," the source-text "Lollius," which presents him with a wide variety of phenomenological blanks; unfortunately, he lacks the desired, direct "experience" of love that, he claims, might allow him to fill them in with confidence. Troilus and Criseyde themselves are also remarkably text-bound as they conduct their love affair, like the narrator and lady of the *Voir-Dit*; but once again, this circumstance is, for Chaucer, at least potentially tragic.

This work from the middle of Chaucer's career, despite the troubled view it takes of such dehumanization, also implies, in the narrator's repeated request to the readers for their more experienced assistance in recreating the story, that texts are not necessarily closed and indecipherable, as they were in *The Book of the Duchess*. Here, the reader is not foredoomed to defeat in the attempt to understand. Instead, *Troilus and Criseyde* suggests that the reader can indeed play this more active role; and our participation in filling in the blanks suggests a way of coping with, if not of transcending, the alienation that textuality still implies.

The central importance of Chaucer's narrating persona in this poem, as in all of Chaucer's works, has frequently been discussed.[20] One of the narrator's most interesting characteristics is his continuous presence in the text, his constant invasion of the love-story with his comments upon it.[21] He is, from one critical perspective, passionately involved in his attempt to tell the story, and even in the story itself as he tells it, which is to say that the narrator offers constant reminders that he is both a reader and a transmitter of the tale. Both of these roles involve acts of interpretation, whether on his part or Criseyde's.

Certain critics in recent years have taken issue with the separation of the poet Chaucer from his personae, as established most influentially by E. Talbot Donaldson. Both Martin Stevens, with regard to *The Canterbury Tales*, and Elizabeth Salter, with regard to *Troilus and Criseyde*, have suggested that the acknowledgments of his own reading and writing are genuine self-presentations on Chaucer's part:[22]

> Here may be the first time in English literature when the poet goes some way toward an acknowledgment, both to himself and to his public, of the controversial and troublesome part he finds himself bound to play in the handling of his received "matere." We are allowed, even encouraged, to speculate upon "workshop" activity. . . . the medieval fiction of "naive narrator" . . . is made to cope with the pressing problems of the poet himself, as he presents a freshly thoughtful version of a narrative familiar to all in general outline if not in literary detail.[23]

In this view, Chaucer (even more directly than Machaut, because the narrator does not literally participate in the poem's actions) obtrudes himself into his own poems as the real writer writing and thus refuses to create an illusion of reality for his story, while in Donaldson's view the illusionary reality of the love story is replaced, or augmented, by an equally illusionary narrator with a coherent psychology (and the latter view has recently received important support from Winthrop Wetherbee).[24] In either case, problems of reading and writing are foregrounded, as in *Troilus and Criseyde*; for reasons that will become obvious, I shall continue to refer to "the narrator."

His position as a reader of the very story he is retelling is kept constantly before his audience by means of the continual acknowledgment of a source: not Chaucer's actual sources, of course, but the presumably fictional author "Lollius." *Troilus and Criseyde*, however, does not even purport to be this narrator's literal transmission of an authoritative text; indeed, one gathers from the narrator's sometimes impatient comments that Lollius is, at least for the man who likes to have things spelled out, a somewhat unsatisfactory author, one who leaves many blanks to be filled in:

> Nought list myn auctour fully to declare
> What that she thoughte whan he seyde so,
> That Troilus was out of towne yfare,
> As if he seyde therof soth or no. (III, 575–78)[25]

It often appears, in fact, despite the narrator's insistence on his source's truth and completeness—

> But soth is, though I kan nat tellen al,
> As kan myn auctour, of his excellence—(III, 1324–25)

that Lollius provides only the bare facts of the story, only the external actions that make up the plot, and that he consistently refuses to explain what they mean or what motivations lie behind the simple, observable behavior of any character. Lollius apparently resembles Marie de France in leaving important details to the reader's imagination; but unlike her inscribed readers or Machaut's, this narrator finds such blanks frustrating rather than inviting, though the final effect may be the same. Variations on the theme of what "myn auctour" chooses not to "declare" or make explicit arise throughout the work, especially when there is some question of possible guilt on the part of one of the characters (usually Criseyde):

> Kan I naught seyn, for she bad hym nought rise,
> If sorwe it putte out of hire remembraunce,
> Or elles that she took it in the wise
> Of dewete, as for his observaunce;
> But wel fynde I she dede hym this plesaunce,
> That she hym kiste, although she siked sore,
> And bad hym sitte adown withouten more. (III, 967–73)

There is a constant tension in this work between what the narrator "finds" in his source and what he "can not say" because it isn't there for him to read; even at the most crucial points in the plot (perhaps especially at those points) the narrator is unable to determine exactly what Lollius, or any other source, really meant. He finds himself consistently frustrated in his attempts to arrive at the truth:

> I fynde ek in the stories elleswhere,
> Whan thorugh the body hurt was Diomede
> Of Troilus, tho wepte she many a teere,
> Whan that she saugh his wyde wowndes blede;
> And that she took, to kepen hym, good hede;
> And for to helen hym of his sorwes smerte,
> Men seyn—I not—that she yaf hym hire herte. (V, 1044–50)

These "stories elleswhere" and "men" are presumably not Lollius, wedged as these lines are between two references to that main source, "the storie"

(V, 1037 and 1051); apparently the supposedly authoritative text is silent on this essential point of Criseyde's fidelity to Troilus, and our narrator must look elsewhere, to even less trustworthy sources, for information that may or may not be true. The conventional appeal to authority is here neatly subverted: on all aspects of the story considered significant by the narrator, the "source" makes no authoritative comment whatsoever. This state of affairs carries the ambiguity of the tale of Alcione and of the knight's speeches in *The Book of the Duchess* to an extreme: Lollius does not even suggest possible interpretations but allows his text to remain completely indeterminate. Once again, the substitution of text for interlocutor prevents communication.

If a reader, then, the narrator is a constantly frustrated reader, one who cannot depend upon the text he reads to tell him what he wants to know about the inner life of its characters, and one for whom a multiplicity of sources only augments the confusion. The effect of this frustration on the narrator is, inevitably, to make him an interpreter, to force him to reflect upon the bare events narrated by Lollius and to extract meaning from them for himself. Throughout *Troilus and Criseyde*, whenever he is confronted with one of these frustrating moments that seem to suggest some meaning or motivation behind themselves but that are always left unexplained in his source, the narrator, rather than simply following that source and retelling the plot, attempts to make sense of what he has read and speculates on what it might all mean. He stubbornly refuses to accept the surface actions of the story as the only way of telling it and insists time and again on engaging himself in an interpretive relationship with his source, on making some meaning out of those surface actions. Whereas mystery or ambiguity can be enjoyed for their own sake in Chrétien's works, or redefined as textual "truth" in Machaut's, for this narrator mysteries require solutions.

In Book I, for example, one of the narrator's earliest protestations that he cannot find out Criseyde's motives from his source also supplies (as do the examples cited above) the possible interpretations that he himself has come up with. Troilus is pretending to have a physical illness in order to disguise his love-sickness:

> But how it was, certeyn, kan I nat seye,
> If that his lady understood nat this,
> Or feynede hire she nyste, oon of the tweye;
> But wel I rede that, by no manere weye,
> Ne semed it as that she of hym roughte,
> Or of his peyne, or whatsoevere he thoughte. (I, 492–97)

Here, as in the "Kan I nought seyn" passage and in the speculations on Criseyde's infidelity, the narrator admits that his reading lacks authority and yet also manages to suggest possible meanings that emerge from that reading: Criseyde might be ignorant or she might be pretending, possibilities casting two different lights on her character. External appearance and surface actions are, as usual, accurately reported according to the source, but the meaning of those surfaces depends solely upon the narrator's own unsure, speculative interpretation of that source. His reading of a previous text, then, becomes a new text: his interpretation of the fictional Lollius in *Troilus and Criseyde* as the inscribed reader reads it, reflecting Chaucer's own transformation of Boccaccio's *Filostrato* for his actual readers.

Besides acknowledging his source and thus his status as a reader and, ultimately, an interpreter, Chaucer's narrator also constantly acknowledges the presence of his audience or readers, and thus his status as a writer or transmitter both of the story he reads and of the interpretation he supplies. The narrator makes no secret of his conception of the audience's position with regard to the text he is in the process of creating: nowhere does he address his readers as passive onlookers simply receiving the story. Instead, every time the narrator acknowledges his readers it is to remind them that they must take some measure of responsibility for the text, that their reading of his work must be an active one that will correct his speculative interpretations (as his own reading completes the source by adding those interpretations). As in Marie's *Lais*, the reader is directly invited to provide meaning; but here the fussy narrator carefully tells us just what changes he has already made to the source, and where our further help is needed. Rather than issuing a general invitation, the narrator sets specific problems to be solved.

That the story is constantly in a state of transition and flux, according to the handling of new writers and readers, is thus constantly emphasized. All readings and writings are insufficient and must be supplemented, as Bruns has shown is true of all literature in a manuscript culture,[26] though few medieval writers are as acutely aware of this fact as Chaucer.

Apostrophes to the reader on just this subject occur at the beginning and approximately in the middle of *Troilus and Criseyde*. The problem that the narrator most needs his audience's help in overcoming, it appears, is his lack of experience in love and the resulting difficulty he has in telling a love-tale:

And ek for me preieth to God so dere
That I have myght to shewe, in som manere,
Swich peyne and wo as Loves folk endure,
In Troilus unsely aventure. (I, 32–35)

The audience here is given indirect responsibility for his creation of the text: by calling his ability into question immediately, this narrator creates the possibility of a kind of collaboration with his presumably more knowledgeable readers. At this point that collaboration is only of the most indirect kind: God as mediator might inspire the narrator if urged to do so by readers who know what they are talking about ("ye loveres, that bathen in gladnesse," I, 22). By the time he has gotten half-way through his story, however, the narrator seems to be losing the little confidence he had in his talents, and divine inspiration is notably lacking; in the course of Book III, another appeal is made to the reader, one that frankly admits the narrator's inadequacy to the task and that requests a much more direct contribution to the work from the reader. He is speaking of the lovers' first night together:

> Of hire delit, or joies oon the leeste,
> Were impossible to my wit to seye;
> But juggeth ye that han ben at the feste
> Of swich gladnesse, if that hem liste pleye!
> I kan namore. . . . (III, 1310–14)

> Why nad I swich oon with my soule ybought,
> Ye, or the leeste joie that was theere?
> Awey, thow foule daunger and thow feere,
> And lat hem in this hevene blisse dwelle,
> That is so heigh that al ne kan I telle!

> But soth is, though I kan nat tellen al,
> As kan myn auctour, of his excellence,
> Yet have I seyd, and God toforn, and shal
> In every thyng, al holy his sentence;
> And if that ich, at Loves reverence,
> Have any word in eched for the beste,
> Doth therwithal right as youreselven leste.

> For myne wordes, heere and every part,
> I speke hem alle under correccioun
> Of yow that felyng han in loves art,
> And putte it al in youre discrecioun
> To encresse or maken dymynucioun
> Of my langage, and that I yow biseche. (III, 1319–36)

It is not clear whether the narrator really believes that "no man" could fully describe love's bliss, but he certainly knows that he cannot do it. What he can do is to make, despite his inexperience in love, an imaginative attempt to understand it, that is, to interpret what his text tells him, to add to it what he can, "for the beste." This very act of interpretation, he makes clear, allows his own readers an enormous freedom of interpretation; because he claims no authority for himself beyond his own imagination, the readers can accept, reject, or modify, in their own readings, everything the narrator says: "myne wordes, heere and every part." The text's words are only one possible way in many of responding to the matter they present; each reader's reading must be slightly different. Readers who have more experience of love than the narrator will use that experience in their reading to create a new textual interpretation of their own. In this fashion, the narrator's imaginative interpretation of his source results in a text that can engage the readers in further interpretations and thus in the creation of new texts or readings.[27]

Throughout *Troilus and Criseyde*, the narrator's ignorance and difficulty in dealing with a love-text, and the freedom of interpretation they allow the audience, are expressed in several different ways. Often, as in lines 1310–14, cited above, he simply admits that descriptions of scenes dealing with love are far beyond his ability, and asks the readers to imagine for themselves what is happening or what the characters are feeling:

> Who koude telle aright or ful discryve
> His wo, his pleynt, his langour, and his pyne?
> Naught alle the men that han or ben on lyve.
> Thow, redere, maist thiself ful wel devyne
> That swich a wo my wit kan nat diffyne.
> On ydel for to write it sholde I swynke,
> Whan that my wit is wery it to thynke. (V, 267–73)

On the other hand, the narrator is very willing, as was noted earlier, to supply one or more possible interpretations of any action left unexplained in his source. Whenever he does so, he is careful to warn the reader that the interpretations are his own and are therefore without authority; the audience is thus reminded both that simple facts demand interpretation and that no single interpretation, the narrator's included, can be guaranteed true. Throughout Book V, for instance, the narrator constantly provides interpretations, carefully labeled as such, that soften Criseyde's character and mitigate her apparently indefensible betrayal of Troilus:

> To hire he wroot yet ofte tyme al newe
> Ful pitously—he lefte it nought for slouthe,—
> Bisechyng hire, syn that he was trewe,
> That she wol come ayeyn and holde hire trouthe.
> For which Criseyde upon a day, for routhe,—
> I take it so,—touchyng al this matere,
> Wrot hym ayeyn, and seyde as ye may here. (V, 1583–89)

The phrase "I take it so" warns the reader that Criseyde's "routhe" has been supplied by the narrator's imagination, and that another interpretation of her motives could as easily be substituted. The readers remain free in their reading of Criseyde's character, as in their reading of the work as a whole; it is quite possible that readers (Shakespeare, for example) might form an impression of her personality entirely opposed to the narrator's lenient one. Certainly, given that each of his speculations on the positive aspects of her character is qualified by its lack of authority, readers must ultimately have more ambiguous feelings about Criseyde than the narrator does;[28] *Troilus and Criseyde* insists on remaining open to interpretation.

The moments when the narrator addresses the audience directly might be seen as the outline of a theory of reading: these moments suggest the extent to which the readers are responsible for the text they read. Such moments orient us toward the possibility and even the necessity of creating our own meaning from the words before us, just as the narrator previously made new sense of old tales, and indeed as the real Geoffrey Chaucer adapted his sources in order to accommodate his own vision.

The problem of interpretation is not confined to those passages dealing directly with the narrator-text-reader relationship; a system of parallels to this relationship can be discovered in the plot of the romance. For example, Pandarus is very much like the narrator, as has been noted before.[29] He is, first, as unsuccessful in love as the narrator is inexperienced (or at least he presents himself as being so): each speaks of himself as not having won favor with ladies. As Troilus says to Pandarus, "'Thow koudest nevere in love thiselven wisse'" (I, 622). This somewhat tenuous connection with the narrator is strengthened by a further parallel, between Pandarus's and the narrator's attitudes toward other, more successful lovers: each sees his role as that of a loyal friend or even servant to lovers. Their reason for acting as they do either in creating the tale or manipulating the course of the love affair is the hope that such actions will make the course of love smoother for others than it has been for themselves. As Pandarus notes when Troilus first reveals to him his love for Criseyde (somewhat bluntly paraphrasing the narrator's words in the prologue to Book I), "A fool may ek a wis-man ofte gide" (I, 630). To accomplish the end of helping Troilus in his suit, Pandarus becomes a sort of stage-manager to the love-affair, constantly plotting means of bringing the lovers together. The narrator, of course, has a similar function: he creates a plot that brings his characters together where and when he chooses. That Pandarus is indeed a reflection within the text of the narrator's task in creating the text is suggested several times in the course of the work. Not only does Pandarus actually invent fictions designed to trap Criseyde into loving Troilus (complete with conventional narrative phrases: "'What sholde I lenger,' quod he, 'do yow dwelle?,'" II, 1614), he also finds himself in situations exactly similar to those in which the narrator finds himself. Pandarus's invocation of the Furies in Book II ("O Furies thre of helle, on yow I crye!," II, 436), echoes the narrator's invocation in Book I:

> To the clepe I, thow goddesse of torment,
> Thow cruwel Furie, sorwynge evere in peyne. (I, 8–9)

More interestingly, Pandarus puts himself into the narrator's position of transmitting a text he does not understand (as he also puts himself into the narrator's position of inexperience in love). As go-between for Troilus and Criseyde, he must deliver messages as the narrator delivers an old and obscure text to Criseyde:

> "This, short and pleyn, th'effect of my message,
> As ferforth as my wit kan comprehende. . . ." (IV, 890–91)

This perhaps feigned difficulty in transmitting a love-message must recall the narrator's similar difficulties, discussed above. The parallel suggests not only Pandarus's similarity to the narrator but a connection between literary and erotic experience as well. The similarity in function of Pandarus and the narrator not only makes Pandarus seem a sort of artist, but also makes the narrator into a sort of pander, a go-between in the erotic encounter between text and reader similar to that which we found in Marie de France's *Lais*. The narrator's invitation to the reader to participate in the text's interpretation is associated, through the figure of Pandarus, with an invitation to love. The dubious nature of Pandarus's invitations, however, renders such participation problematic.[30]

The love affair between Troilus and Criseyde is presented more as a matter of words, texts, and mutual interpretations than as a matter of direct contact or consummation. Pandarus is not the work's only narrator-figure: the lovers themselves experience difficulties in interpreting each other very similar to those experienced by the narrator in his interpretation of the source-text. Their reaction to their difficulties is seldom simply to transcend interpretation and strive for direct contact. Instead, again like the narrator, and like the lovers in the *Lais* and in the *Voir-Dit*,[31] they create texts of one kind or another for the other to interpret. Each of the lovers is thus both narrator and reader, interpreting the other and presenting a self to be interpreted.

Troilus and Criseyde do attain occasional moments of direct contact, notably when their affair is first consummated:

> And Troilus in lust and in quiete
> Is with Criseyde, his owen herte swete. (III, 1819–20)

Such moments of quiet contentment are, however, painfully rare in this romance; more often we are made aware that it is a tale of "double sorwe" (I, 1), of love first unattainable and then lost. Most of the book, indeed, is remarkable for its lack of "quiete"; the three main characters talk incessantly, to one another or to themselves, keeping up a constant stream of interpretation or, usually, misinterpretation, of signs and texts relating to the others. Perhaps the most distressing examples of the creation of an interpretable text by one lover, and of its misinterpretation by the other, occur at the end of the romance, in the form of Criseyde's letters from the Greek camp and of Troilus's reactions to them. By this point, especially when her last letter arrives and is quoted in full by the narrator, it has become clear to the reader that Criseyde will never return. Her precise motives for writing that "Come I wole" (V, 1618) are, as usual, debatable, and are made more so by the narrator's speculations (again as usual, labeled as such):

> For which Criseyde upon a day, for routhe,—
> I take it so,—touchyng al this matere,
> Wrot hym ayeyn, and seyde as ye may here. (V, 1587–89)

To the end, Criseyde's behavior is subject not to any authoritative praise or blame but to interpretation by the narrator, by the reader, and finally by Troilus himself:

This Troilus this lettre thoughte al straunge,
Whan he it saugh, and sorwfullich he sighte.
Hym thoughte it lik a kalendes of chaunge.
But fynaly, he ful ne trowen myghte
That she ne wolde hym holden that she hyghte;
For with ful yvel wille list hym to leve,
That loveth wel, in swich cas, though hym greve. (V, 1632–38)

The difficulty of knowing the truth about Criseyde has been linked to the larger difficulties examined by fourteenth-century epistemology: the unpredictability of the radically individual beings posited in Ockham's brand of nominalism (we have seen what happens to the notion of causality in the context of this separation of individuals) drastically limits the knowledge those individuals can have of one another.[32] Besides the individual's confinement to his or her own isolated consciousness and the resulting inability to verify perceptions with any certainty (a problem raised, as we have seen, by Nicholas of Autrecourt and reflected in *The Book of the Duchess* as well as in Machaut's *Voir-Dit*), Chaucer in this and similar episodes confronts a more basic issue in fourteenth-century Ockhamism (an issue whose source is Ockham himself rather than one of his followers). Not only epistemology but ontology itself, the very question of being, is conditioned by this radical individuality, and that fact has implications not only for knowledge and communication but for all human relations, whether represented as occurring between two fictional characters, or between a narrating voice and the inscribed reader, or actually occurring between the writer and his audience. Whereas Machaut playfully addressed the epistemological issue by redefining "truth" in a purely textual manner, and by suggesting that extra-textual reality is not the concern of a reader while reading, Chaucer still seems at this stage in his career to find these forms of alienation troublesome. Communication rather than interpretation is still the ideal, as it was in *The Book of the Duchess*, and the difficulty of achieving it, the transformation of human relations into ambiguous texts (which seems inevitable after Ockham) therefore has tragic potential, whether that potential is finally realized or not.

At this point, the love relationship as such has clearly ceased to exist except in Troilus's misinterpretation of Criseyde's text. But one might question whether, except in those brief and infrequent scenes of mutual contact such as the scene of consummation, their affair ever consists of anything else. If Pandarus is a narrator, the text that he narrates is frequently an idealized or conventionalized version of Troilus, and the audience for whose benefit he narrates it is Criseyde. His mission as go-between when the affair is first getting under way is precisely to present this version of Troilus to Criseyde for her interpretation and eventual acceptance; he presents it most fully during his first visit to Criseyde, in Book II. Pandarus's awareness that what he says will be interpreted by Criseyde is suggested early in this visit and determines the form his speech will take; his manipulation of her is possible because he can anticipate her ability to interpret him:

> Than thought he thus: "If I my tale endite
> Aught harde, or make a proces any whyle,
> She shal no savour have therin but lite,
> And trowe I wolde hire in my wil bigyle;
> For tendre wittes wenen al be wyle
> Thereas thei kan nought pleynly understonde;
> Forthi hire wit to serven wol I fonde." (II, 267–73)

The story he tells her purports to be that of how he came to learn of Troilus's love for her. The readers have already witnessed that scene in Book I, and must be struck by the dichotomy between the version they have read and the one narrated by Pandarus, despite the latter's claim to use no "subtyl art" (II, 257) in his narration. The version told by Pandarus is a highly conventionalized narrative, making use of traditional courtly-love motifs noticeably absent from the account presented in Book I:

> ". . . This other day, naught gon ful longe while,
> In-with the paleis gardyn, by a welle,
> Gan he and I wel half a day to dwelle." (II, 507–09)

The enclosed garden and the well are instantly recognizable features of the conventional courtly-love landscape; what Pandarus does here is to transform Troilus into a traditional courtly lover rather than the slightly ridiculous figure (not in a garden but in bed) the reader has seen him to be.[33] Whereas Machaut uses literary conventions to redefine "truth" in textual terms, in this episode they appear simply as lies.

Criseyde accepts this false narrative as the truth. She does, as Pandarus predicted she would, engage in a certain amount of interpretation:

> Criseyde aros, no lenger she ne stente,
> But streght into hire closet went anon,
> And set hire doun as stylle as any ston,
> And every word gan up and down to wynde
> That he had seyd, as it com hire to mynde;
>
> And wax somdel astoned in hire thought,
> Right for the newe cas; but whan that she
> Was ful avysed, tho fond she right nought
> Of peril, why she ought afered be. (II, 598–606)

Her interpretation, of course, leads her nowhere near the truth; what she fears, namely being entrapped in a love affair, is precisely what Pandarus has in mind and is what will actually come to pass.

More examples might be cited of how the love affair is a result of deceit and misinterpretation; much of Books II and III is devoted to an account of the various ways Pandarus deceives Criseyde in order to bring her together with Troilus. And it is not only Pandarus's tricks and Criseyde's letters that are misinterpreted; this poem is filled with signs and texts not only generated by the characters but appearing in the lovers' natural world or forming a part of their cultural background as well, all of which are consistently misinterpreted by both of them. One more example of Criseyde's potential for misinterpretation, this time of a natural sign, should suffice. At the beginning of Book II, as Pandarus is about to undertake his mission as go-between, he is awakened and, as it were, sent on his way by a chattering swallow, who is perceived by the narrator as the mythical transformed Procne:

> The swalowe Proigne, with a sorowful lay,
> Whan morwen com, gan make hire waymentynge,
> Whi she forshapen was; and ever lay
> Pandare abedde, half in a slomberynge,
> Til she so neigh hym made hire cheterynge
> How Tereus gan forth hire suster take,
> That with the noyse of hire he gan awake. (II, 64–70)

Just enough of the plot of the myth of Procne, Tereus, and Philomela is here recounted to remind the reader that it is a tale of lust, deceit, and rape. The narrator presents the incident as a simple statement of fact concerning Pandarus's awakening and makes no editorial comment; the reader, however, must be tempted as he or she reads further in Book II to keep this scene in mind and to draw a parallel between the rape of Philomela and the ongoing seduction of Criseyde; Pandarus goes forth to take her as Tereus went forth to take Philomela. The use of this particular myth to send Pandarus out on his mission to deceive Criseyde inevitably creates an atmosphere of sexual misconduct that darkens the apparently light and bantering tone of their encounter. These lines are not the last we hear of the myth in Book II, although it is the last time the narrator refers to it by name or, indeed, appears to have it in mind. At the end of their first interview, Criseyde has decided that to love Troilus might not be entirely out of the question:

> And ay gan love hire lasse for t'agaste
> Than it did erst, and synken in hire herte,
> That she wex somwhat able to converte. (II, 901–03)

It is at this point that the myth of Procne surfaces again, very subtly, as Criseyde goes to sleep:

> A nyghtyngale, upon a cedir grene,
> Under the chambre wal ther as she ley,
> Ful loude song ayein the moone shene,
> Peraunter, in his briddes wise, a lay
> Of love, that made hire herte fressh and gay.
> That herkned she so longe in good entente,
> Til at the laste the dede slep hire hente. (II, 918–24)

Given the context—that his day began with the song of transformed Procne—it is only too appropriate that it end with the song of transformed Philomela, the nightingale. Criseyde and the narrator hear only the traditional love-related song of the nightingale (as it appears, for instance, in Marie de France's "Laüstic"), but the reader hears a warning as well: the voice of Tereus's victim, warning Criseyde that she too could be the victim of lust and deceit. Neither Criseyde nor the narrator hears the warning (although the narrator's "peraunter" might be taken as a clue by the alert reader); Criseyde, indeed, takes the song "in good entente" and is made "fressh and gay" by it. Her love for Troilus is reinforced once again by a possible misinterpretation, the perception of a warning as though it were encouragement.[34]

Troilus, too, consistently misinterprets signs and texts from sources other than Criseyde (as well as misinterpreting hers), especially once the affair has been consummated. The effect of his misinterpretations, like the effect of Criseyde's, is to give false strength to a love built on very shaky foundations. Perhaps the best example is to be found near the end of the poem, in Book V, when Criseyde's infidelity has been established (though reluctantly) by the narrator. Troilus retains a steadfast confidence in his lover until he has a dream that appears to reveal her guilt:

> He mette he saugh a bor with tuskes grete,
> That slepte ayeyn the bryghte sonnes hete.
>
> And by this bor, fast in his armes folde,
> Lay, kissyng ay, his lady bryght, Criseyde. (V, 1238–41)

Troilus's first reaction is a heartfelt and accurate interpretation of the dream:

> "My lady bryght, Criseyde, hath me bytrayed,
> In whom I trusted most of any wight.
> She elliswhere hath now here herte apayed.
> The blysful goddes, thorugh here grete myght,
> Han in my drem yshewed it ful right.
> Thus yn my drem Criseyde have I byholde." (V, 1247–52)

Pandarus, however, counters with another interpretation designed to comfort his friend and incidentally proclaims the difficulty and danger of all interpretation:

> Pandare answerde and seyde, "Allas the while
> That I was born! Have I nat seyd er this,
> That dremes many a maner man bigile?
> And whi? For folk expounden hem amys.
> How darstow seyn that fals thy lady ys,
> For any drem, right for thyn owene drede?
> Lat be this thought; thow kanst no dremes rede.
>
> "Peraunter, ther thow dremest of this boor,
> It may so be that it may signifie,
> Hire fader, which that old is and ek hoor,
> Ayeyn the sonne lith, o poynt to dye,
> And she for sorwe gynneth wepe and crie,
> And kisseth hym, there he lith on the grounde;
> Thus sholdestow thi dreme aright expounde!" (V, 1275–88)

Troilus does appear to be comforted, but later we learn that he continues to engage in interpretation of Criseyde's increasingly suspicious behavior, "Ymagynyng ay that she was unkynde" (V, 1441), and especially that his dream "May nevere come out of his remembraunce" (V, 1444). The second person to whom he turns for yet another interpretation of it is his sister Cassandra, the prophet, doomed, her myth tells us, never to be believed. Cassandra responds initially not with a simple interpretation but with stories justifying the interpretation to come; it is the history of Diomede's family that generates the symbol of the boar that appeared in Troilus's dream:

> "This ilke boor bitokneth Diomede,
> Tideüs sone, that down descended is
> Fro Meleagre, that made the boor to blede.
> And thy lady, wherso she be, ywis,
> This Diomede hire herte hath, and she his.
> Wep if thow wolt, or lef! For, out of doute,
> This Diomede is inne, and thow art out." (V, 1513–19)

Despite such justification for her reading of the boar as Diomede—a much more convincing reading than Pandarus's—Troilus fulfills Cassandra's destiny by refusing to believe her accurate reading:

> "Thow seyst nat soth," quod he, "thow sorceresse,
> With al thy false goost of prophecye!
> Thow wenest ben a grete devyneresse!
> Now sestow nat this fool of fantasie
> Peyneth hire on ladys for to lye?
> Awey!" quod he, "ther Joves yeve the sorwe!
> Thow shalt be fals, peraunter, yet tomorwe!
>
> "As wel thow myghtest lien on Alceste,
> That was of creatures, but men lye,
> That evere weren, kyndest and the beste!
> For whan hire housbonde was in jupertye
> To dye hymself, but if she wolde dye,
> She ches for hym to dye and gon to helle,
> And starf anon, as us the bokes telle." (V, 1520–33)

He substitutes the irrelevant story of Alcestis, which allows a favorable interpretation, for the highly relevant story of Diomede's family. Ultimately,

Cassandra's interpretation of his dream only causes Troilus, by way of reaction, to love the unfaithful Criseyde more than before:

> Cassandre goth, and he with cruel herte
> Foryat his wo, for angre of hire speche;
> And from his bed al sodeynly he sterte,
> As though al hool hym hadde ymad a leche. (V, 1534–37)[35]

Love in *Troilus and Criseyde*, then, is derived from and sustained by the misinterpretation, by both lovers, of various kinds of signs and texts; both act like the Black Knight, desiring communication but presenting themselves as texts that, by their very nature, prevent communication, substituting instead unsatisfactory interpretation as the usual mode of intercourse. And yet Chaucer never, any more than his narrator, labels their misinterpretations directly as such. It is always possible that Criseyde is correct in deriving comfort rather than a warning from the nightingale's song; we are not forced to make the connection with the reference to Procne that occurred so many lines earlier, and indeed her ultimate fate is not as horrifying as Philomela's. Troilus might even be correct to trust in Criseyde's love for him despite her infidelity; as has been demonstrated, her motives are, because of the narrator's speculations, impossible to determine with any certainty. The reader is always provided, though, with enough details unnoticed by the lovers to insure his or her participation in their act of interpretation. As is the case with Cassandra's reading of Troilus's dream, the reader's familiarity with other, older texts (Boccaccio, Boethius, the myth of Procne, etc.) will alter the reading of this poem, will give a standard against which the characters' misinterpretations of one another and of other texts can be judged. This is one of the reader's most important functions in *Troilus and Criseyde*: we must judge the lovers' acts of interpretation in much the same way that we complete or correct the narrator's. Chaucer provides various models of the creation and interpretation of texts in the course of creating his own text; how the readers respond to these models and thus generate a meaning for the poem, an interpretation of their own, is up to them. Both the narrator's professed inadequacy to his task, and the questionable interpretations of the lovers, function to engage the readers in their own acts of interpretation.

The readers' erotic relationship with the text is never assumed; it must be earned by their engagement with it, an interpretive relationship reflecting the lovers' interpretive engagement with each other. The problem here is the frustration involved in this enterprise, the sheer difficulty, illustrated in the text, of interpreting correctly. The reader is free to interpret the text as Troilus and Criseyde interpret each other, but the poem faces up to the dangers of interpretation, indeed, to the danger of this kind of freedom. By concerning itself with a love-relationship consisting more of distanced, mediated signs and texts (created by a go-between as well as by the lovers), and based to a large extent on the misinterpretation of those signs and texts, Chaucer's romance is able to confront once more, as in *The Book of the Duchess*, the very basic problem associated with the use of figurative or literary language: the problem that language, especially interpretable language, conceals at least as much as it reveals. In *Troilus and Criseyde*, interpretable texts are not easily controlled: they may simply hide the truth, finally serving more as a barrier to understanding and union than as the bridge they are intended to be. The reader of *Troilus and Criseyde* engages in interpretation while being reminded constantly what a problematic, even futile, activity it is in the post-Ockhamist world.

That the narrator's concern is with the very worth of language itself as an instrument of communication is signalled early in the text, when he speaks, perhaps somewhat naïvely, of his own "vers, that wepen as I write" (I, 7). The problem is precisely that: how to create words that weep, a language that can fully embody human experience. A later association of texts and tears, when Troilus is writing Criseyde his first love letter, suggests just how difficult a task this might be:

> And with his salte teris gan he bathe
> The ruby in his signet, and it sette
> Upon the wex deliverliche and rathe.
> Therwith a thousand tymes, er he lette,
> He kiste tho the lettre that he shette,
> And seyde, "Lettre, a blisful destine
> The shapyn is: my lady shal the see!" (II, 1086–92)

The letter, a text, is luckier than Troilus himself, its creator, in that it rather than he will have direct contact with Criseyde. It may communicate something of his feelings to her, but it also inevitably stands between them; he kisses the letter, not the woman. Pandarus delivers the letter: "And in hire bosom the lettre down he thraste" (II, 1155). Even in a sexual encounter, Troilus is thus replaced by his text. Texts tend to usurp human relationships rather than to encourage them; the readers of a love-text, especially one that calls the validity of interpretation so drastically into question, must be concerned with how they can get beyond the mere words before them, to some understanding of the truth of human relationships those words try to present.[36] This seemed impossible in *The Book of the Duchess*, but in *Troilus and Criseyde* the interpreting engagement with a text may, for one character at least, be seen as leading to genuine emotional experience.

A more appropriate model than either Troilus or Criseyde for the reader engaged in this attempt might be the narrator: he may be the only presence in the poem to achieve a really meaningful love.[37] If Donaldson is correct in asserting that the narrator loves Criseyde, it would seem equally evident that that love is achieved through his active reading of the older texts whose story he wants to transmit. Clearly, a sort of leap of faith in their own abilities is required of the readers: they must take responsibility for what they learn of love and apply it if the text is to mean something in their own lives. In a sense, they must, like the narrator, fall in love with what they read: truth lies not in the words alone but in the relationship between those words and their engaged reader.

Even the narrator's direct and unmediated vision at the poem's end, and the narrator's apparently unambiguous advice to the reader, signal the necessity not of detachment but of involvement, in love as in the text. The much-discussed reaction of Troilus to his own death is to laugh:

> And in hymself he lough right at the wo
> Of hem that wepten for his deth so faste;
> And dampned al oure werk that foloweth so
> The blynde lust, the which that may nat laste,
> And sholden al oure herte on heven caste. (V, 1821–25)

This seems like an outright rejection of earthly experience; and yet this last appearance of Troilus echoes his first, laughing appearance:

> And in his walk ful faste he gan to wayten
> If knyght or squyer of his compaignie
> Gan for to syke, or lete his eighen baiten
> On any womman that he koud espye.
> He wolde smyle and holden it folye. (I, 190–94)

Troilus moves, then, from an initial laughing detachment, through earthly involvement in love, back to a final laughing detachment. The narrator, however, approves of the distanced, uninvolved attitude only in its final manifestation, advising the reader to imitate Troilus's scorn for the world:

> O yonge, fresshe folkes, he or she,
> In which that love up groweth with youre age,
> Repeyreth hom fro worldly vanyte,
> And of youre herte up casteth the visage
> To thilke God that after his ymage
> Yow made, and thynketh al nys but a faire
> This world, that passeth soone as floures faire. (V, 1835–41)

Troilus's original scorn for love, on the other hand, is just as clearly condemned by the narrator in another direct address to the reader making use of the blindness metaphor that will reappear in V, 1824 (cited above), but in an opposite sense:

> O blynde world, O blynde entencioun!
> How often falleth al the effect contraire
> Of surquidrie and foul presumpcioun;
> For kaught is proud, and kaught is debonaire.
> . . . .
>
> So ferde it by this fierse and proude knyght:
> Though he a worthy kynges sone were,
> And wende nothing hadde had swich myght
> Ayeyns his wille that shuld his herte stere,
> Yet with a look his herte wax a-fere,
> That he that now was moost in pride above,
> Wax sodeynly moost subgit unto love.
>
> Forthy ensample taketh of this man,
> Ye wise, proude, and worthi folkes alle,
> To scornen Love, which that so soone kan
> The fredom of youre hertes to hym thralle;
> For evere it was, and evere it shal byfalle,
> That Love is he that alle thing may bynde,
> For may no man fordon the lawe of kynde. (I, 211–14; 225–38)

It could be argued that the narrator has changed his mind or has become better educated in the ways of the world by writing his book;[38] and yet Chaucer (the author rather than the narrator) has chosen to depict this new frame of mind in such a way as to send the reader, at least imaginatively, back to the beginning of the work. The structural similarities of the two passages—Troilus's laugh followed by the narrator's advice to the reader, which in both cases uses a blindness metaphor—emphasizes not what the narrator says in the second passage but the fact that it clearly contradicts what he says in the first. The readers are thus once again presented with an ambiguity, a choice between two possible truths, and the need for an act of interpretation to decide between them.[39] They are sent back not only to interpretation but to earthly experience as well: even if Troilus and the narrator have at the book's end progressed to a higher plane of understanding than they were on at the beginning, surely it is only their shared experience in loving Criseyde, what they have gone through in living and in writing the book, that can have brought them there. The narrator advises detachment; but his own example in arriving at detachment encourages involvement. Thus one possible reading of the poem would send the reader outside its bounds, back to the real world. Indeed, it has been shown just how closely earthly and heavenly love are related in this poem;[40] Criseyde herself, object of earthly passion, is at least twice described in heavenly terms:

. . . an hevenyssh perfit creature
That down were sent in scornynge of nature; (I, 104–05)

Lo, trewely, they writen that hire syen,
That Paradis stood formed in hire yën. (V, 816–17)

The narrator himself describes earthly love as "hevene blisse" in III, 1322, cited above.

It would be foolish to imply that the book's Christian ending is in any way insincere; Chaucer chose to remind the reader of the book's beginning in its ending, but the narrator chooses to end with a very moving rejection of that beginning. The reader should probably choose the narrator's final advice over his original advice; but the point is precisely that it is the reader's own decision, his or her own interpretation that will determine the book's meaning, and that the text itself encourages such freedom of interpretation, as other critics have suggested.[41] Indeed, the structural circularity I have just outlined may well suggest that a second proper response might be to reread the poem, continuing to oscillate with the narrator between approval and rejection of earthly experience. The danger is that, like the lovers themselves, the reader may allow the textualization of his or her own experience, by which I mean the subversion or usurpation of life by textuality, the substitution of texts for life. Chaucer never loses sight of the problems of textuality, or of freedom. The narrator makes his choice clear at the end and invites the reader to share it; but the reader nevertheless remains free to decide.

St. John, the Wife of Bath, and the Poetics of Misinterpretation

Troilus and Criseyde suggests that textual interpretation can entrap the reader in the alienating textuality demonstrated by its two lovers; to that extent, it reflects the traditional Christian prejudice against secular literature.[42] However, it also suggests that interpretation can overcome textuality and allow a breakthrough to extra-textual experience, either earthly or spiritual. While stressing the potentially tragic dangers of the textual/interpretive mode and continuing to idealize the conversational/communicative mode, like *The Book of the Duchess*, it also, unlike the earlier poem, begins to find a potential value in interpretation for overcoming the isolation of the post-Ockhamist consciousness. This possibility is most fully developed in *The Canterbury Tales*, paradoxically by the most complete textualization of experience, the fullest usurpation of lived experience by texts, or substitution of texts for life. It is in this work that Chaucer appears most clearly to accept textuality and interpretation as the normal mode of human intercourse, a mode that, however, does not necessarily imply solipsism, isolation, or alienation.

The Wife of Bath's Prologue is, of all the subdivisions of *The Canterbury Tales*, the one most overtly concerned with texts, their interpretation, and their relationship with lived experience, as is signalled by its very first line. It is the clearest demonstration in Chaucer's works of a self composed of conflicting texts; indeed, it is a commonplace of Chaucer criticism that the Wife is a living example of the truth of the very texts she argues against. The Wife also perceives other people, and indeed life itself, as texts to be interpreted. The very lucidity with which Chaucer presents these issues in her *Prologue* makes it an ideal introduction to their appearance in *The Canterbury Tales* generally; at the end of this chapter, therefore, I shall briefly suggest some of the implications that this almost schematic demonstration of the text-bound status of lived experience may have for the interpretation of *The Canterbury Tales* as a whole. I would like to approach *The Wife of Bath's Prologue* by means of one of its acknowledged sources, the fourth chapter of St. John's Gospel, which is also concerned with problems of language and interpretation.

The Wife explicitly compares herself, early in the *Prologue*, to the Samaritan woman at the well whom Jesus engages in conversation (III/D, 14–25).[43] This passage has become a *locus classicus* for discussions of Chaucer's views on marriage, but to my knowledge another similarity between the Wife and the Samaritan has not been widely discussed: both are misinterpreters of Christ's words.[44] A comparison of the two women, the reasons for their misunderstandings, and the very different results of their confrontations with divine language, should illuminate Chaucer's presentation of presence and absence in language, of speech and textuality, of communication and interpretation.

The conversation between Jesus and the Samaritan can also be profitably compared with the central conversation in *The Book of the Duchess*. In this case, Jesus plays a role comparable to that of the Black Knight in terms of the nature of their speech, while the Samaritan, in her naïve attempts to understand her interlocutor by direct questioning, resembles the dreamer. In both cases the ignorant questioner succeeds in obtaining an unadorned statement of the truth by forcing the other speaker to abandon his obscure, literary, textual language. The Biblical passage is well worth quoting at length. Jesus, tired out from traveling through Samaria, is resting near Jacob's well:

> 4:7 There cometh a woman of Samaria, to draw water. Jesus saith to her: Give me to drink.
>
> 8 For his disciples were gone into the city to buy meats.
>
> 9 Then that Samaritan woman saith to him: How dost thou, being a Jew, ask of me to drink, who am a Samaritan woman? For the Jews do not communicate with the Samaritans.
>
> 10 Jesus answered, and said to her: If thou didst know the gift of God, and who he is that saith to thee, Give me to drink; thou perhaps wouldst have asked of him, and he would have given thee living water.
>
> 11 The woman saith to him: Sir, thou hast nothing wherein to draw, and the well is deep; from whence then hast thou living water?
>
> 12 Art thou greater than our father Jacob, who gave us the well, and drank thereof himself, and his children, and his cattle?
>
> 13 Jesus answered, and said to her: Whosoever drinketh of this water, shall thirst again; but he that shall drink of the water that I will give him, shall not thirst forever:

14 But the water that I will give him, shall become in him a fountain of water, springing up into life everlasting.

15 The woman saith to him: Sir, give me this water, that I may not thirst, nor come hither to draw.

. . . .

21 Jesus saith to her: Woman, believe me, that the hour cometh, when you shall neither on this mountain, nor in Jerusalem, adore the Father.

22 You adore that which you know not: we adore that which we know; for salvation is of the Jews.

23 But the hour cometh, and now is, when the true adorers shall adore the Father in spirit and in truth. For the Father also seeketh such to adore him.

24 God is a spirit; and they that adore him, must adore him in spirit and in truth.

25 The woman saith to him: I know that the Messias cometh (who is called Christ); therefore, when he is come, he will tell us all things.

26 Jesus saith to her: I am he, who am speaking with thee.[45]

Like the Black Knight, Jesus at first uses figurative, literary language to express his truths, especially the metaphor of "living water"; and like the dreamer, the Samaritan finds such language beyond her comprehension. She interprets it as a reflection of her own experience and assumes that Jesus means literal water; in the same way, the apparently lovesick dreamer understands the knight as meaning that his lady refuses to love him, or sees only his own sorrow in the tale of Alcione. But also like the dreamer, the Samaritan, emphasizing her own incomprehension (that she has not yet been told "all things"), finally induces Jesus to speak the truth directly, and in words that emphasize the conversational situation: "I am he, who am speaking with thee."

That the problem may lie in Christ's language, rather than in one individual's inability to understand it, is suggested by the following verses, in which his own disciples repeat the Samaritan's mistake of interpreting figurative speech as if it were literal:

31 In the mean time the disciples prayed him, saying: Rabbi, eat.

32 But he said to them: I have meat to eat, which you know not.

33 The disciples therefore said one to another: Hath any man brought him to eat?

34 Jesus saith to them: My meat is to do the will of him that sent me, that I may perfect his work.

Once again, Jesus must respond to human incomprehension with a direct statement giving the authoritative interpretation of his metaphor. Similar exchanges take place in John 10:1–18 and 16:25–29, as well as in Matthew 13:1–43.

In the meantime, the Samaritan has been converted by Christ's revelations and proceeds to spread the word. Her countrymen, however, are not convinced by her mediation but only by their own direct experience of hearing Christ speak:

42 And they said to the woman: We now believe, not for thy saying: for we ourselves have heard him, and know that this is indeed the Saviour of the world.

The other Samaritans will not accept Christ's truth in his absence, or through the text-like (because of the absence of the speaker) mediation of the first Samaritan; only the direct presence of both speaker and hearers allows the communication of this truth. In *The Book of the Duchess*, the narrator's interpretation of the Ovidian tale of Alcione lacks authority because of the nature of writing; but face to face with the supreme Authority, the Samaritans and the disciples can receive an authoritative and uninterpretable communication, like the *Queste*'s knights in their meetings with the holy interpreters.

The Wife of Bath's reading of the Gospel of John's fourth chapter is initially similar to the Samaritan's first "reading" of Christ's words but finally has almost the opposite effect. The similarity lies in the Wife's incomprehension of Christ's words. Like the Samaritan, she says she is not sure what he means:

Herkne eek, lo, which a sharp word for the nones,
Biside a welle, Jhesus, God and man,
Spak in repreeve of the Samaritan:

> "Thou hast yhad fyve housbondes," quod he,
> "And that ilke man that now hath thee
> Is noght thyn housbonde," thus seyde he certeyn.
> What that he mente therby, I kan nat seyn;
> But that I axe, why that the fifthe man
> Was noon housbonde to the Samaritan?
> How manye myghte she have in mariage?
> Yet herde I nevere tellen in myn age
> Upon this nombre diffinicioun. (III/D, 14–25)

For the Wife, it is not a question of the obscurity of figurative speech; she cannot understand even Jesus' literal pronouncement on the validity of the Samaritan's fifth marriage. Also like the Samaritan, the Wife asks questions designed, on the surface, to provoke a clear and unequivocal response; but the Wife knows, of course, that a direct response is not available to her as it was to the Samaritan. Because Christ is absent from her, she can question his language for her own purposes, which is to say that she calls it into question knowing that its true and authoritative meaning, which might well not be to her liking, will not be revealed. For the Samaritan, Christ was fully present for questioning, but for the Wife, he is absent except for his written text, which cannot respond to her questions. The Wife reacts to Christ's words neither with the Samaritan's initial, simple incomprehension, nor with the understanding and acceptance of the truth that the Samaritan attains later. The Wife takes a third course that was not an option for her predecessor: she interprets, like *Troilus and Criseyde*'s characters. The lines quoted above are only the first of many examples throughout the *Prologue* of her ability to transform Scripture in such a way as to suit her own unorthodox purposes, as Troilus and Criseyde transform each other's texts. Rather than submitting to Christ's authority as the Samaritan does in recognizing him as the Messiah, the Wife asserts her own authority over his language and that of the rest of the Bible by reinterpreting it until it says what she wants it to say. It is the difference between speech and writing that makes this possible.

Critics have noted many instances of her tendentious Scriptural exegesis;[46] two examples should suffice here. One method of transforming a Scriptural text is selective quotation:

> An housbonde I wol have, I wol nat lette,
> Which shal be bothe my dettour and my thral,
> And have his tribulacion withal
> Upon his flessh, whil that I am his wyf.

> I have the power durynge al my lyf
> Upon his propre body, and noght he.
> Right thus the Apostel tolde it unto me;
> And bad oure housbondes for to love us weel.
> Al this sentence me liketh every deel. (III/D, 154–62)

Her reference is to I Corinthians 7:4, in which St. Paul says that "The wife hath not power of her own body, but the husband. And in like manner the husband also hath not power of his own body, but the wife." By referring only to the second sentence of this verse, and ignoring the first, the Wife is able to interpret it as giving her power over her husband rather than as advising mutual submission.[47] Another way to transform Scripture is to put it into the mouth of one's opponent, as she does with a quotation from I Timothy 2:9:

> Thou seyst also, that if we make us gay
> With clothyng, and with precious array,
> That it is peril of oure chastitee;
> And yet, with sorwe! thou most enforce thee,
> And seye thise wordes in the Apostles name:
> "In habit maad with chastitee and shame
> Ye wommen shul apparaille yow," quod he,
> "And noght in tressed heer and gay perree,
> As perles, ne with gold, ne clothes riche."
> After thy text, ne after thy rubriche,
> I wol nat wirche as muchel as a gnat. (III/D, 337–47)

In the Wife's version, St. Paul's admonitions become the text of the hypothetical husband she is here arguing against, "*thy* text"; thus they lose their authority and can be used for a purpose opposed to St. Paul's.

Unlike the Samaritan, then, the Wife of Bath exerts interpretive power over divine language rather than submitting to it. Her search for a sixth husband suggests that she has rejected Christ's words to the Samaritan, and that the interpretability of those words, stemming from their textuality, is her justification for doing so. Why is Christ's language so unsuccessful in communicating an authoritative truth to the Wife, when the same words did succeed in communicating with the Samaritan? Why is the Wife able to subvert divine language through interpretation, when the Samaritan could only recognize its divinity?

The answer, as I have suggested, lies once again in the nature of textuality. For the Samaritan, Jesus is present, and their interaction follows the conversational mode. He can respond to her confusion and to her questions directly, as is emphasized when he says, "I am he, who am speaking with thee." His physical presence makes communication possible. For the Wife of Bath, on the other hand, Jesus is absent. She can interact only with a text that, as she very well knows, must remain silent before her rhetorical questions (which therefore lose their rhetorical status). Her questions and confusions, whether real or pretended, must go unanswered and uncorrected. Whereas the narrator of *The Book of the Duchess* passively found in the tale of Alcione only a reflection of his own state of mind, the Wife actively makes the Bible into a justification of her own desires. The difference between them demonstrates a second danger of textuality: the text's ambiguity may prevent communication, but so may the intentions of a "bad reader" (and here the Wife of Bath resembles the *Voir-Dit*'s *médisants*). For both of these reasons, nothing is necessarily communicated in the mode of textuality; the interpreter can merely, solipsistically, impose his or her own state of mind on the text, as could not be done to a present speaker. In its comic way, this process also resembles Troilus's deliberate misinterpretation of his dream.

Thus writing, though it preserves speech and gives it an aura of authority, also opens it to interpretation and subversion (and Chaucer thus continues to be concerned with the relationship between textuality and falsehood discerned in non-literary writers by Stock and Clanchy).[48] In fact, it makes interpretation necessary, as *The Wife of Bath's Prologue* consistently emphasizes. The Wife knows that she is only one in a long line of interpreters, none of whom has the final word:

> But me was toold, certeyn, nat longe agoon is,
> That sith that Crist ne wente nevere but onis
> To weddyng, in the Cane of Galilee,
> That by the same ensample taughte he me
> That I ne sholde wedded be but ones; (III/D, 9–13)

> Men may devyne and glosen, up and doun. (III/D, 26)

The Samaritan's countrymen refuse her mediation and need not take her word for it that the man she spoke to at the well is the Messiah; they can go and hear him for themselves. The Wife, on the other hand, in passages like these, acknowledges that other Scriptural exegetes do stand between her and the text, like Pandarus interpreting Troilus to Criseyde, and that the text itself is an unsatisfactory substitute for Christ's presence. Divine language for her is thus doubly mediated, by its written form and by previous interpreters (whose activity is made necessary by the written form), and is thus doubly absent from her own "experience," which alone is present to her in a way that "auctoritee" cannot be.

We can draw analogies among the various linguistic interactions represented in John, *The Book of the Duchess,* and *The Wife of Bath's Prologue.* If the Samaritan is related to Jesus in a conversation comparable to that between the dreamer and the Black Knight, then the Wife of Bath is related to him in a textual mode comparable to that which relates the narrator to Ovid's text, or Chaucer's audience (us) to *The Book of the Duchess* itself. Before considering the reader's relationship with *The Wife of Bath's Prologue,* it should be useful to examine another similar constellation of text, audience, and interpretation that occurs near the end of the *Prologue.*

The Wife's fifth husband, Jankyn, owns a book that might be seen as a secular counterpart to the Biblical texts she subverts at the beginning of the *Prologue.* His "book of wikked wyves" (III/D, 685) also enshrines an ancient authority in written form. Like the Bible, it represents male authority trying to control women (recall St. Paul's injunctions on women's clothing, cited above), and like the Bible, it must be transformed before the Wife can be satisfied with it. Its existence as a physical object rather than as speech ironically leaves it open to an even more direct kind of "interpretation" than the Wife practiced on the Bible:

> And whan I saugh he wolde nevere fyne
> To reden on this cursed book al nyght,
> Al sodeynly thre leves have I plyght
> Out of his book, right as he radde, and eke
> I with my fest so took hym on the cheke
> That in oure fyr he fil bakward adoun. (III/D, 788–93)

This attack on the book as an object demonstrates that for the Wife, writing itself is to some extent the problem in her relationship with Jankyn. It is, however, a problem that contains its own solution: precisely because it is written rather than spoken, Jankyn's volume can be attacked and destroyed. Such violence against the book is only the logical extension of the Wife's earlier interpretations of the Bible: from ignoring that part of the text that offends her (as in her reference to I Corinthians), it is but a short step to the actual tearing-out of the offensive pages, or to burning the book as a whole (as she does in line 816). As usual, this act of violent interpretation is solipsistic: the interpreter's own views are substituted for whatever the author may have hoped to communicate.

There is also a more positive aspect to this destruction of the book, at least in the Wife's view. Textuality in this case has assumed not only the absence of the author or original producer of the text but that of the performer as well. Jankyn, in reading aloud from the book, substituted the text for himself, authority for experience. He did not speak in his own language but absented himself in favor of the text. The Wife's attack on textuality allows a return of presence and of direct communication between husband and wife:

> But atte laste, with muchel care and wo,
> We fille acorded by us selven two.
> He yaf me al the bridel in myn hond,
> To han the governance of hous and lond,
> And of his tonge, and of his hond also;
> And made hym brenne his book anon right tho.
> And whan that I hadde geten unto me,
> By maistrie, al the soveraynetee,
> And that he seyde, "Myn owene trewe wyf,
> Do as thee lust the terme of al thy lyf;
> Keep thyn honour, and keep eek myn estaat"—
> After that day we hadden never debaat.
> God helpe me so, I was to hym as kynde
> As any wyf from Denmark unto Ynde,
> And also trewe, and so was he to me. (III/D, 811–25)

One might regard these lines as an ironic reversal of the Samaritan's conversion in John 4: it is now the Wife's authoritative truth that is communicated in present conversation, and Jankyn who is converted to it. Although the reader may see little improvement for Jankyn in the substitution of his wife's language for that of the book of wicked wives (she now has control of "his tonge"), the Wife herself takes the view that the solipsism of interpretation has here given way before mutual communication, in which Jankyn is rewarded for giving up his text with a loving and faithful wife, just as the Black Knight's abandonment of textuality is rewarded with the dreamer's sympathy.

In *The Book of the Duchess* and *Troilus and Criseyde*, the abandonment of textuality is entirely positive for the time it lasts; but the fact that the reader's perspective on Jankyn's abandonment of it is ironically removed from the Wife's whole-hearted approval suggests that a somewhat different attitude toward textuality may be found in Chaucer's later works. Successful communication in *The Book of the Duchess* is framed in a poem that insists on its own textuality and hence on the absence of communication between author and reader, while the ending of *Troilus and Criseyde* implies that interpretation may be a valid alternative to communication. It should now be asked what kind of frame *The Canterbury Tales* as a whole provides for *The Wife of Bath's Prologue*, and what kind of relationship to the audience it implies. The *Prologue*'s obvious concern with textuality may suggest an approach to other sections of *The Canterbury Tales* that are not so overtly text-bound. As Gellrich suggests, "the desires, fears, and arguments represented by the pilgrims and their tales are first of all problems of language and of reading."[49]

Although the Wife of Bath represents herself as achieving a fully present communication with her husband, she cannot, of course, achieve such presence to the readers of *The Canterbury Tales;* she is, after all, only a fictional character and not a human being (insistent on her "reality" though some critics have been).[50] This is just the problem confronted (and not fully resolved) at the end of both of the other poems I have discussed. And even within the fiction of *The Canterbury Tales*, the Wife and the other pilgrims are remarkably text-bound, and not merely in the sense that Chaucer, like all medieval authors, constructed his works by rewriting older texts. All the pilgrims are like Jankyn reading from his book of wicked wives: although they are given distinctive personalities in the *General Prologue* and the links between the tales, these personalities are always subsumed by the tales they tell, which make up by far the larger portion of the *Tales* as a whole. Certainly, the individual tales are suited to the tellers' distinct personalities as they have previously been developed (though perhaps less fully than Lumiansky believed);[51] but besides expressing the tellers' personalities, the tales also allow the tellers to absent themselves, to substitute fictions for their own presence. Hence the many disclaimers:

> But first I make a protestacioun
> That I am dronke, I knowe it by my soun;
> And therfore if that I mysspeke or seye,
> Wyte it the ale of Southwerk, I you preye; (I/A, 3137–40)

> Thise been the cokkes wordes, and nat myne; (VII, 3265/B, *4455)

> I were right now of tales desolaat,
> Nere that a marchant, goon is many a yeere,
> Me taughte a tale, which that ye shal heere. (II/B1, 131–33)

Many more examples might be cited, including the narrator's frequent apologies and assertions that he is merely a reporter, concerning the *Tales* as a whole. The tale allows the teller precisely *not* to be present in it; it allows the expression of his or her personality, which could be offensive if presented directly, precisely through its stated absence. The individual tales, though represented as having been orally delivered, are thus texts, and must be distinguished carefully from the conversational interludes that punctuate them. Those conversations represented in *The Canterbury Tales* in which both parties are present as themselves, speaking in their own voices, are notably lacking in the sympathy and mutual understanding achieved in the central conversation of *The Book of the Duchess*, or the love scenes in *Troilus and Criseyde*, or represented by the Wife as having been attained by her and Jankyn. Much more frequently they are rancorous and malicious, confirming each party in his or her own prejudiced view of the other, and of the world. Reeve and Miller; Parson, Host, and Shipman; Pardoner and Wife; Friar and Summoner; Clerk and Wife; Host and Pardoner; Host and Chaucer; Host and Monk; Monk and Knight; Canon's Yeoman and Canon; Host, Cook, and Manciple—in none of these cases does communication take place, despite the presence of each pilgrim to the others. Paradoxically, it is only in telling tales from which they can absent themselves, and consequently in treating one another as interpretable texts, that the pilgrims can make any impression on one another.

We can use the Wife's interpretations as a model. Although she transforms the Biblical passages she quotes by interpreting them, she has also internalized them and thus preserved them: she may reject Christ's words to the Samaritan or Paul's admonitions against personal ornament, but she must quote them in order to do so. In a way, she has become a preaching handbook,[52] a compendium of Scriptural passages taken out of context and rearranged by topic. The Wife's incorporation of the very texts she wishes to challenge is even clearer in the case of the antifeminist tradition represented by Jankyn's book: in lines 713–85 she summarizes the book's contents, and incidentally the antifeminist history of the world from Eve (line 715) to a contemporary murder of husband by wife (lines 765–68).[53] Indeed, it is a critical commonplace that the Wife is an embodiment of the very tradition she argues against, that the course her argument takes serves to confirm the antifeminist tradition. The Wife may reinterpret Scriptural passages or destroy an antifeminist text, but again, to do so requires that she internalize them first. To a degree, the Wife becomes the texts she seeks to subvert.

The same process can be observed in the pilgrims' mutual interpretations that structure the entire *Canterbury Tales*. The rancorous arguments that they have with one another are also played out textually, in their revisions of one another's tales. Thus the tales stand in for their tellers in relation to the other pilgrims; instead of arguing with their enemies, the pilgrims take revenge by "rewriting" their enemies' tales. These rewritings, however, also preserve the text being rewritten as the Wife's argument against Jankyn's book also preserves it, and indeed as most medieval works preserve the previous works that they also modify or even attack.[54]

The best example of this phenomenon is to be found in the sequence of tales that Kittredge called "the Discussion of Marriage."[55] According to Kittredge, both the Clerk's and the Merchant's tales are replies to the Wife's, each presenting a view of marriage radically unlike hers. Both specifically absent themselves from their tales: the Clerk learned his story from "Fraunceys Petrak" (IV/E, 31), and so has no personal stake in it, while the Merchant claims that he will not speak "of myn owene soore" (IV/E, 1243). If they refuse presence to themselves in their own tales, they do not refuse it to the Wife of Bath: the Clerk refers to her in lines 1170–71 of his own tale and devotes his Envoy to an ironic restatement of her views. Ironic though it may be, in view of the story of Patient Griselda that precedes it, the Envoy nevertheless repeats point for point the Wife's own argument:

> For which heere, for the Wyves love of Bathe—
> Whos lyf and al hire secte God mayntene
> In heigh maistrie, and elles were it scathe—
> I wol with lusty herte, fressh and grene,
> Seyn yow a song to glade yow, I wene;
> And lat us stynte of ernestful matere. (IV/E, 1170–75)

The Clerk revises the Wife for his own purposes but in doing so also preserves her arguments.

The Merchant begins his own tale by quoting the last line of the Clerk's Envoy:

> Wepyng and waylyng, care and oother sorwe
> I knowe ynogh, on even and a-morwe. (IV/E, 1213–14)

His *Prologue* also refers to the Clerk's tale of Griselda in line 1224, which is thus preserved even as it is refuted, and his tale refers to the Wife of Bath directly:

> The Wyf of Bathe, if ye han understonde,
> Of mariage, which we have on honde,
> Declared hath ful wel in litel space. (IV/E, 1685–97)

Even as he is refuting her view, the Merchant reminds his audience of it, not only in these lines but in many verbal echoes throughout the tale. Something similar happens in other sequences of tales as well: it has often been noted that the Knight's, Miller's, Reeve's, and Cook's tales are all variations on one another,[56] and another such pattern has been discerned in the Wife-Friar-Summoner sequence.[57] Many of the pilgrims can be recognized in the Parson's disquisition on the Seven Deadly Sins and repentance,[58] and indeed not only each of the *Tales* but Chaucer's entire poetic output receives similar treatment in the *Retraction:* the author simultaneously rejects and catalogues his previous works, so that the "sinful" ones are retracted and memorialized at a single stroke (the *Book of the Lion*, in fact, is preserved *only* in its retraction). One aspect of textuality that *The Canterbury Tales* emphasizes is thus its ability to be preserved and repeated, what Derrida calls its "iterability." It allows for the extraordinary intertextuality of most medieval writing, such as Chaucer's own simultaneous quotation and revision of Boccaccio's *Filostrato* in *Troilus and Criseyde*. This intertextuality is also the basis for the Canterbury pilgrims' treatment of one another's tales.

The Canterbury Tales, then, presents a model of verbal interaction very different from those of either *The Book of the Duchess* or St. John's Gospel. The direct conversation, or successful oral communication, that those works present as a difficult but desirable goal to be achieved, is here shown to be a failure, as the pilgrims' arguments serve to reinforce their various solipsisms rather than to communicate anything new. Indeed, Chaucer's presentation of interpretation here goes beyond even the more positive implications it gained at the end of *Troilus and Criseyde*: it is no longer a response that can lead the reader outside the text into secular or spiritual "real life" but has itself become a condition of real life. Involvement in textuality is now identified with involvement in the world. Textuality and interpretation, which seem to be such dead ends in earlier texts, leading only to solipsism or incomprehension, are here presented as a normal mode of human interaction: the Wife may disagree with Jankyn's texts but clearly understands them, as the Clerk in his own disagreement understands the Wife. The pilgrims avoid solipsism in their mutual interpretations as the narrator of *The Book of the Duchess* does not, because in *The Canterbury Tales* interpretation is shown to be a process that never ends. The Miller's "rewriting" of

The Knight's Tale is itself rewritten in The Reeve's Tale, which apparently was to be rewritten in turn by the Cook. The same is true of the other sequences of tales, and indeed of the pilgrimage as a whole, which is rewritten in two different ways by the Parson and in the Retraction: none of the pilgrims is allowed simply to impose his or her own point of view as the true one; all are in a constant state of revision and reinterpretation, reflecting medieval textual mouvance. The narrator of The Book of the Duchess simply accepts Alcione's reading of her dream and self-destructively sympathizes with it; he tells his own audience that they cannot possibly understand his dream-vision correctly. Nowhere is that audience invited to participate in the text's re-creation as it frequently is in The Canterbury Tales:

> And therfore, whoso list it nat yheere,
> Turne over the leef and chese another tale;
> For he shal fynde ynowe, grete and smale,
> Of storial thyng that toucheth gentillesse,
> And eek moralitee and hoolynesse.
> Blameth nat me if that ye chese amys. (I/A, 3176–81)

In passages like this one, the speaker abdicates the creation of his own text to the reader or audience, inviting them not only to interpret but to re-create the text entirely on their own terms, in his absence. The poem is not to be seen as an inviolable whole but as what it is, a collection of fragments that we can rearrange and thus reinterpret at will (as all the critics and editors who argue over the "correct" order of the tales have in fact always done, when the narrator has explicitly stated that the tales' ordering is up to the reader).[59]

We are to treat The Canterbury Tales as its pilgrims treat one another: as texts to be simultaneously preserved and violated, accepted and interpreted. The Tales represents its characters in the process of reification: they turn before our eyes from the historical people on whom some of them are based,[60] into "realistic" characters who converse and argue with one another in rhyme, and then into texts, preserved and interpreted by one another like the writing that, at the most basic level, they really are. The poet himself is subject to a similar process, as Leicester and Ferster have argued: "the poem creates the poet."[61] As writing, they are all available to the interpretations of later readers like us; and especially as manuscript writing, they were available to textual violation like that performed by the Wife upon Jankyn's book. Gellrich points out that meaning shifts from the narrator's voice to "other sources of meaning,"[62] and one such source is the reader.

As long as this process continues, there is no danger of the solipsism evident in *The Book of the Duchess:* no one reading or writing about the *Tales* can feel that his or her reading is final.[63]

Chaucer seems to have abandoned his earliest model of verbal interaction as inappropriate to a writer, that is, to one who would necessarily be absent from most of his readers; direct communication can be represented in a text, but a text can never participate in it. One of the many achievements of *The Canterbury Tales* is that it accepts textuality and interpretability as normal and even shows them to be positive qualities. The *Tales'* vision of human interaction is not at all a humanistic one like that of *The Book of the Duchess* or even of *Troilus and Criseyde.* Whereas the Black Knight, like Jesus in the Gospel of John, moves beyond textuality to direct contact with another person, and whereas *Troilus and Criseyde* can be seen as directing the reader outside the text, *The Canterbury Tales* reverses the process, making interaction indirect and textually mediated. People *are* texts in *The Canterbury Tales*, to be revised and interpreted (rather than merely communicated with), if its readers are open to textualizing their own experience, to entering the textual play, as medieval readers did by writing further tales, and thus themselves becoming texts for further interpretation.[64] *The Canterbury Tales* goes even further than Machaut's *Voir-Dit.* Whereas Machaut's book concerns itself only with what goes on inside the text, Chaucer's suggests that everything that goes on in the world is itself already a text—not a divine, authoritative text like that of the earlier Middle Ages, but one open to constant revision and interpretation.

Our participation in this process is invited not only by the narrator but by one of the tale-telling pilgrims as well. Kittredge suggested that the Discussion of Marriage is concluded by the Franklin, although he does not refer directly to the previous debaters as both the Clerk and the Merchant do.[65] The real conclusion, however, may lie not in the supposed equality of the marriage the *The Franklin's Tale* describes, but in the fact that his tale does not really conclude at all, ending with an invitation to interpretation:

> Lordynges, this question, thanne, wol I aske now,
> Which was the mooste fre, as thynketh yow?
> Now telleth me, er that ye ferther wende.
> I kan namoore; my tale is at an ende. (V/F, 1621–24)

One is reminded of Marie de France's similar conclusion to "Chaitivel": the meaning of the tale will depend upon which of several possible perspectives the interpreter brings to it. Like Marie's narrator, the Franklin refuses to choose. What his *jeu-parti* invites is not simple interpretation but a multiplicity of interpretations; any one that the reader supplies can be, he recognizes, complemented or contradicted by several others. One is reminded more strongly of Nicole Oresme's supplementing of Buridan's explanations of natural phenomena with other equally plausible ones, in order to restore mystery to the created universe. In his own way, Chaucer restores such mystery to the world of human behavior.

Not only the tale itself but any response to it thus becomes a text for further interpretation in an endless chain. In these circumstances, neither communication nor solipsism, as we saw them in *The Book of the Duchess*, is possible. Absence has become a source of pleasure rather than a threat. It does not communicate—*The Canterbury Tales* reminds us that communication is not the true function of a text—but it does invite participation in its textuality. This textuality is not distinct from normal human experience, as it is in Machaut's game/text; rather, and most appropriately in the period after William of Ockham, it is a condition of life.[66]

5

Alterity and Interpretation: From
La Mort le roi Artu to Malory's Closing Books

Several of the preceding chapters touch on the related issues of historical truth and the accurate transmission of knowledge: from Marie de France's assertion that even her most fabulous narratives commemorate true events of the past to the difficulties that *Troilus and Criseyde*'s narrator has in understanding his source and in explaining it to his audience, the writers I consider claim that, at least to some extent, they are writing works of history, and that the temporal distance of the events they recount makes such an undertaking highly problematic. In this chapter, I examine two Arthurian prose romances that exemplify this problem much more directly and completely than most. The first is a French work of the thirteenth century, *La Mort le roi Artu* (or *Mort Artu*), the final section of the prose *Lancelot* (or Vulgate Cycle). The second is largely derived from it: Sir Thomas Malory's fifteenth-century English "reduction" of it and other works in the two closing books of his *Morte Darthur*, identified in the Winchester manuscript as *The Book of Sir Launcelot and Queen Guinevere* and *The Most Piteous Tale of the Morte Arthur Saunz Guerdon* (or *Morte Arthur*).

The thirteenth-century and the fifteenth-century work both exemplify the difficulty of filling in the phenomenological blanks left by the passage of time, a problem also raised by recent literary theorists with regard to the difficulties inevitably encountered by a modern reader attempting to understand literary works of a much earlier period. "Alterity," the otherness of mentalities not our own—especially the essential difference of mentalities historically distant from ours—means that we can never experience medieval literature as its original audience did; its meaning can never be the same for us.[1] This is precisely the problem confronted in the *Mort Artu* and by Malory, and this chapter examines how their respective attempts to deal with alterity draw the reader into the hermeneutic circle. It happens differently in these two works at least in part because of the cultural changes occurring between the thirteenth and the fifteenth centuries. Chapter 3 touches on the impact of similar changes as it moves from Marie to Machaut, but that impact should be even clearer here: the *Mort Artu* and Malory's closing books are of the same genre, and indeed the former served as the main source of the latter, so that Malory's modifications of the earlier material are all the more striking.

The *Mort Artu* is preceded in the prose *Lancelot* by *La Queste del saint Graal*, whose mode of signification and the interpretive method it requires are discussed in some detail in chapter 2. The *Mort Artu* can easily be seen as marking a transition between the essentially neoplatonic attitude of the *Queste* and Malory's more ambiguous and indeterminate work. Signification is much more problematic for its characters than for those in the *Queste*: the *Mort Artu* lacks the God-inspired holy men and women who explain the spiritual meaning of the *Queste*; and indeed the divine immanence that transforms the *Queste*'s chivalric world, giving it a consistent metaphorical meaning simultaneous with the literal, does not appear in the *Mort Artu*, whose characters, though constantly interpreting, do so only on the literal level.[2] On the other hand, the *Mort Artu* shares with the *Queste* an apparent omniscience lacking in Malory's narrative; although its characters may not succeed in understanding the truth about their lives, the text itself claims (and the validity of this claim is one topic I will investigate) a clearer view, as well as the ability to impart it to the reader, unlike Malory's narrator, who frankly admits that he cannot share certain essential pieces of information because he simply does not have them. "Li contes," the source-tale, claims to be an authority that provides a complete picture in the *Queste* and the *Mort Artu*, with few phenomenological blanks, whereas Malory's narrator, despite his many appeals to the "French book," at times finds only blanks that he cannot fill.

Although the *Mort Artu* does not go as far as Malory in emphasizing the necessity for the reader's participation in creating meaning, it does go much further than the *Queste* in problematizing the nature of interpretation. It predates the controversies surrounding Ockham and his followers, whose influence we have traced in earlier chapters; their questioning of certainty and of such concepts as causality had not yet taken place, as it had when Malory wrote, and it is therefore not surprising to find such questions reflected to a lesser degree in the *Mort Artu*. On the other hand, Abelard's reflections on the relation between signs and meaning were already exerting their influence, as was his "ethic of intentions," as well as the rhetoricians' emphasis on expression and on surface rather than on hidden meaning, on words rather than the Word. The author of the *Mort Artu* could not share the very late medieval *mentalité* available to Malory, but that of his own period made possible a concern with the nature of knowledge and interpretation in a world deprived of divine immanence.[3]

One area where these differences can be charted is in the two romances' shared representation of the attempt to describe accurately events that occurred in the past. It is of course only a representation of that project; the Arthurian subject-matter is not literally historical, despite the *Mort Artu*'s elaborate attempts to authenticate itself with reference to its own textual genealogy and production[4] (not unlike Machaut's problematization[5] of "truth," though with a different effect). It is an even riskier project for Malory's narrator: since the possibility of any certain knowledge was called into question more radically in the fourteenth century than ever before in the Middle Ages, knowledge of a distant past may have come to seem especially problematic by the fifteenth. These difficulties created by alterity are of less concern in the *Mort Artu*, though its spurious self-presentation as an historical document creates a different kind of difficulty in historical understanding.

Chapter 5 serves several purposes. First, whereas chapter 4 examines the general problem of textuality in the many different forms it takes in Chaucer's works, this chapter narrows the focus to one specific problem, alterity, within that larger one. Second, it illustrates how the changing cultural context allows a development in the presentation of the ambiguity of signification, which becomes more complete in the later work. Finally, the consideration of Malory will bring us to the very end of the Middle Ages, a chronologically fitting conclusion to our investigations.

The Reader and Textual Omniscience in the Mort Artu

The *Mort Artu* raises the question of meaning most obviously by means of the many epitaphs and other written texts it incorporates. The textual status of these inscriptions is clear: they are fixed writing (literally carved in stone, in the case of the epitaphs) that seeks to preserve authoritative truths, summing up an event, a life, or especially a death. As we have seen in our examination of Chaucer's narratives, however, written texts, precisely because they exist independently of a speaker, are also liable to misinterpretation; the very attempt to make a fixed, unalterable statement in writing allows the alterations in meaning that inevitably come with reading.

The first of many such epitaphs is that of Gaheris:

ICI GIST GAHERIZ LI BLANS DE KARAHEU, LI FRERES MADOR DE LA PORTE, QUE LA REINE FIST MORIR PAR VENIM. (78)[5]

This text is literally true: the queen did give Gaheris the poisoned fruit that caused his death. It gives rise, however, to two quite different interpretations. Mador de la Porte, the dead knight's brother, asks if the epitaph is true and receives this answer from an anonymous knight: "vos voulez que ge vos die se ce est voirs que la reïne ait ocis vostre frere; sachiez que il est einsi comme li escriz le tesmoigne" (84).[6] Mador, seeking legal redress, then makes his formal charge to the king: "Sire, or vos requier ge comme a roi que vos me faciez droit de la reïne qui en traïson a ocis mon frere; et se ele le velt noier et mesconnoistre, que ele traïson n'ait fete et desloiauté, je seroie prez del prouver contre le meilleur chevalier que ele i vodra metre" (85).[7] Gawain, though he agrees with the epitaph's statement, interprets it differently: "Or creroie ge bien que Mador fust en mauvese querele; car comment que ses freres moreust, je jurroie seur seinz au mien escient qu'onques la reïne n'i pensa desloiauté ne traïson" (104).[8] Here not only the epitaph, but the action it commemorates—Guinevere's poisoning of Gaheris—is treated as a text to be interpreted. The question of Guinevere's guilt or innocence, and hence of the meaning of the epitaph, hinges on her intentions; meaning is thus linked with motive. Lancelot, as Guinevere's champion, proves in a trial by battle against Mador that she is indeed innocent, but the reader, unlike the knights, has known this all along, having been informed of her good intentions unequivocally by the text itself: "La reïne prist le fruit, qui de la traïson ne se gardoit; si en dona a un chevalier qui estoit compains de la Table Reonde et avoit non Gaheris de Karaheu" (76).[9] The problematic nature of verbal meaning is suggested here, but the reader who accepts the text's authority does not experience it as a problem in his or her encounter with the text itself; it is only a represented problem, whose solution the reader knows before any character except Guinevere herself. Whether or not the text should be accorded such authority is another issue, to be taken up below.

R. Howard Bloch has suggested that this concern with intentions is not reflected in thirteenth-century French law: "Nus hom doit soffrir painne de sa pensée."[10] It is, however, clearly reflected in the romance itself and in Abelard's ethical system, which predates the *Mort Artu* by a century. The ethic of intentions is another twelfth-century innovation that almost inevitably produces a corollary emphasis on interpretation in the literature of later centuries: unlike actions, intentions cannot be known with certainty by any observer except God. They must be deduced from external signs that, as in Guinevere's case, may be misleading.

The same point can be made about a number of other epitaphs:

CI GIST GAHERIET, LI NIÉS LE ROI ARTU, QUE LANCELOS DEL
LAC OCIST; (133)

CI GIST LUCANS LI BOUTEILLIERS QUI LI ROIS ARTUS ESTEINST
DESOUZ LUI. (251)[11]

The meaning of each is ambiguous; Gawain believes that Lancelot intentionally murdered his brother Gaheriet (despite his earlier, accurate reading of
the epitaph accusing Guinevere), and Lucan's epitaph implies that Arthur
was his murderer, though neither inscription makes such an interpretation
necessary. Another "epitaph," the letter written by the Escalot maiden to
be found with her corpse, does direct its readers to a specific interpretation:
"ge sui morte por le plus preudome del monde et por le plus vilain: ce est
Lancelos del Lac, qui est li plus vilains que ge sache, car onques ne le soi
tant prier o pleurs et o lermes que il volsist de moi avoir merci; si m'en a
tant esté au cuer que g'en sui a ma fin venue por amer loiaument" (89–90).[12]
In all these cases, however, the reader can supply a different and less
accusatory interpretation; we know, for example, that the action that re-
sulted in Lucan's death was intended as an expression of love: "il prent
Lucan qui desarmez estoit et l'embrace et l'estraint, si qu'il li crieve le cuer
el ventre, si qu'onques ne li lut parole dire, einz li parti l'ame del cors. Et
quant li rois a grant piece esté einsi, si le let, car il ne cuide mie qu'il soit
morz" (247).[13] Similarly, we know that Lancelot killed Gaheriet not "en
traïson" but because he failed to recognize him, and that he refused to love
the Escalot maiden not out of cruelty but because of his commitment to
Guinevere. In all these cases, the meaning of a written text within the text
is ambiguous to those who do not know the intentions and motives behind
the actions it describes; the reader, however, is in a position to assert the
one correct interpretation, which can be found by juxtaposing the epitaph
itself with the earlier narration of the actions it describes. Interpretation is
thus a metonymic process for the reader of the *Mort Artu:* true meanings
can be found, not by means of a metaphorical substitution, as in allegory,
but by completing the partial truth found in the written text by comparing
the ambiguous passage with an earlier and fuller version of the same events.
The earlier, definitive narrative must be associated in the reader's mind
with its later, ambiguous summary. The reader must be actively engaged
in this process rather than accepting ambiguities at their face value; and such
engagement is usually rewarded with a definitive reading.[14] Omniscience
concerning human intentions is available only to God in the ethic of intentions; in the *Mort Artu*, it is also available to the reader.

Another of the *Mort Artu*'s sign-systems, and one that is closely related to that of the written texts within the text, is the legal system of trial by battle. It is designed, as we saw in chapter 1, to reveal the truth in an ambiguous situation, physical success in battle signifying legal innocence, the assumption being that God will not allow the innocent to be defeated or the guilty to triumph. It is an essentially metaphorical or even allegorical procedure, as hidden moral worth is revealed publicly by a proportionate physical ability. As Bloch has shown, however, the *Mort Artu* condemns this system of correspondences and demonstrates its inadequacy in signifying guilt or innocence in complex moral circumstances. The ambiguity of Gaheris's epitaph, for example, reflects the ambiguity of Guinevere's legal situation, what Bloch calls "involuntary manslaughter, an ambiguous mixture of guilt in deed and innocence of intent which defies the legal mechanism of Arthur's court."[15] Although Lancelot's defense of Guinevere in battle proves publicly what the reader knows to be true, the innocence of her intentions, Lancelot himself could not know this psychological fact for sure and therefore risks perjury. As Bloch seems unwilling to admit, however, this trial is indeed successful: Mador's accusation, which states that the queen's intentions as well as her actions were guilty, is false, and Lancelot's success in the battle, whether attributable to God's judgment or his own chivalric prowess, is justified.[16] God's judgment and Lancelot's prowess, in fact, coincide with each other and with the reader's perspective, which shares divine omniscience concerning the facts of this case.

A more difficult case is Lancelot's self-defense against Gawain's accusation that he treacherously and intentionally murdered Gawain's brothers. Bloch has pointed out that this accusation is quite true: the reader witnesses Lancelot's ambush of the party assigned to prevent him from rescuing the queen after she has been condemned to death for adultery and specifically witnesses his desire to kill Gawain's brother Agravain, who engineered the plot against the lovers.[17] Gawain charges Lancelot first with "la mort de mes freres que vos oceïstes en traïson" (189) and repeats a similar formula to the king: "Sire, veez me ci prest de prouver que Lancelos ocist desloiaument mes freres" (191).[18] Lancelot's denial of the charge does not really answer it: he names one brother, Gaheriet, whom he did indeed kill in the ambush, though without recognizing him: "vos jurrai seur seinz que onques au mien escient n'ocis Gaheriet vostre frere et que plus m'en pesa qu'il ne fu bel" (191).[19] Gawain's accusation did not name a specific brother but referred generally to "mes freres"; Lancelot himself recognizes that this more general charge is true, and that therefore his own cause is unjust: "moult doutoit qu'il ne li mescheïst envers monseigneur Gauvain por la mort de ses freres qu'il avoit ocis" (194).[20] Nevertheless, Lancelot wins the battle, and not only through a technicality (as Bloch suggests):[21] although Arthur intervenes and stops the battle, declaring Lancelot the winner, the text has already stated that Gawain, despite his miraculous increase in strength at noon, was exhausted by evening, while Lancelot was still strong: "et lors fu tant messire Gauvains traveilliez qu'a peinne puet il tenir s'espee; et Lancelos, qui n'estoit mie trop las et qui pooit encore soufrir, giete seur lui cox et le meinne une eure avant et autre arriere" (201).[22] It seems clear that Lancelot wins the battle—and obscures the truth—despite the injustice (or, at least, the ambiguity) of his cause, simply because of his greater strength. The truth remains concealed; the trial by battle, as a signifying system, has failed.

It is true that Lancelot may not be entirely guilty, at least as charged; Gawain's grief is almost exclusively for Gaheriet, the one brother Lancelot clearly did not intend to kill, and it may well be Gaheriet that he specifically has in mind when making the accusation (despite his use of the oblique plural construction "mes freres"). But in either case, the trial's outcome conceals some part of the truth: Lancelot is indeed guilty of ambushing the guards as a group, including Agravain, Gaheriet, and Gawain's third brother Guerrehet, and is specifically guilty of the intentional killing of Agravain. But he is to some extent innocent of the intentional murder of Gaheriet (as must be taken into account when interpreting the dead knight's epitaph). No matter what the outcome, the trial by battle with its either-or judgments cannot reveal these nuances in the truth, important though they are; it cannot reveal degrees of guilt or innocence. To some extent, it must in this case signify falsely or ambiguously.

Once again, however, this is not true of the romance itself as a signifying system for the reader. By the time the trial takes place, it has already revealed the truth in all its subtlest nuances: we know exactly which brother was Lancelot's intended victim, and which killing was a mistake. We therefore know just to what extent Gawain's accusation is true, and to what extent it is false. The omniscient reader can supply the motives and intentions—the truth—that the trial cannot reveal. As in the *Chanson de Roland*, phenomenological blanks in the characters' experiences can be filled in by the reader's experience of the literary work.[23] The metaphorical method of interpretation used by Arthur's legal system is inadequate to the task of truthful signification; the reader must supplement it with the same metonymic process necessary to the proper interpretation of the epitaphs: the reader must mentally connect the wording of the characters' legal charges and denials with the more complete version of the events that is preserved elsewhere in the text. This is true not only of the trials by battle but of Agravain's attempted capture of Lancelot and Guinevere in the act of adultery. Bloch has demonstrated the unsatisfactory legal outcome of this attempt: although Agravain's suspicions are correct, circumstances (the locked door that gives the lovers time to dress) and Lancelot's physical superiority to his attackers prevent his being taken.[24] His escape might be interpreted as God's verdict that he is innocent; but in a world like the *Mort Artu*'s, which lacks divine immanence, such an inference is not justified, especially because the text itself has already stated generally that Lancelot "rencheï el pechié de la reïne" (3) on his return from the grail quest, and specifically that he "se deschauça et despoilla et se coucha avec la reïne" (115) on this occasion.[25] The characters cannot be sure of the truth, but once again, the text claims that it, and therefore the reader, can. Failures of systems designed to reveal the truth within the text can nevertheless apparently be rectified for the reader by the semiology of the text itself. The narrative is not limited to any merely human perspective; not a narrator, but "li contes" itself tells the story, as in the *Queste* ("Or dit li contes," 119 etc.).[26] "Li contes" in its omniscience claims to preserve the truth about these past events, and to impart it to any reader willing to engage in the metonymic process of interpretation. It should be noted, however, that this text does not share in the divine guarantees of meaning that characterize the *Queste*. The fact that it is merely a *conte*, rather than a holy hermit or angel, that guarantees meaning for the reader may alert us to the continued competition between the determinate truth being claimed and the indeterminate conflict of interpretations being represented. The two modes, determinate and indeterminate, coexist in this romance much more clearly than in the *Queste*.

Lancelot as Text

Formal, verbal constructs such as epitaphs and legal charges are clearly textual and interpretable in nature, but it may be less obvious that Lancelot himself takes on textual status in the course of the romance. Although the *Mort Artu*'s characters cannot always fill in the phenomenological blanks in their experience (as the reader can, if the text's authority is accepted), they never stop trying to do so; many aspects of their world are treated as mysterious texts requiring interpretation. That Lancelot is such a text is suggested at the beginning of the romance, in the episode of the Winchester tournament. Lancelot deliberately fosters the false signs that make accurate interpretation difficult: "Mes Lancelot, qui i beoit a estre en tel maniere que nus nel conneüst, dist a ceus qui entor lui estoient qu'il estoit si deshetiez que il n'i porroit aler en nule maniere" (4); "il ne vouloit pas de jorz chevauchier, qu'il ne fust conneüz par aventure. Quant il vint desoz le chastel, il chevaucha si enbrons que a peinne le peüst l'en connoistre" (7).[27] No motive is suggested for this behavior, though it is not an uncommon motif in medieval romance.[28] It has the effect of turning the other knights, especially Gawain, into readers of Lancelot's text, and thus into figures of the interpreting reader of the *Mort Artu* itself: " 'Sire, par mon chief, cil chevaliers a ces armes vermeilles qui porte la manche seur son hiaume n'est pas li chevaliers que ge cuidoie; einz est uns autres, certeinnement le vos di . . . .' 'Et qui cuidiez vos,' fet li rois, 'que ce soit?' 'Ne sai, sire,' fet messire Gauvains, 'mes il est trop preudom' " (15).[29]

Gawain remains the most dogged pursuer of the truth behind the various surfaces that Lancelot presents to the world throughout the romance. "Pursuer," in fact, is a literally accurate description of Gawain's function in many episodes, because Lancelot's location is frequently as mysterious as his identity (and is sometimes linked with it). Gawain's pursuit of the disguised Lancelot after the Winchester tournament is only the first instance of a frequently recurring motif: "messire Gauvains dit que l'en li amaint son cheval, car il voudra aler savoir qui cil chevaliers est por soi acointier de lui; et ausi dist Gaheriez" (18).[30] Sometimes Gawain knows that it is Lancelot he seeks, while at other times he does not; sometimes he is accompanied or replaced by other knights: Gaheriet, Hector, Bors. In the desire Lancelot awakens in others to find him or to identify him, in the determination with which he is pursued, in the frequent fruitlessness of the search, Lancelot begins to seem analogous to the Holy Grail in the prose *Lancelot*'s preceding branch, *La Queste del saint Graal*: both present mysterious signs, causing a desire to reveal the truth about them.

The truth about Lancelot, however, is psychological and social rather than allegorical. His motives and intentions are the key to accurate interpretation needed by those, both within the text and outside it, who would read him. Lancelot's textuality, and the difficulty of interpreting him, are indicated most clearly in his function as Guinevere's lover. Much of the interpretive activity engaged in by the rest of the characters seeks to answer such questions as: Who is it that Lancelot loves? What does the answer to that question reveal about his fulfillment of the function of courtly lover? Of loyal vassal? Many characters speculate about these questions, but they are of most concern to Arthur and to Guinevere herself, who both conform to a pattern of suspicion, interpretation, and appeasement in their attempts to read Lancelot.[31]

Arthur is established as a reader of Lancelot in the well-known episode of Arthur's visit to Morgan's castle, where he sees the paintings done by Lancelot, with their explanatory text, when the latter was Morgan's prisoner. Words and images together tell the story of Lancelot's love for Guinevere; Arthur thus becomes, quite literally, a reader and interpreter of Lancelot's text:

> si avint que li rois commença a regarder entor lui et vit les paintures et les ymages que Lancelos avoit portretes tandis comme il demora leanz en prison. Li rois Artus savoit bien tant de letres qu'il pooit auques un escrit entendre; et quant il ot veües les letres des ymages qui devisoient les senefiances des portretures, si les conmença a lire, et tant que il connut apertement que cele chambre estoit peinte des oeuvres Lancelot et des chevaleries que il fist tant comme il estoit noviax chevaliers. . . . et quant il voit les ymages qui devisoient l'acointement Galeholt, si en fu touz esbahiz et touz trespansez; si commence a regarder ceste chose et dist a soi meïsmes tout basset: "Par foi," fet il, "se la senefiance de ces letres est veraie, donques m'a Lancelos honni de la reïne, car ge voit tout en apert que il s'en est acointiez; et se il est veritez einsi com ceste escriture le tesmoigne, ce est la chose qui me metra au greigneur duel que ge onques eüsse, que plus ne me pooit Lancelos avillier que de moi honnir de ma fame." (61)[32]

Arthur does not simply accept the pictures or the text as an authoritative truth but treats them as requiring interpretation ("se la senefiance de ces letres est veraie," "se il est veritez"), seeming to realize that signs and texts like this one may falsify the truth rather than revealing it. Even after Morgan has told him that Lancelot himself was the painter, Arthur finds other signs in Lancelot's behavior that suggest an opposite interpretation: "il li estoit avis que se Lancelos amast la reïne de fole amor, si comme l'en li metoit sus, il ne peüst pas la court tant eslongnier ne metre ariere dos tant comme il fesoit; et c'estoit une chose qui moult metoit le cuer le roi a aise et qui moult li fesoit mescroire les paroles que il ot oïes de Morgain sa sereur" (75).[33]

Arthur, indeed, is never able to arrive at any certain knowledge concerning Lancelot's relationship with Guinevere; the pattern exemplified in the scene at Morgan's castle, in which conflicting signs lead first to suspicion and then to appeasement, is repeated throughout the romance. Even after the war caused by Agravain's attempted capture of the lovers in bed together, the pope can induce Arthur to take the queen back, for lack of evidence:

> quant li apostoles ot oï que on ne l'avoit pas prise provee el meffait que
> on li metoit sus, si manda as arcevesques et as esvesques del païs que
> toute la terre que li rois Artus tenoit fust entredite et en escommunica-
> tion, se il ne reprenoit sa fame. . . . Quant li rois ot ce mandement, si
> fu moult courrouciez; et nonpourquant il amoit la roïne de si grant
> amour, tot quidast il bien qu'ele li eüst meffait, que il fu legierement
> vaincus. (153)[34]

If Lancelot is a text requiring interpretation, accurate readings of him are
made difficult by the multiplicity of his conflicting signs. In the absence of
certainty, Arthur must settle for interpretation.

Guinevere, too, is an active reader of Lancelot, and the difficulty of
deducing his true intentions from signs is emphasized in the aftermath of
the Winchester tournament, which records various speculations on the
identity of the disguised knight. Lancelot is disguised at the tournament
not only by his armor but also by the lady's favor that he wears on his
helmet, a sleeve belonging to the Escalot maiden. He wears it with some
annoyance, having been tricked into accepting it. Attempts to identify him
at the tournament are focused on the sleeve, as in Gawain's speculations,
quoted above; but the most direct link between his motivation in wearing
the sleeve and his supposed lover's identity is drawn after the tournament,
when Gawain reports the incident to Guinevere. Gawain himself has
learned who wore the sleeve from the maiden who gave it and has drawn
the obvious, though erroneous, conclusion about Lancelot's motive. He
tells the Escalot maiden that "ge le crois ores mieuz, que il vos aint par
amors, que ge ne fis onques mes, car autrement n'eüst il mie portee tele
enseigne" (27).[35] When reporting on the tournament to the queen, Gawain
conceals what he believes to be the truth (assuming that this is what Lancelot
wants) but does tell her of the mysterious knight with the sleeve: "Et lors
pensa meintenant la reïne que ce ne fu mie Lancelos, car ele ne cuidoit pas
qu'il portast a tornoiement nule enseigne, s'ele ne li eüst bailliee" (31).[36]
Guinevere here draws the essential connection between the knight's identity and that of his lover. It takes another knight's intervention and Gawain's
oath, however, before she can be convinced that the unknown knight was
Lancelot; she then questions, not the sign's meaning, but her lover's fidelity:

> Lors saut avant Girflez et dist a la reïne: "Dame, sachiez veraiement
> que cil as armes vermeilles qui porta la manche desus son hiaume fu
> Lancelos." (31)

> "Messire Gauvain," fet la reïne, "cuidiez vos que il die voir? Par la foi
> que vos devez monseigneur le roi, dites moi ce que vos en savez, se il

est einsi que vos en sachiez nul riens." "Dame," fet il, "vos m'avez tant conjuré que ge ne vos en celeroie riens que g'en seüsse; je vos di veraiement que ce fu il, ses cors meïsmes, qui ot armes vermeilles et qui porta la manche seur son hiaume et veinqui le tournoiement." Et quant la reïne entent ceste parole, si s'en test atant et s'en entre en sa chambre lermoiant des euz del chief. (31–32)[37]

Both Gawain and Guinevere function as interpreters in this sequence of events. The Escalot maiden's sleeve serves as an interpretable sign; Gawain's assumption that it indicates Lancelot's love for the maiden, and Guinevere's initial belief that the knight who carried it could not be Lancelot, are both misreadings that demonstrate the extent to which Lancelot's behavior makes interpretation necessary, as is Guinevere's belief in his infidelity once she learns the facts: "ele cuidoit veraiement que Lancelos amast cele qui manche il avoit portee au tournoiement et qu'il l'eüst lessiee" (32).[38] Lancelot's signs intentionally and unintentionally conceal his true motives; they make interpretation both necessary and extremely difficult.

As in the case of the verbal texts within the text, however, it is less difficult for the reader to interpret Lancelot than it is for the other characters, who do not share our privileged information. Thus even before the Winchester tournament takes place, we have been informed in the passage quoted above that Lancelot will attend it in disguise. "Li contes" also reports the circumstances that allow him to remain incognito: his secret departure from Camelot, his discovery of the unused red armor, the interview with the Escalot maiden that results in his wearing the famous sleeve, and his successful evasion of pursuit after the tournament (1–19). We cannot share the other knights' uneasiness about Lancelot's whereabouts, as we always know where he is (at the home of his companion's aunt, at the hermitage, and so on) as well as his physical and emotional state. We can judge Guinevere's jealousy to be based on a misinterpretation, because we have witnessed the Escalot maiden's manipulation of Lancelot, and therefore understand his motive for wearing the sleeve as Guinevere does not; nor can we share Arthur's wishful misreadings, as the text makes us aware of Lancelot's and Guinevere's sin from the beginning. The text would seem to claim that every attempt by a character to fill in the blanks can be judged by the reader who applies the metonymic procedure outlined above. As models for the actual readers' activity, the text's reader-figures are quite limited—as long as the text's authority is accepted.[39] The time has come, however, for a more detailed examination of the text's claims to provide the truth. Its concern with historical accuracy calls such claims into question, perhaps even more radically than its lack of any divine guarantee of meaning.

The Mort Artu *As "History"*

Because of the provisional omniscience that "li contes" shares with the reader, the *Mort Artu* itself may be regarded as an epitaph for Arthurian society (and to some extent for the genre of romance),[40] similar in intention to the individual epitaphs it records but more successful than they in recording and preserving the truth about past events. The title itself, *La Mort le roi Artu*, suggests this commemorative function as do the supposed circumstances of its composition that, referred to at the text's beginning and end, frame the events it records and give the romance a spurious historical status:

> Aprés ce que mestres Gautiers Map ot mis en escrit des *Aventures del Seint Graal* asez soufisanment si com li sembloit, si fu avis au roi Henri son seigneur que ce qu'il avoit fet ne devoit pas soufire, s'il ne ramentevoit la fin de ceus dont il avoit fet devant mention et conment cil morurent dont il avoit amenteües les proesces en son livre; et por ce commença il ceste derrienne partie. (1)

> Si se test ore atant mestre Gautiers Map de l'*Estoire de Lancelot*, car bien a tout mené a fin selonc les choses qui en avindrent, et fenist ci son livre si outreement que aprés ce n'en porroit nus riens conter qui n'en mentist de toutes choses. (263)[41]

Bloch has pointed out that the text also serves a function like that of the trials by battle and does so in a more satisfactory manner: "Both judicial and literary inquest, that of the courtroom and of the courtly novel, function to assure the displacement of the physical ordeal of battle toward a verbal and, eventually, written equivalent."[42]

Not only is the trial by battle's physical violence sublimated in language; the text, at least in its intentions, establishes the truth as the trials by battle represented within it do not. In this respect, the fixing of an authoritative truth about the events it records, the romance parallels a third kind of text within the text, the prophecy. Sometimes inscribed like epitaphs, prophecies in the *Mort Artu* record the truth about the future as the work itself records the past (and the prophetic future becomes the historical past in the course of the romance).

Gawain's behavior, for example, is fixed by two earlier prophecies: that which, at his baptism, predicted his miraculous increase of strength around noon (we witness an example of this prophecy's fulfillment in his battle with Lancelot), and the vision, recounted earlier in the prose *Lancelot*, that predicted the Arthur-Lancelot war and Gawain's own death. He is reminded of this vision in the *Mort Artu:* "Ore esgardez: ne vos souvient de ce que vos veïstes jadis el Palés Aventurex chiés le Riche Roi Pescheor, en celui point que vos veïstes la bataille del serpent et del liepart? S'il vos souvenist bien des merveilles que vos i veïstes et de la senefiance que li hermites vos devisa, ja ceste guerre ne fust, tant com vos la poïssiez dest-orner" (142).[43] Gawain's failure to heed the prophecy enables it to come true; he comes to seem reified, bound by authoritative texts at the beginning and end of his life. To some extent, the same is true of Arthur himself. The *Mort Artu*'s most striking prophecy is that inscribed by Merlin on a rock, which Arthur discovers years later on Salisbury Plain, on the eve of his final battle against Mordred:

EN CESTE PLAINGNE DOIT ESTRE LA BATAILLE MORTEL PAR QUOI LI ROIAUMES DE LOGRES REMEINDRA ORFELINS. (228)[44]

Unlike Gawain, Arthur makes no attempt to escape the prophecy but consciously chooses to fulfill it, despite the archbishop's attempt to dissuade him: "'Sire,' fet li rois Artus, 'g'en voi tant que, se ge ne fusse tant venuz avant, je retornasse, quel que talent que ge eüsse eü jusques ci. Mes or soit Jhesucrist en nostre aïde, car ge n'en partirai jamés jusques a tant que Nostre Sires en ait donee enneur a moi ou a Mordret'" (229).[45] Like the romance itself, these prophecies give an accurate and inescapable account of its characters' destiny; if Lancelot resembles, in his shifting signs and multiple interpretations, the epitaphs and trials whose true meaning can be judged only by the omniscient reader, Arthur and Gawain resemble instead these fixed prophecies, whose meaning leaves no room for doubt or escape.[46]

The goal of the text itself is to be similarly authoritative, to give the reader a fully accurate account of the events it depicts. We have seen that the reader does share with "li contes" a more omniscient view of those events than is possessed by any of the characters; it should now be appropriate to ask whether the text fully achieves its goal of a fixed, historical truth.

The prophecies' model of inescapable truth is associated with supernatural figures like Merlin, and even with divinity: Gawain's miraculous strength, we are told, is a form of God's grace, granted through the interces-

sion of the holy hermit who baptized him and made the prediction (197–
99). The epitaphs, which are merely human creations, and the Arthurian
legal system, which is shown to depend on human force rather than God's
justice, suggest a descent from the divine authority of the prophecies (and
of an allegorical romance like the *Mort Artu*'s predecessor in the prose
Lancelot, the *Queste del saint Graal*) to a merely human and fallible mode of
signification in a world without divine immanence. The text is an attempt
to regain some of that authority, at least in the realm of history, and to pass
on the truths it discovers to the reader. But like the epitaphs and legal
system it resembles, the text itself is a merely human creation, specifically
Walter Map's. It lacks the holy authority claimed by such texts as the *Estoire
del saint Graal* and the *Perlesvaus*.

Even at the stylistic level, the text subverts its own apparently rigid
causality. Despite the plot's emphasis on inescapable destiny, Jean Rychner
has demonstrated that causality is not syntactically emphasized:

> Il est remarquable que les relations logiques, l'hypothèse, la cause, la
> concession, le but, ne jouent qu'un rôle infime dans l'enchaînement
> des procès principaux; seule la conjonction *mais* y introduit plus
> souvent une démarche logique, d'ailleurs des plus légère et très peu
> chargée de modalité. La *Mort Artu* n'ignore bien sûr ni l'hypothèse, ni
> la conséquence, ni le but, mais, n'apparaissant pas à l'attaque de la
> phrase, ces relations se subordonnent aux relations fondamentales.[47]

Causality tends to appear within sentences rather than to link them together; each sentence is thus a distinct unit whose syntax severs causal
connections with other such units. Such causality must be assumed or
inferred if the romance is to make any sense; but it is the reader who must
assume or infer, and who is thus subtly activated. The text's syntax requires
the reader's conscious or unconscious participation in order for it to become
comprehensible; the reader must supply connections the text itself refuses
to make.

Beyond the stylistic level, two models of the *Mort Artu* within the text
itself suggest that the romance is not completely successful in its attempt
to avoid ambiguity; they place the reader in a position with regard to certain
narrated events similar to that occupied by the fictional reader-figures with
regard to the issues left unresolved by their attempts at interpretation, such
as the guilt or innocence of Lancelot and Guinevere. One such model is
Arthur's death. The text, as we have seen, announces itself as his epitaph;
its main concern is with Arthur's passing. It may thus be compared with
Arthur's actual epitaph, which it quotes:

CI GIST LI ROIS ARTUS QUI PAR SA VALEUR MIST EN SUBJECTION .XII. ROIAUMES. (251)[48]

This statement seems straightforward enough and is confirmed when Girflet questions the resident hermit: "'Sire, est il voirs que ci gist li rois Artus?' 'Oïl, biax amis, il i gist voirement; ci l'aporterent ne sai quex dames'" (251).[49]

And yet King Arthur is the only main character, despite the romance's title, whose death is not narrated directly, not witnessed by the reader; he is last seen through Girflet's eyes, boarding the boat full of ladies. This image inevitably recalls the myth of Arthur's survival in Avalon, which had acquired iconographic details similar to this account's (the presence of Morgan, for example) before the *Mort Artu*'s composition.[50] Once brought to mind, the myth cannot be dispelled by Girflet's discovery of the tomb, since no death scene has been narrated and especially since the reliability of epitaphs has been called into question all along. In interpreting other epitaphs, the reader has learned to look elsewhere in the text for a more definitive version of the truth than they supply; but we look for reliable information on Arthur's death in vain, finding only an equivocation at the beginning of the romance: "en la fin est escrit conment li rois Artus fu navrez en la bataille de Salebieres et conment il se parti de Girflet qui si longuement li fist compaignie que aprés lui ne fu nus hom qui le veïst vivant" (1).[51] The text here achieves a tension that cannot be resolved between the myth and the epitaph. It invites the reader to draw on his or her own knowledge of the Avalon myth (which the text refers to without citing explicitly) rather than on information provided elsewhere in the romance, and to accept or reject it in order to arrive at an interpretation. The reader, not the text, provides this episode's meaning by choosing between two equally possible and mutually exclusive readings.[52]

A second model of the *Mort Artu* is the history of its own composition, provided in the opening and closing passages cited above. It ends with a declaration of its own authority: "aprés ce n'en porroit nus riens conter qui n'en mentist de toutes choses" (263). The text is supposedly fixed, closed to any future interventions, not to be questioned or interpreted. But this pretense of authority is highly ironic: Walter Map, the famous man of letters of Henry II's court and the supposed author of the prose *Lancelot*, actually died in 1209, some twenty years before the composition of the *Mort Artu*. The text says that any sequel will be full of lies, in the very act of lying about its author's identity.[53] In addition, the attempt at closure must be read ironically in light of the opening passage: "Aprés ce que mestres Gautiers Map ot mis en escrit des *Aventures del Seint Graal* assez soufisanment si com li sembloit, si fu avis au roi Henri son seigneur que ce qu'il avoit fet ne devoit pas soufire" (1). The text that denies the possibility of a sequel is itself a sequel. "Walter Map" thought his work was finished once before and was wrong; how can he be so certain that he has reached his conclusion this time? The claims to be truthful and definitive can both be read ironically; the refusal of any interpretation can also be taken as an invitation to intervene and interpret.

"Aprés ce" does not necessarily refer only to sequels; instead, "Walter Map" here attempts to prevent any kind of addition or intervention composed after his closure of the work. But that medieval readers themselves perceived this ending as interpretable rather than definitive is suggested by the additions to the *Lancelot* cycle made after the *Mort Artu*'s completion. Each addition changes the story somewhat with its interpretive foreshadowings of the episodes already written. One such addition is the *Estoire del saint Graal*, added to the beginning of the prose *Lancelot* after the rest was finished. It is the *Estoire* that relates the vision of the divine book, a vision that places the cycle in a new and supernatural context, coloring any subsequent interpretation. In addition, Fanni Bogdanow points out the existence of a subsequent *remaniement* of the *Mort Artu* (with the same title) that reflects a very different conception of the story, omitting the original's reference to fortune, for example, and reducing the part played by Lancelot.[54] A supposedly definitive text with an authoritative meaning thus actually opens itself to subsequent adaptations and interpretations.

Lancelot and the Reader

One final model of this aspect of the text is Lancelot himself, seen from a slightly different perspective than that which showed him to be an interpretable text for the other characters. Issues such as his location and the identity of his lover can be resolved by the "omniscient" reader, and sometimes even by the fictional reader-figures: Guinevere eventually recognizes the truth about his relations with the Escalot maiden; Hector and Bors eventually find him. But what about Lancelot's essential identity? Earlier I suggested that he serves a purpose like that of the Grail in the *Queste:* both are objects of desire, pursuit, interpretation. But the Grail has a distinct meaning: its provision of physical nourishment at the Round Table is an allegory of God's provision of spiritual food, grace, to those who seek it. Lancelot has no such essential significance: he is a rhetorical rather than an allegorical text, one whose shifting surface signs direct the interpreter to no essential truth. One might say that there is no "real" Lancelot: not only his appearance but the very nature of what he is undergoes radical changes in the course of the romance.

One critic has found in this fluidity of identity one of the *Mort Artu*'s structural principles: "Chaque personnage agit en fonction des deux systèmes de valeurs qui se superposent à la cour d'Artus," the courtly function predominating before the scene of Lancelot's and Guinevere's adultery and the feudal function predominating after, when warfare rather than courtly love becomes the main concern, though both functions are present throughout.[55] Blake locates the split in Lancelot's value-system in a specific image: "Le renversement de fonctions de Lancelot est couronné par une image métonymique: lorsqu'il quitte le pays de Logres, il laisse son écu, signe synecdochique du chevalier errant, dans l'église de Kamaalot."[56] The passage in question follows:

> "Pren mon escu en cele chambre et t'en va droit a Kamaalot, et si le porfe en la mestre eglise de Saint Estienne et le lesse en tel leu ou il puisse remanoir et ou il soit bien veüz, si que tuit cil qui des ore mes le verront aient en remenbrance les merveilles que ge ai fetes en ceste terre. Et sez tu por quoi ge faz a cel leu ceste enneur? Por ce que ge i reçui primes l'ordre de chevalerie; si en aing plus la cité que nule autre; et por ce voil je que mes escuz i soit en leu de moi, car je ne sai se jamés aventure m'i amenra, puis que je serai partiz de cest païs." (161)[57]

Lancelot here forsakes his former life and leaves its signs behind; henceforth he will play the role of feudal lord in his own land, rather than that of courtly knight-errant and lover in Arthur's. Two observations should be added to Blake's brilliant analysis: first, Lancelot's signs of identity are radically unstable even within the courtly role he plays in the first half of the text; his disguises render the "real" Lancelot unknowable, at least temporarily. Second, the feudal role of the second half is not Lancelot's final transformation; his final function is neither courtly nor feudal, but religious: "li arcevesques l'avoit ja tant mené que Lancelos avoit ordre de prouvoire, si qu'il chantoit chascun jor messe et qu'il estoit de si grant abstinence qu'il ne menjoit fors pain et eve et racines qu'il cueilloit en la broce" (260).[58] Blake sees this description as a cessation of the reduplication of functions that structure the romance;[59] but the similarity of this transformation to Lancelot's earlier incarnations suggests more plausibly that it represents yet another version of him. All three functions—courtly, feudal, and religious—involve an allegiance to a higher power (lady, lord, God),

signified by difficulties undergone heroically (obedience, warfare, abstinence). The final transformation does not reveal a true, essential Lancelot
who was hidden by false signs in his earlier phases of existence; rather the
essence itself changes each time. The truth about Lancelot is itself fluid,
which is to say that there is no single, essential truth about him. The signifier
"Lancelot" has no fixed signified. Not only is the real Lancelot unknowable;
there is no real Lancelot.

The *Mort Artu* thus leads us far from the transcendent religious meaning
of the allegorical Grail-quest; if Lancelot is a text requiring interpretation,
he resembles more closely those rhetorical texts condemned by Hugh of
St. Victor: "the writings of those fellows whom today we commonly call
'philosophers' and who are always taking some small matter and dragging
it out through long verbal detours, obscuring a simple meaning in confused
discourses—who, lumping even dissimilar things together, make, as it
were, a single 'picture' from a multitude of 'colors' and 'forms.'"[60] A simple
meaning disguised by a variety of forms and figures: this seems as good a
description as any of the *Mort Artu*'s Lancelot.

To a lesser extent, it also defines the *Mort Artu:* if the reader can usually
fill in its phenomenological blanks with information found elsewhere in the
text, there are also passages that defy the attempt to do so. The narration
of Arthur's death is as ambiguous for the reader as other texts within the
text are for the characters; and the ironic declaration of authority that
concludes the romance actually destabilizes it as Lancelot's multiplicity of
roles and functions destabilizes his identity. This tendency to question its
own authority is presented with great subtlety in the *Mort Artu* and is held
in tension with the opposite tendency to establish itself as a definitive
historical document. It is the first of these tendencies that the *Mort Artu*'s
late medieval adapter, Sir Thomas Malory, adopts and develops at the end
of his Arthurian compilation.

Malory

The longest ongoing debate in Malory scholarship concerns the unity or
lack thereof in what is referred to either as *Le Morte Darthur* or as Malory's
Works, depending on whether one aligns oneself with those who see it as
a unified narrative or with those who see it as a collection of eight separate
tales. This is an issue I cannot hope to address in this chapter, as it is both
complex and largely irrelevant to this book's concerns.[61] I would claim that
the issues I discuss here can be fruitfully pursued throughout Malory's

entire output, but I will limit my investigation to a fraction of that output, taking the arguments of those who favor the separate-tales view as my justification for doing so. Indeed, Malory's production as a whole is of such length and complexity that even the defenders of the single-book view usually focus their attention on one segment at a time, tacitly accepting the divisions suggested by the Winchester manuscript, on which Vinaver based his great edition, and from which he derived the theory of eight separate tales.[62] Specifically, the remainder of this chapter examines what Vinaver calls *The Book of Sir Launcelot and Queen Guinevere* and *The Most Piteous Tale of the Morte Arthur Saunz Guerdon* (books 18–21 in Caxton),[63] focusing on the characteristics of Malory's narrative voice and its function as intermediary between the events it recounts and the reader, and especially on the ways it helps or hinders the reader in the interpretation of the work's linguistic signs, as a development of the *Mort Artu's* subtle destabilization of text and meaning. It might be argued that these two tales or four books have a unity of their own, detached from the rest of Malory's output, as they are largely (though not completely) derived from the same French source, the *Mort Artu* itself.[64]

Sir Thomas Malory lived and wrote in the late fifteenth century;[65] he is the last writer this book will consider, and may be seen as the culmination of several medieval literary traditions. Besides summarizing the Arthurian romance in what has become its most widely-read form, Malory also summarizes and unites several of the intellectual concerns we have seen elsewhere. Not only the plot but the concern with the social significance of interpretation and the use of legal mechanisms as one focal point for that concern are derived from the *Mort Artu;* the antisocial nature of Lancelot's relationship with Guinevere comes ultimately from Chrétien (and the unreadable hero is another point of similarity with both these predecessors); the lovers' mutual interpretations might be compared to those in Marie de France's *Lais;* secrecy and the concern with reputation are emphasized as in Machaut's *Voir-Dit,* and as in that work the reader is indirectly invited to interpret sympathetically; the narrator is presented both as reader and as writer, as in *Troilus and Criseyde,* and the production and interpretation of written texts are problematized as in *The Book of the Duchess.*

Many readers coming to Malory's works for the first time are perplexed by the sense usually present in them of mysterious patterns being worked out, of vast structures to which one lacks the key. Knowledge is difficult to attain for Malory's narrator and thus for his readers, especially knowledge of the past; and that the events he recounts are long past is a fact of which the narrator never loses sight (these references to the distance of the past are usually Malory's own additions to the story). Part of the difficulty stems from what often appear to be deliberate confusions in Malory's language, from an attempt to make all statements as ambiguous or equivocal as possible. At one point in Malory's closing pages, Mordred is presented to us not as a single, unified personality but as a network of relationships dizzying in its complexity; the bishop of Canterbury says, "'ys nat kynge Arthur youre uncle, and no farther but youre modirs brothir, and uppon her he hymselffe begate you, uppon hys owne syster? Therefore how may ye wed youre owne fadirs wyff?'" (707–08). Mordred is Arthur's nephew, the son of Arthur's sister, the son of his mother's brother, the lover of his father's wife: it is as though the bishop and Malory are searching for an adequate linguistic formula that would define Mordred, a way of summing him up in language, which proves barely adequate to the task.

Indeed, the inadequacy of language, the difference between language and reality, receives very direct attention in Malory's closing books. His characters speak about one another's speech with remarkable frequency, and their remarks are usually critical. Faced with the duplicity of his characters' language and with the distance of the past, Malory's narrator sometimes admits that he is unsure of what the truth might be; and if the narrator is unable to interpret, the reader must be at an even greater loss.

Abuses and Successes of Signification

One of the reasons that the relationship between language and reality is so problematic for Malory is that Lancelot and Guinevere make it so. As regards their love, a concern of central importance in these final books, Lancelot and Guinevere are, apparently, liars; their love for each other is, among other things, an abuse of language, the use of speech to conceal reality.

The problematization of signs begins in the "Poisoned Apple" episode of *The Book of Sir Launcelot and Queen Guinevere*. Lancelot, on his return from the Grail quest, is unable to preserve the exclusively religious devotion he learned there, and, as in the *Mort Artu*, "began to resorte unto quene Gwenivere agayne and forgate the promyse and the perfeccion that he made in the queste" (611). The lovers' relationship is noticed by other knights; to avoid scandal, Lancelot "withdrew hym fro the company of quene Gwenyvere" (611). This withdrawal sets in motion a series of misinterpretations that nearly prove fatal to the queen. It seems, in fact, that this episode will exemplify the dangers of signification and interpretation, the manipulation of signs in order to disguise the truth. Lancelot's manipulations work entirely too well: he fools not only the court at large but Guinevere herself. "Sir Launcelot, I se and fele dayly that youre love begynnyth to slake, for ye have no joy to be in my presence, but ever ye are oute of thys courte, and quarels and maters ye have nowadayes for ladyes, maydyns, and jantillwomen, more than ever ye were wonte to have beforehande" (611). One misreading, the court's, is intended, but a different one occurs: this Lancelot does not seem to be the deft dissembler we may recall from Chrétien's *Le Chevalier de la charrette*[66] but one whose manipulations immediately escape his control. The same thing happens to Guinevere after her break with Lancelot: she too becomes the victim of her own false signs. As in the *Charrette*, she tries to disguise her true feelings for Lancelot by misleading the rest of her society: "So the quene lete make a pryvy dynere in London unto the knyghtes of the Rownde Table, and all was for to shew outwarde that she had as grete joy in all other knyghtes of the Rounde Table as she had in sir Launcelot" (613). Note the differences between Malory's treatment of the episode and the *Mort Artu*'s: in the French romance, Lancelot does not withdraw from the court in order to deceive the other knights nor is Guinevere's motive in planning this dinner mentioned. Malory invents these intentions and thus emphasizes the attempts to manipulate signification; every action now exemplifies this problem.

Guinevere's scheme, too, has more than the desired effect: although no one divines her true motive in giving the dinner party, a further misinterpretation of it turns the court against the queen as she mistakenly turned against Lancelot. When Sir Pyonell poisons an apple intending that it be given to his enemy Gawain (who "loved well all maner of fruyte," 613) in the course of the dinner, Sir Patryse eats it and dies instead, and "every knyght lepe frome the bourde ashamed and araged for wratthe oute of hir wittis, for they wyst nat what to sey; considerynge quene Guenyvere made the feste and dyner they had all suspeccion unto hir" (614). Like Lancelot, the queen loses control of her false sign, the dinner; although everyone misreads it (as she intended), the misreading is not the one she planned. Only the minor character Sir Pyonell seems to manipulate signs with any success at this point. The irony of the lovers' situation is unwittingly emphasized by King Arthur as he tries to think of a knight who would consent to serve as Guinevere's champion (lacking one, she must suffer the death penalty):

"For well I see," seyde the kynge, "that none of the four-and-twenty knyghtes, that were at your dyner where sir Patryse was slayne, that

> woll do batayle for you, nother none of hem woll sey well of you, and
> that shall be grete sclaundir to you in thys courte."
>
> "Allas," seyde the quene, "and I may not do withalle, but now I
> mysse sir Launcelot, for and he were here he wolde sone putte me in
> my hartis ease."
>
> "What aylith you," seyde the kynge, "that ye can nat kepe sir
> Launcelot uppon youre syde?" (615)

Slander of the queen's character, just what she and Lancelot tried to avoid, will be the result of their very attempts to avoid it with false signs; they have ironically convinced Arthur that they are enemies, and their success in doing so could result in Guinevere's death. The manipulation of signs in order to deceive society at large seems fatal; the lovers' deceptions will serve as their own punishments.

This segment of the story does not, of course, work out that way; Guinevere really is innocent of murder, Lancelot still does love her, and their society's mechanisms for discerning the truth come to their rescue. The most important such mechanism, as in the *Mort Artu*, is the trial by battle: when Mador de la Porte accuses the queen "of the deth of hys cousyn sir Patryse" (614), she must find a champion to defend her, and Sir Bors agrees to do so, reserving the right to step aside should a better knight than he appear. Lancelot takes this opportunity to return to the queen's favor, and in doing so also asserts the efficacy of Arthur's legal system. Mador's accusation is false; Lancelot deservedly wins the battle, and justice is done. Not only is Guinevere's life saved but the true identity of the killer is also finally revealed by a supernatural authority: "And so hit befelle that the Damesell of the Lake that hyght Nynyve . . . . whan she herde how the quene was greved for the dethe of sir Patryse, than she tolde hit opynly that she was never gylty, and there she disclosed by whom hit was done, and named hym sir Pynel, and for what cause he ded hit. There hit was opynly knowyn and disclosed, and so the quene was excused" (620–21). Nymue is clearly a figure to be trusted;[67] because of her revelation, Guinevere's innocence can be literally graven in stone:

HERE LYETH SIR PATRYSE OF IRELONDE, SLAYNE BY SIR PYNELL LE SAVEAIGE THAT ENPOYSYNDE APPELIS TO HAVE SLAYNE SIR GAWAYNE, AND BY MYSSEFORTUNE SIR PATRYSE ETE ONE OF THE APPLIS, AND THAN SUDDEYNLY HE BRASTE. Also there was wrytyn uppon the tombe that quene Gwenyvere was appeled of treson of the deth of sir Patryse by sir Madore de la Porte, and there was made the mencion how sir Launcelot fought with hym for quene

Gwenyvere and overcom hym in playne batayle. All thys was wretyn uppon the tombe of sir Patryse in excusyng of the quene (621).

Just as Malory gives greater emphasis to the potential destabilization of signification, so here he adds emphasis to the re-establishment of truth: the *Mort Artu* lacks the reference to the supernatural authority Nymue and gives the dead knight a far more ambiguous epitaph. Malory heightens the contrast between the failures and the successes of signification; the truth is here revealed with such unambiguous force that later failures to discover it, for both characters and readers, are all the more striking.

What seemed at first, then, to be a story of the dangers of signification and interpretation, of failures to communicate the truth, finally emerges as the portrait of a society's semiotic systems in good working order. The legal mechanism of trial by battle serves to reveal the truth, and written texts like the epitaph preserve that truth permanently and completely. The episode can thus end in reconciliation: "And evermore the quene behylde sir Launcelot, and wepte so tendirly that she sanke allmoste to the grownde for sorow that he had done to her so grete kyndenes where she shewed hym grete unkyndenesse" (620). Lancelot's and Guinevere's original intention, to disguise their relationship from the court, is for the time being forgotten, as more immediate truths are revealed.

And, of course, the reader always knows that there are authoritative truths to be revealed in this episode. As in the *Mort Artu*, the reader witnesses all the secret actions and motives that are concealed from the other characters: Lancelot's love and his departure, Guinevere's jealousy and pride, Sir Pyonel's poisoning of the apple:

So whan sir Launcelot was departed the quene outewarde made no maner of sorow in shewyng to none of his bloode nor to none other, but wyte ye well, inwardely, as the booke seythe, she toke grete thought; but she bare hit oute with a proude countenaunce, as thoughe she felte no thought nother daungere (613).

. . . thys sir Pyonell hated sir Gawayne bycause of hys kynnesman sir Lamorakes dethe; and therefore, for pure envy and hate, sir Pyonell enpoysonde sertayn appylls for to enpoysen sir Gawayne (613).

Like Sir Patryse's tombstone, and like the trial by battle, the text itself of "The Poisoned Apple" reveals the whole truth; the former systems of communication reveal to the characters only what the omniscient narrator has already revealed to his audience, which shares his perspective rather than the court's. Even Sir Bors, who knows the truth about Lancelot and Guinevere and is Lancelot's spokesman (and who to that extent is a figure of the omniscient reader), does not know as much as we do about the murder, though he guesses the truth (as on p. 617). This is a text, in fact, largely lacking in phenomenological blanks: we have all the information we need for an accurate reading and indeed need not even engage in the metonymic process of interpretation required to arrive at one in the *Mort Artu*.

That historical as well as psychological truth can be known is emphasized at several points. The narrator is an historian, confident that he knows the truth about the past and that it can easily be communicated to his readers: "for such custom was used in tho dayes: for favoure, love, nother affinite there sholde be none other but ryghtuous jugemente, as well uppon a kynge as uppon a knyght, and as well uppon a quene as uppon another poure lady" (618). The past was better than the present is, but its difference does not render it unknowable; it can therefore serve as an example.[68] History itself presents no phenomenological blanks for the historian; therefore his transmission of it poses no problems of interpretation for the reader. At this point, Malory's narrator achieves that authoritative depiction of past events to which "Walter Map" aspired in the *Mort Artu*.

Signs continue to function efficiently in the second section of this tale, called "The Fair Maid of Astolat" by Vinaver. There are several structural similarities between it and the preceding section: Lancelot and Guinevere agree to disguise their love for each other; Lancelot unintentionally causes Guinevere's jealousy to revive (when he wears Elaine's sleeve as a token during the famous tournament); the truth is revealed by an authoritative written text (the letter that accompanies Elaine's corpse on its journey down the river) that causes the lovers to be reconciled. Here as in "The Poisoned Apple," Lancelot's attempt to manipulate signs, by wearing the sleeve in order not to be recognized, gets out of hand and is misinterpreted by Guinevere in a way he did not intend; the letter, however, in its textual authority, sets matters right. That Elaine might have composed a false letter is not a possibility anyone considers, so great is the authority of a text. Once again, Malory increases our sense of knowing the whole truth: whereas the Escalot maiden in the French romance did in fact include false accusations in her letter, which the reader had to rectify by recalling earlier scenes, in Malory's version her letter truthfully recapitulates those scenes. There is no disjunction between the original narration of events and their repetition in inserted texts (epitaphs, letters), and therefore our sense of the efficacy of verbal or at least written signification is, for the moment, heightened.

As before, the reader is allowed psychological omniscience (we are told Lancelot's true motive for wearing Elaine's token, for example), and the narrator is presented as an admiring historian, with accurate knowledge of the past: "For in thos dayes hit was nat the gyse as ys nowadayes; for there were none ermytis in tho dayes but that they had bene men of worship and of prouesse, and tho ermytes hylde grete householdis and refreysshed people that were in distresse" (629). The past can be presented to a present reader even when the passage of time has altered its identifying signs: "and than they rode so longe tylle that they cam to Camelot, that tyme called Wynchester" (624). Here as in "The Poisoned Apple," "the booke" (623) that the narrator is translating is an authoritative text revealing psychological and historical truths to be passed on to future readers, similar to the *Mort Artu's* "li contes" (and as in that text, we may also wish to question whether the book can really have such authority; Malory himself poses the question in later episodes).

At this point, Malory departs from the *Mort Artu* to add three episodes whose plots are invented or derived from other sources.[69] In them, the optimistic view of signification found in the early episodes begins to give way to a more problematic presentation. Lancelot and Guinevere learn their lesson in the first two sections: the episode called "The Great Tournament" by Vinaver opens with them working out a basic semiotic system of their own:

> Than quene Gwenyver sent for sir Launcelot and seyd thus: "I warne you that ye ryde no more in no justis nor turnementis but that youre kynnesmen may know you, and at thys justis that shall be ye shall have of me a slyeve of golde. And I pray you for my sake to force yourselff there, that men may speke of you worshyp. But I charge you, as ye woll have my love, that ye warne your kynnesmen that ye woll beare that day the slyve of golde uppon your helmet." (642)

This sign will identify Lancelot to his kinsmen and thus avoid the misinterpretations that led to Guinevere's jealousy previously. It is unclear whether these kinsmen are to know that the token is Guinevere's this time; perhaps it is also to function as a private sign of their love, for themselves alone. By the time we get to the next episode, in any case, called "The Knight of the Cart" by Vinaver, they are able to communicate with each other very effectively, partly by means of such direct verbal negotiations as that which opens "The Great Tournament," and partly by an apparently intuitive reading of each other's signs, even of those that mislead other interpreters:

> "A! se, madam," seyde the lady, "where rydys in a charyot a
> goodly armed knyght, and we suppose he rydyth unto hangynge."
> "Where?" seyde the quene.
> Than she aspyed by hys shylde that hit was sir Launcelot. . . .
> "Alas!" seyde the quene, "now I may preve and se that well ys
> that creature that hath a trusty frynde. A ha!" seyde quene Gwenyver,
> "I se well that ye were harde bestad whan ye ryde in a charyote." And
> than she rebuked that lady that lykened sir Launcelot to ryde in a
> charyote to hangynge: "Forsothe hit was fowle-mowthed," seyde the
> quene, "and evyll lykened, so for to lyken the moste noble knyght of
> the worlde unto such a shamefull dethe." (654)

Such a passage must remind us of the similarly successful mutual interpretations by pairs of lover in Marie de France's *Lais,* or in the final section of its
ultimate source, Chrétien's *Chevalier de la charrette;* but we are far from the
capriciously cruel Guinevere of the corresponding passage in that romance.
We are also far from the lovers' misinterpretations that caused such problems in the earlier sections of this tale of Malory's.[70] When Lancelot comes
to rescue the queen from her kidnapper, Sir Mellyagaunce, she is anxious
to make peace although he wants revenge; their conflicting motives are
brought into accord by direct discussion rather than by the external authorities (Nymue, Elaine's letter) needed earlier:

> "Madame," seyde sir Launcelot, "syth hit ys so that ye be accorded
> with hym, as for me I may nat agaynesay hit, howbehit sir Mellya
> gaunte hath done full shamefully to me and cowardly. And, madame,"
> seyde sir Launcelot, "and I had wyste that ye wolde have bene so
> lyghtly accorded with hym I wolde nat a made such haste unto you."
> "Why say ye so?" seyde the quene. "Do ye forthynke youreselff
> of youre good dedis? Wyte you well," seyde the quene, "I accorded
> never with hym for no favoure nor love that I had unto hym, but of
> every shamefull noyse of wysedom to lay adoune." . . .
> "Madame," seyde sir Launcelot, "so ye be pleased! As for my
> parte, ye shall sone please me." (655–56)

Antisocial Uses of Language

This discussion also suggests the queen's motive in making peace: she
wishes to conceal their love, as usual, from society at large. The disturbing
implication, which will become stronger from this point on, is that the
better they communicate with each other, the better they are able to conceal

the truth from everyone else. It is at this point that the antisocial nature of their love and of their private sign-systems, glossed over in the earlier episodes, is first emphasized. It is examined from this point on, most clearly in terms of their abuses of language.

Malory provides a foil for the lovers in the person of the uncouth Sir Mellyagaunce, whose habitual suspicion of their speech serves to emphasize its problematic nature. He constantly suggests that the lovers' words do not correspond to reality and seems contemptuous of their language for that reason. The first instance of his attack on their language does not imply what alternative reality might be hidden by it but only suggests that Guinevere's high-flown words on honor have little to do with his own earthier reality. He is in the process of abducting her: "'As for all thys langayge,' seyde sir Mellyagaunte, 'be as hit be may. For wyte you well, madame, I have loved you many a yere, and never ar now cowde I gete you at such avayle. And therefore I woll take you as I fynde you'" (651). "All thys langayge" clearly counts for little in Mellyagaunce's view of reality.

A similar but somewhat later attack on their mode of speech has more serious implications for Lancelot and Guinevere, because their enemy has found tangible evidence of a truth their words try to conceal. As he says to Guinevere's knights, "'Away with youre proude langayge! For here ye may all se that a wounded knyght thys nyght hath layne by the quene.' Than they all loked and were sore ashamed whan they saw that bloode" (658). The proud language of the queen's knights cannot stand before this tangible evidence. Lancelot, too, tries to distract Mellyagaunce with words, and has a similar lack of success: "'Sir, I wote nat what ye meane,' seyde sir Mellyagaunce, 'but well I am sure there hath one of hir hurte knyghtes layne with her thys nyght'" (658). Mellyagaunce here admits that he cannot understand Lancelot's words; but he interprets signs of a different kind dangerously well. Indeed, Mellyagaunce is undone only when he accepts Lancelot's words, during their battle to determine Guinevere's guilt or innocence. Lancelot has offered to do battle partially unarmed and bound: "Than sir Mellyagaunce sterte up and seyde on hyght, 'Take hede, my lorde Arthur, of thys proffir, for I woll take hit. And lette hym be dissarmed and bounden accordynge to hys proffir'" (662). Lancelot still kills him easily; Mellyagaunce's mistake is in allowing himself to be seduced by Lancelot's language, which before he quite properly scorned.

Lancelot, of course, legally deserves to win this battle, because of the wording of the charge, which the linguistically sophisticated Lancelot has manipulated for his own ends. Whereas Mellyagaunce's original charge, quoted above, accused one of the queen's hurt knights—a category that could include Lancelot himself—Lancelot narrows the accusation so as to exclude himself:

> "But as to that I say nay playnly, that thys nyght there lay none of thes ten knyghtes wounded with my lady, quene Gwenyver, and that woll I prove with myne hondys that ye say untrewly in that. Now, what sey ye?" seyde sir Launcelot.
>
> "Thus I say," seyde sir Mellyagaunce, "here ys my glove that she ys a traytoures unto my lord kynge Arthur, and that thys nyght one of the wounded knyghtes lay wyth her." (659)

If Lancelot's cause here is just, its justice is severely technical: the queen has indeed slept with a wounded knight as Mellyagaunce says, with Lancelot himself (who hurt his hand breaking into her room), though not with one of the ten Lancelot specifies. Although the trial may, then, be strictly correct, it must weaken whatever confidence the reader may have had in a legal system based on such minute distinctions in wording. This way of revealing the truth has degenerated, as it did in the *Mort Artu*, since the more clearly just outcome of Lancelot's battle with Mador de la Porte; that degeneration will be directly recognized in the final tale.

The fact that Lancelot is a liar would not be so disturbing if his lies had no larger function than protecting his guilty secret, or if all members of society were as perceptive as Mellyagaunce. Unfortunately, more than his love-affair depends upon the concealment of reality. Malory makes it quite clear that the well-being of the Round Table fellowship, indeed of Arthurian society as a whole, rests at least partially upon the misinterpretation of Lancelot's behavior, that is, upon the acceptance of his lies as the truth, of his language as though it truly represented reality.

To this extent, Lancelot is similar to the fictional or rhetorical text, as he was in the *Mort Artu*. E. Jane Burns has pointed out of that earlier romance that "Arthur dies when artifice ceases" because the Arthurian world is composed only of artifice, of fictions or literary lies.[71] This is, of course, equally true of Malory's version, and indeed of all versions of this legend: Arthurian society literally exists only because writers tell lies about it, make fictions. Lancelot's lies in Malory thus resemble the lies of fiction at least in their function: they defer the final dissolution of Arthur's world.

The dependence of Arthur's society upon its conception of Lancelot is illustrated continually in the two final tales. Sir Bors, having wounded Lancelot in a tournament, in apologizing gives his cousin an almost supernatural status as leader of the Round Table fellowship: "'I drede me that

God ys gretely displeasyd with me, that He wolde suffir me to have such a shame for to hurte you that ar all oure ledar and all oure worship; and therefore I calle myselff unhappy. . . . I mervayle,' seyde sir Bors, 'that my herte or my bloode wolde serve me'" (634). It is as though, in Bors's view, God himself had ordained Lancelot as a synecdoche for the court and its "worship": in harming Lancelot, even unintentionally, he has harmed himself. Lancelot is so much a part of him that his very body should have refused to do so. Bors—frequently the most perceptive interpreter among the knights—also draws the crucial connection between Lancelot's status as representative of the Round Table and his role as the queen's lover, during one of Guinevere's attacks of jealousy: "'A, sir Bors! Have ye nat herde sey how falsely sir Launcelot hath betrayed me?' 'Alas, madame,' seyde sir Bors, 'I am aferde he hath betrayed himselff and us all'" (632). In appearing to betray Guinevere's love, Lancelot betrays their entire social organization. Ironically, Lancelot's adultery with the queen—his betrayal of Arthur—is here construed, quite accurately, as the force that sustains Arthur's society. Lancelot's presence at court binds the Round Table together; but only his relationship with Guinevere guarantees that presence, a relationship that, were it known, would cause this society's dissolution.

Lancelot and Society in "The Healing of Sir Urry"

That Arthur's society has come to base itself upon the false signs that conceal this relationship is the point of the final episode of the seventh tale, an episode apparently invented by Malory and that Vinaver called "The Healing of Sir Urry," usually best remembered for its puzzling catalogue of knights, covering two and a half pages, along with several inserted anecdotes about some of the knights named. The catalogue lists those who handle the wounds of a Hungarian knight, Sir Urry, who because of a spell laid on him can supposedly be cured only by "the beste knyght of the worlde" (663). Although this catalogue is well known it has received little critical attention, perhaps because it seems to have been inserted rather arbitrarily, serving no clear purpose in the plot and indeed digressing from it unnecessarily in the apparently irrelevant recounting of certain experiences chosen at random.[72]

Seen in the context of Arthurian society's dependence upon its conception of Lancelot as leader and exemplar, however, the episode makes more sense, for the catalogue sums up that society, presenting a complete picture of it at a crucial juncture, just preceding its final dissolution. All the knights currently at court are named, frequently grouped by family or clan: "Than cam in sir Gawayne wyth hys three sunnes, sir Gyngalyn, sir Florence, and sir Lovell (thes two were begotyn uppon sir Braundeles syster), and all they fayled. Than cam in sir Aggravayne, sir Gaherys, and sir Mordred, and the good knyght sir Gareth that was of verry knyghthod worth all the brethirn" (665). In addition to this synchronic portrait of the court as it exists at one specific moment, the inserted anecdotes give a sense of the court's history as well, a diachronic portrait that also emphasizes relations among the knights, sometimes familial (giving an account of how a specific knight was begotten) and sometimes of other kinds, as in the story of Lancelot's friendship with Sir Severause le Brewse, or the enmity to King Mark shared by Sir Bellyngere's father with Tristram (665–66). The inserted anecdotes thus bring the Round Table's past into contact with its present and even temporarily resurrect dead knights like Tristram for a total portrait of Arthurian society in history as well as at a single moment. Past and present are here united on a single continuum, as the various knights present are also united, by this episode's emphasis on fellowship: to Lancelot's modest refusal to try and heal Sir Urry, Arthur replies that "ye shall nat do hit for no presumpcion, but for to beare us felyshyp" (668).[73] Even the absence of some knights, who "were that tyme away" (664), suggests that history is continuing, as represented by those who are off pursuing new adventures; the future is thus brought into the historical continuum as well, to complete this picture of a synchronically and diachronically unified society that can be summed up in a text.

The "Sir Urry" episode thus serves to remind us what it is that depends upon its image of Lancelot as the world's best knight: this unified fellowship itself. The entire community concurs in Arthur's assessment: "and ye prevayle nat and heale hym, I dare sey there ys no knyght in thys londe that may hele hym. And therefore I pray you do as we have done" (668). Only Lancelot can bring this collective adventure, the adventure that has, in the narrator's recounting of it, defined and unified the court in time and space, to its successful conclusion. Only he can successfully represent Arthurian society as a whole at this crucial moment. To do so, he must demonstrate that he is what his society perceives him to be, the best knight in the world.

In the eyes of the other knights, and indeed of most readers, Lancelot does so.[74] Sir Urry is healed at the moment Lancelot touches his wounds, and the court celebrates this demonstration of their representative's perfection. What is not usually noticed is that Lancelot himself repeatedly refuses this identification, both in his oral exchanges with Arthur and in his mental prayer:

"My most renowmed lorde," seyde sir Launcelot, "I know well I dare nat, nor may nat, disobey you. But and I myght or durste, wyte you well I wolde nat take uppon me to towche that wounded knyght in that entent that I shulde passe all othir knyghtes. . . ." (667–68)

And than he hylde up hys hondys and loked unto the este, saiynge secretely unto hymselff, "Now, Blyssed Fadir and Son and Holy Goste, I beseche The of Thy mercy that my symple worshyp and honesté be saved, and Thou Blyssed Trynyté, Thou mayste yeff me power to hele thys syke knyght by the grete vertu and grace of The, but, Good Lorde, never of myselff." (668)

Sir Urry is to be healed by God's power, not by Lancelot's virtue, which Lancelot himself knows to be an illusion. The many critics who follow Arthur's knights in seeing the healing as proof of Lancelot's superiority are not attending to the content of Lancelot's prayer, in which that superiority is denied; what he requests is that the *appearance* of virtue be granted to him, that his reputation, "worship," be preserved. His famous tears following the healing—"And ever sir Launcelote wepte, as he had bene a chylde that had bene beatyn!"—surely one of Malory's most effective lines—are caused by the recognition that he is not what the others think him, that his adultery with Guinevere prevents him from being the best knight. His tears show him to be just the opposite: a beaten child.[75]

Although Malory is usually regarded as an intellectually unsophisticated writer, this episode suggests a possible awareness of post-Ockhamist theology. For Ockham and his followers God could suspend natural law, causing directly by his absolute power (*potentia absoluta*) effects usually associated with secondary causes (*potentia ordinata*).[76] This appears to be what has happened in Sir Urry's miraculous healing: God consents to heal him directly rather than through any secondary agent, including Lancelot himself. Such a reading, and such a theology, are also consistent with Malory's style in the passage describing the actual healing:

And than sir Launcelot prayde sir Urré to lat hym se hys hede; and than, devoutly knelyng, he ransaked the three woundis, that they bled a lytyll; and forthwithall the woundis fayre heled and semed as they had bene hole a seven yere. And in lyke wyse he serched hys body of other three woundis, and they healed in lyke wyse. And than the laste of all he serched hys honde, and anone hit fayre healed. (668)

This paratactic syntax refuses to draw causal connections among the events being described; nowhere is it said that the wounds healed *because* Lancelot

touched them but only that he touched them *and* they healed. P. J. C. Field
has suggested that such a lack of syntactical subordination is typical of
Malory's style;[77] causality is thus, at the most basic level, left to the reader's
discretion. Whereas the *Mort Artu* stylistically weakened causal links between sentences while preserving subordination within them, Malory's
style tends to eliminate even that internal subordination. That causality is
unknowable is also a basic tenet of much late medieval theology, and is a
logical development of Ockham's assertion of the radical individuality of
everything that exists, found, for example, in Nicholas of Autrecourt:

> "If you understand by natural agents, 'agents which are next to their
> patients and are not impeded posit the existence of their action,' I
> concede that it follows logically: A natural agent is next to its patient
> and there is no impediment, therefore there is an action. But I say that
> it is neither evident to anyone that there are such agents in the universe
> of things nor is it evident that such agents may be assumed to exist."
> This and many other texts make it plain that we do not perceive nor
> can we logically infer the efficacy of those efficient causes which fall
> within our experience. We can and do perceive the coexistence and the
> succession of appearances. Hence, we have evident knowledge of this
> coexistence and succession. The knowledge thus obtained is not of
> causal connection, but only of conjunction. It is, then, quite clear that
> Nicolaus of Autrecourt denied that causal connections are perceived or
> justifiably inferred.[78]

Thus Malory's view of Lancelot's "miracle" can, like many more overtly
mysterious events in his book (the story of Balin, for example), be associated
with the theology of an unknowable God, while his very style may reflect an
unknowable causality, returning a sense of mystery to the created universe.

In a similar way, Malory recreates that sense in the reader: the book
becomes a mysterious event in our own lives, and its meanings cannot be
known with Augustinian certainty. The reader can choose to see Lancelot's
agency as necessary to the healing of Sir Urry, but nothing in the text itself
nor in the intellectual context of Malory's period, from the most basic
syntactical structure to the most abstract epistemological speculations, imposes such a reading, and indeed much evidence points in a different
direction. Lancelot's chivalric superiority, which the court associates with
its own identity and cohesion, is an illusion. Social unity rests on his false
appearances, on the deceptive signs of virtue and loyalty that conceal a
very different reality. A very curious passage near the end of *The Book of Sir
Launcelot and Queen Guinevere* suggests that Lancelot himself is tiring of

those false appearances: "because of dispyte that knyghtes and ladyes called hym 'the Knyght that rode in the Charyot,' lyke as he were juged to the jybett, therefore, in the despite of all them that named hym so, he was caryed in a charyotte a twelve-monethe" (669). If the miraculous healing imposes the appearance of "best knight" upon him, Lancelot himself chooses to be identified with an opposite sign, the cart, sign of criminality. He may force a re-evaluation of the socially agreed-upon reading of a knight in a cart; but he may also be flaunting what he knows to be the truth about himself.

The preceding passage suggests that the unity of the Round Table, represented by Lancelot's supposed superiority, is itself an illusion: "But every nyght and day sir Aggravayne, sir Gawaynes brother, awayted quene Gwenyver and sir Launcelot to put hem bothe to a rebuke and a shame" (669). The generally comic structure of the "Sir Urry" section, with its final recovery of health and even a wedding, conceals a potential tragedy; the signs of social health and unity are as illusory as those of Lancelot's virtue.

History and the Abuse of Language

Until this point, the reader has usually retained the privileged position granted in the seventh tale's earlier sequences: we are privy to Lancelot's internal as well as his externally expressed doubts; we alone witness his prayer and are in a position to interpret it. Whatever deceitful manipulations of signs have been represented as occurring in the past at Arthur's court, the reader's own present experience of the text itself is still complete and satisfying; it tells us the whole truth about the past in a fuller way than the characters living in it ever experience. At the very end of *The Book of Sir Launcelot and Queen Guinevere*, however, occurs a disturbing suggestion that the text itself is losing authority: "And bycause I have loste the very mater of Shevalere de Charyot I departe frome the tale of sir Launcelot; and here I go unto the morte Arthur, and that caused sir Aggravayne" (669). Our attention is directed to a large "blank" in the history; the narrator has lost his source, and the reader is left to his or her own conjectures about what it might have contained (similar omissions occur elsewhere in Malory's output, notably at the end of the tale of Tristram, 511). The difficulty of writing an accurate history, and the danger of depending upon a written "mater" that can be destroyed or misplaced, indeed the gap between past and present that can be bridged only by such fragile texts (as Orderic Vitalis pointed out much earlier),[79] is here called to our attention for the first time in the books derived from the *Mort Artu*. This problem, the problem of alterity,[80] becomes insoluble in the final tale, the *Morte Arthur*. This gap merely epitomizes a problem prevalent throughout Malory's works: the conflict we have been observing between signifying systems that cannot be reconciled.

It also represents one point at which Malory's narrative voice can be distinguished from that of Malory the author.[81] Vinaver has convincingly demonstrated that the author's method of "reducing" his source, the long French prose romances, in the production of such tales as the *Noble Tale of Sir Launcelot du Lake* was precisely to choose for translation only such parts of the original as could form a coherent work:

> The *Tale* falls into three distinct sections of approximately equal length, each corresponding roughly to two folio leaves of Malory's "French book." The three sections belong to three different parts of the text. It is tempting, but perhaps not very realistic, to speculate that Malory's source was simply a gathering of three sheets which had dropped out of a volume of the Prose *Lancelot*. The alternative, and the more likely, explanation is that he deliberately chose those three sections in order to give a reasonably continuous account of Lancelot's adventures and so avoid the necessity of interweaving a variety of different themes.[82]

The narrator, at the end of the seventh tale, claims just such an accidental loss of portions of his source as that which Vinaver dismisses as unlikely. By doing so, he can return to his first source for the seventh tale, the *Mort Artu*, at the beginning of the eighth, and thus produce that sense of continuity that Vinaver mentions. Surely Malory the author is disingenuous in claiming that an accidental loss caused him at this point to use the narrative technique that usually characterizes his style anyway; it is a fictional narrator who makes this claim, one whose other characteristics emerge clearly in the *Morte Arthur*.

Lancelot's continuing duplicity, and especially his abuse of language, cause this narrator progressively to lose confidence in his ability to transmit history to his audience by means of a text. This duplicity remains dangerous to Arthurian society as well, as is suggested by its continued dependence upon its conception of Lancelot. Various characters echo the opinion of Lancelot's knights: " 'For by the noble felyshyp of the Rounde Table was kynge Arthur upborne, and by their nobeles the kynge and all the realme was ever in quyet and reste. And a grete part,' they sayde all, 'was because of youre moste nobeles, sir Launcelot' " (699). The threat posed by any possible change in this society's perspective on Lancelot is clearly perceived by Gawain when Agravain admits his plan to reveal the love-affair: "and there aryse warre and wrake betwyxte sir Launcelot and us, wyte you well, brothir, there woll many kynges and grete lordis holde with sir Launcelot. . . . and the beste of us all had bene full colde at the harte-roote had nat sir Launcelot bene bettir than we" (673). Lancelot, as the Round Table's supposed best knight, has maintained this society almost single-handedly; the revelation of the facts about him could destroy it.[83]

Lancelot's chief means of preventing such a revelation is his false language, the lies that continue to conceal reality even after Agravain's report to the king: " 'And therefore, my good and gracious lorde,' seyde sir Launcelot, 'take your quene unto youre good grace, for she ys both tru and good' " (688). The essential fact of his adultery with the queen, that aspect of his personality which sets him against society while paradoxically preserving it, is never directly admitted; indeed, Lancelot attacks the language of others when his own is at its most duplicitous: "For they that tolde you tho talys were lyars, and so hit felle uppon them . . . for I was sente unto my lady, youre quyne, I wote nat for what cause" (694). Words about others' words proliferate; in the *Morte*, Gawain takes on the function served by Mellyagaunce in *Launcelot and Guinevere*, as the scorner of Lancelot's sophisticated language:

> "Now, fy on thy proude wordis," seyde sir Gawayne (689).

> "Sir Launcelot," seyde sir Gawayne, "I have ryght well harde thy langayge and thy grete proffirs. But wyt thou well, lat the kynge do as hit pleasith hym, I woll never forgyff the my brothirs dethe" (696).

> "Make thou no more langayge," seyde sir Gawayne (697).

> "And thou darste do batayle, leve thy babelynge and com off, and lat us ease oure hartis!" (703).

The distinction between babble and battle is an essential one; although Gawain's quarrel concerns not the queen's guilt but his brothers' deaths, he perceives Lancelot as Mellyagaunce did: as one who prefers fine words to any harsh reality.

The abuse of language would be less destructive, and less disturbing to the reader, if any other objective standards of judgment remained; but, as in the *Mort Artu*, the breakdown of language as a means of communicating the truth also heralds the breakdown of the Arthurian society's legal mechanism as a means of determining the truth. Lancelot's victory over Mellya-gaunce was, in a strict sense, perhaps legally correct; but his victories, both potential and actual, over those who wish to reveal the truth about his relations with the queen, are not. When Agravain and the others surprise the lovers in Guinevere's chamber, Lancelot threatens them with a legal formula: "hydir I cam to the quene for no maner of male engyne, and that woll I preve and make hit good uppon you wyth my hondys" (677). As he himself later notes, his defeat of them proves them legally wrong: " 'My lorde, sir Gawayne,' seyde sir Launcelot, 'in their quarell they preved nat hemselff the beste, nother in the ryght' " (694). On returning the queen to Arthur, Lancelot openly threatens the assembled knights: "Now lat se whatsomever he be in thys place that dare sey the quene ys nat trew unto my lorde Arthur, lat se who woll speke and he dare speke" (698). As in the *Mort Artu*, Lancelot is always able to prove himself legally right, whether his words are true or not; as Arthur sums it up when Gawain suggests that Lancelot can prove Guinevere's innocence in a trial by battle, " 'That I beleve well,' seyde kynge Arthur, 'but I woll nat that way worke with sir Launcelot, for he trustyth so much uppon hys hondis and hys myght that he doutyth no man. And therefore for my quene he shall nevermore fyght, for she shall have the law' " (682–83). Lancelot is beyond the law; his abuse of language causes Arthur's legal system to cease functioning. The two semiotic systems that worked so efficiently at the beginning of the seventh tale, language and the law, are now both unable to communicate the truth.[84]

The community is thus bound together by words that have become meaningless, by language, represented by both Lancelot's personal statements and his legal formulae, that conceals the truth. In such an atmosphere, correct interpretation, the understanding and revelation of the truth, can only be destructive; Gawain's prediction that Agravain's presentation of the facts will divide the kingdom proves accurate. Agravain, the true interpreter, is seen as Mellyagaunce was: as a villain.

Until this point, I have been assuming that Agravain is, in fact, the knight who tells the truth, and that Lancelot is a liar, but it should now be stressed that the narrator himself does not make this assumption. His admission that he does not actually have the crucial piece of information is quite straightforward and has provoked an ongoing critical debate about the exact nature of the relationship between Lancelot and Guinevere.[85] In each of the two final tales, the narrator suggests different answers to the question of whether or not the lovers are guilty.

In the "Knight of the Cart" section of *Launcelot and Guinevere*, virtuous love seems to preclude sexual expression, and Guinevere is held up as a prime example of such virtue:

> And ryght so faryth the love nowadayes, sone hote sone colde. Thys ys no stabylyté. But the olde love was nat so. For men and women coude love togydirs seven yerys, and no lycoures lustis was betwyxte them, and than was love trouthe and faythefulnes. And so in lyke wyse was used such love in kyng Arthurs dayes.
>   . . . And therefore all ye that be lovers, calle unto youre remembraunce the monethe of May, lyke as ded quene Gwenyver, for whom I make here a lytyll mencion, that whyle she lyved she was a trew lover, and therefor she had a good ende. (649)

Guinevere, then, apparently felt no "lecherous lust" for Lancelot; and yet, a few pages later she is in bed with him: "So, to passe uppon thys tale, sir Launcelot wente to bedde with the quene and toke no force of hys hurte honde, but toke hys plesaunce and hys lykynge untyll hit was the dawnyng of the day" (657). Pleasure and liking in bed would seem to include sexual satisfaction, but if so, which of the narrator's statements is to be believed? The problem is further compounded in the *Morte*, in which the nature of the lovers' relationship when discovered by Agravain is an issue of central importance. It is an issue the narrator is frankly unable to resolve: "For, as the Freynshhe booke seyth, the quene and sir Lancelot were togydirs. And whether they were abed other at other maner of disportis, me lyste nat thereof make no mencion, for love that tyme was nat as love ys nowadayes" (676). Gawain provides one possible interpretation but admits that it is only a possibility: "thoughe hyt were so that sir Launcelot were founde in the quenys chambir, yet hit myght be so that he cam thydir for none evyll" (682). It is, in fact, ultimately impossible to decide with certainty what the precise nature of their relationship is; the central issue of the two tales is thus left deliberately unresolved. Lancelot's and the queen's behavior remains as mysterious to the reader as it is to the other characters. In fact, Lancelot's language has had precisely the effect he desired: it has successfully concealed the true nature of his relationship with Guinevere from those most anxious to understand it, from the narrator of these tales and from us, his readers. We are placed in the same position as the members of Arthur's court: we understand the various possibilities but lack the information necessary to judge which possibility is true. Note the important distinction between Malory and his source: as Vinaver points out, the

"French book" is actually more explicit, as is the other English version.[86] The *Mort Artu* states clearly that the lovers are indeed in bed together. The ambiguity of this passage, which Malory takes such pains to emphasize, is apparently his alone. As earlier he heightened the authority with which the truth about Guinevere was revealed, so here he heightens the difficulty or impossibility of knowing the truth. The failure of signification is all the more poignant because it reverses an earlier success.

It is not only the abuse of language in itself that causes the narrator's, and the reader's, inability to comprehend these events; rather, it is the abuse of language complicated by the temporal distance of the realities this abuse conceals. It is the narrator's consciousness of alterity, that life in the past was not as it is in the present, that makes it impossible for us simply to label Lancelot's words as lies, or simply to label Agravain's interpretations as the truth. Time's passage and Lancelot's language both conceal past reality from us as from the narrator; history, at least in verbal and textual form, comes to seem as ambiguous as other semiotic systems.[87]

Indeed, this supposed history comes to seem like what it really is: fiction. The fictionality of Arthurian society that is reflected in Lancelot's lies becomes more and more overt as the book draws to a close because the narrator, like Machaut's in the *Voir-Dit*, finds himself creating fictional interpretations of "history"; fictional because there is no evidence that any one of them is true. These fictional speculations are the text as we read it; they replace "historical" truth.

Whereas in the early portions, at least, of the seventh tale, all misunderstandings and false accusations were eventually cleared up by the orderly working of those semiotic systems, in the eighth tale such misunderstandings become more and more extreme. In the earlier tale, Lancelot's many disguises eventually came off and he was recognized; by the end of the *Morte*, as in the *Mort Artu*, his appearance and his personality have both undergone a radical change: "Thenne syr Launcelot never after ete but lytel mete, nor dranke, tyl he was dede, for than he seekened more and more and dryed and dwyned awaye. For the Bysshop nor none of his felowes myght not make hym to ete and lytel he dranke, that he was waxen by a kybbet shorter than he was, that the peple coude not knowe hym" (723). Malory once again goes further than the *Mort Artu*: here, not even the body is a reliable text. Ironically, Lancelot becomes physically unknowable after his intentional manipulation of signs has ceased, after the destruction of Arthurian society, a destruction whose most direct cause is itself a mass misunderstanding:

Ryght so cam oute an addir of a lytyll hethe-buysshe, and hit stange a knyght in the foote. And so whan the knyght felte hym so stonge, he loked downe and saw the adder; and anone he drew hys swerde to sle the addir, and thought none othir harme. And whan the oste on bothe partyes saw that swerde drawyn, than they blewe beamys, trumpettis, and hornys, and shoutted grymly, and so bothe ostis dressed hem togydirs. (712–13)

It seems that human intentions to deceive or to be truthful no longer matter; the world's chance occurrences themselves cause signs to be misread most destructively.[88]

The Reader's Role in Malory

Misinterpretation in itself is not all that happens in Malory, however; the narrator's very insistence on his lack of an authoritative perspective on the past, his acknowledgment of the distance of the past and of the inadequacy of language, may allow the reader a different kind of perspective. The emphasis on our lack of objective understanding also functions as an invitation to achieve another kind of understanding.

The narrator's admission that he cannot tell us precisely what kind of relationship Lancelot and Guinevere have is only one of several instances presented in Malory's tales of a concern with the difficulty of contact between past and present. Lancelot himself is worried about how he will be perceived by posterity: "And now I had levir than to be lorde of all Crystendom that I had sure armour uppon me, that men myght speke of my dedys or ever I were slayne" (677). This is a development of Lancelot's and Guinevere's concern with their "worship" or reputation, a constant worry throughout these tales, but the emphasis is new: Lancelot is here concerned not with what other members of Arthur's court may think of him but with posterity's judgment. He wants to leave an impression of knightliness and fears this may be impossible. Again, when sent into exile, his thoughts turn to posterity's perception of him: "And that ys to me grete hevynes, for ever I feare aftir my dayes that men shall cronycle uppon me that I was fleamed oute of thys londe. And ellis, my fayre lordis, be ye sure, and I had nat drad shame, my lady quene Gwenyvere and I shulde never have departed" (698). Lancelot's use of the words "speke" and "cronycle" when referring to future interpretations of his acts suggests that the inadequacy of language (for which he himself is at least partly to blame in this context) is what concerns him most. He sees himself in linguistic terms, as an inaccurate chronicle, a text that future readers will inevitably misinterpret. Other characters also seem aware of their own textuality (like the lovers in Machaut's *Voir-Dit*) and are concerned with how they will be interpreted:

> ". . . and than lat us fresshly set uppon them and shrede hem downe as shepe in a folde, that ever aftir alyauntis may take ensample how they lande uppon oure londys!" (700)

> "Woll ye now turne agayne, now ye ar paste thys farre uppon youre journey? All the worlde woll speke of you vylany and shame." (701)

These knights see themselves for what they are: characters in a text, examples that will be interpreted by sympathetic or unsympathetic future readers.

It is this awareness of the textuality of these events and characters, and of the difficulty future readers may have in interpreting them, that allows the narrator to move toward a more positive presentation of them to the reader. This awareness establishes just such a link with future interpreters as Lancelot feared would be impossible: the present reader is indeed Lancelot's, and the other characters', posterity, the one interpreting the text they are aware of becoming, the one whose evaluation of their example is both feared and desired.[89]

The characters' fear that such interpretation will be difficult is fully justified: communication between text and reader has, in fact, become problematic because of the past's distance and the abuse of language. The admission that objective knowledge of the past is unavailable to us, however, can also be seen as an invitation to recreate it, and Malory's narrator presents several examples of readers in his present attempting to do just that:

> And so they shypped at Cardyff, and sayled unto Benwyke: som men calle hit Bayan and som men call hit Beawme, where the wyne of Beawme ys. (699)

> . . . Joyous Garde. (Somme men say it was Anwyk, and somme men say it was Bamborow). (724)

Note the difference from the narrator's earlier confidence that past locations could be pinpointed exactly in the present world.[90] Here, "some men" are interpreters like the reader, trying to arrive at the historical reality behind the text's uncertainty on even such minor matters. "Some men," these figures of the interpreting reader, also appear in a far more important context. The issue of Arthur's supposed death and possible survival becomes far more ambiguous in Malory's hands than it is in his French source. Sir Bedivere at the unmarked tomb assumes that it is Arthur's, but the hermit who witnessed the entombment is less certain than his French counterpart: " 'Fayre sunne,' seyde the ermyte, 'I wote nat veryly but by demynge' " (716). The narrator too is unsure and admits that he has no authoritative information, but he raises the legend of Arthur's survival:

> Now more of the deth of kynge Arthur coude I never fynde, but that thes ladyes brought hym to hys grave, and such one was entyred there whych the ermyte bare wytnes that sometyme was Bysshop of Caunturbyry. But yet the ermyte knew nat in sertayne that he was veryly the body of kynge Arthur; for thys tale sir Bedwere, a knyght of the Table Rounde, made hit to be wrytten.
>
> Yet som men say in many partys of Inglonde that kynge Arthure ys nat dede, but had by the wyll of oure Lorde Jesu into another place; and men say that he shall com agayne, and he shall wynne the Holy Crosse. Yet I woll nat say that hit shall be so, but rather I wolde sey: here in thys worlde he chaunged hys lyff. And many men say that there ys wrytten uppon the tumbe thys:
> HIC IACET ARTHURUS, REX QUONDAM REXQUE FUTURUS. (717)

"Some men," "many men": these readers of the past are making imaginative contact with the reality that has been concealed from them and from us. The narrator does not determine our reading but uses the phrase "chaunged hys lyff" to refer to Arthur's passing, a phrase more suggestive of a new identity than of death.[91]

Once again, Malory has given greater emphasis than the *Mort Artu* to this passage's indeterminacy; whereas the French romance uses certain iconographic details to suggest the myth of Arthur's survival to the reader, Malory's narrator cites the myth more explicitly, though without affirming or denying its truth. And the *Mort Artu*'s epitaph, which clearly states that Arthur is buried there, here becomes more mysterious: if it is the one Bedivere sees, the tomb is unmarked; if not, no one actually sees it, and the legendary inscription implies a future for Arthur, not only a past.

Malory's refusal to give his narrator an authoritative resolution to such important issues, the act of withholding necessary information from the reader, places us in a position like that of these interpreters within the text: we are invited to participate in the (fictional) recreation of the past as they do.[92] The characters' concern with posterity has warned us of the dangers of such speculations, and especially of the dangers of unsympathetic interpretation (and note, again, the similarity to Machaut's *Voir-Dit*). Mysteries, however, by their very nature invite us to provide solutions. The inadequacy of language and the distance of the past are presented in such a way as to allow the reader to overcome them imaginatively, through sympathetic acts of interpretation.

The narrator, or perhaps Malory himself, makes a direct appeal for such imaginative participation in a less distant past, his own era, in his final *explicit*, which epitomizes the text-reader relationship with great poignancy: "I praye you all jentylmen and jentylwymmen that redeth this book of Arthur and his knyghtes from the begynnyng to the endynge, praye for me whyle I am on lyve that God sende me good delyveraunce. And whan I am deed, I praye you all praye for my soule" (726). We are asked to project ourselves into the narrator's time not as individuals but as an orderly and unified society of gentlemen and gentlewomen. A community of readers is asked to participate imaginatively in the narrator's deliverance, as we participated in the imaginative revival of Arthur. Past and present, text and reader, are here brought together in a final acknowledgment that one cannot exist without the other, that the past survives only in texts, by means of its present readers, however fragile and fictional the texts and lacking in information the readers. The literary portrayal of a past community split by the abuse of language can create a present community of gentlefolk united in the acts of reading and of prayer. Participation in this community arises from participation in the text.

One of Malory's early readers, William Caxton, took a similar view. Though much of his famous preface is devoted to a justification of printing Malory's book on the grounds of its historical value, he eventually works his way to the view that history is in the eye of the beholder: "And for to passe the tyme thys book shal be plesaunte to rede in, but for to gyve fayth and byleve that all is trewe that is conteyned herin, ye be at your lyberté" (xv). His view of Malory's "history" is like the narrator's view of the legend of Arthur's survival, or of Lancelot's relationship with Guinevere; he does not know the truth but suggests that sympathetic reading of fiction can *create* a history for its readers:

> Thenne, to procede forth in thys sayd book, whyche I dyrecte unto alle noble prynces, lordes and ladyes, gentylmen or gentylwymmen, that desyre to rede or here redde of the noble and joyous hystorye of the grete conquerour and excellent kyng, Kyng Arthur, somtyme kyng

of thys noble royalme thenne callyd Brytaygne, I, Wyllyam Caxton, symple persone, present thys book folowyng whyche I have enprysed t'enprynte: and treateth of the noble actes, feates of armes of chyvalrye, prowesse, hardynesse, humanyté, love, curtosye, and veray gentyl- nesse, wyth many wonderful hystoryes and adventures. (xv)

Caxton invokes those same gentlemen and gentlewomen who appeared in Malory's final *explicit*, but now in their proper hierarchical place in an organized society consisting also of princes, lords, and ladies. This unified society is united precisely in the role of readers, specifically as readers of their own legendary national past. Having invoked that present society of readers, Caxton can finally assert that Arthur was indeed "king of this noble realm." The text will unite its readers in a national and social organization whose past it represents; the readers in turn can validate that past and the text by means of their sympathy and belief.[93]

If Machaut divorced textuality from life and encouraged the enjoyment of such a separation, Malory and Caxton urge the acceptance of fictional textuality and interpretation as a condition of life. Moving even beyond Chaucer's acceptance of textuality in interpersonal relations, they expand its implications into the (broadly defined) political sphere. In this new and positive presentation of textuality (and reading), it can recreate the past; and the acceptance of that recreated, textual, fictional past can also transform present reality.

Conclusion

Certain recent developments in literary theory, discussed in chapter 1, can now be seen to have opened up the possibility of reading pre-modern literature in a postmodern way. Although medieval thinkers would not, like Derrida, have denied the "transcendental signified" in favor of the endless chain of signifiers, some of them were willing to bracket the question of the divine control of human signification, with results that may seem startlingly familiar to a late twentieth-century reader. Indeed, the reader's creation of meaning, recently rediscovered by such theorists as Iser, would not have surprised medieval writers like Marie de France or Chaucer, who ask explicitly for such participation, or like Machaut or Malory, who make it possible even without directly requesting it.

The preceding chapters demonstrate some of the ways determinate and indeterminate modes of thought compete with, and impinge upon, each other in a number of medieval literary narratives of a variety of genres, cultures, and periods. In the twelfth century, Abelard, the rhetoricians, and other thinkers, responding to the new Aristotelian focus on the visible reality of this world in itself and on the recent interest in the literal level of Scripture, were willing to bracket the question of divine immanence and thus to react against the previously dominant neoplatonic mode of thought. Writers like Chrétien de Troyes also participate in this new *mentalité*, responding to it with works that question the validity of determinate allegory in such an intellectual climate. His *Conte del Graal* presents a world to be dealt with not by decoding its signs allegorically and determinately but by constantly readjusting one's methods of interpretation according to concrete circumstances. In a world of constantly shifting signification such interpretation must accept indeterminacy, that is, the probability that no authoritative truth can be discovered; instead, a more practical approach is needed, one that is flexible enough to adapt to the partial, changing, unstable reality of the visible universe. Paradoxically, these problems are themselves thematized in Chrétien's works, suggesting that some degree of determinate linguistic communication is still a goal to be pursued. Knowledge is still possible for the reader.

A similar conflict of the determinate and the indeterminate is also visible in the works of Chrétien's contemporary, Marie de France. The *Lais* draw her readers into the hermeneutic circle by suggesting that they can participate in the works' creation of meaning, which is thus not predetermined by the author. Nevertheless, this participation is, again, itself thematized; in a sense, semantic determinacy is not eliminated but simply raised to a meta-semantic level, as in Chrétien's romance.

In the thirteenth century, the Vulgate Cycle exemplifies a similar competition between the two modes. One of its component sections, the *Queste del saint Graal*, is evidence that determinate, neoplatonic allegory, in which this world can be confidently decoded as symbolic of the invisible things of God, because God himself controls human signification directly, retains much of its power in the high Middle Ages. The following section, however, the *Mort Artu*, immediately challenges this predetermined signification with a wealth of apparently authoritative signs and texts whose relation to reality is nevertheless consistently questioned. One such text is the *Mort Artu* itself: apparently omniscient, its concern with historical truth calls that omniscience radically into question, as does its emphasis on purely human text-production rather than the divine symbolism of the *Queste*. Here at last is a literary narrative that does not thematize the indeterminacy of signification but builds it into its very structure. The *Mort Artu* thus reproduces in itself the competition between determinate and indeterminate meanings that characterizes the Vulgate Cycle generally.

Not until the fourteenth century, with its radical questioning of the possibility of knowledge, as proposed by William of Ockham and the later philosophers he influenced, do we find a writer in whose works the indeterminate mode predominates almost completely. Guillaume de Machaut's *Livre du Voir-Dit*, with its playful destabilization of all meaning, including its own claims to truth, is the most sophisticated literary response to the indeterminate, post-neoplatonic *mentalité* yet to appear. In Machaut's hands, even allegory appears as an indeterminate mode, concealing rather than revealing a supposed truth (that may not, in fact, exist at all outside the confines of the text). Like Marie, Machaut carefully draws the reader into the hermeneutic circle, but he does not thematize this process as she does, preferring, like the author of the *Mort Artu*, to build indeterminacy into the very fabric of his text.

Machaut, however, does not represent the final triumph of the indeterminate mode of thought. The fourteenth century, too, can be seen as a period of competition between the two modes. Soon after Machaut's career, Chaucer began exploring the problems that indeterminate signification raises.

His poetry demonstrates the conflict in a single writer's career as the Vulgate Cycle demonstrates it in a single work, and as the movement from the twelfth to the fourteenth century demonstrates it for the entire period. Whereas an early poem like *The Book of the Duchess* finds indeterminacy and interpretation dangerous and suggests a nostalgia for full presence and communication, and whereas *Troilus and Criseyde* finds interpretation uncontrolled by divine authority tragic in life (but perhaps valuable in literature), the *Canterbury Tales*, written at the end of his life, goes even further than Machaut's *Voir-Dit* in accepting the textual nature of experience: absence, indeterminacy, and never-ending interpretation comically triumph over presence and communication.

Malory, in the fifteenth century, summarizes all these trends and suggests that, even this late in the Middle Ages, the competition between determinate and indeterminate had not been resolved. Although the reader must supply much of his book's meaning, this indeterminacy is seen as an historically "modern" phenomenon, caused in part by the distance of the past; that distant period itself is shown to have been characterized by the possibility, at least, of fully adequate sign systems. On the other hand, even the Arthurian past is also characterized by the competition among differing interpretations; the two modes compete in the past, and their competition means that the indeterminate one predominates in the present.

These observations suggest that a more nuanced view of medieval narrative than has so far appeared is needed. Medieval culture outside of literature is not simply dominated by determinate modes of thought nor does medieval literature simply escape from those modes and propose an indeterminate alternative, as Gellrich suggests. Neither is there a simple movement from early, determinate modes to later, indeterminate ones, as Bloch implies (see chapter 1). Instead, the competition between determinate and indeterminate must be seen as dominating high and late medieval culture and literature both (though in different ways at different points in medieval cultural history). Indeterminacy would seem to gain ground as we move from the twelfth to the fifteenth centuries, but the nostalgia, at least, for a world in which meaning was directly controlled by God, is still present in all the works we have investigated (possibly excepting the *Voir-Dit* and *The Canterbury Tales*). On the other hand, the very fact that there is a conflict between the modes in these works at all may finally suggest that indeterminacy, the refusal to choose, ultimately prevails.

In any case, with Caxton, discussed at the end of chapter 5, we come to the end of the Middle Ages. His edition of Malory was printed in 1485, the year Henry VII became king of England, ushering in the Renaissance. The printing press may be the more important factor: the experience of reading a printed book is decisively different from that of reading a manuscript. No longer can readers literally affect the work they are reading as the Wife of Bath affected Jankyn's book. While her removal of three leaves from it would have meant that future scribes copying it would produce a text very different from that of the original, nothing the reader of a printed book may do can affect the many other copies of it. No longer can a reader become a writer simply by writing between the lines. With the advent of the Renaissance, the indeterminacy of meaning must be separated from the indeterminacy of texts, and interpretation must thus become less overt and participatory, must be taken less for granted. With the printing press, we are on the threshold of the modern world; nothing like the medieval experience of reading will reappear until the postmodern.

Notes
Bibliography
Index

Notes

1. Indeterminacy of Literary Meaning and Medieval Culture, 1100–1500

1. Hartman, "Interpreter," 12.

2. Chrétien, *Perceval*, lines 3190–3209. This passage will be discussed in more detail in chapter 2.

3. John Stevens, *Romance*, 21.

4. Iser, *Act*, 43; see also 163–231. Such "gaps" have been theorized by other phenomenological critics; for example, Ingarden, *Work*, 336–55.

5. See Kristeva, *Text*; Greimas, *Dictionnaire*; Todorov, *Grammaire*; Eco, *Aesthetics* (first published in Italy in 1970); Jauss, *Aesthetic*.

6. Spivak, Introduction, lxxxi.

7. Derrida, *Grammatology*, 7.

8. See Norris, *Deconstruction*, 49.

9. For good visual examples of commentary in late medieval manuscripts, see Parkes, *Book Hands*, plates 19–20, and commentary. Derrida, *Glas*.

10. On *mouvance*, see Zumthor, *Essai*, 70–75, and his "Intertextualité."

11. See Frappier, *Etude*, 27–146. Other relevant discussions of medieval authorship include Zumthor, *Essai*, 64–106, and Grigsby, "Ontology."

12. See Rossetti, *Chaucer's Troylus*.

13. See Kane's convincing argument against multiple or anonymous authorship in *Authorship*.

14. Coleman, *Readers and Writers*, 171–72. For a specific example of the effect of this phenomenon on literary composition, see Allen, "*Detractor*."

15. Minnis, *Authorship*, 191–210; Stock, *Literacy*, 414.

16. For a discussion of scribal interventions in literary works, see E. Kennedy, "Scribe."

17. Marie de France, *Lais*, Prologue, lines 9–16.

18. On the additions to *The Canterbury Tales*, and on their elimination by post-medieval editors, see the commentary on the major editions in *Critical Heritage*, 1, 33–38. On the perception of commentary as integral to the text, see Caie, "Glosses."

19. Derrida, "Limited, Inc a b c . . . ." This article is a reply to Searle,

"Reiterating the Differences," which in turn is a response to Derrida's "Signature Event Context."

20. Fish, "Poem," 327.

21. Foucault, "What Is an Author?"; Ricoeur, "What Is a Text?" For Bonaventure's speculations on authorship, see Minnis, 94–95 etc.

22. Hanning, "Harassment," 29.

23. Vinaver, *Rise*, cited by Bruns, *Inventions*, 51.

24. Bruns, 55–56.

25. Bloch, *Etymologies*; Gellrich, *Idea*; Ferster, *Interpretation*; Burns, *Arthurian Fictions*; Shoaf, *Currency*; Minnis, *Authorship*.

26. Gellrich, 17–138. Minnis falls into a similar trap because he considers only a single context for literary authorship, that of Biblical exegesis. Bloch discusses the movement from one mentality to another in his third chapter, 92–127; though he would probably deny having taken an essentialist point of view, his presentation of the two modes suggests a complete break between them. Stock, 12–87.

27. Ferster, *Interpretation*, 4–15.

28. Burns's interpretation of the *Queste*, for example, rests on a misunderstanding of Auerbach, "Figura." Burns originally suggested that in medieval typology, the antitype could refer back to the type: see "Allegory," 354. Auerbach makes it clear, however, that referentiality moves only from type to antitype, never the reverse: the fulfillment is *veritas*, while the figure is merely *umbra* or *imago* ("Figura," 34). Although the mistake is corrected in Burns's book, 55–77, the interpretation to which it gave rise (that the *Queste* is not allegorical, because the "spiritual" level refers back to the "historical") remains. The need to demonstrate the free play of signification overwhelms historical sensitivity.

29. See Colish, *Mirror*, 7–54, especially 26.

30. Trans. Pine-Coffin, IX.10, 197. The Latin text follows: "et dum loquimur et inhiamus illi, attingimus eam modice toto ictu cordis; et suspiravimus, et relinquimus ibi religatas primitias spiritus, et remeavimus ad strepitem oria nostri" (ed. Rouse, 2, 48).

31. Bloch, 50. Two articles by Vance trace the entire process by which language provides the impetus for transcendence: "Augustine's *Confessions*" and "Language."

32. Pine-Coffin, XII.18, 295–96. "quid mihi obest, cum diversa in his verbis intellegi possint, quae tamen vera sint? quid, inquam, mihi obest, si aliud ego sensero, quam sensit alius eum sensisse, qui scripsit? omnes quidem, qui legimus, nitimur hoc indagare atque conprehendere, quod voluit ille quem legimus, et cum eum veridicum credimus, nihil, quod falsum esse vel novimus vel putamus, audemus eum existimare dixisse. dum ergo quisque conatur id sentire in scripturis sanctis, quod in eis sensit ille qui scripsit, quid mali est, si hoc sentiat, quod tu, lux omnium veridi-

carum mentium, ostendis verum esse, etiamsi non hoc sensit ille, quem legit, cum et ille verum nec tamen hoc senserit?" (Rouse, 2, 328–30).

33. Knapp, "Wandrynge," 149.

34. Curtius, *Literature*, 159–62.

35. Gellrich, 98.

36. Gellrich, 100.

37. Cited in translation by Pelikan, *Growth*, 96. The Latin text follows: "nihil enim visibilium rerum corporaliumque est, ut arbitror, quod non incorporale quid et intelligibile significet" (Eriugena, *De divisione naturae*, col. 865–66).

38. *Ecclesiastical History of Orderic Vitalis*, ed. and trans. Chibnall, 3, 213. The Latin text follows: "Humani acumen ingenii semper indiget utili sedimine competenter exerceri, et preterita recolendo presentiaque rimando ad futura feliciter uirtutibus instrui. . . . Plerumque multa quae uelut inaudita putantur rudium auribus insonant, et noua modernis in repentinis casibus frequenter emanant, in quibus intellectuales inexpertorum caligant (VI, prologue; Chibnall, 3, 212).

39. Stock, 74.

40. Stock, 457.

41. Gregory of Tours, *History*, trans. Thorpe, 247. "In eo anno fulgor per caelum discurrisse visus est, sicut quondam ante mortem Chlotharii factum vidimus" (ed. Omont and Collon, IV.XXXVI (51), 147).

42. Thorpe, 247–48. "Si abieris et fratrem tuum interficere nolueris, vivus et victor redis; sin autem aliud cogitaveris, morieris. Sic enim Dominus per Salomonem dixit: *Foveam quae fratri tuo parabis, in ea conrues*" (Omont and Collon, IV.XXXVI (51), 147–48). And see De Nie, *Views*.

43. Bloch, 83–87.

44. Curtius, 23; Gellrich, 17–28.

45. Chibnall, 3, 285. "Codicibus autem perditis antiquorum res gestae obliuioni traditae sunt, quae a modernis qualibet arte recuperari non possunt, quia ueterum monimenta cum mundo praetereunte a memoria presentium deficiunt" (VI.9; Chibnall, 3, 284).

46. Stock, 88–240

47. Jauss, *Aesthetic*; Fish, *Is There a Text?*

48. On *historia*, see C. Benson, *History*, 6–15.

49. Nichols, *Signs*, 11.

50. Nichols, 12.

51. Nichols, 164. For an example of "directed vision" in another *chanson de geste*, see Nichols, "Sign as (Hi)story," 1–9.

52. My discussion of trends in exegesis is indebted throughout to Smalley, *Study*.

53. Smalley, 28, paraphrasing Cassian's *Conlationes*.

54. Minnis, 72.

55. Smalley, 196.

56. Hugh of St. Victor, *Didascalicon*, trans. Taylor, VI, 3, 136. The Latin text follows: "neque ego te perfecte subtilem posse fieri puto in allegoria, nisi prius fundatus fueris in historia. noli contemnere minima haec. paulatim defluit qui minima contemnit" (ed. Buttimer, 114).

57. "Sententia divina" is the phrase translated as "divine deeper meaning." Taylor, VI, 11, 149–50. "sententia nullam admittit repugnantiam, semper congrua est, semper vera" (Buttimer, 128).

58. Taylor, VI, 11, 150. "cum sana fide concordat" (Buttimer, 129).

59. Eco, 145.

60. Smalley, 101; Taylor, VI, 11, 149. "cum in sensu, ut dictum est, multa inveniantur contraria" (Buttimer, 128).

61. Taylor, VI, 10, 148–49. "quid dicere voluerit propheta, bonum promiserit an malum minatus fuerit, ignoras" (Buttimer, 127).

62. Smalley, 299–300.

63. Minnis, 84.

64. St. Thomas Aquinas, *Summa Theologiae*, Blackfriars translation, 60. The Latin text follows: ". . . sensus litteralis est, quem auctor intendit: auctor autem sacrae Scripturae Deus est, qui omnia simul suo intellectu comprehendit: non est inconveniens, ut dicit Augustinus (XII *Confessionum*), si etiam secundum litteralem sensum in una littera Scripturae plures sint sensus" (*Summa Theologiae* [1962, Prima pars, qu. I, art. 10, 10).

65. Minnis, 91.

66. Minnis, 158.

67. Eco, 152–53.

68. Murphy, *Rhetoric*, 49ff. See also Burns, *Arthurian Fictions*, 21–27.

69. Clanchy, *Memory*, 249.

70. Clanchy gives the example of forged Arthurian charters, 249–50.

71. Alain de Lille, *The Complaint of Nature*, trans. Moffat, 39. The Latin text follows: "An ignoras, quomodo poetae sine omni palliationis remedio, auditoribus nudam falsitatem prostituunt, ut quadam mellita dulcedine velut incantatas audientium aures inebrient? Quomodo ipsem falsitatem quadam probabilitatis hypocrisi palliant?" (Alanus de Insulis, *De planctu naturae*, col. 451). See also Bloch, 133–36.

72. On the classicizing friars, see Allen, *The Friar as Critic*.

73. Taylor, III, 4, 88. "Hujus modi sunt omnia poetarum carmina, ut sunt tragoediae, comoediae, satirae, heroica quoque et lyrica, et iambica, et didascalica quaedam; fabulae quoque et historiae; illorum etiam scripta, quos nunc philosophos appellare solemus, qui est brevem materiam longis verborum ambagibus extendere consueverunt, et facilem sensum perplexis sermonibus obscurare, vel etiam diversa simul compilantes, quasi de multis coloribus et formis, unam picturam facere" (Buttimer, 54).

74. Geoffrey of Vinsauf, *Poetria nova*, trans. Nims, 50. The Latin text follows:

> Quando venit tali sententia culta paratu,
> Ille sonus vocum laetam dulcesit ad aurem,
> Et fricat interius nova delectatio mentem.

(*Poetria nova* IV, 11, 949–51, in *Les Arts poétiques,* ed. Faral, 226). See also Leupin, *Le Graal,* 9–20. Trimpi, *Muses,* suggests that rhetoric has a long non-theological history.

75. Leupin, "Reflexivity," 141.

76. "Ponit tres opiniones more philosophi sed nullam soluit aut affirmate, more poete" (I.412); "Non affirmat uerum esse ut historiographus sed tangit ut poeta" (II.410). (*Arnulfi Aurelianensis Glosule super Lucanum,* ed. Marti, 55 and 128). Cited by Marti in her introduction, xxxviii, to which I am indebted for this entire discussion.

77. Marti, Introduction, xxxviii.

78. Bloch, 142, quoting Abelard's *Historia calamitatum.*

79. De Rijk, *Logica Modernorum,* 2, 186.

80. Bloch, 146, citing Abelard, *Dialectica.* See also De Rijk, *Logica,* 2, 186–206, for a more technical discussion.

81. Stock, 377.

82. Gilson, *Christian Philosophy,* 161. See Abelard, *Scito teipsum,* 2, 592–642; *Abailard's Ethics,* trans. McCallum.

83. Vinaver, *Rise,* 1.

84. Ker, *Epic and Romance.*

85. *La Chanson de Roland,* ed. Bédier, lines 3543–54. *The Song of Roland,* trans. Goldin. See Goldin, 150n., and Bédier's "note critique" on line 3546 in his edition. And cf. Gerard J. Brault's commentary: *The Song of Roland: An Analytical Edition,* 1, 307–09 and 465n. 45 and 46.

86. *Roland,* ed. Bédier, line 3554. "he is wrong . . . Charlemagne is right." Trans. Goldin.

87. Bloch, *Law,* 11 and 37–39.

88. See *Roland,* lines 3931–33, and Bloch, *Law,* 46.

89. Nichols, 39.

90. Pine-Coffin, X.3, 208. "sed quia caritas omnia credit, (inter eos utique, quos conexos sibimet unum facit,) ego quoque, domine, etiam sic tibi confiteor, ut audiant homines, quibus demonstrare non possum, an vera confiteor; sed credunt mihi, quorum mihi aures caritas aperit" (Rouse, 2, 78).

91. Parker, *Inescapable Romance,* 4.

92. Frye, *Anatomy of Criticism,* cited by Parker, 13.

93. Parker, 13.

94. See Leupin, *Le Graal,* 20.

95. On the date of *Roland,* see Bédier, *La Chanson de Roland commentée,* 40–59. On the date of the *Charrette,* see Frappier's essay on Chrétien in *ALMA,* 180–81.

96. Chrétien, *Charrette,* lines 333–38. "Whoever was convicted of any crime was placed upon a cart and dragged through all the streets, and he lost

henceforth all his legal rights, and was never afterward heard, honoured, or welcomed in any court" (*Lancelot*, trans. Comfort, 274).

97. Chrétien, lines 4483–93. Here and throughout this book, conventions for indicating dialogue follow modern American usage. "Then the queen replies: 'What? Did you not hesitate for shame to mount the cart? You showed you were loath to get in, when you hesitated for two whole steps. That is the reason why I would neither address nor look at you.' 'May God save me from such a crime again,' Lancelot replies, 'and may God show me no mercy, if you were not quite right!' " (Comfort, 327).

98. Hanning, *Individual*, 15 and 17–34.

99. Chrétien, lines 5773–82. "Thus they talk among themselves: 'Do you see that knight yonder with a golden band across the middle of his red shield? That is Governauz of Roberdic. And do you see that other one, who has an eagle and a dragon painted side by side upon his shield? That is the son of the king of Aragon, who has come to this land in search of glory and renown' " (Comfort, 343).

100. Chrétien, lines 7093–97. "The King and all the others there are jubilant and express their joy. Happier than they ever were before, they relieve Lancelot of his arms, and lead him away exultingly" (Comfort, 359).

101. See *Roland*, lines 3993–4002.

102. For a review of the mutually exclusive readings of the *Charrette* published in one ten-year period, see Shirt. See also the negative opinions of Lancelot reviewed by Rychner, "Prologue." Rychner's own assessment is positive: see his "Le Sujet," a good example of the difficulties encountered by a critic who attempts to assert a single aspect of Lancelot's character as the poem's meaning, while still trying to account for those aspects which do not accord with his reading. Rychner is forced, for example, into the position of suggesting that Lancelot represents his community although he rejects its values, 71. A more general discussion of the self-contradictory romance hero is Sklute, "Ambiguity," which also links this problem with medieval epistemological concerns. Adler draws a similar conclusion for a later period in "Problems." "A chacun son Lancelot" is from Imbs, "La Charrette," cited by Shirt, 50.

103. Grant, "Scientific Thought." Oresme's paradoxical method of demonstrating that there is no logical reason either to accept or to reject a given proposition is illustrated at several points in a convenient volume of selections from Duhem: *Cosmology*. See, e.g., 472–79. Duhem cites Oresme's *Livre du ciel et du monde*, which has since been published. See also Kruger, "Dreams," 601–49, for another detailed examination of Oresme's indeterminate mode of scientific thought as expressed in a more literary format.

104. Quoted in translation by Gilson, 491. The Latin text follows: "quaelibet res extra animam seipsa est singularis" (*Ordinatio* 2, I.ii.6, 197).

105. Leff, *Ockham*, 359–82.

106. *Potentia absoluta* as the central issue in nominalist and Ockhamist

thought has been described most clearly by Oberman. For Ockham's position, see Adams, *Ockham*, 2, 1186–1207, and Leff, *Ockham*, 14–18.

107. "notitia intuitiva, tam sensitiva quam intellectiva, potest esse de re non existente" (Ockham, *Ordinatio* 1, Prologue, i.1, 38). See also Gilson's discussion of this passage, 490.

108. Adams, 2, 1235–36; see also Leff, *Ockham*, 18.

109. Scott, "Nicholas," 19.

110. Scott, "Ockham," 46.

111. Minnis, 74. Minnis refers to Ockham, *De sacramento altaris*.

112. *Ockham's Theory of Terms*, trans. Loux, 50. The Latin text follows: "conceptus sive passio animae naturaliter significat; terminus autem prolatus vel scriptus nihil significat nisi secundum voluntariam institutionem. Ex quo sequitur alia differentia, videlicet, quod terminus prolatus vel scriptus ad placitum potest mutare suum significatum, terminus autem conceptus non mutat suum significatum ad placitum cuiuscumque" (*Summa Logicae, Pars I*, I).

113. Bursill-Hall, *Speculative Grammars*, describes another theory of language roughly contemporary with Ockham's, that of the speculative grammarians. This theory has been seen both as a determinate one, because it attempts to describe a universal grammar for all languages (Gellrich, 102–09), and as an indeterminate one, because it emphasizes the gap between language and reality (Bloch, *Etymologies*, 151–58). It is perhaps more useful to see it as another example of the competition between the two modes: thus, even the attempt to discover determinate laws that work in all cases has the effect of destabilizing signification.

114. *The Universal Treatise*, 119. The Latin text follows: "Tertia decima conclusio est quod de scitis per experimentiam . . . habetur solum habitus conjecturavitus, non certitudo" (*Exigit ordo executionis*, ed. O'Donnell, 237).

115. Scott, "Nicholas," 29.

116. Moody, "Parisian Statutes," 122.

117. Leff, *Ockham*, 53–54.

118. Moody, "Parisian Statutes," 122.

119. See Scott, "Ockham," especially 39, and "Nicholas," especially 24.

120. Searle, "The World," 78.

121. Searle, 78–79.

2. Modes of Signification in Two Grail Romances

1. De Man, "Pascal's Allegory," 2. See also his *Allegories of Reading*, and J. Hillis Miller, "Two Allegories."

2. De Man, "Pascal's Allegory," 10–11.

3. Quilligan, "Allegory," 186. See also her "Words and Sex."

4. Minnis, *Theory*, 73–159.

5. Frappier, "Cortège," 191. Frappier's most thorough refutation of the allegorical reading is "Le *Conte du Graal* est–il une allégorie judéo-chrétienne?"

6. Guiette, "Li conte." See also Duggan, "Ambiguity," and Freeman, "Jean Frappier," which also gives further references to Frappier's views on this point.

7. On this latter point, see Wetherbee, *Platonism*, 36–48.

8. Fletcher, *Allegory*, 179–303.

9. Robertson, "Historical Criticism," 14.

10. Robertson, *Preface*.

11. This theory was originated by Holmes, *New Interpretation*, and has been pursued by Holmes and Klenke in *Chrétien, Troyes, and the Grail*, and by Klenke alone in a series of studies, the most recent of which is *Chrétien de Troyes and* Le Conte del Graal.

12. Bloomfield, "Symbolism," 78. For a review of other negative responses to Holmes and Klenke, see Levy, "Literary Criticism."

13. Examples can be found in the work of the "classicizing friars" described by Smalley, *English Friars*, and by J. Allen, *Friar as Critic*. The well-known Christian interpretation of Virgil's "Fourth Eclogue" is discussed by de Lubac, *Exégèse*, part 2, vol. 2, 233–62.

14. Dante, "Epistola X"; "Letter to Can Grande," trans. Haller, *Literary Criticism of Dante Alighieri*, 95–111. For a survey of late medieval allegorical interpretations of the *Commedia*, see Pépin, *Dante et la tradition de l'allégorie*, 127–29, where it is also noted that Boccaccio claims allegorical meanings for some of his own contemporaries. See his *Genealogie deorum gentilium libri*, XIV, 22: "Plures enim ex nostris poete fuere et adhuc sunt, qui sub tegminibus fictionum suarum Christiane religionis devotos sacrosque sensus commendavere"(ed. Romano, 2, 748). "Many even of our own tongue have been poets—nay, still survive—who, under cover of their compositions, have expressed the deep and holy meaning of Christianity" (*Boccaccio on Poetry*, trans. Osgood, 99). Pépin surveys the debate on the authenticity of the "Letter," 59–60, n. 6.

15. Pépin, 126.

16. Auerbach, "Dante's Addresses to the Reader," especially 151 ff. See also his "Figurative Texts," 94, n. 6.

17. Eco, *Aesthetics*, 162.

18. Minnis, 214–17. Cf. Mazzotta, *Dante*, who places Dante in a very different tradition, one that destabilizes meaning and emphasizes the ambiguity resulting from the distance between signs and meanings.

19. *Glossa ordinaria*, trans. Rollinson in his *Classical Theories*, 78. The Latin text follows: "Habet tamen iste liber hoc speciale quod una littera continet plures sensus. Cujus ratio est quia principalis hujus libri auctor est ipse Deus: in cujus potestate est non solum uti vocibus ad aliquid significandum (quod etiam hominis facere possunt et faciunt), sed etiam rebus significatis

per voces utitur ad significandum alias res: et ideo commune est omnibus libris, quod voces aliquid significent, sed speciale est huic libro quod res significatae per voces aliud significent" (*PL* 113, col. 8).

20. "Unde in nulla scientia, humana industria inventa, proprie loquendo, potest inveniri nisi litteralis sensus; sed solum in ista Scriptura, cujus Spiritus sanctus est auctor, homo vero instrumentum" (St. Thomas Aquinas, *Quaestiones quodlibetales*, ed. Mandonnet, VII, qu. 6, art. 16, 280).

Both Bloomfield, 77, n. 17, and Pépin, 71–72, cite two further texts that imply the same prohibition on allegorical readings of human creations: Hugh of St. Victor, *Didascalicon*, ed. Buttimer, V, 3, 96; trans. Taylor, 121–22; and St. Thomas Aquinas, *Summa Theologiae*, Pauline ed., I, qu. 1, art. 10, 10; Blackfriars translation, 59.

21. The most convincing modern expositions of the Augustinian influence are Huppé, *Doctrine and Poetry*, 3–63, and Robertson, *Preface*, 52–137. A somewhat more tendentious exposition may be found in these authors' collaborative *Fruyt and Chaf*, 3–31.

22. See Rollinson, 54–64; see also D. Allen, *Mysteriously Meant*, 16, and Marrou, *Saint Augustin*, 345–50 (for the negative view of allegorizing the classics), and 497 (for the positive).

23. St. Augustine, *Confessions*, trans. Pine-Coffin, 62. "quantum enim meliores grammaticorum et poetarum fabellae quam illa decipula! nam versas et carmen et Medea volans utiliores certe, quam quinque elementa, varie fucata propter quinque antra tenebrarum, quae omnino nulla sunt et occidunt credentem. nam versum et carmen etiam ad vera pulmenta transfero" (ed. Rouse, 1, 118).

24. Huppé, 3–63, surveys patristic and early medieval views of allegory. Like both Augustine and Aquinas, Hugh of St. Victor gives different opinions of secular literature and its interpretation in different passages.

25. Cited in Pézard, *Dante sous la pluie de feu*, 400. The text of St. Eucher he refers to is the *Liber formularum spiritalis intellegentiae*, PL 50, col. 727–28. Pézard quotes the relevant passages, 383.

26. *Summa theologiae*, Pauline ed., I, qu. 1, art. 10, 10; Blackfriars translation, 60. See Pépin, 74–82.

27. Dante, *Convivio*, ed. Busnelli and Vandelli, *passim*. The theoretical discussions of allegory are translated by Haller, *Literary Criticism*, 112–14 and 123–30. See also Pépin, 53–57.

28. See Misrahi, "Symbolism," especially 557 and 564; Guiette; and Jung, *Etudes*, 15, 19, and 182–86. Nitze, *"Sans,"* suggests that Chrétien adapted the techniques of Scriptural exegesis in composing his own works but rendered his meanings non-allegorical for his courtly audience.

29. Olson, *Literature as Recreation*, 19–127.

30. J. Allen, *Ethical Poetic*.

31. Tuve, *Allegorical Imagery*, 408. Rollinson also makes the point that "the assumption that a perfectly satisfactory literal text will never indicate on its

own anything beyond its obvious literal implications seems sound, if not inevitable," 26, and goes on to suggest that "suitable meanings must be similar and not unlike the text they interpret," according to Augustine, 47.

32. Roques, "Le Graal"; see also Lot-Borodine, "Le *Conte del Graal*."

33. Both Olschki, *Grail Castle*, and Gallais, "Perceval," have seen the *Conte del Graal* as an allegorical confrontation of orthodoxy and the Cathar heresy, while Adolf, *Visio Pacis*, and Carmody, "Les Sources orientales" and "Le *Perceval*," respectively find political allegories of the Crusades and of Philip of Flanders' activities in the Orient. Grill, "Château," and Mahoney, "*Conte del Graal*," find symbolic relations between the romance and a religious order. Misrahi, "Symbolism," finds the initiator of such allegorical readings in Bezzola, *Le Sens de l'aventure*, and surveys a number of them, as does Payen, *Motif*, 391–92. Both declare allegorical readings unjustifiable.

34. Critics who have continued to defend the allegorical view in the 1980's include Klenke, *Chrétien de Troyes*, and Ribard, "Ecriture symbolique."

35. For two further examples of a non-allegorical response, see *The Continuations of the Old French* Perceval, ed. Roach, Ivy, and Foulet. See also Roach, "Transformations," and Marx, "Quelques remarques," especially 472–73.

36. Wolfgang, "Perceval's Father," argues that the religious overtones of the Grail-quest (which are necessary for most allegorical interpretations) are not present in Chrétien's work but were added by Robert de Boron.

37. See chapter 1.

38. Frappier, in *ALMA*, 159, dates the *Conte del Graal* between 1181 and 1190. Smalley finds the beginnings of a renewed interest in the literal level of Scripture in the late twelfth and early thirteenth centuries; see *Study*, 292–308. De Lubac describes the process by which allegory became detached from Scriptural study, which itself became primarily historical, after Hugh of St. Victor: *Exégèse médiévale*, part 2, vol. 1, 418–35.

39. However, for an ingenious attempt to demonstrate that the *Conte del Graal* is actually complete, despite appearances, see Dragonetti, *La Vie*, especially 241–64.

40. See chapter 1. Ollier, "Modernité," points out that the twelfth century "annonce la querelle des universaux," 431, and implies that this may also help account for the problematic nature of knowledge in Chrétien's romances; see also 435–36.

41. Quilligan, *Language of Allegory*, 225–26. I am also indebted to Quilligan's book for the distinction between "readers of allegory" and "allegorical critics," 227. For the view of allegory as primarily didactic, see Clifford, *Transformations*, 36–93.

42. Leupin, *Graal*, 9–20 and 211–13.

43. On semiotic disruption, see Grigsby, "Sign." For an opposite, and unusual, view of Perceval as an agent of "collective social destiny," see Sturm-Maddox, "Prophetic Fool." Grigsby also supports my contention

that Chrétien does not reject rhetoric as he rejects allegory, by situating his works in the rhetorical tradition. See also Kelly, "Psychologie/pathologie."

44. Pickens, *Welsh Knight*, makes a similar point, 138–39. See also Grigsby, "Sign," 39–40. Obviously I believe that Perceval's and Gawain's adventures both genuinely belong to a single romance, and that the Good Friday episode is authentic, though the fact that they were perceived as a unit by medieval scribes and readers is in my opinion reason enough for us to perceive them as a unit too, whether or not Chrétien wrote all the episodes himself. For the opposite view see D. Owen, *Grail Legend*, and Hofer, "Structure." Arguments in favor of the entire work's unity and authenticity include Delbouille, "Genèse"; Hoffman, "Structure"; Hoggan, "Péché"; and Saly, "L'Itinéraire."

45. Chrétien de Troyes, *Le Roman de Perceval ou le Conte du Graal*, ed. Roach. Line numbers will be cited parenthetically in the text. "The youth hears and does not see those who are coming at more than a pace. He marvels at it and says:

'By my soul, my mother, my lady, told me true, who told me that devils are more noisy than anything in the world. And she said, to teach me, that because of them one ought to cross himself. But this instruction I shall disdain, for never indeed will I cross myself; rather will I strike the strongest so quickly with one of my javelins that never, as I believe, will any of the others approach me' " (5–6; *The Story of the Grail*, trans. Linker). Quotations from this translation, with citations by page number, will continue to appear as notes. I prefer Linker's translation, for my purposes here, to several more elegant and recent ones because Linker's, despite its stylistic awkwardness, is the most literal.

46. As is noted by Crow, "Some Observations," especially 84–86.

47. " 'Ah! Lord God, thanks! These are angels that I see here. Ah! truly have I sinned much, now have I acted very badly in saying that they were devils. My mother did not tell me a fable, who told me that angels were the most beautiful things there are, except God Who is more beautiful than all. Here I see the Lord God, I believe, for I perceive one of them so beautiful that the others, if God keep me, haven't the tenth of beauty.' " (6)

48. Bloch, *Etymologies*, 203.

49. "He reaches out his hand to his lance, grasps it and says: 'Fair dear lord, you who are named knight, what is this you hold? . . .'

'. . . I shall tell you: this is my lance.'

'Do you say,' says he, 'that one throws it just as I do my javelins?'

'No, indeed, youth, you are quite foolish. Rather does one strike with it on the spot.'

'Then one of these three javelins is worth more; for I slay whatever I wish with it, birds and beasts at need, and I slay them as far as one could draw a bolt' (7).

'He doesn't know all the laws,' says the lord, 'if God help me, for he never answers rightly anything I ask him. Rather he asks of whatever he sees, what is its name and what one does with it' " (8).

50. "The youth understands very little of what his mother is saying. 'Give me,' says he, 'something to eat! I don't know of what you speak to me, but I should very willingly go to the King who makes knights. And I shall go, no matter whom it may worry' " (13).

51. Bloch, *Etymologies*, 204.

52. 578–79. ". . . a beautiful and most holy house both of holy bodies and of treasures" (15).

53. "There were two minsters in the town which were two abbeys, the one of trembling nuns, the other of dejected monks. He did not find the minsters well adorned nor well tapestried; rather he saw the walls cracked and split and the towers uncovered" (42).

54. " 'Rather will I kiss you, by my head,' says the youth, 'whomever it may grieve; as my mother taught me.'

'I, truly, will never kiss you,' says the maiden, 'if I can help it. Flee, so that my friend does not find you; because, if he finds you, you are dead.'

The youth had strong arms and he embraces her very sillily, for he did not know how to do otherwise" (18).

55. " 'There is more to it, lord,' says she, 'my ring is in the quarrel; for he has taken it from me, and carries it away: I would rather be dead than that he should have thus carried it away.'

Behold him discomforted and in anguish in his heart. 'By my faith,' says he, 'here is an outrage! And since he carries it away, let him have it; but I think that he did more' " (20).

56. For example, Nitze, *Perceval and the Holy Grail*, 290–305. See also Hoffman; Payen, *Motif*, 391–403; and Ribard, "L'Ecriture romanesque." Haidu, *Aesthetic Distance*, suggests that Perceval does not really progress, 255.

57. "The youth who had come therein that night saw this marvel, but held himself from asking how that thing came about, for he remembered the warning of the one who made him a knight, who showed and taught him that he should keep himself from too much talking" (69).

"But he keeps silent more than is fitting, for at each dish which was served he sees the grail completely uncovered pass in front of him, but he does not know whom they serve with it and he would very much like to know, but he will ask, truly, this he says and thinks, before he turns away, of one of the youths of the court, but he will wait until morning when he takes his leave of the lord and of all the other household" (71).

58. " 'You have told me a felonious tale. Since she is put in the earth what should I go forward to seek? For nothing was I going there except for her whom I wished to see. I must hold another way, but if you wished to

come with me I should like it well, for this one who lies here dead will never more be worth anything to you, I pledge it to you: "The dead to the dead, the living to the living." Let us go away, you and I together. It seems to me great folly of you that here alone you watch this dead man; but let us follow the one who killed him, and I promise and grant you either that he will make me recreant or I him, if I can reach him' " (77).

59. "Next Perceval says quite differently that he will not lie in a hostel two nights in all his life, nor will he hear news of strange passage without going there to pass, nor of knight who is worth more than another knight or more than two, without going to combat him, until he knows of the grail whom they serve with it, and until he has found the lance which bleeds, and until the proven truth is told him why it bleeds; never will he leave it for any pain" (99).

60. "Thus he remained five years, nor for this did he leave off seeking chivalry and strange adventures, the felonious and harsh ones he went seeking and found so many of them that well did he prove himself. . . . Within the five years he sent sixty knights of worth to the court of King Arthur as prisoners. Thus he employed the five years that he never remembered God" (129).

Linker translates several lines omitted from Roach's edition, hence the ellipsis above. Rutledge, "Perceval's Sin," finds in Perceval's lack of response to his mother and cousin "an absence of affect," 58.

61. Potters, "Blood Imagery," sees the romance as an ironic condemnation of the chivalric values of Arthur's court.

62. " 'He whom they serve with it is my brother; my sister and his was your mother, and of the rich Fisher I believe that he is son to that King who has himself served with the grail. But do not believe that he has pike nor lampreys nor salmon; with a single host, which is carried to him in this grail, the holy man sustains and comforts his life. So holy a thing is the grail' " (122–23).

63. Lyons, "Beauté et lumière," concludes that the Grail is not "une chose sacrée ou mystique mais . . . une chose surprenante," 110.

64. "Brother, much has a sin harmed you of which you do not know a word: that was the grief that your mother had of you when you departed from her; for she fell to the ground in a faint at the head of the bridge before the portal, and of this grief she died. Because of the sin that you have of this, it befell you that you did not ask of the lance nor of the grail, and there befell you many an ill for that" (132).

Other critics have found non-allegorical religious meanings in this romance: see Baumgartner, "Le Défi"; Imbs, "L'Elément religieux"; Jodogne, "Le Sens chrétien"; and Laurie, "Some New Sources."

65. Armstrong, "Blood Drops," especially 137 ff.

66. "In the looking that he was doing, it seemed to him, it pleased him so much, that he saw the new color of the face of his beautiful friend" (89).

67. Freeman notes that this episode represents the first time Perceval interprets without referring to rules imposed upon him from without, 132.

68. " 'Now has my lord Gawain, your nephew, the prize and the honor of it. The battle was very perilous and grievous, if I am not lying; for he returns just as healthy as he moved out, for never did he receive there another's blow nor any other feel blow of his' " (95).

69. " 'Sire, if the Lord God help me, it is not reasonable, well do you know it, as you yourself have always said and rightly judged, that a knight should as these two have done, take another knight from his thought, whatever it may be. If they were wrong, that I do not know, but ill has befallen them for it, that is a certain thing' " (92).

70. " 'Lord, I should have greeted you, if I had known your heart as well as I do my own' " (93).

71. On Abelard's ethics, see chapter 1.

72. Cf. Bloch, *Etymologies*, 203–12; Leupin, *Graal*, 55–92.

73. Grigsby, "Sign," suggests that this pattern "contributes to the semiotic breakdown" in the romance, 39, but as Gawain continues to assert his true character successfully, this suggestion is only partly true.

74. "Whoever had good shield, whoever good lance, whoever good helm and good sword presented it to him; but it did not please him to carry anything of another's; he leads seven squires with him and seven chargers and two shields" (101).

75. " 'God!' says one of the damsels, 'this knight beneath that hornbeam, what is he waiting for that he does not arm himself?'

Another more arrogant said in turn: 'He has sworn the peace.'

And another said after her: 'He is a merchant; don't say again that he is to wait to tourney: he is leading all those horses to sell.'

'Rather he is a changer,' says the fourth, 'he has no inclination to divide today with the poor knights that wealth that he bears with him'" (106).

76. " '. . . he is a knight and well does he resemble one.'

And all the ladies together say to her: 'Then, fair friend, if he resembles one, he is not. But he makes himself resemble one because he thinks thus to steal costumes and passages. He is a fool, and yet he thinks to be wise, for in this way he will be taken, will be accused as a thief and blamed for villainous and foolish theft and he will have a halter around his neck for it'" (106).

77. " 'But the sea will be all of ice before such a knight may be found who can remain in the palace; for he would have to be perfectly wise and generous, without covetousness, handsome and noble, bold and loyal, without villainy and without any evil' " (156).

78. Stock, 488.

79. On this point, see Nitze, "The Character of Gauvain."

80. Minnis, 73–117.

81. J. Stevens, 21; Grigsby, "Sign," 39.
82. Quilligan, *Language of Allegory*, 227.
83. See Crow; see also Freeman, 131.
84. Iser, 182–203.
85. Cf. Iser's views on aesthetic response, 20–50.
86. Bloch, *Etymologies*, 207.
87. Bruns, 56.
88. See the works by Bursill-Hall and De Rijk cited in chapter 1.
89. See chapter 1.
90. See chapter 1.
91. See Pauphilet, *Etudes*, 3 and 192. For the *Queste*'s many Biblical references, see Le Hir, "L'Elément biblique," and Matarasso, *Redemption*, 245–55. Matarasso convincingly argues for the work's Biblical structure and suggests that "the *Queste* participates in the authority of Scripture," 243. She goes on to suggest that the *Queste* is unique in its relation to Scriptural allegory: "The use of allegory based on Scripture is not peculiar to the *Queste*, but the maintenance of two continuous and distinct levels does seem to be," 243. Hennessy, "Romance and Allegory," also notes its "attempt to claim divine sanction," 196. See also Baumgartner, *L'Arbre*, 83–95, who sees in the *Queste* a third period of Biblical history with Galahad not as Christ's "type" but as his successor.
92. *Lestoire del saint Graal*, ed. Sommer, 4–12. The other major self-allegorizing romance also claims divine inspiration: see *Perlesvaus*, ed. Nitze and Jenkins, 1, 23.
93. *La Queste del saint Graal*, ed. Pauphilet, 167–68. Page numbers of this edition will be cited parenthetically in the text.
94. "The bird signifies our Maker, who created man in His own image. When Adam was expelled from Paradise for his transgression, he found himself on earth, and there he met with death, in life's default. The tree without leaves or fruit plainly signifies the world, where in those days was nothing but adversity and poverty and want. The young birds signify the human race whose members, unredeemed as yet, went every one to hell, the good men with the sinners, being equal in deserts. When the Son of God saw this, He climbed onto the tree, which is the Cross" (*The Quest of the Holy Grail*, trans. Matarasso, 196).

Quotations from this translation, and citations by page number, will continue to appear as notes.

95. Pauphilet, *Etudes*, suggests that only the central adventures are given direct allegorical interpretations, 172. Hennessy believes that the reader is trained by earlier sections to provide his or her own interpretations for the later ones, 196.
96. Burns, "Feigned Allegory," points out, 355, that the *Queste*'s interpretations are never anagogical; anagogy does, however, seem to become

the text's literal level in its final sections, which deal with the ultimate experiences of the Grail. See also the revised version of Burns's article in her book *Arthurian Fictions*, 55–77.

97. "I have shown you that your hardness is inordinate, and where there is such hardness, sweetness can find no room, nor should we think that anything remains save bitterness; thus you are bitter where you should be sweet and in equal measure. You resemble in that the dead and rotten wood whose sweetness has given place to gall. Now have I shown you how it is that you are harder than stone and more bitter than wood" (92).

98. "For this service in which you are entered does not pertain in any way to things of earth, but of heaven" (134).

99. "The adventures that you are now to seek concern the nature and manifestations of the Holy Grail; these signs will never appear to sinners or men sunk deep in guilt, and never therefore to you, for you are most heinous sinners. Do not imagine moreover that the adventures now afoot consist in the murder of men or the slaying of knights; they are of a spiritual order, higher in every way and much more worth" (174). For Baumgartner, *L'Arbre*, the *Queste* is a rewriting of Christian mythology intended for the use of the chivalric class alone, whose supposed origins and ultimate transformation it celebrates: it is "un nouvel Evangile de la chevalerie," 79. See also 89, 125, and 141–54. Both Chènerie, " 'Ces curieux chevaliers' " and Savage, "Father and Son," find a generally positive view of chivalry in the *Queste*.

100. "Had you not been so hardened a sinner, the seven brothers would never have perished by your hand nor with your help, but would even now be doing penance for the wicked custom they established in the Castle of the Maidens and making their peace with God. He whom you seek, Galahad the Good Knight, did not act thus: he overcame without destroying them" (79).

101. "By the Castle of Maidens you are to understand hell, and by the maidens the souls of the just that were undeservedly imprisoned there before the Passion of Jesus Christ; and for the seven knights you should read the seven deadly sins. . . . But when the heavenly Father saw the corruption of all that He had made, He sent His son to earth to ransom the maidens, which is to say the souls of the just. And even as He sent His son, who was with Him before the beginning of the world, even so did He send Galahad" (79).

102. Both Cornet, "Trois épisodes," and Hennessy, 192, miss the point of this disjunction, finding in it only inconsistency and arbitrariness.

103. See Baumgartner, "Aventures," especially 27.

104. *Queste*, 277–79.

105. Quilligan, *Language of Allegory*, 24; both Pauphilet and Hennessy make this point specifically about the *Queste*. See above, note 91.

106. *Queste*, 91–105.

107. "Do not despise me for my blackness, but know that my black hues are better worth than others' whiteness" (184).

108. "The lady was restored to health that very day. For as soon as she was

washed in the blood of the holy maid she was cleansed and healed of her leprosy and her flesh that had been blackened and hideous to look on recovered all its bloom" (249).

109. Matarasso's translation, 300, note 67. This adventure provides another example of characters simultaneously living on different levels of meaning: for Perceval's sister her sacrifice is allegorical, whereas for the leper herself it is literal and thus punishable. See *Queste*, 244–45. On the moral view of the sacrifice, see Rémy, "La Lèpre," especially 226. For further examples of allegorical elements that the text refrains from interpreting, see Matarasso, *Redemption, passim*. See also Jonin, "Un Songe."

110. "Le Graal, c'est la manifestation romanesque de Dieu," *Etudes*, 25.

111. Gilson, "Mystique"; *Queste*, 158–59.

112. Lot-Borodine, "Les grands secrets," 173.

113. Hamilton, "L'Interprétation."

114. Matarasso, *Redemption*, 180–204. Ihle, *Malory's Grail Quest*, 33–40, defines the process by which these various meanings appear: for her, the Grail is defined periphrastically, each mention demonstrating a different facet of its meaning. On the Cistercian influence, see Pauphilet, *Etudes*, 11–12 and 53–84. The extent of this influence has been re-examined by Payen, *Motif*, 446–47.

115. C. Morse, *Pattern of Judgment*, 65. See also Ribard, "De Chrétien de Troyes à Guillaume de Lorris," and Todorov, "La Quête."

116. See Pelikan, *Growth*, 202–204; he shows that the concept of transubstantiation first appears around 1140, that is, shortly before Chrétien's period, and was officially promulgated by the Fourth Lateran Council in 1215, 203. Cf. Stock's extensive discussion, 241–325.

117. Cf. Boletta, "Sustenance."

118. On the relation of sensory experience to spiritual reality, see Baumgartner, *L'Arbre*, 121–30, in which the Grail is also seen as part of this pattern. On transubstantiation, see Pelikan, cited above, note 115, and on its place in the *Queste*, see Lot-Borodine, "Les Apparitions," and Whitaker, "Christian Iconography."

119. "He believed it was a woman he spoke to, yet he erred, for it was none other than the enemy, agog to trick him and bring him to that pass where he should lose his soul eternally" (112).

120. "So he raised his hand to his forehead and made the sign of the cross. When the enemy felt himself weighted down with the burden of the cross, which was exceedingly heavy and hateful to him, he gave a great shake, and freeing himself of Perceval, rushed into the water howling and shrieking and making a yammer such as was never heard. And it came about then that bright sheaves of fire and flame shot up from the river in several places, so that the water itself appeared to burn.

Observing this phenomenon, Perceval understood in a trice that it was the enemy that carried him thither" (113).

121. *Queste*, 177.

122. *Queste*, 210–26. Burns, *Arthurian Fictions*, discusses the importance of *li contes*, especially in chapter 2, 35–54.

123. "Good sir, such things cannot be void of meaning, and since I crave, if possible, to understand, I beg you to explain what I have seen" (105).

124. "When [Parlan] had found this sword he unsheathed it by as much as you can see (for nothing of the blade was visible before), and would have lost no time in baring the remainder, had he not been transfixed at that moment by a flying lance which pierced him through the thighs, inflicting a wound that never healed but left him maimed, as to this day he is and shall remain until you come to him" (221).

125. "The king said then to Galahad:

'Sir, here is the adventure I told you of. Some of the most valiant knights of my household have today failed to pluck this sword from the stone.'

'Sire,' said Galahad, 'that is not to be wondered at, for the adventure was not theirs but mine. I was so sure of this sword that I came to court without one, as you may have seen.'

Then he took hold of the sword and drew it as easily from the stone as if it had never been fast; and he sheathed it in the scabbard" (41).

126. See Todorov, "La Quête," 138–45.

127. "you may be sure that if he gave himself to mortal sin—from which Our Lord preserve him in His pity—he would get no further in this Quest than any other ordinary knight" (134).

128. See note 8, above.

129. Of the few critics who find any degree of indeterminacy in the *Queste*, the most interesting is Burns. As I suggested in chapter 1, she places the *Queste* in a deconstructive tradition derived from Derrida; but Derrida himself claims that his project is possible only at its own historically determined moment: see *Of Grammatology*, 7 and 15. To find a thirteenth-century romance writer writing deconstructively is surely anachronistic, even in deconstructive terms. Bourquin, "Saint Bernard," makes the same mistake. Locke, *The Quest*, 1–11, finds the *Queste* ambiguous but nevertheless proceeds to interpret the Grail in a single specific way, as an "initiation into mysteries foreshadowing the life to come"; see 101.

130. Hynes-Berry, "Language and Meaning," 310. For a similar view of Malory's method of adapting the *Queste*, see Tucker, "The Place of the 'Quest.' "

3. Marie de France and Guillaume de Machaut

1. Rothschild, *Narrative Technique*.

2. Rothschild, 15.

3. On the distinction between the worlds of magic and of realism, see

Solano, "Love and the Other World"; but cf. Green, "Fusion," which argues that both worlds are actually parts of the same human reality.

4. Rychner dates the *Lais* between 1160 and 1178 in the introduction to his edition: Marie de France, *Lais*, x–xii. The earliest of the *artes* is Matthew of Vendôme's *Ars versificatoria*, dated "before 1175" by Parr in his translation, 8. On the rhetoricians, see chapter 1.

5. Quotations are from Rychner's edition. Line numbers are cited parenthetically in the text.

> I've often heard
> that one could once find
> adventures in this land
> that brought relief to the unhappy.
> Knights might find young girls
> to their desire, noble and lovely;
> and ladies find lovers so handsome, courtly, brave, and valiant
> that they could not be blamed,
> and no one else would see them.
> If that might be or ever was,
> if that has ever happened to anyone,
> God, who has power over everything,
> grant me my wish in this!

The Lais of Marie de France, trans. Hanning and Ferrante. Quotations from this translation, whose line numbering generally follows that of the original, will continue to appear as notes.

> 6. Then I thought of the *lais* I'd heard,
> I did not doubt, indeed I knew well,
> that those who first began them
> and sent them forth
> composed them in order to preserve
> adventures they had heard.
> I have heard many told;
> and I don't want to neglect or forget them.
> To put them into word and rhyme
> I've often stayed awake.
> 7. There, beside a tomb,
> they would hear the story of his death,
> how he was wrongfully killed.
> There she would give her son the sword.
> The adventure would be recited to him,
> how he was born and who his father was;
> then they'd see what he would do.
> 8. The people began to weep
> and, weeping, to recount
> that it was the best knight,

the strongest, the most fierce,
the most handsome and the best loved,
that had ever lived.
"He was king of this land;
no one was ever so courtly.
At Caerwent he was discovered
and killed for the love of a lady.
Since then we have had no lord,
but have waited many days,
just as he told and commanded us,
for the son the lady bore him."
When the lady heard the news,
she called aloud to her son.
"Fair son," she said, "you hear
how God has led us to this spot.
Your father, whom this old man murdered,
lies here in this tomb.
Now I give and commend his sword to you.
I have kept it a long time for you."
Then she revealed, for all to hear,
that the man in the tomb was the father and this was his son,
and how he used to come to her,
how her lord had betrayed him—
she told the truth.

9. The custom among the ancients—
as Priscian testifies—
was to speak quite obscurely
in the books they wrote,
so that those who were to come after
and study them
might gloss the letter
and supply its significance from their own wisdom.

10. Spitzer, "Prologue"; Robertson, "Marie de France."

11. Spitzer, 100.

12. Hunt, "Glossing." Hunt points out that Spitzer's claims are supported by evidence drawn from a period later than Marie's, and that Robertson's Christian translation of "le surplus mettre" is arbitrary, and demonstrates that medieval interpretation was not always doctrinal. He suggests that Marie refers not to exegesis but to the idea of intellectual progress, and that she believes her own works will be surpassed as she surpassed he predecessors.

13. Hunt, 412.

14. Two earlier critics have also suggested that lines 9–16 refer both to

Marie's treatment of her predecessors and to the treatment of her own
works by future generations: see Meissner, *Die Strengleikar*, 208 ff., and
Brät, "Marie de France et l'obscurité." See also Pickens, "La Poétique": "un
poème . . . est à la fois la glose d'un texte ancien et un nouveau texte à
interpréter," 373. Foulet and Uitti, "The Prologue," review some recent
readings of the prologue, 242–43.

15. I should like very much
       to tell you the truth
       about the *lai* men call *Chievrefoil*—
       why it was composed and where it came from.

       For the joy that he'd felt
       from his love when he saw her,
       by means of the stick he inscribed
       as the queen had instructed,
       and in order to remember the words,
       Tristan, who played the harp well,
       composed a new *lai* about it.

16. Mermier, "En relisant," summarizes and compares the various arguments on this topic.

17. "This was the message of the writing / that he had sent to her."

18. With the two of them it was just
       as it is with the honeysuckle
       that attaches itself to the hazel tree:
       when it has wound and attached
       and worked itself around the trunk,
       the two can survive together;
       but if someone tries to separate them,
       the hazel dies quickly
       and the honeysuckle with it.
       "Sweet love, so it is with us:
       You cannot live without me, nor I without you."

19. Bullock-Davies, "Form," says that the term *lai* refers to a purely
musical composition, but cf. Donovan, *Breton Lay*, who suggests that both
musical and narrative *lais* were composed, and that only the narrative type
is extant, 44–64. In any case, Tristan is an artist whose works require
interpretation. I use the term *lai* interchangeably with "tale."

20. I have given you the truth
       about the *lai* that I have told here.

21. Cf. Huchet, "Nom de femme": "Ecrire au XIIe siècle, c'est avant tout
lire," 409; and cf. Bruns, *Inventions*, cited in chapter 1.

22. "Beloved, I need your promise.
       Give me your shirt;

I'll make a knot in the tail.
You have my leave to love the woman,
whoever she may be,
who will be able to undo it."
He gave her the shirt, and his promise;
she made the knot in such a way
that no woman could untie it
except with scissors or knife.
She gave him back the shirt,
and he took it on condition
that she would make a similar pledge to him,
by means of a belt
that she would wear next to her bare flesh,
tightened about her flanks.
Whoever could open the buckle
without breaking it or severing it from the belt,
would be the one he would urge her to love.

23. "Is this," he said, "my dear love,
my hope, my heart, and my life—
my beautiful lady who loved me?
Where did she come from? Who brought her here?
Now, that was a foolish thought!
I know it can't be she;
women often look alike—
I got all excited for no reason."

24. When she heard his order,
she took his shirttail
and easily untied the knot.
Guigemar was thunderstruck;
he knew her very well, and yet
he couldn't bring himself to believe firmly it was she.
So he spoke to her in this way:
"Beloved, sweet creature,
is that you? Tell me truly!
Let me see your body,
and the belt I put on you."

25. The knight reassured her,
gave her a ring,
and explained to her
that, as long as she kept it,
her lord would not remember
anything that had happened—
he would imprison her no longer.
He gave her his sword

and then made her swear
no man would ever possess it,
that she'd keep it for their son.
26. [She] saw the piece of wood; she knew what it was.
She recognized all the letters.
27. The knights who were accompanying her,
who were riding with her,
she ordered to stop:
she wanted to dismount and rest.
They obeyed her command.
She went far away from her people.
28. See above, note 21, for the translation.
29. Cf. Fitz, "Desire."
30. See above, note 6.
31. He lay awake all night,
sighing and in distress.
32. She'd been awake all night, that was her complaint.
It was the fault of love, pressing her hard.
33. "stayed awake until daybreak";

"I still don't even know
if she will take me as her lover."
34. All night she was awake;
she couldn't rest or sleep.
35. "Alas," she said, "now I must suffer.
I won't be able to get up at night
or go and stand in the window."

In a piece of samite,
embroidered in gold and writing,
she wrapped the little bird.
She called one of her servants,
charged him with her message,
and sent him to her love.
36. When everything had been told and revealed to the knight,
after he had listened well,
he was very sad about the adventure,
but he wasn't mean or hesitant.
He had a small vessel fashioned,
with no iron or steel in it;
it was all pure gold and good stones,
very precious and very dear;
the cover was very carefully attached.
He placed the nightingale inside.

37. Another very explicit substitution of text-making and reading for sex occurs in "Milun," though without the reference to wakefulness that relates the other tales to one another.

38. See chapter 1.

39. See chapter 1.

40. He was gloomy and worried,
    concerned about the lovely girl,
    the daughter of his lord, the king,
    because she had summoned him so sweetly,
    because she had sighed.

    He remembered his wife
    and how he had assured her
    that he'd be faithful to her,
    that he'd conduct himself loyally.

41. "Lady," he said, "since you love him,
    send something to him,
    a belt, a ribbon, or a ring;
    send it, he will like that.
    If he receives it well,
    if he is happy that you sent it,
    you may be sure of his love."

    When she heard his advice,
    the girl answered:
    "How can I know from my present
    if he has any desire to love me?
    I've never seen a knight
    who had to be begged—
    whether he loved or hated—
    who would not willingly take
    a present that was offered to him."

42. . . . the chamberlain was moving quickly.
    He came to Eliduc
    and greeted him in secret
    with what the girl had sent;
    he presented the ring
    and gave him the belt.
    The knight thanked him.
    He put the gold ring on his finger,
    pulled the belt around him;
    the youth said no more,
    nor did Eliduc ask anything,
    except that he offered him something of his.
    But the chamberlain took nothing and departed.

43. This adventure was told,
    it could not be concealed for long.
    The Bretons made a *lai* about it
    which men call *The Nightingale.*

44. Huchet suggests that the very act of writing the *Lais* is a way to maintain mystery, 409, but he does not address the problem of this writing's explicitly public nature.

45. . . . do not let any man know about this.
    I shall tell you why:
    you would lose me for good
    if this love were known;
    you would never see me again
    or possess my body.

46. Although critical attempts to do so have been made: see Wathelet-Willem, "Le Mystère," who agrees that the ritual objects are there simply to be mysterious and to point to the Other World; and Koubichkine, "Lanval," who sees in them signs "de beauté, de richesse, de jeunesse, de diligence," suggesting that Lanval will now receive all that he has been denied at court, including an identity and a homeland.

47. "Lanval," she said, "sweet love,
    because of you I have come from my land;
    I came to seek you from far away. . . ."

48. ". . . No man but you will see me
    or hear my words."

49. She dismounted before the king
    so that she was well seen by all.
    And she let her cloak fall
    so they could see her better.

50. The term is a critical commonplace: see Koubichkine; Maraud, "Structure narrative"; and Davison, "*Lanval.*"

51. ". . . he didn't know who they were,
    where they came from or where they were going."

52. No man heard of him again
    and I have no more to tell.

53. My discussion of "Chaitivel" is indebted to a remark made in passing by J. Stevens, "The *granz biens*": he agrees that Marie leaves an unresolved tension at the end of this tale but sees it as a defect. For another view of the ending, see Cowling, "Image."

54. ". . . Because I have loved you so,
    I want my grief to be remembered:
    I shall compose a *lai* about the four of you
    and call it *The Four Sorrows.*"

55. ". . . but I, who escaped alive,
    the one I could love most in the world

> I see coming and going frequently,
> speaking with me morning and evening,
> but I can have no joy from her,
> from kisses or embraces,
> nor any other good but talk.
> You make me suffer a hundred such ills,
> that it would be better for me to die.
> If the *lai* is to be named for me,
> let it be called *The Unfortunate One*. . . ."

> 56. So the *lai* was begun
> and then perfected and performed.
> Of those who traveled about with it,
> some called it *The Four Sorrows;*
> either name is apt,
> both suit the subject.
> *The Unfortunate One* is the common name.

> 57. Here it ends, there is no more;
> I've heard no more and I know no more about it;
> I shall tell you no more of it.

58. Vitz, "The *Lais* of Marie de France," suggests that the lover's creation of the casket in "Laüstic" is a similarly indecipherable action: we know that it is an "act of meaning," but just what the meaning may be cannot be determined, 401.

59. *Arnvlfi Avrelianensis Glosvle svper Lvcanvm*, ed. Marti, xxv. See chapter 1.

60. Calin, *A Poet*. Two important earlier studies are Hanf, "Uber Guillaume de Machauts *Voir Dit*," and Eichelberg, *Dichtung*, and more recent ones are Brownlee, *Poetic Identity*, and Cerquiglini, *Un Engin*. Collections of articles include *Machaut's World*, ed. Cosman and Pelner, and *Guillaume de Machaut*, ed. Imbs. See also Kelly, *Medieval Imagination*.

61. For example, on poetic constructions of the self, see Brownlee's book; on writing and absence, see two articles by Cerquiglini: "Ethique de la totalisation" and "Syntaxe et syncope."

62. Eichelberg argues that the *Voir-Dit* is largely autobiographical; Calin and Brownlee follow Hanf in suggesting instead that the entire work is the product of Machaut's imagination and of literary conventions. See also Poirion, "Le Monde imaginaire": "La dame du *Voir-Dit* représente trop bien la création poétique pour que son existence réèlle n'apparaisse pas comme une merveilleuse coincidence," 224–25. Poirion does imply, however, in his earlier *Le Poète et le prince*, 199–200, that the book can be seen as autobiographical to the extent that it reflects the more general tension between the court-poet's emotional and professional lives. The extent to which this question is still a live issue is demonstrated by the round-table discussion

in *Guillaume de Machaut*, 215–22. Opinions on specific, relevant points in this general debate will be cited in the notes.

63. But see Calin, *A Poet*, 167–202; Beer, "Ambiguity"; and Cerquiglini, "Ethique."

64. See Brownlee's chapter on the *Voir-Dit*, 94–156. Because Brownlee's analytical method is an episode-by-episode investigation, discussing the questions that concern him along the way, it is difficult to give precise page references for each of the issues he raises; they all appear over and over again throughout the chapter. I make my references as precise as possible.

65. On Machaut's social standing, see Poirion, *Le Poète et le prince*, 193–95. Marie's identity is disputed, but all suggestions agree that she was of noble birth. See Mickel, *Marie de France*, for a review of the theories.

66. Poirion, *Le Poète et le prince*, 198.

67. On the notion of "poetic truth," see Brownlee, *Poetic Identity*, 123–27. On the pseudo-autobiographical component of the *dit* as a genre, see Cerquiglini, "Le Clerc," especially 160–65.

68. See chapter 1.

69. Williams, "Author's Role," 434. Williams develops this remark further in her "Machaut's Self-Awareness."

70. He suggests that "art triumphs over life," 200.

71. The long-awaited edition of the *Voir-Dit* by Imbs has not yet appeared as I write; I therefore quote from the 1875 edition of Paris. Citations by page number appear parenthetically in the text. It should be noted that this edition is woefully incomplete, Paris having inexplicably omitted a number of passages. The longest of these was published by Thomas, "Guillaume de Machaut et l'*Ovide moralisé*." Calin, *A Poet*, has also published three short passages omitted by Paris, one of which affects the plot: see 176n. See also Brownlee, *Poetic Identity*, 155. In any case, all studies of the *Voir-Dit* should be considered tentative until the Imbs edition appears. My own inelegant but literal translations will appear in the notes. "And also, I promise and swear to you, that as far as I am concerned, Lancelot never loved Guinevere, nor Paris Helen, nor Tristan Iseult more faithfully than you will be loved and served by me."

72. Eichelberg and Paris both argue that the lady actually wrote the poems and letters attributed to her; see Paris's introduction to his edition. This position has received recent support from Musso, "Comparaison." As usual, Hanf, Calin, and Brownlee disagree with them and agree with one another: see Calin, "Le Moi," especially 249. Calin's own interpretation of Musso's statistics appears in *Guillaume de Machaut*, 215–16.

73. "And as for what you wrote me, that if you were a man you would see me quite often, I beg you for God's sake and on all the love you have for me that you be pleased to hold me excused, if I do not see and have not

come to you; because, by my soul, God knows that this has not been through lack of love or of good will."

74. "And if I wrote to you that I would see you quite often were I a man, by my faith I spoke truly; but nevertheless, it was not because I wish you would come to see me except in comfort and good health."

75. On the question of naturalistic description in this work, see Calin, *A Poet*, 172–78, where he sums up both sides of the argument. Williams, "Author's Role," uses the *Voir-Dit* as documentation of how manuscripts were really produced.

76. Paris provided this identification of the lady in his introduction, xviii–xxvi, and it is generally accepted, though all he has to say about her is not. Cf. Calin, "Le Moi," 249.

77. Brownlee, *Poetic Identity*, 107–23.

78. "Gentle Thought calmed and healed my pains, without having had sight of her. I had never seen her; but Imagination depicted her in my heart. . . . Thus I fell in love, by means of these sweet, gentle thoughts."

On courtly-love conventions, see Brownlee, *Poetic Identity*, 94–156; see also Kelly.

79. "She who never saw you, and who loves you faithfully, makes you a gift of all her heart."

80. "But when Love pricks a lover, he isn't always of one mind, but has various thoughts, both gentle and perverse. I was taken by melancholy, which was foolish; for I thought about the greatness of my lady, and my own littleness. And in my heart I imagined that compared to her I was nothing, and that it was great stupidity to think she was my friend; and that in the place where she was staying, every day she saw forty or even, by God, a hundred better than I; and that the eye frequently constrains the heart, and masters and takes power over it through pleasure, which instructs it, so that it loves with a fine love."

81. "For I will change your pains through true love, and through gentle speech, when I see you."

82. Calin, *A Poet*, 199; but cf. Cerquiglini, "Syntaxe," in which writing, especially the lyrics but to some extent the letters as well, appears as a fairly satisfactory substitute for physical gesture, 66–72. Given the frustrations caused by the lack of physical contact throughout the *Voir-Dit*, Calin's argument seems to me more persuasive; Cerquiglini herself admits that even physical gestures can be ambiguous in this work, 63.

83. "Do not write me anything until you hear news of me."

84. "So that I did not know if she forbade my writing for some ruse, or through lack of love."

85. "While sleeping, I dreamed a dream, and saw within my dream that while I was adoring her lovely portrait, it turned its head and face away; it did not deign to look at me, for which my heart complained most strongly; and it was all dressed in green, which signifies infidelity."

86. "Fair friend, this is great foolishness of thought; for it seems that you are both sleeping and speaking, and in my opinion you are dreaming. One should not believe in dreams."

87. Brownlee, *Poetic Identity*, 133–34. On the influence of the *Roman de la Rose*, see also two articles in *Machaut's World*: Uitti, "From *Clerc* to *Poète*"; and Brownlee, "Poetic *Oeuvre*."

88. But cf. Brownlee, *Poetic Identity*, who suggests that the plot line verifies her fidelity, 134. This seems to me an unwarranted assumption; instead, the narrator chooses to act as if it had been verified.

89. "And Fortune is against me, because it is nearly nine weeks since I heard certain news of her, so that I wonder if she doesn't have some grievance against me, or if her heart might not be elsewhere."

90. Weinberg, *Nicolaus*, 103; and see chapter 1. Weinberg, 7, dates all of Nicholas's writings before 1340, and Calin, *A Poet*, suggests a date of 1363–65 for the *Voir-Dit*, 16.

91. Cerquiglini, "Syntaxe," finds disjunctions rather than similarities between the reader's experience and that of the characters, 72–74.

92. Poirion, *Le Poète et le prince*, 192–205.

93. Calin, *A Poet*, discusses these vacillations but categorizes the lovers too rigidly: he believes that the narrator desires only discretion and the lady only fame, 175 and 198.

94. "And because such a noble thing should not be hidden or shut away, I will tell you, without deletion or addition, what was in the letter."

95. "But you, be my confidant, to speak discreetly and to be silent."

96. "A number of great lords know of our love, and have sent me a chaplain who is a great friend of mine, and have commanded that I send to them by him some of your poems and my responses, especially 'She who never saw you'; I have obeyed their command. For I sent several of your things and mine to them, and they wished to know if it is true that I have your portrait, and I showed it to their messenger, well and richly decorated and placed above my bed; so that they all marvel that this could be. And know that they are aware of how you revived me, and returned joy and health to me without having seen me."

97. "But, for God's sake, do nothing to please me that might cause people to talk; for, by the God who made me, I would rather die or that I should never see you (from which God preserve me!) for if it came to that, I would truly die."

98. "And it would be no great dishonor to my pretty, gentle lady, if I dare put nothing in this book except as it is, and without gloss. For to do otherwise would be against her command: and since it pleases her, it pleases me. I will obey her desire."

99. "And if I call you my friend in front of people, it is a precaution, so that I may speak with you more easily, and come to you and go."

100. "And, by God, I never did anything to let anyone know of the love I had for you."

101. "They think as well of you, of your gentleness and humility, as of any lady of whom they ever heard spoken."

102. "Friend, by God, it's a true saying that there's more than one ass at the fair. For your lady has several lovers, young, handsome, graceful, and lovable, who visit her often. And also I promise you that she shows and flaunts your letters everywhere so indiscriminately that it is a mockery, and there are few who don't laugh about it."

103. "And do you believe she loves you because she calls you her friend? She would also call any stranger from Castile her friend."

104. "Thus everyone reported to me things that advised my heart to forget my worthy lady, whom I love, respect, praise, and adore, and value. But while walking in the street, everyone made me the butt, saying in mockery, 'I see one who has a fine friend!' "

105. "It seems to me certain that in all ways you have rejected me and left me in jeopardy and that you have never had any love for me. . . . You know that our love has been made known to several worthy people, so that, if they knew your love were gone, they would believe that I had been false to you, or that you had found in me some wickedness or folly, for which you did this."

106. "I won't tell her anything of what everyone says."

107. "My very dear and only lady, if I write you what has been said to me, I pray that it may not displease you. Please know that a rich man, very much my lord and friend, told me for certain that you show everyone what I send you, which seems a mockery to many."

108. "Thus we were reconciled, as I have here recorded it for you, in a most agreeable peace. I have great joy when I recall it, and it is a great good to record it when one sees people in accord, and an even greater good to bring those who were into discord into accord, and therefore I will still record briefly what is left to tell: how All-Beautiful took my heart, when she was reconciled to me."

Most of this passage was omitted from Paris's edition; it is published in Calin, *A Poet*, 192–93. The corresponding page in Paris's edition is 370.

109. "I beg you, as lovingly and humbly as I may, that all relations, everything done, said, or written between us, be forgotten and forgiven with the true heart of lover and lady, and never be remembered."

110. Scholars have tried to reconstruct her journeys; Paris provides one hypothesis in his notes. As for her name, Paris deduced it from the concluding anagram; others have been misled, and Paris takes issue with some mistaken identifications in his introduction, but see my discussion of this anagram below.

111. "For she whom Love guards wishes that I put into this *True Story* all

I have done and said for her, and all she has done to me, without concealing anything relevant."

112. "The goddess was there immediately, for at that moment she descended, covered by an obscure cloud full of incense and fine balm, which censed and scented the room. And there she performed a clear miracle, so well and openly that I was filled with joy and my desires were fulfilled, so well that I asked for nothing more, nor desired anything else."

113. Calin, *A Poet*, 190. His position has apparently changed somewhat since this book's publication: cf. the round-table discussion in *Guillaume de Machaut*, 263, in which he finds this scene deliberately ambiguous.

114. Paris, Introduction, xxxii.

115. "There was neither vice nor stain."

116. "And if I have said too much or too little, don't blame me, for, by Saint Paul, my lady wished me to do it thus, on pain of losing her favor."

117. See the works by de Man cited in chapter 2, note 1. Brownlee discusses the implications of another allegorical scene important for the *Voir-Dit*'s truth status, *Poetic Identity*, 123–27.

118. "And I truly wish you would not write to me at all, except songs, or unless it were by your servant who was here before, and who knows how to do it. In my opinion, this is best."

119. "And although I have always accustomed you to writing openly, and many know of our love, there is no one who knows the truth about it perfectly, except one other and me and your confidant."

120. Calin, *A Poet*, 196–97.

121. Paris's edition, 370n. Cerquiglini, "Syntaxe," suggests that the reader must decode the text like an anagram, 74—an ironic statement, given this anagram's indecipherability.

122. "I do not know who will speak of it, but it will not be otherwise for all that."

123. "And those who will think evil of it will be traitors and malicious ones."

124. "From now on I wish to be silent about that which I spoke of before; because I well know that the vicious ones do not like such matters, because they wish to hide their malice if they can, and their vice."

125. See Brownlee, *Poetic Identity*, 94–156.

126. "And it is a sin against nobility to believe something so wounding that one might lose from it honor and life and the love of one's dear lover."

127. "Thus did I think and think again, and in my thoughts I thought I had been wrong."

128. "By that God who made me, I had a heart so troubled and troubled myself so strongly that little kept me from splitting in two."

4. Communication and Interpretation

1. See chapter 1.

2. On the dramatic structure of *The Canterbury Tales*, see Lumiansky, *Of Sundry Folk;* on the therapeutic nature of *The Book of the Duchess*, see Bronson, "The *Book of the Duchess* Reopened"; on emotional response in *Troilus and Criseyde*, see Donaldson, "Criseide and Her Narrator."

3. Gellrich, 167–247, deals with several Chaucerian texts in terms of their reaction against neoplatonic medieval language theory. Ferster approaches Chaucer through modern hermeneutic theory, focusing on interpretation. Shoaf, 105–227, concentrates specifically on the problem of linguistic referentiality. Individual articles by Leicester and Vance will be cited where appropriate, as will all of the above critics. Criticism of Chaucer's poetry is so extensive that I make no attempt to cite all of it that is relevant to the issues I discuss. Articles and books I do cite fall generally into three categories: those that initiated discussion of an issue and/or established the terms in which it has been conducted; those that summarize or review the critical debate on an issue; and important recent contributions to the discussion of the issues that are my central concerns.

4. For the standard dating of Chaucer's works, which I follow here, see Robinson's edition, xxix. This chronology is still for the most part accepted in more recent editions. Palmer, "Historical Context," suggests a slightly earlier date for *The Book of the Duchess*, on the basis of new documentary evidence.

5. Line numbers from Robinson's edition will be cited in the text.

6. Aers, "Art," sees a related pattern but suggests that the value of art itself is problematic. Johnson, "Art as Discovery," takes an opposite view, suggesting that grief is "sublimated through aesthetic discovery," 60. It should be clear that I am more sympathetic to Aers, but the problem is less one of aesthetics than of textuality. See also an important article by Edwards, "Beginnings," that links the problems of subjective psychology to those of language and aesthetics. Like Johnson, Edwards reads the creation of a work of art as a positive and therapeutic act, an assumption I dispute below.

7. On the nature of the narrator's illness, see Spearing, *Dream-Poetry*, 51–52; but cf. Severs, "Self-Portrait," who sees it as a spiritual problem.

8. The distinction between dreamer and narrator was first drawn by Kreuzer, "Dreamer," and has proven useful to many critics over the years.

9. Arguments for the dreamer's naïveté originate with Kittredge, *Chaucer and His Poetry*, 48–51; the case for his tactful understanding is well made by Kreuzer and by Bronson. Phillips, "Structure," provides a useful summary of various nuances other critics have contributed to this debate, 107 and notes.

10. Boardman, "Courtly Language"; R. Morse, "Understanding"; see

especially 206, on the ambiguous meaning of the word "fers." For an argument similar to Morse's, and which she cites, see French, "Lyric."

11. Aers, 202. R. Morse points out that the song "may very well appear to be a *planh* sung to reflect the singer's mood, his mental rather than his actual state," 204.

12. For the poem's many sources, see Robinson's explanatory notes, 772–78, and Edwards, *passim*. On its rhetorical structure, see Spearing, 72. On the *dit* as a genre, including its use of the pseudo-autobiographical first person, see Cerquiglini, "Le Clerc."

13. Derrida, *Of Grammatology*, 7–8.

14. Derrida, 24.

15. Derrida, 14–15.

16. Cf. Edwards, 197.

17. Ferster, "Intention," somewhat anachronistically suggests an equation, reminiscent of Derrida, of *all* speech with writing (in terms of the speaker's "absence"); but as we have seen, Derrida himself claims both that his deconstruction of their opposition is possible only at this moment in history, and that this opposition was perceived as especially acute in the Middle Ages. Ferster's argument is developed further in *Chaucer on Interpretation;* we discuss similar issues but reach very different conclusions.

18. On Chaucer's "realism," see Kittredge, *Chaucer and His Poetry*, 152 ff., and Lumiansky, *Of Sundry Folk;* on his traditionalism, see two standard texts: Muscatine, *Chaucer and the French Tradition*, 173–97, and Robertson, *Preface*, especially 228–85.

19. Ferster, *Chaucer on Interpretation*, 46–68; Gellrich, 167–201.

20. For a classic example, see Bethurum, "Point of View."

21. See Bethurum, and two articles by Donaldson: "Masculine Narrator" and "Criseide and Her Narrator."

22. See Donaldson, "Ending"; M. Stevens, "Chaucer and Modernism," especially 210–12; and Salter, "Poet and Narrator."

23. Salter, 284.

24. See Wetherbee, *Chaucer and the Poets*, 195–204, for a detailed and critical examination of the psychology of the fictional narrator's response to the love-affair as he describes it.

25. Quotations follow Robinson's edition. Book and line numbers will be cited parenthetically in the text.

26. See chapter 1.

27. On textual "blanks" requiring the audience's engagement, and on how they make us aware of the variety of possible readings, see Mehl, "Audience." Mehl feels, however, that Chaucer's own point of view can be discerned, 228. See also an important article by Carton, "Complicity," which argues, as I do, that Chaucer requires the reader to take responsibility for the text, though it gives little attention to just how that is to come about. A further application of Carton's insights to one specific passage is Rudat,

"Narrator-Reader Complicity." A more general discussion of Chaucer's audiences is Strohm, "Chaucer's Audience(s)," while Patterson, "Ambiguity," considers an actual medieval response and has some relevant comments on the process of "disambiguating" the text.

28. On the narrator's feelings for Criseyde, see Donaldson, "Criseide and Her Narrator."

29. See Donaldson, "Three 'P's' "; and Fyler, "Fabrications," for similar views of Pandarus. Van, "Chaucer's Pandarus," draws a further connection, between Pandarus and God.

30. Wetherbee's discussion of the narrator suggests some very disturbing implications of this parallel: *Chaucer and the Poets*, 195–204.

31. Wimsatt, "Guillaume de Machaut," demonstrates Machaut's direct influence on the poem.

32. See Eldredge, "Boethian Epistemology," which argues, however, that Chaucer presents analogues of late medieval skepticism only to show that they need correction by Boethian epistemology, and that the final ascent of Troilus is a metaphor for the neoplatonic epistemological ascent. Peck, "Nominalist Questions," is a more sympathetic presentation of Chaucer's response to late medieval philosophy, though it does not consider *Troilus and Criseyde*.

33. Van makes this point, 91.

34. Mudrick, "Chaucer's Nightingales," mentions in passing the mythological connection between the birds Pandarus and Criseyde hear, 94, but consider only Criseyde's view, not the reader's. See also R. Miller, "Pandarus and Procne," whose positive view of Pandarus causes him to reject this connection.

35. On Chaucer's alteration of Boccaccio's treatment of Cassandra, see Knapp, "Boccaccio and Chaucer."

36. On the unreliability of language, see Stokes, "Wordes White."

37. "The most obvious, and all-important, fact about the narrator is that he loves Criseide," Donaldson, "Criseide and Her Narrator," 68. But cf. Wetherbee's more critical view of the narrator's love as compared with that of Troilus, *Chaucer and the Poets*, 195–204.

38. Covella, "Audience as Determinant of Meaning," holds that Chaucer rather than the narrator changed his intentions: the poem as a whole, for a courtly audience, celebrates love, while the conclusion condemning it was tacked on later for a more general, and more moralistic, audience. This reading demands that the epilogue be seen as contrary, and inferior, to the rest of the poem, and would find few supporters among recent critics.

39. Elbow, *Oppositions*, finds that oppositions in which both sides are affirmed are an important structural and thematic feature throughout Chaucer's works. His chapter on *Troilus and Criseyde* focuses on two antithetical speeches, 49–72. Gordon, *Double Sorrow*, finds that such oppositions are

usually resolved. My reasons for favoring Elbow's view should become clear.

40. See Kirk, " 'Paradis.' " Kirk also reviews the long-lived debate on the poem's ending in the course of her article.

41. Shoaf, 107–57, has worked out the problem of linguistic referentiality in *Troilus and Criseyde;* Vance takes a route comparable to mine but reaches a different conclusion, suggesting in "Mervelous Signals" that the narrator abandons equivocal poetic language. It should be clear why I think the ending considerably more equivocal than Vance allows.

42. See chapter 1.

43. Fragment and line numbers from Robinson's edition will be cited in the text.

44. The comparison of the gospel and *The Wife of Bath's Prologue* evolved during a conversation with Marlena G. Corcoran, to whom I am grateful for pointing out the problematic nature of figurative language in the gospel.

45. Biblical quotations are taken from the Douay-Rheims translation.

46. The most exhaustive analysis of the Wife's faulty exegesis is Robertson, *Preface*, 317–31 and 380–82. Justman, "Literal and Symbolic," situates it in a larger historical context. But cf. Ferster's fine analysis of the Wife's proper interpretations, *Chaucer on Interpretation*, 123–28.

47. See Robertson, *Preface*, 329.

48. See chapter 1.

49. Gellrich, 245.

50. The practice of treating Wife of Bath as though she had some real existence outside the text still appears in some fairly recent articles: both Rowland, "Timely Death," and Palomo, "Tale," suggest that she "really" murdered her fourth husband with Jankyn's help.

51. Lumiansky, *Of Sundry Folk*, is the most exhaustive demonstration of the tales' suitability to their tellers; but cf., for example, the annual sessions at the International Congress on Medieval Studies held at Western Michigan University on "tales ill-suited to their tellers."

52. See Coleman, 171–72, and chapter 1, above. Ferster discusses the Wife's textual and contextual identity, *Chaucer on Interpretation*, 128.

53. On the Wife's reference to a recent murder case see, besides Rowland and Palomo, Hamel, "Contemporary Murder."

54. Thus the opinions of the twelfth-century philosopher Roscelin de Compiègne, for instance, have survived almost exclusively in references by other philosophers attacking him, from which modern scholars have nevertheless been able to deduce the essentials of his nominalist views. See Gilson, *History*, 154–60, and notes.

55. The "Marriage Group" was first identified by Kittredge, "Discussion of Marriage"; see also his *Chaucer and His Poetry*, 185–211. Its existence was challenged by Hinckley, "Debate," and the critical argument has continued

to the present day; but in any event, the Wife, Clerk, and Merchant are clearly linked by direct quotation and allusion. Ferster discusses a similar phenomenon—the relations between the Host and the "pilgrim Chaucer"—in *Chaucer on Interpretation*, 154–55.

56. This arrangement was first noticed by Frost, "Interpretation," and has been elaborated by Stokoe, "Structure," and by C. Owen, "Aesthetic Design." See also Owen's *Pilgrimage and Storytelling*, 99–110, and Ruggiers, *Art*, 55.

57. Different aspects of this pattern have been discerned by Carruthers, "Letter and Gloss," and by Szittya, "Green Yeoman."

58. Baldwin, *Unity*, includes many examples of how the Parson's generalizations can be applied to specific pilgrims; see especially 83–110.

59. The various proposals for ordering the fragments are too numerous to catalogue here; the most indefatigable rearranger is C. Owen, whose *Pilgrimage and Storytelling* both defends his own view and summarizes some others. See also Robinson's comments in his edition, 2.

60. Still the best investigations of various pilgrims' historical bases are Manly, *New Light*, and Bowden, *Commentary*.

61. *Chaucer on Interpretation*, 151; and see Leicester, "Impersonation."

62. Gellrich, 232.

63. Ferster, *Chaucer on Interpretation*, 156, confirms this point.

64. Cf. Gellrich, 234–40.

65. *Chaucer and His Poetry*, 205–10. Many scholars, especially Robertson, *Preface*, 275–76, have criticized Kittredge's favorable view of the Franklin and his tale. For a review of the controversy and a vindication of the Franklin, see White, "The Franklin's Tale." On inconclusiveness as a basic principle of Chaucer's poetry, see Sklute, *Virtue*.

66. See Middleton, "Chaucer's 'New Men,' " for some other subtly argued relations among poetry, truth, understanding, and fourteenth-century culture.

5. Alterity and Interpretation

1. On alterity, see Jauss, "Alterity," and Warning, "Drama," as well as the responses to these articles by various scholars in *New Literary History* 10 (1979): 367–416.

2. Adler, "Problems," outlines the philosophical transition from neoplatonic figuralism to Aristotelianism taking place at the time of the *Mort Artu*'s composition; the former mode is exemplified in the *Queste*, the latter in the *Mort Artu*: see especially 933–36. Despite its essentially non-allegorical nature, certain critics have discerned in the *Mort Artu* isolated examples of symbolism: see Pensom, "Rapports." One of the examples he cites has also been noticed by Frappier, *Etude*, 318, and by Imbs, "La Journée," 285. The

importance of religious values despite the absence of allegory is emphasized by Frappier and by Larmat, "Les Idées morales."

3. On the date of the *Mort Artu*, see Frappier, *Etude*, 20 and 134–38.

4. On the ambiguity of this self-authentication throughout the prose *Lancelot*, see Burns, *Arthurian Fictions*, 7–21.

5. Quotations from the *Mort Artu* follow Frappier's edition. Page numbers will be cited parenthetically in the text.

> HERE LIES GAHERIS LE BLANC OF KARAHEU, THE BROTHER OF MADOR DE LA PORTE, WHOM THE QUEEN KILLED WITH POISON. (84)

The Death of King Arthur, trans. Cable. Quotations from this translation, its page numbers cited parenthetically, will continue to appear as notes.

6. "You want me to say whether it is true that the queen killed your brother. In fact it is just as the inscription says" (89).

7. "My Lord, now I request you as a king to grant me justice concerning the queen who [treacherously] killed my brother; if she wishes to deny and disavow that she has acted treacherously and dishonourably, I shall be pleased to prove my case against the finest knight she wishes to represent her" (90).

Cable's translation omits the first occurrence of the term "en traïson," which is important, as we shall see.

8. "I think now that Mador was in the wrong, because, however his brother died, I would swear on the relics of the saints that to my knowledge the queen never had dishonour or treachery in mind" (106).

9. "The queen took the fruit, because she was not on her guard against treachery, and she gave it to a knight who was a companion of the Round Table, called Gaheris de Karaheu" (82).

10. "No man should suffer penalty for his thoughts," *Le Livre de jostice et de pletz*, ed. Rapetti, cited and translated by Bloch, *Law*, 33.

11. HERE LIES GAHERIET, KING ARTHUR'S NEPHEW, WHO WAS KILLED BY LANCELOT DEL LAC. (129–30)

> HERE LIES LUCAN THE BUTLER, WHOM KING ARTHUR CRUSHED TO DEATH. (225)

12. "I died for the noblest man in the world, and also the wickedest: Lancelot del Lac. He is the wickedest as far as I know because however much I begged him with tears and weeping he refused to have mercy on me, and I took it so much to heart that as a result I died from loving faithfully" (94).

13. "He took Lucan, who was unarmed, and embraced him, holding him so tightly that he burst his heart inside him. Lucan was unable to say a word before his soul left his body. When the king had been in that position for some time, he released his hold, because he did not realize he was dead" (221–22).

14. But cf. Zuurdeeg, who suggests that the epitaphs read sequentially tell "the whole story in a nutshell," apparently finding no need for interpretation in them: *Narrative Technique*, 59.

15. Bloch, *Law*, 41.

16. Noble makes this point, "Some Problems," 519.

17. Bloch, *Law*, 42–46. Adler believes, like Bloch, that the second trial by battle shows Lancelot defending a less justifiable position than the first, 931. Muir disagrees: see her objections to Bloch's argument (originally published in "From Grail Quest to Inquest"), and Bloch's convincing refutation of them, in their joint article "Further Thoughts." York, "Concept," gives legal information useful in interpreting all these trials.

18. "the deaths of my brothers whom you killed treacherously and disloyally" (175); "My Lord, here I am, ready to prove that Lancelot killed my brother[s] treacherously." (176).

19. "I will swear on the saints that I never killed Gaheriet knowingly, and that I greatly regretted his death" (176).

20. "He was very worried that things might turn out badly for him against Sir Gawain, because of Gawain's brothers that he had killed" (178).

21. Bloch, *Law*, 44–45.

22. "Sir Gawain was so exhausted that he could hardly hold his sword. Lancelot, not yet too weary and still able to fight, rained blows on him and drove him now forward and now back" (184).

23. Bloch, *Law*, suggests that this assembling of information is the function of the text itself, 203; this point will be discussed further below.

24. Bloch, *Law*, 53–62.

25. "He fell back into sin with the queen" (24); "He took off his shoes and undressed and climbed into bed with the queen" (115).

26. On "li contes" in the prose *Lancelot*, see Burns, *Arthurian Fictions*, 13–43.

27. "However, Lancelot, planning to go in disguise, told all those around him he felt so unwell that he definitely would not be able to go" (25); "He did not want to travel during the day, in case he were recognized. When he arrived beneath the castle, he rode with his head so low that he could hardly be identified" (27–28).

28. Like many such "blanks," this lack of motivation has given rise to several mutually exclusive interpretations by critics: Frappier, *Etude*, sees religious scruples as Lancelot's reason for the disguise, that is, his shame at having taken up again the search for earthly glory after his mystical experiences in the grail quest. A. Kennedy, "Lancelot Incognito," on the other hand, agrees with Arthur's speculation within the text that Lancelot fears others will be afraid to fight him if he is recognized; thus confidence in his worldly accomplishments, rather than shame, motivates him. Frappier sees no reason at all for Lancelot's refusal to reveal his whereabouts after the tournament is over (*Etude*, 348, n. 5), while Lyons, "An Interpreta-

tion," finds in that decision Lancelot's discretion because of his recent injuries, 141.

29. "My Lord, that knight with red arms and the sleeve on his helmet is not who I thought it was, I swear it; it is someone else, I am quite sure. . . ."

"And who do you think it is?" asked the King.

"I do not know, my Lord," said Sir Gawain, "but he is very noble" (34).

30. "Sir Gawain ordered his horse to be brought to him, because he wanted to go and find out the identity of the knight so that he could become acquainted with him. Gaheriet said he would go too" (36).

31. Lacy, "Spatial Form," examines the manner in which the first half of this romance is structured on these alterations between suspicion and appeasement, as does Zuurdeeg, 8–10 and 89.

32. "It happened that the king began looking around him and saw the pictures which Lancelot had painted long before, when he was a prisoner there. King Arthur knew his letters well enough to be able to make out the meaning of a text, and when he had seen the inscriptions with the pictures that explained their meaning, he began to read them. So he found out that the room was illustrated with all Lancelot's deeds of chivalry since he had been made a knight. . . . and when he examined the paintings which related the meeting arranged by Galeholt, he was completely astounded and taken aback. He looked again and said under his breath:

"In faith, if these inscriptions tell the truth, then Lancelot has dishonoured me through the queen, because I can see quite clearly that he has had an association with her. If it is as the writing says, it will be the cause of the greatest grief that I have ever suffered, since Lancelot could not possibly degrade me more than by dishonouring my wife" (70–71).

33. "He was sure that if Lancelot loved the queen adulterously as had been alleged, he could not be absent from the court and turn his back on it for as long as he did. This was a thing which went a long way to set the king's mind at rest, and which led him to discount what he had heard his sister Morgan say" (82).

34. "When the Pope heard that she had not been proved guilty of the crime of which she was accused, he ordered the archbishops and bishops of the country to excommunicate and lay under an interdict the whole of the land that Arthur held, unless he took his wife back. . . . When the king heard this order he was very angry; and yet he loved the queen so much, although he was sure she had sinned against him, that he was easily persuaded to obey it" (146).

35. "I now believe even more certainly than before that he loves you truly, because otherwise he would not have worn the sleeve" (43).

36. "Then the queen felt sure it was not Lancelot, because she did not think he would bear any token at a tournament that she had not given to him" (47).

37. "Then Girflet jumped forward and said to the queen:
'My lady, I can assure you that the knight with red arms who wore the sleeve on his helmet was Lancelot . . . '" (47).

'Sir Gawain,' asked the queen, 'do you think he is right? By the faith you owe my lord the king, tell me what you know, if you do know anything.'

'My lady,' he said, 'you have begged me in such serious terms that I shall not hide from you anything I know; I can tell you truthfully that it was Lancelot himself who had red arms, who wore the sleeve on his helmet and who won the tournament.'

When the queen heard this, she immediately fell silent, and went into her room crying" (47–48).

38. "She really imagined that Lancelot had deserted her, and loved the girl whose sleeve he had worn at the tournament" (48).

39. Lyons, "An Interpretation," suggests that the atmosphere of concealment creates greater interest on the reader's part, 142; but she seems to be confusing the response of the reader, from whom very little is actually concealed, with that of the characters.

40. As Lepick points out, "History," especially 518. But cf. Burns, *Arthurian Fictions*, 165–67.

41. "After Walter Map had put down in writing as much as he thought sufficient about the *Adventures of the Holy Grail*, his lord King Henry II felt that what he had done would not be satisfactory unless he told about the rest of the lives of those he had previously mentioned, and the deaths of those whose prowess he had related in his book. So he began this last part" (23).

"At this point Walter Map will end the *Story of Lancelot*, because he has brought everything to a proper conclusion according to the way it happened; and he finished his book here so completely that no one can afterwards add anything to the story that is not complete falsehood" (235).

The *Mort Artu*'s commemorative function is also discussed by Bloch, *Law*, 202 ff., and by Lepick throughout her article. Richard Hartman, *La Quête et la croisade*, situates the *Mort Artu* within a major change in the *Zeitgeist* around 1200: "la perte d'un goût pour une vérité pooétique, associée la plupart du temps aux récits versifiés, et le développement d'une double exigence: celle d'une vérité à la fois historique et exhaustive," 202. Both Lepick and Hartman deal with the tension between this desire for historical truth and the difficulty of achieving it. For Hartman, the *Mort Artu* is among "des oeuvres dans lesquelles les moyens traditionnels de savoir la vérité devinrent inéfficaces, et où des poteaux indicateurs du droit chemin ne donnent que des renseignements trompeurs," 203.

42. Bloch, *Law*, 209.

43. "Now think: do you not remember what you once saw in the Adventurous Palace of the Rich Fisher King, at the time you witnessed the battle

of the serpent and the leopard? If you had remembered correctly the marvels you saw and the interpretation of them the hermit gave you, this war would never have taken place as long as you could have avoided it" (137).

44. ON THIS PLAIN WILL TAKE PLACE THE MORTAL BATTLE WHICH WILL ORPHAN THE KINGDOM OF LOGRES (207).

45. " 'My Lord,' said King Arthur, 'now I see so much that if I had not come so far I should turn back, whatever my plans had been up to now. But may Jesus Christ help us now, because I shall never leave until Our Lord has granted victory to me or to Mordred' " (207).

46. Blaess, "Predestination," draws a somewhat different connection between prophecy and predestination, as does Zuurdeeg, 59, while Mac-Rae, "Appearances and Reality," finds possibilities for the exercise of free-will at every crucial juncture. Frappier attempts to steer a middle course; see his "La Bataille": "Fortune a sous sa Loi, sur le plan terrestre, dans l'ordre historique et temporel, la puissance et la gloire des hommes, con-damnées à ne pas durer, tandis que Dieu n'a confié à aucune entité la juridiction du spirituel, de la grace et du salut des âmes," 1022. See also his *Etude*, 258–88.

47. Rychner, *L'Articulation*, 235. See also Bloch's discussion of this pas-sage, "Text as Inquest," 113–14, and Lepick on parataxis in the romance, 519.

48. HERE LIES KING ARTHUR WHO THROUGH HIS VALOR CON-QUERED TWELVE KINGDOMS. (225)

49. " 'My Lord, is it true that King Arthur lies here?'
'Yes, my friend, he truly lies there; he was brought here by some ladies whom I did not know' " (226).

50. On the dissemination of this myth, see Loomis, *ALMA*, 64–65.

51. "The end of it relates how King Arthur was wounded at the battle of Salisbury and left Girflet who had long been his companion, and how no one ever again saw him alive" (23).

52. Noble, "Fairy Mythology," argues that the *Mort Artu*'s use of the myth denies any possibility of Arthur's survival.

53. Lepick points out that Map had been called a liar in Hugh of Rutland's *Ipomedon* and asks whether the supposedly closed text contains hints of its own "undoing," but finally decides that the use of Map's name is not ironic, 524–25.

54. Bogdanow, "Post-Vulgate."

55. Blake, "Etude," 737–38.

56. Blake, 738. Fox, *Etude sur les manuscrits*, suggests that consistent characterization is of little interest to the *Mort Artu*'s author, 224–25, while Adler finds its inconsistency of character to be compatible with the Aristote-lian theology he describes, 935–36. Lyons, "An Interpretation," on the other hand, makes the surprising claim that the *Mort Artu* contains no character development and even that Lancelot's character is stable, 146–47. Frappier,

Etude, presents the more plausible view that character changes are due to consistent psychological development, 289–343, a position with which Noble, "Some Problems," agrees, 520. Zuurdeeg, 13–27, like Blake, sees the characters as collections of conflicting ideologies rather than as coherent individuals. See also Burns, *Arthurian Fictions*, 160–61.

57. "Take my shield from that room and go straight to Camelot; carry it to St. Stephen's Cathedral and leave it in a place where it can remain and be seen, so that everyone who sees it in the future will remember my adventures in this country. Do you know why I am paying that place such an honour? It is because I first received the order of chivalry there, and I love that city more than any other; and also because I want my shield to be there to compensate for my absence, as I do not know if it will ever happen that I shall return there, once I have left this country" (152).

58. "The archbishop had already taken him so far that he had been ordained a priest; he sang mass every day and led a life of such great abstinence that he ate and drank only bread and water and roots he collected in the bushes" (233).

59. Blake, 743.

60. Hugh of St. Victor, *Didascalicon*, trans. Taylor, 88. "scripta quos nunc philosophos apellare solemus, qui et brevem materiam longis verborum ambagibus extendere consueverunt, et facilem sensum perplexis sermonibus obscurare. vel etiam diversa simul compilantes, quasi de multis coloribus et formis, unam picturam facere" (ed. Buttimer, III, 4, 54).

61. The argument that Malory's works comprise eight separate tales was first proposed by Vinaver in his original three-volume edition of Malory's *Works*; it is restated in the second edition, xxxv–lvi. The most ambitious attempt to assert their unity is a collection of essays by various scholars, *Malory's Originality*, ed. Lumiansky. Perhaps the most balanced view is achieved in a series of three articles in the collection *Essays on Malory*, ed. Bennett: Lewis, "The English Prose *Morte*"; Vinaver, "Art and Nature"; and Brewer, " 'the hoole book.' " Brewer was an early opponent of the separate-tales view, and this article should be compared with an earlier one, "Form."

62. I will be quoting from the one-volume edition, *Malory's Works*, ed. Vinaver, the text of which was reproduced in the final three-volume edition of 1973. Page numbers for both Malory's text and Caxton's preface will be cited parenthetically in the text.

63. See *Caxton's Malory*, ed. Spisak and Matthews, for the division into books and chapters rather than tales.

64. Although material derived from other sources or invented by Malory is also included. Vinaver himself admits a degree of unity between these two tales, pointing out that the *explicit* concluding the seventh tale also forms a link with the eighth, "and suggests no interruption in the process of writing." See the three-volume edition of 1967, 1, xxxviii; see also xciv.

65. No matter which Thomas Malory is considered the author. For the

debate on his identity, see Spisak's useful summary in *Caxton's Malory*, 2, 606–12.

66. See chapter 1.

67. See Holbrook, "Nymue."

68. Snyder, " 'Historial' Adaptation," argues that Malory searches for present relevance in past reality; Pochoda, *Arthurian Propaganda*, suggests that Malory originally intended to present Arthurian society as a political model for his contemporaries.

69. See Vinaver's 1967 edition, 3, 1591–94.

70. Some critics have argued that the opposite is true, that tension between Lancelot and Guinevere increases throughout the seventh tale. For two examples, see Lumiansky, "Suspense," and Walsh, "Characterization."

71. Burns, *Arthurian Fictions*, 165.

72. The most perceptive reading of this episode to date is Atkinson, " 'Healing.' " Although Atkinson over-emphasizes this segment's relationship with the Grail quest (for which there is little direct textual evidence), and hence the contrast between earthly and spiritual chivalry, his reading coincides with mine at several points, which will be indicated in the subsequent notes.

73. Cf. Atkinson, 344–45.

74. See, for example, Bradstock, "Juxtaposition," in which Lancelot's spirituality is compared with Galahad's, 218–19; and Lambert, *Malory*, who sees in this episode "supernatural confirmation" of Lancelot's supremacy, 57. Atkinson reviews some other critical responses, 348.

75. Atkinson contrasts Lancelot's negative response with Arthur's positive one and finds the episode's significance in their juxtaposition, 351.

76. For a further discussion of this point, see chapter 1 and two articles cited there: Moody, "Parisian Statutes," and Scott "Nicholas," especially 20–27. Bradstock notes that God is free to choose Lancelot as his agent regardless of his morality or immorality, 215.

77. Field, "Description"; see especially 478–79, and, on how this style activates the reader, 482–83. See also Field's expansion of these points in *Romance and Chronicle*, especially 36–82. Vinaver has applied Field's observations on syntax to Malory's plot structure: "A Note."

78. Weinberg, *Nicolaus*, 48–49. See also 215. The passage Weinberg quotes is his translation of this part of a letter from Nicholas to Egidius: "Dico hic, quod, si per agentia naturalia intelligatis: 'Ista agentia, que sunt approximata passivis et non impediata sunt, ponunt suas actiones esse,' quia dicendo, quod optime sequitur: Agens naturale est approximatum passivo et non est impeditum, ergo est actio. Sed dico, quod non est evidens evidentia descripta alicui, quod in rerum universitate sint talia agentia, ymo nec, quod sint ponibilia." (Lappe, *Nicholaus von Autrecourt*, 2, 29*, ll. 3–9. [Lappe distinguishes the pagination of Nicholas's texts from his own with an asterisk]). Brewer, "Traditional Writer," believes that there is a greater

sense of cause and effect in the later books than in the earlier (see 117–18) and even identifies causality with the tragic modernity that overtakes Malory's idealized archaic world, 119; and cf. Knight, *Structure,* on the change of style between early and late books, 86–91. But Mann has argued convincingly that Malory consciously eliminated causal explanations from the story, making it the reader's responsibility to provide aesthetic, rather than logical, connections. See her " 'Taking the Adventure,' " especially 78–79. Her example is the early story of Balin, but her argument can be applied to the final sections as well and accords better than Brewer's or Knight's with the investigations of Field and Vinaver. Malory may be indifferent to theological issues, as Lambert claims, 117–18; this does not mean, however, that the current theological *mentalité* had no influence on him.

79. See chapter 1.

80. Several critics have discussed what Brewer, "Traditional Writer," calls "the pastness of the past," 109. Pochoda argues that Malory came to realize that a past ideal could not be revived in present circumstances, 102–09; see also Lambert, 125–38, for a more general discussion.

81. Brewer, "Traditional Writer," claims that there is no distinction between Malory and the narrator; see 108. This is an overstatement in line with the widely held view of Malory as an unconscious and unsophisticated artist, a view most fully defended in Brewer's article. Both Field, *Romance and Chronicle,* 147–51, and Mahoney, "Narrative Treatment," draw a clear distinction, demonstrating, for example, that the narrator's point of view, unlike the author's, is frequently limited to that of his characters.

82. Vinaver, 1971 edition, 744–45.

83. Riddy, "Structure and Meaning," mentions both the Round Table's dependence on secrecy about Lancelot, 359–60, and Lancelot's ambivalent language, 362; neither is her subject, however.

84. For a similar view of Arthur's legal system, see Holbrook, 775–76, and cf. Bloch's discussion of the *Mort Artu, Law,* 13–53.

85. A brief selection of articles on this topic, each defending a different reading: Davies, " 'Vertuouse Love,' " argues that the lovers are virtuous because they are faithful to each other, but Jurovics, "Definition," finds that their adultery is condemned. Lumiansky, "Relationship," believes that they are not yet lovers in the *Tale of Launcelot,* but Davis, "Unity," believes the opposite. Moorman, "Courtly Love," presents perhaps the wisest approach, maintaining that courtly love in Malory is paradoxical; more recently, L. Benson, *Malory's Morte Darthur,* 230–33, also finds the relationship "contradictory." The whole debate is reviewed by a recent participant in it: see B. Kennedy, "Malory's Lancelot," 454–55, n. 89. Kennedy finds in the "Sir Urry" episode evidence of the efficacy of Lancelot's repentance for his single adulterous act with Guinevere, which occurs in "The Knight of the Cart."

86. See Vinaver's 1967 edition, 3, 1629–30.

87. On the narrator as historian, see Lambert, 125–38, and the other material cited in his note 76; see also Field, *Romance and Chronicle:* Malory "is putting romance material into chronicle form," 37.

88. McCaffrey, "Adder," reads the adder as a symbol of the reasons for Arthur's downfall: "lust, adultery, hypocrisy, and political treason," 23. This symbolic weight seems to me too heavy for the brief reference to bear.

89. Cf. Lambert's observations on the characters' concerns with record-keeping, 134–38.

90. Stewart, "Geography," suggests that place-names are used for an effect of greater realism; but cf. Field, "Description," 482–84: this argument that Malory's style generally weakens the realistic effect perhaps accords better with the uncertainty about place-names in these passages.

91. A useful article on this point is Lappert, "Treatment," which points out the lengths to which Malory went, in revising his sources, to achieve ambiguity rather than the negative view perceived by many critics, whose arguments Lappert also summarizes. He specifically discusses the phrase "chaunged hys lyff," 355–60, pointing out that only Perceval's passing is described in similar terms, and that Perceval does not die, but is translated. See also L. Benson, 241, and Holbrook, 776–77, for similar views, and cf. Kimball, "Merlin's Miscreation," for a forceful psychoanalytical statement of the opposite view, that no cyclical rebirth is possible.

92. Schroeder, "Hidden Depths," presents a view of characterization similar to my view of plot: the reader must supply the connections between circumstances and behavior that reveal character.

93. My remarks on Caxton are in part indebted to Kirk, " 'Clerkes.' "

Bibliography

Abbreviations

ALMA: *Arthurian Literature in the Middle Ages: A Collaborative History*, ed. Roger Sherman Loomis. Oxford: Oxford UP, 1959.
BBSIA: *Bulletin bibliographique de la société internationale arthurienne*
CFMA: Classiques français du Moyen Age
CR: *Chaucer Review*
CSEL: Corpus scriptorum ecclesiasticorum latinorum
MLR: *Modern Language Review*
MP: *Modern Philology*
PL: *Patrologiae cursus completus, series latina*. Ed. J.P. Migne. 221 vols. Paris: 1844–64.
RP: *Romance Philology*
TLF: Textes littéraires français

Primary Sources

Abelard, Peter. *Abailard's Ethics*. Trans. J. Ramsay McCallum. Oxford: Blackwell, 1935.

———. *Scito teipsum. Petri Abelardi opera*. Ed. Victor Cousin. Vol. 2. Paris: Durand, 1859. 592–642. 2 vols.

Alain de Lille. *The Complaint of Nature*. Trans. Douglas M. Moffat. Yale Studies in English 36. New Haven: Yale UP, 1908. Rpt. Hamden, CT: Archon, 1972.

Alanus de Insulis. *De planctu naturae*. PL 210, col. 431–82.

Aquinas, St. Thomas. *The Existence of God, Part One*. Ed. and trans. Thomas Gilby, Timothy McDermott, and Herbert McCabe. London: Eyre & Spottiswoode, 1964. Vol. 1 of *Summa theologiae*. Blackfriars translation. 60 vols. 1964–76. Rpt. Garden City, NY: Image-Doubleday, 1969.

———. *Quaestiones quodlibetales*. Ed. R. P. Mandonnet. Paris: P. Lethellieux, 1926.

———. *Summa theologiae*. Rome: Editiones Paulinae, 1962.

Arnulf of Orléans. *Arnvlfi Avrelianensis glosvle svper Lvcanvm*. Ed. Berthe M.

Marti. Papers and Monographs of the American Academy in Rome. Rome: 1958.

Augustine, St. *Confessions.* Trans. R. S. Pine-Coffin. New York: Penguin, 1961.

———. *St. Augustine's Confessions.* Ed. W. H. D. Rouse. 2 vols. Loeb Classical Library 26–27. Cambridge, MA: Harvard UP, 1912.

Boccaccio, Giovanni. *Boccaccio on Poetry: Being the Preface and the Fourteenth and Fifteenth Books of Boccaccio's* Geneologia deorum gentilium. Trans. Charles G. Osgood. Princeton: Princeton UP, 1930. Rpt. Library of Liberal Arts. New York: Bobbs-Merrill, 1956.

———. *Genealogie deorum gentilium libri.* Ed. Vincenzo Romano. 2 vols. Bari: Gius, Laterza & Figli, 1951.

La Chanson de Roland. Ed. Joseph Bédier. Paris: H. Piazza, 1937.

Chaucer, Geoffrey. *The Works of Geoffrey Chaucer.* Ed. F. N. Robinson. 2nd ed. Boston: Houghton Mifflin, 1957.

Chrétien de Troyes. *Le Chevalier de la charrette.* Ed. Mario Roques. CFMA 86. Paris: Champion, 1975.

———. *Lancelot. Arthurian Romances.* Trans. W. W. Comfort. Everyman's Library 698. New York: Dutton, 1914. Rpt. 1978.

———. *Le Roman de Perceval ou le conte du Graal.* Ed. William Roach. TLF. Paris: Droz, 1959.

———. *The Story of the Grail.* Trans. Robert White Linker. Chapel Hill: U of North Carolina P, 1952.

The Continuations of the Old French Perceval. Ed. William Roach, Robert H. Ivy, Jr., and Lucien Foulet. 6 vols. Philadelphia: American Philosophical Society, 1949–83.

Dante Alighieri. *Convivio.* Ed. G. Busnelli and G. Vandelli. 2nd ed. 2 vols. Florence: Felice Le Monnier, 1937–57.

———. "Epistola X." *Dantis Alagherii Epistolae.* Ed. and trans. Paget Toynbee. 2nd ed. Oxford: Oxford UP, 1967. 160–211.

———. "Letter to Can Grande." *Literary Criticism of Dante Alighieri.* Trans. Robert S. Haller. Regents Critics. Lincoln: U of Nebraska P, 1973. 95–111.

The Death of King Arthur. Trans. James Cable. Baltimore: Penguin, 1971.

Eriugena, John Scotus. *De divisione naturae.* PL 122, col. 441–1022.

Lestoire del Saint Graal. Ed. H. Oskar Sommer. Vol. 1 of *The Vulgate Version of the Arthurian Romances.* 6 vols. Carnegie Institution of Washington Publications 74. Washington, D. C.: Carnegie Institution, 1908. Rpt. New York: AMS, 1979.

Geoffrey of Vinsauf. *Poetria nova. Les Arts poétiques du XIIe et XIIIe siècles.* Ed. Edmond Faral. Bibliothèque de l'école des hautes études 238. Paris: 1924.

———. *Poetria nova.* Trans. Margaret F. Nims. Toronto: Pontifical Institute of Mediaeval Studies, 1967.

Glossa ordinaria. Prologue. PL 113, col. 1–62.

Grégoire de Tours. *Histoire des francs*. Ed. Henri Omont and Gaston Collon. Rev. René Poupardin. Collection de textes pour servir à l'étude et à l'enseignement de l'histoire 47. Paris: Picard, 1913.

Gregory of Tours. *The History of the Franks*. Trans. Lewis Thorpe. Harmondsworth: Penguin, 1974.

Le Haut Livre du Graal: Perlesvaus. Ed. William A. Nitze and T. Atkinson Jenkins. 2 vols. Chicago: U of Chicago P, 1932–37.

Hugh of St. Victor. *Didascalicon*. Ed. Charles Henry Buttimer. Studies in Medieval and Renaissance Latin 10. Washington, D. C.: Catholic U of America P, 1939.

———. *Didascalicon*. Trans. Jerome Taylor. New York: Columbia UP, 1961.

Isidore of Seville. *Etymologiae*. Ed. W. M. Lindsay. Oxford: Oxford UP, 1911.

Machaut, Guillaume de. *Le Livre du Voir-Dit*. Ed. Paulin Paris. Paris: Société des Bibliophiles françois, 1875. Rpt. Geneva: Slatkine, 1969.

Malory, Sir Thomas. *Caxton's Malory*. Ed. James W. Spisak and William Matthews. 2 vols. Berkeley: U of California P, 1983.

———. *Malory: Works*. Ed. Eugène Vinaver. 2nd ed. Oxford: Oxford UP, 1971.

———. *Works*. Ed. Eugène Vinaver. 2nd ed. 3 vols. Oxford: Oxford UP, 1967.

Marie de France. *Les Lais*. Ed. Jean Rychner. CFMA 93. Paris: Champion, 1973.

———. *The Lais of Marie de France*. Trans. Robert Hanning and Joan Ferrante. Durham, NC: Labyrinth, 1978.

Matthew of Vendôme. *Ars versificatoria (The Art of the Versemaker)*. Trans. Roger Parr. Milwaukee: Marquette UP, 1981.

La Mort le roi Artu. Ed. Jean Frappier. 3rd ed. TLF. Geneva: Droz, 1964.

Nicholas of Autrecourt. *Exigit ordo executionis*. Ed. J. Reginald O'Donnell. *Mediaeval Studies* 1 (1939): 179–280.

———. *The Universal Treatise of Nicholas of Autrecourt*. Trans. Leonard A. Kennedy, Richard E. Arnold, and Arthur E. Millward. Mediaeval Philosophical Texts in Translation 20. Milwaukee: Marquette UP, 1971.

Ockham, William of. *Ockham's Theory of Terms: Part 1 of the Summa Logicae*. Trans. Michael J. Loux. Notre Dame: U of Notre Dame P, 1974.

———. *Scriptum in librum primum sententiarum ordinatio*. Ed. Gedeon Gal and Stephen Brown. 2 vols. Vols. 1–2 of *Opera theologica*. St. Bonaventure, NY: St. Bonaventure U, 1967.

———. *Summa logicae: Pars Prima*. Ed. Philotheus Boehner. Franciscan Institute Publications, Text Series 2. St. Bonaventure, NY: Franciscan Institute, 1951. Rpt. 1957.

Orderic Vitalis. *The Ecclesiastical History of Orderic Vitalis*. Ed. and trans. Marjorie Chibnall. 6 vols. London: Oxford UP, 1969–80.

Oresme, Nicole. *Livre du ciel et du monde*. Ed. A. D. Menut and A. J. Denomy. Trans. A. D. Menut. Madison: U of Wisconsin P, 1968.

The Quest of the Holy Grail. Trans. Pauline Matarasso. Baltimore: Penguin, 1969.

La Queste del saint Graal. Ed. Albert Pauphilet. CFMA 33. Paris: Champion, 1923. Rpt. 1978.

The Song of Roland. Trans. Frederick Goldin. New York: Norton, 1978.

The Song of Roland: An Analytical Edition. Ed. Gerard J. Brault. 2 vols. University Park: Pennsylvania State UP: 1978.

Secondary Sources

Adams, Marilyn McCord. *William Ockham.* 2 vols. Publications in Medieval Studies 26–27. Notre Dame: U of Notre Dame P, 1987.

Adler, Alfred. "Problems of Aesthetic versus Historical Criticism in *La Mort le roi Artu.*" *PMLA* 65 (1950): 930–43.

Adolf, Helen. *Visio Pacis: Holy City and Holy Grail.* [University Park?]: The Pennsylvania State UP, 1960.

Aers, David R. "Chaucer's *Book of the Duchess*: An Art to Consume Art." *Durham University Journal* n.s. 38 (1977): 201–05.

Allen, Don Cameron. *Mysteriously Meant: The Rediscovery of Pagan Symbolism and Allegorical Interpretation in the Renaissance.* Baltimore: Johns Hopkins UP, 1970.

Allen, Judson Boyce. *The Ethical Poetic of the Later Middle Ages: A Decorum of Convenient Distinctions.* Toronto: U of Toronto P, 1982.

———. *The Friar as Critic: Literary Attitudes in the Later Middle Ages.* Nashville: Vanderbilt UP, 1971.

———. "Langland's Reading and Writing: *Detractor* and the Pardon Passus." *Speculum* 59 (1984): 342–62.

Armstrong, Grace. "The Scene of the Blood Drops on the Snow: A Crucial Narrative Moment in the *Conte du Graal.*" *Kentucky Romance Quarterly* 19 (1972): 127–47.

Atkinson, Stephen C. B. "Malory's 'Healing of Sir Urry': Lancelot, the Earthly Fellowship, and the World of the Grail." *Studies in Philology* 78 (1981): 341–52.

Auerbach, Erich. "Dante's Addresses to the Reader." *RP* 7: 268–79. Rpt. *Gesammelte Aufsätze zur romanischen Philologie.* Bern: Francke, 1967. 144–55.

———. "Figura." *Scenes from the Drama of European Literature.* 1959. Rpt. Theory and History of Literature 9. Minneapolis: U of Minnesota P, 1984. 11–76.

———. "Figurative Texts Illustrating Certain Passages of Dante's *Commedia.*" *Speculum* 21 (1946): 474–89. Rpt. *Gesammelte Aufsätze zur romanischen Philologie.* Bern: Francke, 1967. 93–108.

Baldwin, Ralph. *The Unity of the* Canterbury Tales. Spec. issue of *Anglistica* 5. Copenhagen: 1955.

Barney, Stephen, ed. *Chaucer's* Troilus: *Essays in Criticism*. Hamden, CT: Shoe String P, 1980.

Baumgartner, Emmanuèle. *L'Arbre et le pain: essai sur la* Queste del saint Graal. Bibliothèque du Moyen-Age. Paris: CDU; SEDES, 1981.

———. "Les Aventures du Graal." *Mélanges de langue et littérature du Moyen Age et de la Renaissance offerts à Monsieur Charles Foulon*. Ed. Michel Denis et al. Vol. 1. Rennes: Institut de français, Université de Haute-Bretagne, 1980. 23–38. 2 vols.

———. "Le Défi du chevalier rouge dans *Perceval* et dans *Jaufré*." *Moyen Age* 83 (1977): 239–54.

Bédier, Joseph. *La Chanson de Roland commentée*. Paris: Piazza, 1928. Rpt. 1968.

Beer, Jeanette A. M. "The Ambiguity of Guillaume de Machaut." *Parergon* 27 (1980): 27–31.

Bennett, J. A. W., ed. *Essays on Malory*. Oxford: Oxford UP, 1963.

Benson, C. David. *The History of Troy in Middle English Literature: Guido delle Colonne's* Historia Destructionis Troiae *in Medieval England*. Totowa, NJ: Rowman and Littlefield, 1980.

Benson, Larry D. *Malory's* Morte Darthur. Cambridge, MA: Harvard UP, 1976.

Bethurum, Dorothy. "Chaucer's Point of View as Narrator in the Love Poems." *PMLA* 74 (1959): 511–20.

Bezzola, Reto R. *Le Sens de l'aventure et de l'amour (Chrétien de Troyes)*. Paris: La Jeune Parque, 1947.

Blaess, Madeleine. "Predestination in Some Thirteenth-Century Prose Romances." *Currents of Thought in French Literature: Essays in Memory of G. T. Clapton*. Oxford: Blackwell, 1965. 3–19.

Blake, H. "Etudes sur les structures narratives dans la *Mort Artu* (XIIIe siècle)." *Revue belge de philologie et d'histoire* 50 (1972): 733–43.

Bloch, R. Howard. *Etymologies and Genealogies: A Literary Anthropology of the French Middle Ages*. Chicago: U of Chicago P, 1983.

———. "From Grail Quest to Inquest: The Death of King Arthur and the Birth of France." *MLR* 69 (1974): 40–55.

———. *Medieval French Literature and Law*. Berkeley: U of California P, 1977.

———. "The Text as Inquest: Form and Function in the Pseudo-Map Cycle." *Mosaic* 8 (1975): 107–19.

Bloomfield, Morton W., ed. *Allegory, Myth, and Symbol*. Harvard English Studies 9. Cambridge, MA: Harvard UP, 1981.

———. "Symbolism in Medieval Literature." *MP* 56 (1958): 73–81.

Boardman, Philip C. "Courtly Language and the Strategy of Consolation in the Book of the Duchess." *ELH* 44 (1977): 567–79.

————. "The Post-Vulgate *Mort Artu.*" *BBSIA* 6 (1954): 106–07.

Boletta, William L. "Earthly and Spiritual Sustenance in *La Queste del saint Graal.*" *Romance Notes* 10 (1968–69): 384–88.

Bourquin, Emmanuelle. "Saint Bernard héritier du Graal: le silence du 'nice' et l'écrit du diable." *Littérature* 41 (1981): 119–28.

Bowden, Muriel. *A Commentary on the General Prologue to the* Canterbury Tales. 2nd ed. New York: Macmillan, 1967.

Bradstock, E. M. "The Juxtaposition of 'The Knight of the Cart' and 'The Healing of Sir Urry.' " *AUMLA* 50 (1978): 208–23.

Brät, Hermann. "Marie de France et l'obscurité des anciens." *Neuphilologische Mitteilungen* 79 (1978): 180–84.

Brewer, D. S. "Form in the *Morte Darthur.*" *Medium Aevum* 21 (1952): 14–24.

————. " 'the hoole book.' " Bennett 41–63.

Brewer, Derek. "Malory: The Traditional Writer and the Archaic Mind." *Arthurian Literature 1*. Ed. Richard Barber. Totowa, NJ: Rowman & Littlefield, 1981. 94–120.

————, ed. *Chaucer: The Critical Heritage*. 2 vols. London: Routledge and Kegan Paul, 1978.

Bronson, Bertrand H. "*The Book of the Duchess* Reopened." *PMLA* 67 (1952): 863–81.

Brownlee, Kevin. *Poetic Identity in Guillaume de Machaut*. Madison: U of Wisconsin P, 1984.

————. "The Poetic *Oeuvre* of Guillaume de Machaut: The Identity of Discourse and the Discourse of Identity." Cosman and Chandler 219–33.

Bruns, Gerald. *Inventions: Writing, Textuality, and Understanding in Literary History*. New Haven: Yale UP, 1982.

Bullock-Davies, Constance. "The Form of the Breton Lay." *Medium Aevum* 42 (1973): 18–31.

Burns, E. Jane. *Arthurian Fictions: Rereading the Vulgate Cycle*. Columbia: Ohio State UP for Miami U, 1985.

————. "Feigned Allegory: Intertextuality in the *Queste del saint Graal.*" *Kentucky Romance Quarterly* 29 (1982): 347–63.

Bursill-Hall, G. L. *Speculative Grammars of the Middle Ages: The Doctrine of Partes Orationis of the Modistae*. Approaches to Semiotics 2. The Hague: Mouton, 1971.

Caie, Graham D. "The Significance of the Early Chaucer Manuscript Glosses (with Special Reference to the *Wife of Bath's Prologue*)." *CR* 10 (1976): 350–60.

Calin, William. "Le *Moi* chez Guillaume de Machaut." Imbs 241–52.

————. *A Poet at the Fountain: Essays on the Narrative Verse of Guillaume de Machaut*. Lexington: UP of Kentucky, 1974.

Carmody, Joseph. "Le *Perceval* de Chrétien de Troyes et les affaires orientales." *Revue de littérature comparée* 40 (1966): 22–47.

————. "Les Sources orientales du *Perceval* de Chrétien de Troyes." *Revue de littérature comparée* 39 (1965): 497–545.

Carruthers, Mary. "Letter and Gloss in the Friar's and Summoner's Tales." *Journal of Narrative Technique* 2 (1972): 208–14.

Carruthers, Mary, and Elizabeth D. Kirk, eds. *Acts of Interpretation: The Text in its Contexts, 700–1600. Essays on Medieval and Renaissance Literature in Honor of E. Talbot Donaldson.* Norman, OK: Pilgrim, 1982.

Carton, Evan. "Complicity and Responsibility in Pandarus's Bed and Chaucer's Art." *PMLA* 94 (1979): 46–61.

Cerquiglini, Jacqueline. "Le Clerc et l'écriture: Le *Voir Dit* de Guillaume de Machaut et la définition du *dit.*" *Literatur in der Gesellschaft des Spätmittelalters.* Ed. Hans Ulrich Gumbrecht. Heidelberg: Carl Winter; Universitätsverlag, 1980. 151–68. Vol. 1 of *Begleitreihe zum Grundriss der romanischen Literaturen des Mittelalters.*

————. *"Un Engin si soutil": Guillaume de Machaut et l'écriture au XIVe siècle.* Geneva: Slatkine, 1985.

————. "Ethique de la totalisation et esthétique de la rupture dans le *Voir Dit* de Guillaume de Machaut." Imbs 253–62.

————. "Syntaxe et syncope: langage du corps et écriture chez Guillaume de Machaut." *Langue française* 40 (1978): 60–74.

Chènerie, Marie-Luce. " 'Ces curieux chevaliers tournoyeurs . . .' des fabliaux aux romans." *Romania* 97 (1976): 327–68.

Clanchy, M. T. *From Memory to Written Record: England 1066–1307.* London: Edward Arnold, 1979.

Clifford, Gay. *The Transformations of Allegory.* London: Routledge and Kegan Paul, 1974.

Coleman, Janet. *Medieval Readers and Writers 1350–1400.* New York: Columbia UP, 1981.

Colish, Marcia L. *The Mirror of Language: A Study in the Medieval Theory of Knowledge.* Rev. ed. Lincoln: U of Nebraska P, 1983.

Cornet, Luc. "Trois épisodes de la *Queste del saint Graal.*" Dethier 2, 983–98.

Cosman, Madeleine Pelner, and Bruce Chandler, eds. *Machaut's World: Science and Art in the Fourteenth Century.* Spec. ed. of *Annals of the New York Academy of Sciences* 314 (1978).

Covella, Sr. Francis Dolores. "Audience as Determinant of Meaning in the *Troilus.*" *CR* 2 (1968): 234–45.

Cowling, Samuel T. "The Image of the Tournament in Marie de France's *Chaitivel.*" *Romance Notes* 16 (1974–75): 686–91.

Crow, A. D. "Some Observations on the Style of the Grail Castle Episode in Chrétien's *Perceval.*" *History and Structure of French: Essays in Honor of Professor T. B. W. Reid.* Ed. F. J. Barnett et al. Totowa, NY: Rowman & Littlefield, 1972.

Curtius, Ernst Robert. *European Literature and the Latin Middle Ages.* Trans. Willard R. Trask. Bollingen Series 36. Princeton: Princeton UP, 1953.

Davies, R. T. "Malory's 'Vertuouse Love.' " *Studies in Philology* 53 (1956): 459–69.

Davis, Gilbert R. "Malory's 'Tale of Sir Launcelot' and the Question of Unity in the *Morte Darthur*." *Publications of the Michigan Academy of Science, Arts, and Letters* 49 (1964): 523–30.

Davison, Muriel. "Marie de France's *Lai de Lanval*, 31–38." *The Explicator* 21 (1962): item 12.

Delbouille, Maurice. "Genèse du *Conte del Graal*." *Les Romans du Graal* 83–91.

De Lubac, Henri. *Exégèse médiévale: Les quatre sens de l'écriture.* 2 parts printed as 4 vols. Théologie 42. Paris: Aubier, 1964.

De Man, Paul. *Allegories of Reading: Figural Language in Rousseau, Nietzsche, Rilke, and Proust.* New Haven: Yale UP, 1979.

———. "Pascal's Allegory of Persuasion." *Allegory and Representation.* Ed. Stephen J. Greenblatt. Baltimore: Johns Hopkins UP, 1981. 1–25.

De Nie, Giselle. *Views from a Many-Windowed Tower: Studies of Imagination in the Works of Gregory of Tours.* Diss. Rijksuniversiteit Utrecht, 1987. Amsterdam: Rodopi, 1987.

De Rijk, L. M. *Logica Modernorum: A Contribution to the History of Early Terminist Logic.* Vol. 2. Assen: Van Gorcum, 1967. 2 vols. printed as 3.

Derrida, Jacques. *Glas.* 2 vols. Paris: Denoël/Gonthier, 1981.

———. "Limited, Inc a b c . . . ." *Glyph* 2 (1977): 162–254.

———. *Of Grammatology.* Trans. Gayatri Chakravorty Spivak. Baltimore: Johns Hopkins UP, 1976.

———. "Signature Event Context." *Glyph* 1 (1977): 172–97.

Dethier, Fred, et al., eds. *Mélanges offerts à Rita Lejeune.* 2 vols. Gembloux: Duculot, 1969.

Donaldson, E. Talbot. "Chaucer's Three 'P's': Pandarus, Pardoner, and Poet." *Michigan Quarterly Review* 14 (1975): 282–301.

———. "Criseide and Her Narrator." *Speaking of Chaucer.* New York: Norton, 1970. 65–83.

———. "The Ending of Chaucer's *Troilus*." *Early English and Norse Studies Presented to Hugh Smith.* Ed. Arthur Brown and Peter Foote. London: Methuen, 1963. Rpt. *Speaking of Chaucer.* New York: Norton, 1970. 84–101.

———. "The Masculine Narrator and Four Women of Style." *Speaking of Chaucer.* New York: Norton, 1970. 46–64.

———. "Patristic Exegesis in the Criticism of Medieval Literature." *Speaking of Chaucer.* New York: Norton, 1970. 134–53.

Donovan, Mortimer J. *The Breton Lay: A Guide to Varieties.* Notre Dame: U of Notre Dame P, 1969.

Dragonetti, Roger. *La Vie de la lettre au Moyen Age: Le Conte du Graal.* Connexions au champ freudien. Paris: Seuil, 1980.

Duggan, Joseph J. "Ambiguity in Twelfth-Century French and Provençal

Literature: A Problem or a Value?" *Jean Misrahi Memorial Volume: Studies in Medieval Literature.* Ed. Hans Runte, Henri Niedzielski, and William L. Hendrickson. Columbia, SC: French Literature Publications, 1977. 136–49.

Duhem, Pierre. *Medieval Cosmology: Theories of Infinity, Place, Time, Void, and the Plurality of Worlds.* Ed. and trans. Roger Ariew. Chicago: U of Chicago P, 1985.

Eco, Umberto. *The Aesthetics of Thomas Aquinas.* Trans. Hugh Bredin. Cambridge, MA: Harvard UP, 1988.

Edwards, Robert. "The *Book of the Duchess* and the Beginnings of Chaucer's Narrative." *New Literary History* 13 (1982): 189–204.

Eichelberg, Walther. *Dichtung und Wahrheit in Machauts "Voir Dit."* Frankfurt: Duren, 1935.

Elbow, Peter. *Oppositions in Chaucer.* Middletown, CT: Wesleyan UP, 1975.

Eldredge, Lawrence. "Boethian Epistemology and Chaucer's *Troilus* in the Light of Fourteenth-Century Thought." *Mediaevalia* 2 (1976): 49–75.

Ferster, Judith. *Chaucer on Interpretation.* Cambridge: Cambridge UP, 1985.

———. "Intention and Interpretation in the 'Book of the Duchess.' " *Criticism* 22 (1980): 1–24.

Field, P. J. C. "Description and Narration in Malory." *Speculum* 43 (1968): 476–86.

———. *Romance and Chronicle: A Study of Malory's Prose Style.* London: Barrie & Jenkins, 1971.

Finke, Laurie A., and Martin Schichtman, eds. *Medieval Texts and Contemporary Readers.* Ithaca, NY: Cornell UP, 1987.

Fish, Stanley. "How to Recognize a Poem When You See One." *Is There a Text in This Class?: The Authority of Interpretive Communities.* Cambridge, MA: Harvard UP, 1980. 322–37.

———. "Is There a Text in This Class?" *Is There a Text in This Class?: The Authority of Interpretive Communities.* Cambridge, MA: Harvard UP, 1980. 303–21.

Fitz, Brewster E. "Desire and Interpretation: Marie de France's *Chievrefoil.*" *Yale French Studies* 58 (1979): 182–89.

Fletcher, Angus. *Allegory: The Theory of a Symbolic Mode.* Ithaca, NY: Cornell UP, 1964.

Foucault, Michel. "What Is an Author?" *Language, Counter-Memory, Practice: Selected Essays and Interviews.* Ed. Donald Bouchard. Ithaca, NY: Cornell UP, 1977. 113–38. Rpt. in Lambropoulos and Miller 124–42.

Foulet, Alfred, and K. D. Uitti. "The Prologue to the *Lais* of Marie de France: A Reconsideration." *RP* 35 (1981–82): 242–49.

Fox, Marjorie B. La Mort le roi Artu: *Etude sur les manuscrits, les sources et la composition de l'oeuvre.* Paris: E. de Boccard, 1933.

Frappier, Jean. "La Bataille de Salesbières." Dethier 2, 1022.

————. "Le *Conte du Graal* est-il une allégorie judéo-chrétienne?" *RP* 16 (1962–63): 179–213.

————. "Le Cortège du Graal." Nelli 175–221.

————. *Etude sur la* Mort le roi Artu: *Roman du XIIIe siècle*. 3rd ed. Publications romanes et françaises 70. Paris: Droz, 1972.

Freeman, Michelle. "Jean Frappier et le mythe du Graal." *Oeuvres et critiques* 5.2 (1980–81): 129–33.

French, W. H. "The Man in Black's Lyric." *Journal of English and Germanic Philology* 56 (1949): 231–41.

Frost, William. "An Interpretaion of Chaucer's Knight's Tale." *Review of English Studies* 25 (1949): 290–304.

Fyler, John M. "The Fabrications of Pandarus." *Modern Language Quarterly* 41 (1980): 115–30.

Gallais, Pierre. "Perceval et la conversion de sa famille: à propos d'un article récent." *Cahiers de civilisation médiévale* 4 (1961): 475–80.

Gellrich, Jesse M. *The Idea of the Book in the Middle Ages: Language Theory, Mythology, and Fiction*. Ithaca, NY: Cornell UP, 1985.

Gilson, Etienne. *History of Christian Philosophy in the Middle Ages*. 1955. Rpt. London: Sheed and Ward, 1980.

————. "La Mystique de la grace dans la *Queste del saint Graal*." *Romania* 51 (1925): 321–47.

Gordon, Ida L. *The Double Sorrow of Troilus: A Study of Ambiguities in* Troilus and Criseyde. Oxford: Oxford UP, 1970.

Grant, Edward. "Scientific Thought in Fourteenth-Century Paris: Jean Buridan and Nicole Oresme." Cosman and Chandler 105–24.

Green, Robert B. "The Fusion of Magic and Realism in Two Lays of Marie de France." *Neophilologus* 59 (1975): 324–36.

Greimas, A. J. *Dictionnaire de l'ancien français*. Paris: Larousse, 1968.

Grigsby, John L. "The Ontology of the Narrator in Medieval French Romance." *The Nature of Medieval Narrative*. Ed. Minnette Grunmann-Gaudet and Robin F. Jones. Lexington: French Forum, 1980. 159–71.

————. "Sign, Symbol, and Metaphor: Todorov and Chrétien de Troyes." *L'Esprit créateur* 18 (1978): 28–40.

Grill, Leopold. "Château du Graal: Clairvaux." *Analecta sacri ordinis Cisterciensis* 17 (1961): 115–26.

Guiette, Robert. "Li conte de Bretaigne sont si vain et plaisant." *Romania* 88 (1967): 1–12.

Haidu, Peter. *Aesthetic Distance in Chrétien de Troyes: Irony and Comedy in* Cligès *and* Perceval. Geneva: Droz, 1968.

Hamel, Mary. "The Wife of Bath and a Contemporary Murder." *CR* 14 (1979): 132–39.

Hamilton, W. E. M. C. "L'Interprétation mystique de *La Queste del saint Graal*." *Neophilologus* 17 (1942): 94–110.

Hanf, Georg. "Über Guillaume de Machauts Voir Dit." *Zeitschrift für roman-ischen Philologie* 22 (1898): 145–96.

Hanning, Robert W. *The Individual in Twelfth-Century Romance.* New Haven: Yale UP, 1977.

———. " 'I Shal Finde It in a Maner Glose': Versions of Textual Harassment in Medieval Literature." Finke and Schichtman 27–50.

Hartman, Geoffrey H. "The Interpreter: A Self-Analysis." *The Fate of Reading and Other Essays.* Chicago: U of Chicago P, 1975. 3–19.

Hartman, Richard. *La Quête et la croisade: Villehardouin, Clari et le* Lancelot *en prose.* New York: Postillion P, 1977.

Hennessy, Helen. "The Uniting of Romance and Allegory in *La Queste del saint Graal.*" *Boston University Studies in English* 4 (1960): 189–201.

Hinckley, H. B. "The Debate on Marriage in the *Canterbury Tales.*" *PMLA* 32 (1917): 292–305.

Hofer, Stefan. "La Structure du *Conte del Graal* examinée à la lumière de l'oeuvre de Chrétien de Troyes." *Les Romans du Graal* 15–30.

Hoffman, Stanton de V. "The Structure of the *Conte del Graal.*" *Romanic Review* 52 (1961): 81–98.

Hoggan, David G. "Le Péché de Perceval: pour l'authenticité de l'épisode de l'ermite dans le *Conte du Graal* de Chrétien de Troyes." *Romania* 93 (1972): 50–76, 244–75.

Holbrook, S. E. "Nymue, the Chief Lady of the Lake, in Malory's *Le Morte Darthur.*" *Speculum* 53 (1978): 761–77.

Holmes, Urban T. *A New Interpretation of Chrétien's* Conte del Graal. North Carolina Studies in the Romance Languages and Literatures 8. Chapel Hill: U of North Carolina P, 1948.

Holmes, Urban T., and Amelia Klenke. *Chrétien, Troyes, and the Grail.* Chapel Hill: U of North Carolina P, 1959.

Huchet, Jean-Charles. "Nom de femme et écriture féminine au Moyen Age: Les *Lais* de Marie de France." *Poétique* 12 (1981): 407–30.

Hunt, Tony. "Glossing Marie de France." *Romanische Forschungen* 86 (1974): 396–418.

Huppé, Bernard F. *Doctrine and Poetry: Augustine's Influence on Old English Poetry.* New York: State U of New York, 1959.

Hynes-Berry, Mary. "Language and Meaning: Malory's Translation of the Grail Story." *Neophilologus* 60 (1976): 309–19.

Ihle, Sandra Ness. *Malory's Grail Quest: Invention and Adaptation in Medieval Prose Romance.* Madison: U of Wisconsin P, 1983.

Imbs, Paul. "La *Charrette* avant la *Charrette:* Guenièvre et le roman d'*Erec.*" Payen and Régnier 1, 423–32.

———. "L'Elément religieux dans le *Conte del Graal* de Chrétien de Troyes." *Les Romans du Graal* 31–58.

———. "La Journée dans la Queste del saint Graal et la Mort le roi Artu."

Mélanges de philologie romane et de littérature médiévale offerts à Ernest Hoepf-fner. Publications de la faculté des lettres de l'Université de Strasbourg 113. Paris: Les Belles Lettres, 1949. 279–93.

————, ed. *Guillaume de Machaut: poète et compositeur*. Actes et colloques 23. Paris: Klincksieck, 1982.

Ingarden, Roman. *The Literary Work of Art*. Trans. George C. Grabowicz. Northwestern Uinversity Studies in Phenomenology and Existential Philosophy. Evanston, IL: Northwestern UP, 1973.

Iser, Wolfgang. *The Act of Reading: A Theory of Aesthetic Response*. Baltimore: Johns Hopkins UP, 1978.

Jauss, H. R. "The Alterity and Modernity of Medieval Literature." *New Literary History* 10 (1979–80): 181–229.

————. *Toward an Aesthetic of Reception*. Trans. Timothy Bahti. Theory and History of Literature 2. Minneapolis: U of Minnesota P, 1982.

Jodogne, Omer. "Le Sens chrétien du jeune Perceval dans le 'Conte du Graal.' " *Les Lettres romanes* 14 (1960): 111–21.

Johnson, William C., Jr. "Art as Discovery: The Aesthetics of Consolation in Chaucer's 'Book of the Duchess.' " *South Atlantic Bulletin* 40 (1975): 53–62.

Jonin, Pierre. "Un Songe de Lancelot dans la *Queste du Graal*." Dethier 2, 1053–61.

Jung, Marc-René. *Etudes sur le poème allégorique en France au moyen age*. Romanica Helvetica 82. Bern: Francke, 1971.

Jurovics, Raachel. "The Definition of Virtuous Love in Malory's *Morte Darthur*." *Comitatus* 2 (1971): 27–43.

Justman, Stewart. "Literal and Symbolic in the *Canterbury Tales*." CR 14 (1980): 199–214.

Kane, George. *Piers Plowman: The Evidence for Authorship*. London: Athlone; U of London, 1965.

Kelly, Douglas. *Medieval Imagination: Rhetoric and the Poetry of Courtly Love*. Madison: U of Wisconsin P, 1978.

————. "Psychologie/pathologie et parole dans Chrétien de Troyes." *Oeuvres et critiques* 5.2 (1980–81): 31–37.

Kennedy, Angus J. "Lancelot Incognito at Winchester in the *Mort Artu*." *BBSIA* 27 (1975): 170–71.

Kennedy, Beverly. "Malory's Lancelot: 'Trewest Lover, of a Synful Man.' " *Viator* 12 (1981): 409–56.

Kennedy, Elspeth. "The Scribe as Editor." Payen and Régnier 1, 523–31.

Ker, W. P. *Epic and Romance: Essays on Medieval Literature*. 1908. Rpt. New York: Dover, 1957.

Kimball, Arthur Samuel. "Merlin's Miscreation and the Repetition Compulsion in Malory's *Morte Darthur*." *Literature and Psychology* 25 (1975): 27–33.

Kirk, Elizabeth D. " 'Clerkes, Poetes and Historiographs': The *Morte Darthur* and Caxton's 'Poetics' of Fiction." *Studies in Malory*. Ed. James W. Spisak. Kalamazoo: Medieval Institute Publications, 1985. 275–95.

———. " 'Paradis Stood Formed in Hire Yën': Courtly Love and Chaucer's Revision of Dante." Carruthers and Kirk, 257–77.

Kittredge, George Lyman. *Chaucer and His Poetry*. Cambridge, MA: Harvard UP, 1915.

———. "Chaucer's Discussion of Marriage." *MP* 10 (1911–12): 435–67.

Klenke, Amelia. *Chrétien de Troyes and* Le Conte del Graal. Studia humanitatis. Madrid: José Porrua Turanzas, S. A., 1981.

Knapp, Peggy A. "Boccaccio and Chaucer on Cassandra." *Philological Quarterly* 56 (1977): 413–17.

———. "Wandrynge by the Weye: On Alisoun and Augustine." Finke and Schichtman 142–57.

Knight, Stephen. *The Structure of Sir Thomas Malory's Arthuriad*. Australian Humanities Research Council Monographs 14. Sydney: Sydney UP, 1969.

Koubichkine, Michèle. "A propos du Lai de Lanval." *Moyen Age* 78 (1972): 467–88.

Kreuzer, James R. "The Dreamer in the Book of the Duchess." *PMLA* 66 (1951): 543–47.

Kristeva, Julia. *Le Texte du roman*. The Hague: Mouton, 1970.

Kruger, Steven. "Dreams in Search of Knowledge: The Middle Vision of Chaucer and His Contemporaries." Diss. Stanford U, 1988.

Lacy, Norris J. "Spatial Form in the *Mort Artu*." *Symposium* 31 (1977): 337–45.

Lambert, Mark. *Malory: Style and Vision in* Le Morte Darthur. Yale Studies in English 186. New Haven: Yale UP, 1975.

Lambropoulos, Vassilis, and David Neal Miller, eds. *Twentieth-Century Literary Theory: An Anthology*. Albany: State U of New York P, 1987.

Lappe, Joseph. *Nicholaus von Autrecourt: sein Leben, seine Philosophie, seine Schriften*. Beiträge zur Geschichte der Philosophie des Mittelalters: Texte und Untersuchungen 6.2. Munich: Aschendorff, 1908.

Lappert, Stephen F. "Malory's Treatment of the Legend of Arthur's Survival." *Modern Language Quarterly* 36 (1975): 354–68.

Larmat, Jean. "Les Idées morales dans *La Mort le roi Artu*." *Annales de la faculté des lettres et sciences humaines de Nice* 2 (1967): 49–60.

Laurie, Helen C. R. "Some New Sources for Chrétien's *Conte du Graal*." *Romania* 99 (1978): 550–54.

Leff, Gordon. *William of Ockham: The Metamorphosis of Scholastic Discourse*. Manchester: Manchester UP, 1975.

Le Hir, Yves. "L'Elément biblique dans la *Queste del saint Graal*." Nelli 101–110.

Leicester, H. Marshall. "The Art of Impersonation: A General Prologue to the *Canterbury Tales*." *PMLA* 95 (1980): 213–24.

Lepick, Julie Ann. "History and Story: The End and Ending of *La Mort le roi Artu.*" *Michigan Academician* 12 (1980): 517–26.

Leupin, Alexandre. "Absolute Reflexivity: Geoffroi de Vinsauf." Trans. Kate Cooper. Finke and Schichtman 120–41.

———. *Le Graal et la littérature: Etude sur la vulgate Arthurienne en prose.* Lausanne: L'Age d'Homme, 1982.

Levy, Raphael. "Literary Criticism of the *Conte del Graal.*" *Homage to Charles Blaise Qualia.* Ed. John Clarkson Dowling et al. Lubbock: Texas Tech P, 1962. 39–46.

Lewis, C. S. "The English Prose *Morte.*" Bennett 7–28.

Locke, Frederick W. *The Quest for the Holy Grail: A Literary Study of a Thirteenth-Century French Romance.* Stanford Studies in Language and Literature 21. 1960. Rpt. New York: AMS, 1967.

Loomis, Roger Sherman, ed. *Arthurian Literature in the Middle Ages: A Collaborative History.* Oxford: Oxford UP, 1959.

Lot-Borodine, Myrrha. "Les Apparitions du Christ aux messes de l'*Estoire* et de la *Queste del saint Graal.*" *Romania* 72 (1951): 202–23.

———. "Le *Conte del Graal* de Chrétien de Troyes et sa présentation symbolique." *Romania* 77 (1956): 235–88.

———. "Les grands secrets du saint-Graal dans la 'Queste' du pseudo-Map." Nelli 151–74.

Lumiansky, Robert M. "The Relationship of Lancelot and Guinevere in Malory's 'Tale of Sir Launcelot.' " *Modern Language Notes* 68 (1953): 86–91.

———. *Of Sundry Folk: The Dramatic Principle in the Canterbury Tales.* Austin: U of Texas P, 1955.

———. " 'The Tale of Lancelot and Guinevere': Suspense." Lumiansky 205–32.

——— , ed. *Malory's Originality: A Critical Study of* Le Morte Darthur. Baltimore: Johns Hopkins UP, 1964.

Lyons, Faith. "Beauté et lumière dans le *Perceval* de Chrétien de Troyes." *Romania* 86 (1965): 104–11.

———. "La Mort le roi Artu: An Interpretation." *The Legend of Arthur in the Middle Ages: Studies Presented to A. H. Diverres.* Ed. P. B. Grout et al. Arthurian Studies 7. Cambridge: D. S. Brewer, 1983. 138–48.

MacRae, Donald C. "Appearances and Reality in *La Mort le roi Artu.*" *Forum for Modern Language Studies* 18 (1982): 266–77.

Mahoney, Dhira B. "Narrative Treatment of Name in Malory's *Morte Darthur.*" *ELH* 47 (1980): 646–56.

Mahoney, John F. "The *Conte del Graal* and the Praemonstratensian Order." *Analecta Praemonstratensia* 31 (1955): 166–67.

Manly, John M. *Some New Light on Chaucer.* New York: Holt, 1926.

Mann, Jill. " 'Taking the Adventure': Malory and the *Suite du Merlin.*" Takamiya and Brewer 71–91.

Maraud, André. "Le Lai de *Lanval* et la *Chastelaine de Vergi:* la structure narrative." *Romania* 93 (1972): 433–59.

Marrou, Henri-Irénée. *Saint Augustin et la fin de la culture antique.* Bibliothèque des écoles françaises d'Athènes et de Rome 145. Paris: E. de Boccard, 1938.

Marx, Jean. "Quelques remarques au sujet de récents travaux sur l'origine du Graal." *Moyen Age* 63 (1957): 469–80.

Matarasso, Pauline. *The Redemption of Chivalry: A Study of the* Queste del saint Graal. Histoire des idées et critique littéraire 180. Geneva: Droz, 1979.

Mazzotta, Giuseppe. *Dante, Poet of the Desert: History and Allegory in the Divine Comedy.* Princeton: Princeton UP, 1979.

McCaffrey, Phillip. "The Adder at Malory's Battle of Salisbury: Sources, Symbols, and Themes." *Tennessee Studies in Literature* 22 (1977): 17–27.

Mehl, Dieter. "The Audience of Chaucer's 'Troilus and Criseyde.' " *Chaucer and Middle English Studies in Honour of Rossell Hope Robbins.* Ed. Beryl Rowland. London: Allen & Unwin, 1974. 173–89. Rpt. Barney 211–29.

Meissner, Rudolf. *Die Strengleikar: Ein Beitrag zur Geschichte der altnordischen Prosaliteratur.* Halle: Niemeyer, 1902.

Mermier, Guy R. "En relisant le *Chevrefoil* de Marie de France." *French Review* 48 (1975): 864–70.

Mickel, Emmanuel J. *Marie de France.* Twayne World Authors 306. New York: Twayne, 1974.

Middleton, Anne. "Chaucer's 'New Men' and the Good of Literature in the *Canterbury Tales." Literature and Society: Selected Papers from the English Institute, 1978.* Ed. Edward W. Saïd. Baltimore: Johns Hopkins UP, 1980. 15–56.

Miller, J. Hillis. "The Two Allegories." Bloomfield 355–70.

Miller, Ralph N. "Pandarus and Procne." *Studies in Medieval Culture.* Ed. John R. Sommerfeldt. Kalamazoo: Western Michigan U, 1964. 65–69.

Minnis, A. J. *Medieval Theory of Authorship: Scholastic Literary Attitudes in the Later Middle Ages.* London: Scolar, 1984.

Misrahi, Jean. "Symbolism and Allegory in Arthurian Romance." *RP* 17 (1963–64): 555–69.

Moody, Ernest A. *The Logic of William of Ockham.* London: Sheed and Ward, 1935.

———. "Ockham, Buridan, and Nicholas of Autrecourt: The Parisian Statutes of 1339 and 1340." *Franciscan Studies* n.s. 7 (1947): 113–46.

Moorman, Charles. "Courtly Love in Malory." *ELH* 27 (1960): 163–76.

Morse, Charlotte C. *The Pattern of Judgment in the* Queste *and* Cleanness. Columbia, MO: U of Missouri P, 1978.

Morse, Ruth. "Understanding the Man in Black." *CR* 15 (1981): 204–08.

Mudrick, Marvin. "Chaucer's Nightingales." *Hudson Review* 10 (1957): 88–95. Rpt. Barney 91–99.

Muir, Lynnette R., and R. Howard Bloch. "Further Thoughts on the 'Mort Artu.' " *MLR* 71 (1976): 26–30.

Murphy, James J. *Rhetoric in the Middle Ages*. Berkeley: U of California P, 1974.

Muscatine, Charles. *Chaucer and the French Tradition: A Study in Style and Meaning*. Berkeley: U of California P, 1957.

Musso, Noel. "Comparaison statistique des lettres de Guillaume de Machaut et de Péronne d'Armentières dans le *Voir-Dit*." Imbs 175–93.

Nelli, René, ed. *Lumière du Graal: Etudes et textes*. Paris, 1951. Rpt. Geneva: Slatkine, 1977.

Nichols, Stephen G., Jr. *Romanesque Signs: Early Medieval Narrative and Iconography*. New Haven: Yale UP, 1983.

———. "Sign as (Hi)story in the *Couronnement de Louis*." *Romanic Review* 71 (1980): 1–9.

Nitze, William A. *Perceval and the Holy Grail: An Essay on the Romance of Chrétien de Troyes*. U of California Publications in Modern Philology 28, no. 5. Berkeley: U of California P, 1949.

———. "*Sans* et *matiere* dans les oeuvres de Chrétien de Troyes." *Romania* 44 (1915–17): 14–36.

Noble, Peter. "The Role of Fairy Mythology in 'La Mort le roi Artu.' " *Studi francesi* 45 (1971): 480–83.

———. "Some Problems in 'La Mort le roi Artu.' " *MLR* 65 (1970): 519–22.

Norris, Christopher. *Deconstruction: Theory and Practice*. New York: Methuen, 1982.

Oberman, Heiko A. "Some Notes on the Theology of Nominalism, with Attention to its Relation to the Renaissance." *Harvard Theological Review* 53 (1960): 47–76.

Ollier, Marie-Louise. "Modernité de Chrétien de Troyes." *Romanic Review* 71 (1980): 413–44.

Olschki, Leonardo. *The Grail Castle and its Mysteries*. Ed. Eugène Vinaver. Trans. J. A. Scott. Berkeley: U of California P, 1966.

Olson, Glending. *Literature as Recreation in the Later Middle Ages*. Ithaca, NY: Cornell UP, 1982.

Owen, Charles A., Jr. "Chaucer's *Canterbury Tales*: Aesthetic Design in Stories of the First Day." *English Studies* 35 (1954): 49–56.

———. *Pilgrimage and Storytelling in the* Canterbury Tales: *The Dialectic of "Ernest" and "Game."* Norman: U of Oklahoma P, 1977.

Owen, D. D. R. *The Evolution of the Grail Legend*. St. Andrews U Publications 58. Edinburgh: Oliver and Boyd, 1968.

Palmer, John N. "The Historical Context of the *Book of the Duchess*: A Revision." *CR* 8 (1974): 253–61.

Palomo, Dolores. "The Fate of the Wife of Bath's 'Bad Husbands.' " *CR* 9 (1975): 303–19.

Parker, Patricia A. *Inescapable Romance: Studies in the Poetics of a Mode.* Princeton: Princeton UP, 1979.

Parkes, M. B. *English Cursive Book Hands, 1250–1500.* London: Oxford UP, 1969. Rpt. Berkeley: U of California P, 1980.

Patterson, Lee W. "Ambiguity and Interpretation: A Fifteenth-Century Reading of *Troilus and Criseyde.*" *Speculum* 54 (1979): 297–330.

Pauphilet, Albert. *Etude sur la* Queste del saint Graal *attribuée à Walter Map.* Paris: Champion, 1921.

Payen, Jean-Charles. *Le Motif du repentir dans la littérature française médiévale.* Publications romanes et françaises 98. Geneva: Droz, 1968.

Payen, Jean-Charles, and M. C. Régnier, eds. *Mélanges de langue et de littérature du Moyen Age et de la Renaissance offerts à Jean Frappier.* 2 vols. Publications romanes et françaises 112. Geneva: Droz, 1970.

Peck, Russell A. "Chaucer and the Nominalist Questions." *Speculum* 53 (1978): 745–60.

Pelikan, Jaroslav. *The Growth of Medieval Theology (600–1300).* Chicago: U of Chicago P, 1978. Vol. 3 of *The Christian Tradition: A History of the Development of Doctrine.* 4 vols. to date. 1971-.

———. *Reformation of Church and Dogma.* Chicago: U of Chicago P, 1984. Vol. 4 of *The Christian Tradition: A History of the Development of Doctrine.* 4 vols. to date. 1971–.

Pensom, Roger. "Rapports du symbole et de la narration dans *Yvain* et dans la *Mort Artu.*" *Romania* 94 (1973): 398–407.

Pépin, Jean. *Dante et la tradition de l'allégorie.* Conférence Albert-le-Grand 1969. Paris: Vrin, 1970.

Pézard, André. *Dante sous la pluie de feu (Enfer, chant XV).* Etudes de philosophie médiévale 40. Paris: Vrin, 1950.

Phillips, Helen. "Structure and Consolation in the Book of the Duchess." *CR* 16 (1981): 107–18.

Pickens, Rupert T. "La Poétique de Marie de France d'après les prologues des *Lais.*" *Les lettres romanes* 32 (1978): 367–84.

———. *The Welsh Knight: Paradoxicality in Chrétien's* Conte del Graal. French Forum Monographs 6. Lexington, KY: French Forum, 1977.

Pochoda, Elizabeth T. *Arthurian Propaganda:* Le Morte Darthur *as an Historical Ideal of Life.* Chapel Hill: U of North Carolina P, 1971.

Poirion, Daniel. "Le Monde imaginaire de Guillaume de Machaut." Imbs 223–34.

———. *Le Poète et le prince: l'évolution du lyrisme courtois de Guillaume de Machaut à Charles d'Orléans.* Université de Grenoble publications de la faculté des lettres et sciences humaines 35. Paris: Presses universitaires de France, 1965.

Potters, Susan. "Blood Imagery in Chrétien's *Perceval.*" *Philological Quarterly* 56 (1977): 301–09.

Quilligan, Maureen. "Allegory, Allegoresis, and the Deallegorization of

Language: The *Roman de la Rose*, the *De planctu naturae*, and the *Parliament of Foules.*" Bloomfield 163–86.

———. *The Language of Allegory: Defining the Genre.* Ithaca, NY: Cornell UP, 1979.

———. "Words and Sex: The Language of Allegory in the *De planctu naturae*, the *Roman de la Rose*, and Book III of *The Faerie Queene.*" *Allegorica* 2 (1977): 195–216.

Rémy, Paul. "La Lèpre, thème littéraire au moyen âge: commentaire d'un passage du roman provençal *Jaufré.*" *Moyen Age* 52 (1946): 195–242.

Ribard, Jacques. "De Chrétien de Troyes à Guillaume de Lorris: ces quêtes qu'on dit inachevées." *Voyage, Quête, Pèlerinage* 313–21.

———. "L'Ecriture romanesque de Chrétien de Troyes d'après le *Perceval.*" *Marche romane* 25 (1975): 71–81.

———. "Ecriture symbolique et visée allégorique dans *Le Conte du Graal.*" *Oeuvres et critiques* 5.2 (1980–81): 103–09.

———. "Les Romans de Chrétien de Troyes sont-ils allégoriques?" *Cahiers de l'association internationale des études françaises* 28 (1976): 7–20.

Ricoeur, Paul. "What Is a Text?: Explanation and Understanding." *Hermeneutics and the Human Sciences: Essays on Language, Action, and Interpretation.* Ed. and trans. John B. Thompson. Cambridge: Cambridge UP, 1981. Rpt. in Lambropoulos and Miller 331–49.

Riddy, Felicity. "Structure and Meaning in Malory's 'The Fair Maid of Astolat.' " *Forum for Modern Language Studies* 12 (1976): 354–66.

Roach, William. "Transformations of the Grail Theme in the First Two Continuations of the Old French *Perceval.*" *Proceedings of the American Philosophical Society* 110 (1966): 160–64.

Robertson, D. W., Jr. "Historical Criticism." *English Institute Essays: 1950.* Ed. Alan S. Downer. New York: Columbia UP, 1951. 3–31.

———. "Marie de France, *Lais*, Prologue, 13–16." *Modern Language Notes* 64 (1949): 336–38.

———. *A Preface to Chaucer: Studies in Medieval Perspectives.* Princeton: Princeton UP, 1962.

Robertson, D. W., Jr., and Bernard F. Huppé. *Fruyt and Chaf: Studies in Chaucer's Allegories.* Princeton: Princeton UP, 1963. Rpt. Port Washington: Kennikat P, 1972.

Robertson, Howard S. "Love and the Other World in Marie de France's *Eliduc.*" *Essays in Honor of Louis Francis Solano.* Ed. Raymond J. Cormier and Urban T. Holmes. North Carolina Studies in the Romance Languages and Literatures 92. Chapel Hill: U of North Carolina P, 1970. 167–76.

Rollinson, Philip. *Classical Theories of Allegory and Christian Culture.* Pittsburgh: Duquesne UP, 1981.

Les Romans du Graal dans la littérature des XIIe et XIIIe siècles. Colloques internationaux du Centre national de la recherche scientifique 3. Paris: Editions du CNRS, 1956.

Roques, Mario. "Le Graal de Chrétien de Troyes et la demoiselle au Graal." *Romania* 76 (1955): 1–27.

Rossetti, William Michael. *Chaucer's* Troylus and Cryseyde *Compared with Boccaccio's* Filostrato. 2 vols. Chaucer Society, First Series 44–45. London: 1875–83.

Rothschild, Judith Rice. *Narrative Technique in the* Lais *of Marie de France: Themes and Variations.* North Carolina Studies in the Romance Languages and Literatures 139. Chapel Hill: U of North Carolina P, 1970.

Rowland, Beryl. "On the Timely Death of the Wife of Bath's Fourth Husband." *Archiv* 209 (1972): 273–82.

Rudat, Wolfgang E. H. "Chaucer's *Troilus and Criseyde:* Narrator-Reader Complicity." *American Imago* 40 (1983): 103–13.

Ruggiers, Paul G. *The Art of the* Canterbury Tales. Madison: U of Wisconsin P, 1967.

Rutledge, Amelia A. "Perceval's Sin: Critical Perspectives." *Oeuvres et critiques* 5.2 (1980–81): 53–60.

Rychner, Jean. *L'Articulation des phrases narratives dans la* Mort Artu. Formes et structures de la prose française médiévale. Université de Neuchâtel receuil de travaux publiés par la faculté des lettres 32. Geneva: Droz, 1970.

———. "Le Prologue du *Chevalier de la charrette* et l'interprétation du roman." Dethier 2, 1121–35.

———. "Le Sujet et la signification du 'Chevalier de la charrette.' " *Vox romanica* 27 (1968): 50–76.

Salter, Elizabeth. "*Troilus and Criseyde:* Poet and Narrator." Carruthers and Kirk, 281–91.

Saly, Antoinette. "L'Itinéraire intérieur dans le Perceval de Chrétien de Troyes et la structure de la quête de Gauvain." *Voyage, Quête, Pèlerinage* 353–61.

Savage, Grace Armstrong. "Father and Son in the *Queste del saint Graal.*" *RP* 31 (1977): 1–16.

Schroeder, Peter R. "Hidden Depths: Dialogue and Characterization in Chaucer and Malory." *PMLA* 98 (1983): 374–87.

Scott, T. K. "Nicholas of Autrecourt, Buridan, and Ockhamism." *Journal of the History of Philosophy* 9 (1971): 15–41.

———. "Ockham on Evidence, Necessity, and Intuition." *Journal of the History of Philosophy* 7 (1969): 27–49.

Searle, John R. "Reiterating the Differences." *Glyph* 1 (1977): 198–208.

———. "The World Turned Upside Down." Rev. of *On Deconstruction: Theory and Criticism After Structuralism*, by Jonathan Culler. *New York Review of Books* 27 Oct. 1983: 74–79.

Severs, J. Burke. "Chaucer's Self-Portrait in the Book of the Duchess." *Philological Quarterly* 43 (1964): 27–39.

Shirt, David J. "Chrétien's 'Charrette' and its Critics, 1964–74." *MLR* 73 (1978): 38–50.

Shoaf, R. A. *Dante, Chaucer, and the Currency of the Word: Money, Images, and Reference in Late Medieval Poetry.* Norman, OK: Pilgrim, 1983.

Sklute, Larry M. "The Ambiguity of Ethical Norms in Courtly Romance." *Genre* 11 (1978): 315–32.

———. *Virtue of Necessity: Inconclusiveness and Narrative Form in Chaucer's Poetry.* Columbus: Ohio State UP, 1984.

Smalley, Beryl. *English Friars and Antiquity in the Early Fourteenth Century.* New York: Barnes and Noble, 1960.

———. *The Study of the Bible in the Middle Ages.* 3rd ed. Oxford: Blackwell, 1983.

Snyder, Robert Lance. "Malory and 'Historial' Adaptation." *Essays in Literature* 1 (1974): 135–48.

Spearing, A. C. *Medieval Dream-Poetry.* London: Cambridge UP, 1976.

Spitzer, Leo. "The Prologue to the *Lais* of Marie de France and Medieval Poetics." *MP* 41 (1943–44): 96–102.

Spivak, Gayatri Chakravorty. Translator's Preface. *Of Grammatology.* By Jacques Derrida. Trans. Spivak. Baltimore: Johns Hopkins UP, 1976. ix–lxxxvii.

Stevens, John. "The *granz biens* of Marie de France." *Patterns of Love and Courtesy: Essays in Memory of C. S. Lewis.* Ed. John Lawlor. London: Edward Arnold, 1966. 1–25.

———. *Medieval Romance: Themes and Approaches.* New York: Norton, 1973.

Stevens, Martin. "Chaucer and Modernism: An Essay in Criticism." *Chaucer at Albany.* Ed. Rossell Hope Robbins. New York: Burt Franklin, 1975. 193–216.

Stewart, George R., Jr. "English Geography in Malory's 'Morte Darthur.' " *MLR* 30 (1935): 204–09.

Stock, Brian. *The Implications of Literacy: Written Language and Models of Interpretation in the Eleventh and Twelfth Centuries.* Princeton: Princeton UP, 1983.

Stokes, Myra. "Wordes White: Disingenuity in *Troilus and Criseyde.*" *English Studies* 64 (1983): 18–29.

Stokoe, W. C. "Structure and Intention in the First Fragment of the *Canterbury Tales.*" *University of Toronto Quarterly* 21 (1952): 120–27.

Strohm, Paul. "Chaucer's Audience(s): Fictional, Implied, Intended, Actual." *CR* 18 (1983–84): 137–45.

Sturm-Maddox, Sara. "King Arthur's Prophetic Fool: Prospection in the *Conte du Graal.*" *Marche romane* 29 (1979): 102–08.

Szittya, Penn R. "The Green Yeoman as Loathly Lady: The Friar's Parody of the Wife of Bath's Tale." *PMLA* 90 (1975): 386–94.

Takamiya, Toshiyuki, and Derek Brewer, eds. *Aspects of Malory*. Arthurian Studies 1. Totowa, NJ: Rowman & Littlefield, 1981.

Thomas, Antoine. "Guillaume de Machaut et l'*Ovide moralisé*." *Romania* 41 (1912): 382–400.

Todorov, Tzvetan. *Grammaire du* Décaméron. The Hague: Mouton, 1969.

————. "La Quête du récit." *Poétique de la prose*. Paris: Seuil, 1971. 129–50.

Trimpi, Wesley. *Muses of One Mind: The Literary Analysis of Experience and Its Continuity*. Princeton: Princeton UP, 1983.

Tucker, P. E. "The Place of the 'Quest of the Holy Grail' in the 'Morte Darthur.' " *MLR* 48 (1953): 391–97.

Tuve, Rosemond. *Allegorical Imagery: Some Medieval Books and their Posterity*. Princeton: Princeton UP, 1966.

Uitti, Karl D. "From *Clerc* to *Poète*: the Relevance of the Romance of the Rose to Machaut's World." Cosman and Chandler 209–16.

Van, Thomas A. "Chaucer's Pandarus as an Earthly Maker." *Southern Humanities Review* 12 (1978): 89–97.

Vance, Eugene. "Augustine's *Confessions* and the Poetics of the Law." *Mervelous Signals: Poetics and Sign Theory in the Middle Ages*. Lincoln: U of Nebraska P, 1986. 1–33.

————. "Mervelous Signals: Sign Theory and the Politics of Metaphor in Chaucer's *Troilus and Criseyde*." *Mervelous Signals: Poetics and Sign Theory in the Middle Ages*. Lincoln: U of Nebraska P, 1986. 256–310.

————. "Saint Augustine: Language as Temporality." *Mervelous Signals: Poetics and Sign Theory in the Middle Ages*. Lincoln: U of Nebraska P, 1986. 34–50.

Vinaver, Eugène. "A Note on Malory's Prose." Takamiya and Brewer 9–15.

————. "On Art and Nature: A Letter to C. S. Lewis." Bennett 41–63.

————. *The Rise of Romance*. Oxford: Oxford UP, 1971.

Vitz, Evelyn Birge. "The *Lais* of Marie de France: 'Narrative Grammar' and the Literary Text." *Romanic Review* 74 (1983): 383–404.

Voyage, Quête, Pèlerinage dans la littérature et la civilisation médiévales. Spec. issue of *Senefiance* 2. Cahiers du CUER MA. Aix-en-Provence: Université de Provence; Paris: Champion, 1976.

Walsh, John Michael. "Malory's Characterization of Elaine of Astolat." *Philological Quarterly* 59 (1980): 146–48.

Warning, Rainer. "On the Alterity of Medieval Religious Drama." *New Literary History* 10 (1979–80): 265–92.

Wathelet-Willem, J. "Le Mystère chez Marie de France." *Revue belge de philologie et d'histoire* 39 (1961): 661–86.

Weinberg, Julius Rudolph. *Nicolaus of Autrecourt: A Study in 14th Century Thought*. Princeton: Princeton UP for the U of Cincinnati, 1948.

Wetherbee, Winthrop. *Chaucer and the Poets: An Essay on* Troilus and Criseyde. Ithaca, NY: Cornell UP, 1984.

————. *Platonism and Poetry in the Twelfth Century: The Literary Influence of the School of Chartres.* Princeton: Princeton UP, 1972.

Whitaker, Muriel. "Christian Iconography in The Quest of the Holy Grail." *Mosaic* 12.2 (1978–79): 11–19.

Williams, Sarah Jane. "An Author's Role in Fourteenth-Century Book Production: Guillaume de Machaut's 'Livre ou je met toutes mes choses.' " *Romania* 90 (1969): 433–54.

————. "Machaut's Self-Awareness as Author and Producer." Cosman and Chandler 189–97.

Wimsatt, James I. "Guillaume de Machaut and Chaucer's *Troilus and Criseyde.*" *Medium Aevum* 45 (1976): 277–93.

Wolfgang, Leonora D. "Perceval's Father: Problems in Medieval Narrative Art." *RP* 34 (1980): 28–47.

York, Ernest C. "The Concept of Treason in the Prose *Lancelot.*" *Kentucky Foreign Language Quarterly* 12 (1965): 117–23.

Zumthor, Paul. *Essai de poétique médiévale.* Paris: Seuil, 1972.

————. "Intertextualité et mouvance." *Littérature* 412 (1981): 8–16.

Zuurdeeg, Atie Dingmans. *Narrative Techniques and their Effects in "La Mort le roi Artu."* York, SC: French Literature Publications Company, 1981.

Index

ROBERT S. STURGES was educated at the University of Bridge-port and at Brown University, where he earned his Ph.D. in comparative literature. He has taught at M.I.T. and Wesleyan University, and is currently assistant professor of English at the University of New Orleans. He has published articles on medieval literature in *Romanic Review, Romance Quarterly, Modern Language Studies, Exemplaria, Manuscripta,* and other scholarly journals, and recently completed an edition of the Middle English pseudo-Augustinian *Soliloquies*. His next book will be entitled *Speech and Writing in the Canterbury Tales*.